VIDEO GAMES
AND GAMING CULTURE

VIDEO GAMES
AND GAMING CULTURE

Critical Concepts in Media and Cultural Studies

Edited by
Mark J. P. Wolf

Volume IV
Cultural Contexts

Routledge
Taylor & Francis Group

LONDON AND NEW YORK

First published 2016
by Routledge
2 Park Square, Milton Park, Abingdon, Oxon OX14 4RN

and by Routledge
711 Third Avenue, New York, NY 10017

Routledge is an imprint of the Taylor & Francis Group, an informa business

British Library Cataloguing in Publication Data
A catalogue record for this book is available from the British Library

Library of Congress Cataloging in Publication Data
A catalog record for this book has been requested

ISBN: 978-1-138-81125-6 (Set)
ISBN: 978-1-138-81131-7 (Volume IV)

Typeset in Times New Roman
by Book Now Ltd, London

Publisher's Note
References within each chapter are as they appear in the original complete work

CONTENTS

CONTENTS

ACKNOWLEDGEMENTS

The Publishers would like to thank the following for permission to reprint their material:

Education and Health for permission to reprint Mark Griffiths, 'The Educational Benefits of Videogames', *Education and Health*, 20(3), 2002, 47–51.

Association for Computing Machinery for permission to reprint James Paul Gee, 'What Video Games Have to Teach Us about Learning and Literacy', *Computers in Entertainment (CIE) – Theoretical and Practical Computer Applications in Entertainment*, 1(1), October 2003. © 2003 Association for Computing Machinery, Inc. Reprinted by permission

Kurt Squire, 'Video Games in Education', *International Journal of Intelligent Games & Simulation*, 2(1), 2003, 49–62.

Sage for permission to reprint Kurt Squire, 'From Content to Context: Video-games as Designed Experience', *Educational Researcher*, 35(8), November 2006, 19–29.

Springer for permission to reprint Michele D. Dickey, 'Game Design and Learning: A Conjectural Analysis of How Massively Multiple Online Role-Playing Games (MMORPGs) Foster Intrinsic Motivation', *Educational Technology Research and Development*, 55(3), June 2007, 253–273.

David Williamson Shaffer, Kurt R. Squire, Richard Halverson, and James P. Gee, 'Video Games and the Future of Learning', *The Phi Delta Kappan*, 87(2), October 2005, 104–111.

Adrienne Shaw, 'What Is Video Game Culture? Cultural Studies and Game Studies', *Games and Culture*, 5(4), 2010, 403–424, originally published on-line May 7, 2010.

Sage for permission to reprint Celia Pearce, 'Productive Play: Game Culture from the Bottom Up', *Games and Culture*, 1(1), January 2006, 17–24.

Heikki Tyni and Olli Sotamaa, 'Material Culture and Angry Birds', *Proceedings of Nordic DiGRA 2014 Conference*, Digital Games Research Association DiGRA, 2014.

Sage for permission to reprint Mary Fuller and Henry Jenkins, 'Nintendo® and New World Travel Writing: A Dialogue', in Steven G. Jones (ed.), *Cybersociety: Computer-Mediated Communication and Community* (Thousand Oaks, CA: Sage Publications, 1995), pp. 57–72.

New York University Press for permission to reprint Ted Friedman, 'Civilization and its Discontents: Simulation, Subjectivity, and Space', in Greg M. Smith (ed.), *On a Silver Platter: CD-ROMs and the Promises of a New Technology* (New York: New York University Press, 1999), pp. 132–150.

David Myers, 'Social Play', *Play Redux: The Form of Computer Games* (Ann Arbor, MI: University of Michigan Press, 2010), pp. 116–130.

Mia Consalvo, 'Gaining Advantage: How Videogame Players Define and Negotiate Cheating', *Cheating: Gaining Advantage in Videogames* (Cambridge, MA: The MIT Press, 2009), pp. 83–105.

Sage for permission to reprint Gareth R. Schott and Kirsty R. Horrell, 'Girl Gamers and their Relationship with the Gaming Culture', *Convergence*, 6(4), December 2000, 36–53.

Mark J. P. Wolf, 'Introduction' (excerpt), in Mark J. P. Wolf (ed.), *Video Games around the World* (Cambridge, MA: The MIT Press, 2015), pp.1–12.

F. Ted Tschang, 'Balancing the Tensions between Rationalization and Creativity in the Video Games Industry', *Organization Science: Innovation at and across Multiple Levels of Analysis*, 18(6), November–December, 2007, 989–1005.

Mia Consalvo, 'Convergence and Globalization in the Japanese Videogame Industry', *Cinema Journal*, 48(3), Spring 2009, 135–141.

John Wiley and Sons for permission to reprint Simon Gottschalk, 'Videology: Video-Games as Postmodern Sites/Sights of Ideological Reproduction', *Symbolic Interaction*, 18(1), Spring 1995, 1–18.

Routledge for permission to reprint Trevor Elkington, 'Too Many Cooks: Media Convergence and Self-Defeating Adaptations', in Bernard Perron and Mark J. P. Wolf (eds), *The Video Game Theory Reader 2* (New York, NY: Routledge, 2008), pp. 213–235.

James Newman, 'The Centrality of Play', *Best Before: Videogames, Supersession and Obsolescence* (excerpt) (New York and London: Routledge, 2012), pp. 149–160.

Disclaimer

The publishers have made every effort to contact authors/copyright holders of works reprinted in *Video Games and Gaming Culture* (Critical Concepts in Media and Cultural Studies). This has not been possible in every case, however, and we would welcome correspondence from those individuals/companies whom we have been unable to trace.

INTRODUCTION TO VOLUME IV

Mark J. P. Wolf

Part 9: Video games and education

When players play video games, they must learn the game controls, the game rules, and have a good idea as to how a game's algorithm works in order to play a game well; because of the different types of learning that are required, it might be said that games are inherently educational in nature, while gameplay itself can be seen as a form of trial-and-error learning. If games are deliberately designed with educational purposes in mind, the interactive capabilities of games can offer tools for education that extend beyond traditional tools. Thus, it should not be surprising that the use of video games in education is a topic that has a long history and a vast amount of existing literature.

The first essay in this section, "The Educational Benefits of Videogames" (2002), is written by Mark Griffiths, a professor of gambling studies, and is an early defense of the use of video games in education. Next is James Paul Gee's "What Video Games Have to Teach Us about Learning and Literacy" (2003), a short essay which summarizes his book of the same title, which argues that we have a lot to learn about learning from video games and that schools, workplaces, and families can make use of games for learning. Kurt Squire's essays, "Video Games in Education" (2003) and "From Content to Context: Videogames as Designed Experience" (2006), examine the history of games in educational research, making an argument for the use of games in education, and looks at them as designed experiences which "instantiate particular theories of the world". Both essays suggest that games can communicate ideas to learners and actively support learning through interaction.

Michele D. Dickey's essay, "Game Design and Learning: A Conjectural Analysis of How Massively Multiple Online Role-Playing Games (MMORPGs) Foster Intrinsic Motivation" (2007), focuses specifically on the educational possibilities of MMORPGs and the ways they foster an environment that can support motivation and promote education. Finally, the section ends with a look at the future of virtual worlds in education in the essay "Video Games and the Future of Learning" (2005) by David Williamson Shaffer, Kurt R. Squire, Richard Halverson, and James P. Gee, which has a message that, although now ten years old, is one that schools still have yet to take to heart and apply to education in the classroom.

Part 10: Video games and culture

Like other types of games, video games are a part of culture and an increasingly large part of popular culture and transmedial franchises. They also have a growing culture surrounding them, with gaming communities, online and offline, magazines and other publications, and a wide spectrum of gamers from hardcore gamers and professional players to the most casual of players who fill spare minutes with simple games on mobile devices. The first two essays of this section deal directly with defining what video game culture is. Adrienne Shaw's "What Is Video Game Culture? Cultural Studies and Game Studies" (2010) explores what is meant by the term "video game culture", the discourse surrounding it, and how definitions can limit video game studies and how it advances. Next, Celia Pearce's essay, "Game Culture From the Bottom Up" (2006), argues against the notion that gameplay is necessarily "unproductive", considering forms of productive play and examining the culture around the *MMOG Uru: Ages beyond Myst* (2003).

Culture is built within and dependent upon the physical world, and the next three essays consider the relationship between video games and the physical world with its objects, spaces, and geography. Heikki Tyni and Olli Sotamaa's essay, "Material Culture and Angry Birds" (2014), looks at how material culture is still an important component of video games, despite the move toward digital distribution, and uses *Angry Birds* (2009) as a case study. In "Nintendo® and New World Travel Writing: A Dialogue" (1995), Mary Fuller and Henry Jenkins compare the ways fictional spaces are traversed, mapped, and mastered in Nintendo games to the way European explorers and travelers mapped and explored physical spaces during the sixteenth and seventeenth centuries, and the similarities between the resulting narratives resulting from each type of geographical exploration. Also concerned with geography, Ted Friedman's essay, "Civilization and Its Discontents" (1999), broadly considers how video games suggest new ways of mapping and understanding the world, including a detailed analysis of *Sid Meier's Civilization II* (1996) to illustrate his arguments.

Culture also inevitably contains a social element, aspects of which are the subjects of the next three essays. David Myers's "Social Play", from his book *Play Redux: The Form of Computer Games* (2010), examines the social element of play in MMOs and some of the contexts and misconceptions surrounding it, seeing social play as an extension of individual gameplay. Mia Consalvo's "Gaining Advantage: How Videogame Players Define and Negotiate Cheating", from her book *Cheating: Gaining Advantage in Videogames* (2009), considers how players define cheating, why they do it, and what the consequences are, within and without a social context. Finally, Gareth R. Schott and Kirsty R. Horrell's essay, "Girl Gamers and their Relationship with the Gaming Culture" (2000), focuses specifically on female gamers and the particular ways that they connect with gaming culture and their playing orientation and style of play.

As a national and global phenomenon, culture also influences the companies and industries in which games are designed and made, and these aspects are explored in the next three essays. The first essay is an excerpt from the Introduction from my book *Video Games around the World* (2015), which looks at the infrastructures necessary for a national industry to develop and the various tensions found in all national video game industries, such as those between indigenous productions and foreign imports, legitimate industry and piracy, mainstream and independent productions, national marketplace and global marketplace, and video games and other media. Also examining tensions within the industry, F. Ted Tschang's essay, "Balancing the Tensions between Rationalization and Creativity in the Video Games Industry" (2007), looks more specifically at the processes of game creation as a balance between creativity and business concerns and how they are negotiated. Using Bandai Namco, Square Enix, and Konami as case studies, Mia Consalvo's essay, "Convergence and Globalization in the Japanese Videogame Industry" (2009), examines how Japanese companies deal with convergence culture and the growing globalization of the video game industry.

On a broader cultural scale, like any other media objects, video games are enmeshed in ideology with their own assumptions and representations which can be used to advance ideas. Simon Gottschalk's essay, "Videology: Video-Games as Postmodern Sites/Sights of Ideological Reproduction" (1995), looks at some of these assumptions, describing eight central assumptions which he collectively refers to as the "videology" that organizes games and how it is connected to post-modernism. With an awareness of differences between media despite the so-called convergence, Trevor Elkington's essay, "Too Many Cooks: Media Convergence and Self-Defeating Adaptations" (2008), examines why so many games which are adaptations often end up disappointing audiences who are fans of their source material. Finally, an excerpt from James Newman's *Best Before: Videogames, Supersession and Obsolescence* (2012) explores gameplay preservation, the death of video games, and what might be done about it.

Part 9

VIDEO GAMES AND EDUCATION

THE EDUCATIONAL BENEFITS
OF VIDEOGAMES

Mark Griffiths

Source: *Education and Health*, 20(3), 2002, 47–51.

Abstract

Videogames have great positive potential in addition to their entertainment value and there has been considerable success when games are designed to address a specific problem or to teach a certain skill.

Most reported effects of videogames—particularly in the popular press-appear to centre upon the alleged negative consequences. These have included my own research into video game addiction,[1,2] increased aggressiveness,[3] and the various medical and psychosocial effects.[4] However, there are many references to the positive benefits of videogames in the literature.[5,6] Research dating right back to the early 1980s has consistently shown that playing computer games (irrespective of genre) produces reductions in reaction times, improved hand-eye co-ordination and raises players' self-esteem. What's more, curiosity, fun and the nature of the challenge also appear to add to a game's educational potential.[7] This paper briefly overviews some of the educational benefits of videogame playing.

Videogames as educational research tools

Videogames can clearly consume the attention of children and adolescents.[8] However, it is important to assess the extent that videogame technology had an impact on childhood education. Since videogames have the capacity to engage children in learning experiences, this has led to the rise of "edu-tainment" media. Just by watching children it becomes very clear that they prefer this type of approach to learning. However, it appears that very few games on the commercial market have educational value.

Some evidence suggests that important skills may be built or reinforced by videogames. For example, spatial visualization ability (i.e., mentally, rotating and manipulating two- and three-dimensional objects) improve with video game playing.[9] Videogames were also more effective for children who started out with relatively poor skills. It has also been suggested that videogames may be useful in equalizing individual differences in spatial skill performance. For over 20 years researchers have been using videogames as a means of researching individuals. Many of these reasons also provide an insight as to why they may be useful educationally. For instance:

- Videogames can be used as research and/or measurement tools. Furthermore, as research tools they have great diversity
- Videogames attract participation by individuals across many demographic boundaries (e.g., age, gender, ethnicity, educational status)
- Videogames can assist children in setting goals, ensuring goal rehearsal, providing feedback, reinforcement, and maintaining records of behavioural change
- Videogames can be useful because they allow the researcher to measure performance on a very wide variety of tasks, and can be easily changed, standardized and understood
- Videogames can be used when examining individual characteristics such as self-esteem, self-concept, goal-setting and individual differences
- Videogames are fun and stimulating for participants. Consequently, it is easier to achieve and maintain a person's undivided attention for long periods of time.[10] Because of the fun and excitement, they may also provide an innovative way of learning
- Videogames can provide elements of interactivity that may stimulate learning
- Videogames also allow participants to experience novelty, curiosity and challenge. This may stimulate learning
- Videogames equip children with state-of-the art technology. This may help overcome technophobia (a condition well-known among many adults). Over time it may also help eliminate gender imbalance in IT use (as males tend to be more avid IT users)
- Videogames may help in the development of transferable IT skills
- Videogames can act as simulations. These allow participants to engage in extraordinary activities and to destroy or even die without real consequences
- Videogames may help adolescents regress to childhood play (because of the ability to suspend reality in videogame playing)

There of course some disadvantages to researching videogames in an educational context. For instance:

- Videogames cause participants to become excited and therefore produce a whole host of confounding variables such as motivation and individual skill[11]
- Videogame technology has rapidly changed across time. Therefore, videogames are constantly being upgraded which makes it hard to evaluate educational impact across studies

- Videogame experience and practice may enhance a participant's performance on particular games, which may skew results

Despite the disadvantages, it would appear that videogames (in the right context) may be a facilitatory educational aid.

Videogames and the development of skills among special need groups

Video games have been used in comprehensive programmes to help develop social skills in children and adolescents who are severely retarded or who have severe developmental problems like autism.[12,13] Case studies such as those by Demarest[14] are persuasive. Demarest's account of her own autistic 7-year old son reported that although he had serious deficiencies in language and understanding, and social and emotional difficulties, videogame playing was one activity he was able to excel. This was ego-boosting for him and also had a self-calming effect. Videogames provided the visual patterns, speed and storyline that help children's basic skills development. Some of the therapeutic benefits Demarest outlined were language skills, mathematics and reading skills, and social skills.

Language skills

These included videogame play being able to facilitate (i) discussing and sharing, (ii) following directions (understanding prepositions etc.), (iii) giving directions, (iv) answering questions, and (v) having a discussion topic with visual aides to share with others.

Basic maths skills

These included videogame playing promoting basic maths skills as children learn to interact with the score counters on videogames.

Basic reading skills

These included videogames' character dialogue which are printed on the screen ('Play', 'Quit', 'Go', 'Stop', Load' etc.).

Social skills

Videogames provided an interest that was popular with other children makes talking and playing together so much easier. At school there are always other children who share a passion for videogame play.

Horn[15] used videogames to train three children with multiple handicaps (e.g., severely limited vocal speech acquisition) to make scan and selection responses. These skills were later transferred to a communication device. Other researchers have used videogames to help learning disabled children in their development of spatial abilities,[16] problem-solving exercises[17] and mathematical ability.[18] Other researchers have offered comments on how best to use computer technology for improved achievement and enhanced motivation among the learning disabled.[19,20]

There are now a few studies that have examined whether video games might be able to help in the treatment of another special needs group–children with impulsive and attentional difficulties. Kappes[21] tried to reduce impulsivity in incarcerated juveniles (ages 15 to 18 years) by providing either biofeedback or experience with a videogame. Impulsivity scores improved for both conditions. Improvement was also noted in negative self-attributions and in internal locus of control. The authors concluded that most likely explanation for the improvement in both experimental conditions was the immediate feedback. Clarke[22] also used videogames to help adolescents learn impulse control. A videogame was used for four weeks with four subjects (11 to 17 years) diagnosed with impulse control problems. After the experimental trial, the participants became more enthusiastic and co-operative about treatment.

Brain-wave biofeedback

New (as yet unpublished) research[23] suggests videogames linked to brain-wave biofeedback may help children with attention deficit disorders. Biofeedback teaches patients to control normally involuntary body functions such as heart rate by providing real-time monitors of those responses. With the aid of a computer display, attention-deficit patients can learn to modulate brain waves associated with focusing. With enough training, changes become automatic and lead to improvements in grades, sociability, and organizational skills. Following on from research involving pilot attentiveness during long flights, a similar principle has been developed to help attention-deficit children stay focused by rewarding an attentive state of mind. This has been done by linking biofeedback to commercial videogames.

In their trial, Pope[24] selected half a dozen 'Sony PlayStation' games and tested 22 girls and boys between the ages of 9 and 13 who had attention deficit disorder. Half the group got traditional biofeedback training, the other half played the modified video games. After 40 one-hour sessions, both groups showed substantial improvements in everyday brain-wave patterns as well as in tests of attention span, impulsiveness, and hyperactivity.

Parents in both groups also reported that their children were doing better in school. The difference between the two groups was motivation. The video-game group showed fewer no-shows and no dropouts. The researchers do warn that the 'wrong kinds of videogame' may be detrimental to children with attention disorders. For instance, 'shoot 'em up' games may have a negative effect on children who already have a tendency toward short attention and impulsivity. They also state that the technique is an adjunct to drug therapy and not a replacement for it.

Videogames and health care

Videogames have also been used to improve children's health care. Several games have been developed specifically for children with chronic medical conditions. One of the best-studied is an educational game called 'Packy and Marlon'.[25] This game was designed to improve self-care skills and medical compliance in children and adolescents with diabetes. Players assume the role of characters who demonstrate good diabetes care practices while working to save a summer camp for children with diabetes from rats and mice who have stolen the supplies. 'Packy and Marlon' is now available through 'Click Health' (www.clickhealth. com), along with two additional health-related software products, 'Bronkie the Bronchiasaurus' (for asthma self-management) and 'Rex Ronan' (for smoking prevention).

In a controlled study using 'Packy and Marlon',[26] 8- to 16-year olds were assigned to either a treatment or control group. All participants were given a 'Super Nintendo' game system. The treatment group was given 'Packy and Marlon' software, while the control subjects received an entertainment videogame. In addition to more communication with parents and improved self-care, the treatment group demonstrated a significant decrease in urgent medical visits.

Rehabilitation

There are also several case reports describing the use of videogames for rehabilitation. In one application, an electronic game was used to improve arm control in a 13 year old boy with Erb's palsy.[27] The authors concluded that the game format capitalized on the child's motivation to succeed in the game and focused attention away from potential discomfort.

Electronic games have also been used to enhance adolescents' perceived self-efficacy in HIV/AIDS prevention programs.[28] Using a time travel adventure game format, information and opportunities for practice discussing prevention practices were provided to high-risk adolescents. Game-playing resulted in significant gains in factual information about safe sex practices, and in the participants' perceptions of their ability to successfully negotiate and implement such practices with a potential partner.

Concluding remarks

It is vital that we continue to develop the positive potential of videogames while remaining aware of possible unintended negative effects when game content is not prosocial. At the present time, the most popular games are usually violent. Given current findings, it is reasonable to be concerned about the impact of violent games on some children and adolescents. Game developers need support and encouragement to put in the additional effort necessary to develop interesting games which do not rely heavily on violent actions.

Relationships between playing violent electronic games and negative behaviors and emotions may never be proven to be causal by the strictest standard of "beyond a reasonable doubt," but many believe that we have already reached the still-compelling level of "clear and convincing evidence."

Finally, most parents would probably support the use of videogames if they were sure they helped their children learn about school subjects. There are several elements which the teacher, parent, or facilitator should evaluate when choosing a health promoting/educational or helping videogame (adapted from Funk[29]).

- **Educational or therapeutic objective.** The objective of the game should be clear. Professional helpers and developers should have a known goal in mind for the players of the game. The outcomes they are seeking should be clear to the teacher and to the player
- **Type of game.** There are many types of activity content: games, puzzles, mazes, play, fantasy/adventure, simulations, and simulation games. Some games require physical skill and strategy, while others are games of chance. Some videogames are board or adventure game, while others involve simulation involving real events or fantasy. No evidence supports a greater therapeutic or educational effect in either situation
- **Required level and nature of involvement.** The evaluator should assess whether the videogame player is passive or active. In some games, the computer plays the game while the participant watches the results. In computer-moderated games, the computer provides the environment for the game to occur and presents decisions or questions to the player at key points during the game. The computer then reveals the consequences of the decisions made by the player
- **Information and rules.** Some games allow the player to have a range of knowledge and information about past experiences with the game. Others provide minimal amounts of information to the player. Part of the strategy may involve the player's response to this lack of information. Rules and player participation in setting rules may vary among games
- **The role of luck.** Some games are driven by chance. It is assumed that the greater the influence of chance in the working of the game, the less educational and therapeutic in nature. However, some players prefer games of chance over games of strategy
- **Difficulty.** Some games allow the player to choose the difficulty level. Others adjust difficulty level based on the progression of the player. This approach allows the game to become progressively more interesting as it becomes more challenging
- **Competition.** Many games build in competition. Some players are attracted by competition. Teachers may wish to examine if the competition is presented in such a way that all can win and that one does not win at the expense of all others
- **Duration.** Some games have very short duration, while others may go on at length. Making of user rewards, personal challenges, or changes in color

or graphical surroundings to maintain interest some games can hold player interest for long periods of time

- **Participant age and characteristics.** Computerized games have been developed for a range of ages. It assumes that the participant can understand the rules of the game and has the skill level to accomplish the motor aspects of playing the game. Some games allow for modification of text to meet the needs of poorly sighted players
- **Number of players.** Some videogames are solitary in nature. Others pit players against each other or the computer. Solitary games may meet the needs of those who find group work difficult
- **Facilitator's role.** In some videogames, the teacher or facilitator merely observes. In others, the facilitator may be an important part of the game format
- **Setting.** Fully prepare staff to integrate these games into the curriculum. Without proper acceptance, the games may be used primarily as a game or toy rather than as a therapeutic or educational tool

Videogame technology brings new challenges to the education arena. Videogames represent one technique that may be available to the classroom teacher. Care should be taken that enthusiastic use of this technique does not displace other more effective techniques. Video and computer-based games may possess advantages not present in other learning strategies. For example, the ability to choose different solutions to a difficult problem and then see the effect those decisions have on a fictional game allows students to experiment with problem-solving in a relative safe environment.

Videogames have great positive potential in addition to their entertainment value. There has been considerable success when games are specifically designed to address a specific problem or to teach a certain skill. However, generalizability outside the game-playing situation remains an important research question. What is also clear from the empirical literature is that the negative consequences of playing almost always involve people who were excessive users of videogames. From prevalence studies in this area, there is little evidence of serious acute adverse effects on health from moderate play. Adverse effects are likely to be relatively minor, and temporary, resolving spontaneously with decreased frequency of play, or to affect only a small subgroup of players. Excessive players are the most at-risk from developing health problems although more research appears to be much needed.

References

1 Griffiths, M.D. & Hunt, N. (1995). Computer game playing in adolescence: Prevalence and demographic indicators. *Journal of Community and Applied Social Psychology*, 5, 189–194.
2 Griffiths, M.D. & Hunt, N. (1998). Dependence on computer game playing by adolescents. *Psychological Reports*, 82, 475–480.

3 Griffiths, M.D. (1998). Video games and aggression: A review of the literature. *Aggression and Violent Behavior*, 4, 203–212.

4 Griffiths, M.D. (1996). Computer game playing in children and adolescents: A review of the literature. In T. Gill (Ed.), *Electronic Children: How Children Are Responding To The Information Revolution*. pp.41–58. London: National Children's Bureau.

5 Lawrence, G.H. (1986). Using computers for the treatment of psychological problems. *Computers in Human Behavior*, 2, 43–62.

6 Griffiths, M.D. (1997). Video games and clinical practice: Issues, uses and treatments. *British Journal of Clinical Psychology*, 36, 639–641.

7 op cit (above, n.1).

8 Malone, T.W. (1981). Toward a theory of intrinsically motivated instruction. *Cognitive Science*, 4, 333–369.

9 Subrahmanyam, K. & Greenfield, P. (1994). Effect of video game practice on spatial skills in boys and girls. *Journal of Applied Developmental Psychology*, 15, 13–32.

10 Donchin, E. (1995). Video games as research tools: The Space Fortress game. *Behavior Research Methods, Instruments, & Computers*, 27, 217–223.

11 Porter, D.B. (1995). Computer games: Paradigms of opportunity. *Behavior Research Methods, Instruments, & Computers* 27 (2), 229–234.

12 Gaylord-Ross, R.J., Haring, T.G., Breen, C. & Pitts-Conway, V. (1984). The training and generalization of social interaction skills with autistic youth. *Journal of Applied Behaviour Analysis*, 17, 229.

13 Sedlak, R. A., Doyle, M. and Schloss, P. (1982) "Video Games–a Training and Generalization Demonstration with Severely Retarded Adolescents", *Education and Training in Mental Retardation and Developmental Disabilities*, 17 (4), pp.332–336.

14 Demarest. K. (2000). Video games—What are they good for? Located at:http://www. lessontutor.com/kd3.html

15 Horn, E., Jones, H.A. & Hamlett, C. (1991). An investigation of the feasibility of a video game system for developing scanning and selection skills. *Journal for the Association for People With Severe Handicaps*, 16, 108–115.

16 Masendorf, F. (1993). Training of learning disabled children's spatial abilities by computer games. *Zeitschrift fur Padagogische Psychologie*, 7, 209–213.

17 Hollingsworth, M. & Woodward, J. (1993). Integrated learning: Explicit strategies and their role in problem solving instruction for students with learning disabilities. *Exceptional Children*, 59, 444–445.

18 Okolo, C. (1992a). The effect of computer-assisted instruction format and initial attitude on the arithmetic facts proficiency and continuing motivation of students with learning disabilities. *Exceptionality*, 3, 195–211.

19 Blechman, E. A., Rabin, C., McEnroe, M. J. (1986). *Family Communication and Problem Solving with Boardgames and Computer Games*. In C. E. Schaefer & S. E. Reid (Ed.), GAME PLAY: Therapeutic Use of Childhood Games pp. 129–145. New York, NY: John Wiley & Sons.

20 Okolo, C. (1992b). Reflections on "The effect of computer-assisted instruction format and initial attitude on the arithmetic facts proficiency and continuing motivation of students with learning disabilities". *Exceptionality*, 3, 255–258.

21 Kappes, B. M., & Thompson, D. L. (1985). Biofeedback vs. video games: Effects on impulsivity, locus of control and self-concept with incarcerated individuals. *Journal of Clinical Psychology*, 41, 698–706.

22 Clarke, B. & Schoech, D. (1994). A computer-assisted game for adolescents: Initial development and comments. *Computers in Human Services*, 11(1–2), 121–140.

23 Wright, K. (2001). Winning brain waves: Can custom-made video games help kids with attention deficit disorder? *Discover*, 22. Located at http://www.discover.com/mar_01/featworks.html

24 Pope, A. & Palsson, O. In Wright, K. (2001). Winning brain waves: Can custom-made video games help kids with attention deficit disorder? *Discover*, 22. Located at http://www.discover.com/mar_01/featworks.html

25 Brown, S. J., Lieberman, D. A., Germeny, B. A., Fan, Y. C., Wilson, D. M., & Pasta, D. J. (1997). Educational video game for juvenile diabetes: Results of a controlled trial. *Medical Informatics* 22, 77–89.

26 ibid.

27 Krichevets, A.N., Sirotkina, E.B., Yevsevicheva, I.V. & Zeldin, L.M. (1994). Computer games as a means of movement rehabilitation. *Disability and Rehabilitation: An International Multidisciplinary Journal*, 17, 100–105.

28 Thomas, R., Cahill, J., & Santilli, L. (1997). Using an interactive computer game to increase skill and self-efficacy regarding safer sex negotiation: Field test results. *Health Education and Behavior*, 24, 71–86.

29 Funk, J.B., Germann, J.N. & Buchman, D.D. (1997). Children and electronic games in the United States. *Trends in Communication*, 2, 111–126.

WHAT VIDEO GAMES HAVE TO TEACH US ABOUT LEARNING AND LITERACY

James Paul Gee

Source: *Computers in Entertainment (CIE) – Theoretical and Practical Computer Applications in Entertainment*, 1(1), October 2003.

Good computer and video games like *System Shock 2*, *Deus Ex*, *Pikmin*, *Rise of Nations*, *Neverwinter Nights*, and *Xenosaga: Episode 1* are learning machines. They get themselves learned and learned well, so that they get played long and hard by a great many people. This is how they and their designers survive and perpetuate themselves. If a game cannot be learned and even mastered at a certain level, it won't get played by enough people, and the company that makes it will go broke. Good learning in games is a capitalist-driven Darwinian process of selection of the fittest. Of course, game designers could have solved their learning problems by making games shorter and easier, by dumbing them down, so to speak. But most gamers don't want short and easy games. Thus, designers face and largely solve an intriguing educational dilemma, one also faced by schools and workplaces: how to get people, often young people, to learn and master something that is long and challenging— and enjoy it, to boot.

In my book, *What Video Games Have to Teach Us About Learning and Literacy* (New York: Palgrave/Macmillan,2003); http://www.amazon.com/exec/obidos/ASIN/1403961697/qid=1062706188/sr=21/ref=sr 2 1 /002-5282466-9651248, I argue that schools, workplaces, families, and academic researchers have a lot to learn about learning from good computer and video games. Such games incorporate a whole set of fundamentally sound learning principles, principles that can be used in other settings, for example in teaching science in schools. In fact, the learning principles that good games incorporate are all strongly supported by contemporary research in cognitive science—the science that studies human thinking and learning through laboratory research, studies of the brain, and research at actual learning sites like classrooms and workplaces [e.g., see Bruer 1993; Clark 1997; Cognition and Technology Group at Vanderbilt 1997; Lave 1996; New London Group 1996; Lave and Wenger 1991].

Beyond using the learning principles that good games incorporate, I also argue that schools, workplaces, and families can use games and game technologies to enhance learning. Further, I believe that use of games and game technologies for learning content in schools and skills in workplaces will become pervasive. Many parents, by getting their sometimes quite young children to play games while actively thinking about the game's connections to other games, media, texts, and the world are already doing so. In field studies we are conducting at the University of Wisconsin, we have watched seven-year-olds play *Age of Mythology*, read about mythology inside and outside the game on web sites, borrow books on mythology from the library, and draw pictures and write stories connected to the game and other mythological themes. They think about the connections between *Age of Mythology* and *Age of Empires*, between mythological figures and popular culture superheroes, and the connections of all of them to history and society. This is education at its best, and it is happening at home, outside of school.

Let me give a few examples of the good learning principles that are incorporated in good games (36 principles are discussed in my book). Good games give information "on demand" and "just in time," not out of the contexts of actual use or apart from people's purposes and goals, something that happens too often in schools. *System Shock 2*, for instance, spreads, throughout the game, the sort of information typically found in a manual. As they move through the initial levels of the game, players can request just the right information (by pressing on a little green kiosk) and make use of it or see it applied soon after having read it. People are quite poor at understanding and remembering information they have received out of context or too long before they can make use of it [Barsalou 1999; Brown et al. 1989; Glenberg and Robertson 1999]. Good games never do this to players, but find ways to put information inside the worlds the players move through, and make clear the meaning of such information and how it applies to that world.

Good games operate at the outer and growing edge of a player's competence, remaining challenging, but do-able, while schools often operate at the lowest common denominator [diSessa 2000]. Since games are often challenging, but do-able, they are often also pleasantly frustrating, which is a very motivating state for human beings. To achieve this, good games allow players to customize the game to their own levels of ability and styles of learning. For instance, Rise of Nations lets players tweak almost every element in the game, and offers skills tests as well, to ensure that nearly everyone can find the outer edge of their competence. Furthermore, players can continually adjust the game as their competence grows.

Games allow players to be producers and not just consumers. Along with the designer, the player's actions co-create the game world. As players make choices about what to build in *Rise of Nations*, what skills and missions to choose in *The Elder Scrolls: Morrowind*, or what moral decisions to make in *Star Wars: Knights of the Old Republic* players are as much designers of the game as the original innovators. Furthermore, players can use software that comes with the game to build new scenarios, maps, or episodes (for example, a scenario in *Age of Mythology* or a skateboard park in *Tony Hawk*). Too often, students in schools

17

consume, but do not produce, knowledge, and rarely get to help design the curriculum [Brown 1994].

Good games confront players in the initial game levels with problems that are specifically designed to allow players to form good generalizations about what will work well later when they face more complex problems. Often, in fact, the initial levels of a game are in actuality hidden tutorials. Work in cognitive science has shown that people need to be presented with problems in a fruitful order, getting initial problems that set up good generalizations for later problems. If they are confronted too early with problems that are too complex, they often come up with creative solutions, but ones that turn out, in the end, not to be very helpful for working on other problems later on [Elman 1993]. Good games don't do this, but order problems in helpful ways.

At the same time, games create "a cycle of expertise" [Bereiter and Scardamalia 1989].

At the outset, the game repeatedly confronts players with a similar type of problem, for example, enemies like the head crabs in *Half-Life*, until players achieve a routinized, taken- for-granted mastery of certain skills. Then the game confronts players with a new problem, for instance, a new type of enemy or a boss, which forces the players to rethink their now taken-for-granted mastery and to integrate their old skills with new ones. Then these new sorts of problems are practiced until a new higher-order routinized, taken-for-granted mastery occurs. This cycle is repeated throughout the game. In many a game, the last boss requires a last re-opening of one's taken-for-granted tool kit. This cycle is the basis for producing expertise in any area. Good games are models for the production of expertise.

Motivation is the most important factor that drives learning. When motivation dies, learning dies and playing stops. Cognitive science has had a hard time defining motivation, though one definition is a learner's willingness to make an extended commitment to engage in a new area of learning [diSessa 2000]. Since good games are highly motivating to a great many people, we can learn from them how motivation is created and sustained.

In computer and video games, players engage in "action at a distance," much like remotely manipulating a robot, but in a far more fine-grained fashion. Cognitive research suggests that such fine-grained action at a distance actually causes humans to feel as if their bodies and minds have stretched into a new space [Clark 2003], a highly motivating state. Books and movies, for all their virtues, cannot do this. The more a player can manipulate a game character and make decisions that impact on the character, the more the player invests in the character and the game at a deep level. This investment appears to be the deepest foundation of a player's motivation in sticking with and eventually mastering a game.

In a sense, all learning involves "playing a character." In a science classroom, learning works best if students think, act, and value like scientists. Games can show us how to get people to invest in new identities or roles, which can, in turn, become powerful motivators for new and deep learning in classrooms and workplaces.

Finally, we can state that when players play in massive multiplayer games, they often collaborate in teams, each using a different, but overlapping, set of skills, and share knowledge, skills, and values with others both inside the game and on various Internet sites. In the process, they create distributed and dispersed knowledge within a community in ways that would please any contemporary high-tech, cross-functional-team-centered workplace [Wenger et al. 2002]. In this respect, games may be better sites for preparing workers for modern workplaces than traditional schools. However, in the end, the real importance of good computer and video games is that they allow people to re-create themselves in new worlds and achieve recreation and deep learning at one and the same time.

References

BARSALOU, L. W. 1999. Language comprehension: Archival memory or preparation for situated action. *Discourse Process. 28* (1999), 61–80.

BEREITER, C. AND SCARDAMALIA, M. 1993. *Surpassing Ourselves: An Inquiry into the Nature and Implications of Expertise*. Open Court, Chicago:

BROWN, A.L. 1994. The advancement of learning. *Eduational Res. 23* (1994), 4–12.

BROWN, A. L., COLLINS, A., AND DUGUID 1989. Situated cognition and the culture of learning. *Educational Res.18* (1989), 32–42.

BRUER, J. T. 1993. *Schools for thought: A Science of Learning in the Classroom*. MIT Press, Cambridge, MA.

CLARK, A. 1997. *Being There: Putting Brain, Body, and World Together Again*. MIT Press, Cambridge, MA.

CLARK, A. 2003. *Natural-Born Cyborgs: Why Minds and Technologies Are Made to Merge*. Oxford University Press, Oxford, UK.

COGNITION AND TECHNOLOGY GROUP AT VANDERBILT. 1997. *The Jasper Project: Lessons in Curriculum, Instruction, Assessment, and Professional Development*. Erlbaum, Mahwah, NJ.

DISESSA, A. A. 2000. *Changing Minds*. MIT Press, Cambridge, MA.

ELMAN, J. 1991. *Incremental learning, or the importance of starting small*. Tech. Rep. 9101, Center for Research in Language, Univ. of California at San Diego.

GLENBERG, A. M. AND ROBERTSON, D. A. 1999. Indexical understanding of instructions. *Discourse Process. 28* (1999), 1–26.

LAVE, J. 1996. Teaching, as learning, in practice. *Mind, Culture, and Activity 3* (1996), 149–164.

LAVE, J. AND WENGER, E. 1991. *Situated Learning: Legitimate Peripheral Participation*. Cambridge University Press, Cambridge, UK.

NEW LONDON GROUP. 1996. A pedagogy of multiliteracies: Designing social futures. *Harvard Educational Rev. 66* (1996), 60–92.

PELLIGRINO, J. W., CHUDOWSKY, N., AND GLASER, R. 2001. *Knowing What Students Know: The Science and Design of Educational Assessment*. National Academy Press, Washington, DC.

WENGER, E., MCDERMOTT, R., AND SNYDER, W. M. 2002. *Cultivating Communities of Practice*. Harvard Business School Press, Cambridge, MA.

73

VIDEO GAMES IN EDUCATION

Kurt Squire

Source: *International Journal of Intelligent Games & Simulation*, 2(1), 2003, 49–62.

Abstract

Computer and video games are a maturing medium and industry and have caught the attention of scholars across a variety of disciplines. By and large, computer and video games have been ignored by educators. When educators have discussed games, they have focused on the social consequences of game play, ignoring important educational potentials of gaming. This paper examines the history of games in educational research, and argues that the cognitive potential of games have been largely ignored by educators. Contemporary developments in gaming, particularly interactive stories, digital authoring tools, and collaborative worlds, suggest powerful new opportunities for educational media.

Video games in American culture

Now just over thirty years old, video games have quickly become one of the most pervasive, profitable, and influential forms of entertainment in the United States and across the world[1]. In 2001, computer and console game software and hardware exceeded $6.35 billion in the United States, and an estimated $19 billion worldwide (IDSA 2002). To contextualize these figures, in October 23, 2001, the Sony PlayStation system debuted in the US, netting well over $150 million in twenty-four hours, over six times the opening day revenues of *Star Wars: The Phantom Menace*, which netted $25 million. Twenty-five million Americans or, one out of every four households, owns a Sony Playstation (Sony Corporate website 2000). Not only are video games a powerful force not only in the entertainment and economic sector, but in the American cultural landscape, as well.

Nintendo's *Pokemon*, which, like *Pac-Man and The Mario Brothers*, before it, has evolved from a video game into a cultural phenomena. In the past few years, *Pokemon* has spun off a television show, a full feature film, a line of toys, and a series of trading cards, making these little creatures giants in youth culture.

Given the pervasive influence of video games on American culture, many educators have taken an interest in what the effects these games have on players, and how some of the motivating aspects of video games might be harnessed to facilitate learning. Other educators fear that video games might foster violence, aggression, negative imagery of women, or social isolation (Provenzo 1991). Other educators see video games as powerfully motivating digital environments and study video games in order to determine how motivational components of popular video games might be integrated into instructional design (Bowman 1982; Bracey 1992; Driskell & Dwyer 1984). Conducted during the age of Nintendo, these studies are few in number and somewhat outdated, given recent advancements in game theory and game design. These studies also tend to focus on deriving principles from traditional action (or "twitch") games, missing important design knowledge embodied in adventure, sports, strategy, puzzle, or role-playing games (RPGs), as well as hybrid games which combine multiple genres (Appleman & Goldsworthy 1999; Saltzman 1999). Likewise, they fail to consider the social contexts of gaming and more recent developments in gaming, such as the Internet.

In this paper, I argue that video games are such a popular and influential medium for a combination of many factors. Primarily, however, video games elicit powerful emotional reactions in their players, such as fear, power, aggression, wonder, or joy. Video game designers create these emotions by a balancing a number of game components, such as character traits, game rewards, obstacles, game narrative, competition with other humans, and opportunities for collaboration with other players. Understanding the dynamics behind these design considerations might be useful for instructional technologists who design interactive digital learning environments. Further, video game playing occurs in rich socio-cultural contexts, bringing friends and family together, serving as an outlet for adolescents, and providing the "raw material" for youth culture. Finally, video game research reveals many patterns in how humans interact with technology that become increasingly important to instructional technologists as they become designers of digital environments. Through studying video games, instructional technologists can better understand the impact of technology on individuals and communities, how to support digital environments by situating them in rich social contexts.

Learners as "Pac-Man" players: using video games to understand engagement

Since the widespread popularity of PacMan in the early 1980s, some educators have wondered if "the magic of 'Pac-Man- 'cannot be bottled and unleashed in the classroom to enhance student involvement, enjoyment, and commitment" (Bowman 1982, p. 14). A few educators have undertaken this project, defining elements of game design that might be used to make learning environments more engaging (Bowman 1982; Bracey 1992; Driskell & Dwyer 1984; Malone 1981). Through a series of observations, surveys, and interviews, Malone (1981) generated three main elements that "Make video games fun": Challenge, fantasy,

21

and curiosity. Malone uses these concepts to outline several guidelines for creating enjoyable education programs. Malone (1981) argues that educational programs should have:

- clear goals that students find meaningful,
- multiple goal structures and scoring to give students feedback on their progress,
- multiple difficulty levels to adjust the game difficulty to learner skill,
- random elements of surprise,
- an emotionally appealing fantasy and metaphor that is related to game skills.

In a case study of *Super Mario Brothers 2*, Provenzo (1991) finds this framework very powerful in explaining why *Super Mario Brothers 2* has become one of the most successful video games of all time. Bowman's checklist provides educators an excellent starting point for understanding game design and analyzing educational games, but at best, it only suggests an underlying theoretical model of why games engage users.

Bowman (1982) offers a very similar framework to Malone, developed through an analysis of *Pac-Man* players. Using Csikzentmihalyi and Larson's (1980) discussion of "flow," Bowman describes the power of video games as their ability to place users in "flow states; " That is,

> It (Pac-Man) is an action system where skills and challenges are progressively balanced, goals are clear, feedback is immediate and unambiguous, and relevant stimuli can be differentiated from irrelevant stimuli. Together, this combination contributes to the formation of a flow experience (Bowman, 1982 p. 15).

"Pac-Man," players are in control of their actions, actively pursue their own goals, are challenged to the optimal extent of their abilities, and they are given clear feedback on their performance. Csikszentmihalyi (1990) describes flow as a state of optimal experience, whereby a person is so engaged in activity that self-consciousness disappears, time becomes distorted, and people engage in complex, goal-directed activity not for external rewards, but for simply the exhilaration of doing. By situating his discussion of video games within flow, Bowman gives educators a theoretical framework for understanding the underlying mechanisms of video games, and a starting place for designing more engaging learning environments.

Bowman contrasts video gamers, who are engaged in states of flow, with students in traditional school environments. Students in traditional, teacher led classes have little control over what they learn, are passive recipients of material chosen by teachers, must conform to the pace and ability level of the group (group instruction), and are given shallow, imprecise, normative feedback on their work (See also Sizer 1989). Contrasting characteristics of video game playing and traditional schooling are expanded in Appendix 1.

Bowman suggests that educators could use video games as a model for improving learning environments, by providing clear goals, challenging students, allowing for collaboration, using criterion based assessments, giving students more control over the learning process, and incorporating novelty into the environment.[2] Bowman acknowledges that well designed learning environments use many of these design features in order to engage learners in states of "flow"; educational approaches such as problem-based learning environments, case based reasoning, learning through participation in communities of practice (i.e. apprenticeships), or inquiry-based learning all place learners in active roles, pursuing goals meaningful to them. Advances in assessment, such as peer-based assessment or performance-based assessment provide learners multiple sources of feedback based on their performance in authentic contexts. Indeed, considering recent developments in the new paradigm of instruction, students are beginning to resemble "Pac-Man" players more than ever (Reigeluth 1999; Reigeluth & Squire 1998).

More recently, Cordova and Lepper (1996) have begun linking these basic underlying factors of games: choice, fantasy, and challenge to specific learning outcomes. Cordova and Lepper compared students who choices in fantasies with those who did not and found that students who could choose what fantasies were represented in games outperformed those who did not. For Cordova and Lepper, fostering intrinsic motivation is a complex design process that hinges on individuals' tastes and preferences, and educators need to carefully consider whose fantasies are represented in computer games and be sure that they are not excluding students by creating fantasy situations for their games.

Of course, educators and educators have used simulations and games to foster learning for decades, and many are already leveraging advancements in gaming and technology (Gredler 1996; Heinich, Molenda, Russell, & Smaldino 1996; Reigeluth & Schwartz 1989). Simulations and drill and practice games already are used in the military, schools, and industry for learning (Thiagarajan 1998). In the military for example, commercial games have been used to measure learners' eye-to-hand abilities, simulators are used to train pilots, and simulator technology is sold to commercial developers to be implemented into flight or tank simulators. Further, many "edutainment" products such as *Gettysburg*, *SimEarth*, or *Railroad Tycoon* have already made their way into K-12 classrooms, as they allow students to explore the complex dynamics of microworlds. The past ten years have seen tremendous advancements in gaming technology that have not been explored within the instructional technology community. In the next section, I discuss some of the advancements in gaming over the past decade and describe how they are being used in educational settings.

Videogames in educational settings

Over the past ten years, videogames have begun to mature as an entertainment form. Most obviously, tremendous advancements in technology have enabled designers to create rich digital worlds with vastly improved sound and graphics.

Developments in video game design go much further, as today's contemporary gaming experience is much richer than "PacMan." Video games still include action games, but they also include simulations, strategy, role playing, sports, puzzles and adventure. Good video game design across these genres immerses users in a rich interactive digital microworlds. Video gamers can be at the helm of an F-14 fighter or an entire civilization (*Civilization, Age of Empires, Alpha Centauri*); they can raise a family (*The Sims*), socially engineer a race of creatures (*Creatures*), explore rich interactive environments (*Shenmue*), or engage in fantasy/role play (*Final Fantasy VIII*). As software companies market titles with educational potential as "edutainment" educators have begun using video games, particularly simulations in classrooms. However, very little empirical study has been done on how these games are used, and the existing research has failed to yield a useful research framework (Gredler 1996). This section describes some of the unique attributes of existing video games and simulations, suggests where they might be useful for educators.[3]

Games: drill and practice

Historically, computers have been used in education primarily as tools for supporting drill and practice for factual recall (Jonassen 1988). Drill and practice games such as *AlgaBlaster, Reader Rabbit,* or *Knowledge Munchers* have been popular because they can easily be integrated into a traditional, didactic curriculum as "enrichment exercises" during independent study time. Good drill and practice games use the "action" genre of video games to engage learners (Bowman 1982; Malone 1980). Little, if any research has been done on the effectiveness of these games, but there is little reason to believe that a well designed video game will produce results which are substantially different from non-computer based games (Clark 1983). Although drill and practice games can have an important role in student-centered learning environments such as problem-based learning (Savery & Duffy 1995), using video games to support student exploration of microworlds or as a construction tool (Papert 1980; Rieber 1996) is more consistent with the emerging paradigm of instruction.

Simulations and strategy games

Unlike games, which suspend the rules of reality in order to use the rules of a game, simulations attempt to model a system in a manner that is consistent with reality (Heinich, et al. 1996). Simulations model physical systems or social systems through another symbol system, such as a computer interface. Thiagarajan (1998) distinguishes between high and low fidelity simulations.[4] Hi-fidelity simulations attempt to model every interaction in a system in as life-like a manner as possible, whereas low fidelity simulations simplify a system in order to highlight key components of the system. Because they are expensive to produce, hi-fidelity simulations are usually used when engaging in the actual activity is either cost-prohibitive or too dangerous, such as in training pilots (Thiagarajan 1992). The military makes extensive use of these simulations, often repackaging and selling them as commercial entertainment software (Herz 1997). The strength in hi-fidelity simulations lies in their ability to produce particular situations consistent with other situations in which learners are expected to participate.

Low -fidelity simulations are also used when the emphasis is on developing a conceptual understanding because they allow students to interact with complex systems while reducing or eliminating extraneous variables. Many low-fidelity simulations do not use computer technology; they use board games or role-playing to simulate a system, such as in *Ghetto*! or *Consultants* (Thiagarajan 1999). However, computerized simulations, or edutainment video games can be powerful tools for learning.[5] They allow learners to:

a   Manipulate otherwise unalterable variables. With simulations of natural systems such as *SimEarth*, learners can observe the effects of changing the globes oxygen levels, or raising the global temperature.

b   Enable students to view phenomena from new perspectives. In the simulation *Hidden Agenda*, learners can assume the position of a president in a Central American country, learning about economics, history, politics, sociology, and culture in the process.

c   Observe systems behavior over time. For example, in simulations like *SimCity* or *Civilization*, learners can observe social systems' behavior over years or centuries. Similarly, in a Virtual Solar System course, students created models of the Solar System where they could observe the solar system in motion, examining rotations, revolutions, and eclipses (Barnett, Barab, & Hay in review). Whereas most physical models tend to be static, computer based simulations allow you to manipulate time (Herz 1997). Simulation games, such as Railroad Tycoon, add a gaming element in order to bolster student engagement.

d   Pose hypothetical questions to a system. In historical simulations, such as *Antietam*, learners can simulate hypothetical events, such as what if

e   Visualize a system in three dimensions (Barab, Hay, & Duffy 1999). In the *Digital Weather Station*, learners use special 3-D tools to visualize weather systems in three dimensions (Hay 1999).

f   Compare simulations with their understanding of a system. Simulations do not represent reality; they reflect a designers conception of reality (Thiagarajan 1998). For example, *SimCity* is weighted heavily toward public transportation, reflect author Will Wright's fondness for public transportation (Herz 1997). Educators can capitalize on this discrepancy and have students examine a simulation for bias or inaccuracies.

By enabling them to interact directly with a model of a complex system, simulations place learners in a unique position to understand a system's dynamics. However, the educational value of simulations does not necessarily lie in the program itself, but rather in the overall experience of the simulation. Simply using a simulation does not ensure that learners will generate the kinds of understandings that educators might desire (Thiagarajan 1998). Rather, learners need opportunities to debrief and reflect, and the amount of time spent on reflection should equal the amount of time engaging in a game or simulation (Heinich, et al, 1996; Thiagarajan 1998). Instructors play an important role in this process fostering collaboration, promoting reflection, and coordinating extension activities (Hawley, Lloyd, Mikulecky, & Duffy 1997). Reigeluth and Schwartz (1989) provide an "instructional theory for the design of computer-based simulations" that offers thorough guidance for developing simulations *and* the instructional overlays that accompany them.

While video games and simulations (edutainment) are becoming more and more widespread in education, very little is known about how they work. Much of the research in this area has focused on comparing game playing to lecturing, which is often inappropriate because each is a different pedagogical technique which usually embodies different values on the part of the instructional designer and is suited for different types of learning experiences. Instead of isolating variables which contribute to good game design or comparing games versus other instructional approaches, instructional technologists would benefit from studying programs that use simulations, in the form of case studies, or design experiments (Brown 1992). Design experiments use case study techniques to understand and improve a design. Design experiments do not necessarily yield generalizable knowledge, but they can serve to inspire other designers in similar situations (Bracey 1992). Educators can also use Reigeluth and Schwartz's instructional-design theory for simulations (1989) as a framework for understanding the dynamics of educational applications of simulations. Regardless, more grounded research is needed to help educators understand the dynamics of using simulations to promote learning.

A world of video kids?

Many educators have expressed concern about the effects of video games on learners, and at the wisdom of bringing more video game technology into the classroom (Provenzo 1991). Provenzo, the most outspoken and oft-quoted of video game critics, raises four main concerns with video games. Video games:

a   can lead to violent, aggressive behavior,
b   employ destructive gender stereotyping,
c   promote unhealthy "rugged individualist" attitudes, and
d   stifle creative play (Provenzo 1991; 1992).

Certainly, some of Provenzo's concerns are justified. The plot of many video games still consists of little more than "kill or be killed," and many games incorporate themes, which, if accepted uncritically are potentially destructive.

Thusfar, video game research has found no relationship between video game usage and social maladjustment. The rapidly evolving nature of video game graphics, violence, and realism cautions against any definitive statement about the impact of video games on social behavior. However, I maintain that concern about video games effects is largely unfounded, and there is very little cause for concern about their effects on players. In fact, recent developments in video game design are beginning to reverse these trends; thematically, video games are increasing in complexity, incorporating story, character development, and collaboration in the game design. Educators should pay attention to these emerging developments in video gaming, as they hold promise for generating many new theories of engaging learners in interactive digital environments.

Aggression, violence, social maladjustment, and video games

If educators are going to embrace the idea of using video games to support learning, it is difficult to avoid the topic of aggression and social maladjustment due to video games, a concern most clearly articulated by Eugene Provenzo (1991) in *Video Kids*. Research on the impact of video games on aggression and violent behavior has consisted primarily of two types of studies: a) experimental designs where players' amounts of aggression are measured before and after playing violent games versus non-violent games, and (b) correlational studies that look for patterns of behavior in frequent video game players. The majority of these studies took place in the early 1990s, which means that video game research is approximately two generations behind home console developments. Regardless, research thusfar has been inconclusive. Some research (Anderson and Ford 1986; Calvert & Tan 1994; Graybill, Kirsch, & Esselman 1985) suggests that video games cause some increase in violent thoughts or feelings as measured by inventories. Others have examined children's free play after playing violent video games. Schutte, Malouff, PostGorden, and Rodasta (1988) found increased violent play in children who played violent games compared to those who played nonviolent games, and Cooper and Mackie (1986) found increased in aggressive play in girls, but not in boys. Silvern and Williamson (1987) found increased amounts of aggressive play in children who played *Space Invaders* when compared to children who had not played games, but *no* effect when compared to those who had watched television cartoons. On the other hand, Graybill, Strawniak, Hunter, and O'Leary (1987) found no increases in violent thoughts in children who played violent video games.

In an attempt to determine if there are any connections between regular video game use and violent behavior or poor school performance, researchers have conducted survey studies looking for correlations between video game play and violent behavior, or video game play and poor academic performance (Dominick 1984; Lin & Lepper 1987). None of these studies uncovered any correlations between regular video game play and violence, aggression, anti-social behavior, or poor academic performance, although Lin and Lepper did find small negative correlations around (.30) between regular arcade play and school performance. Perhaps, not surprisingly, children who spent more than 15 hours per week in arcades did not do well in school. In summary, research on video game violence has failed to show that video games cause violent, anti-social, or aggressive behavior or poor school performance.

27

As Nikki Douglass, a video game designer points out, cultural critics should hesitate before dismissing the competitive nature of most video games as unhealthy (Jenkins 1998). Assertiveness is a socially redeeming quality, is promoted in video games (Graybill et al. 1987). Video game players learn to interact with digital technology at an early age, developing technological literacy which can serve them later in a digital economy (Subrahmanyam & Greenfield 1998). Although there is no thorough research supporting this claim, there is substantial antidotal evidence that video game playing often leads to a fascination with technology, which then can lead to an interest in technology related fields (Herz 1997; Subrahmanyam & Greenfield 1998). In fact, this concern has led some researchers design games which might attract girls, and thus, close the technology gender gap (Cassell & Jenkins 1998b; Greenfield 1984; Kafai 1998). Indeed, if this logic is valid, then playing video games (in moderation) might actually have possible social benefits.

From Barbie and Mortal Combat to interactive fiction

Since Donkey Kong, the game where Mario attempted to rescue a princess from Kong, video games have relied on storylines familiar to popular entertainment. Much like in King Kong or in silent films, women have been often portrayed as a prize in video games (Provenzo 1991). Outside of Ms. Pac-Man, few women protagonists have been featured in games. There are women characters in fighting games, although with their exaggerating sexual features and high heeled stilettos, they overwhelming resemble adolescent male fantasies rather than any well-rounded female character. In 1996, Core Design attempted to reverse this pattern by creating Lara Croft, the Indiana Jones of Playstation and the star of *Tomb Raider*. Lara, however, has also evolved into a sexually exaggerated character who has served to alienate many women (Jenkins 1998). As Herz (1997) describes in her interview with Brenda Garno, a software designer, none of these patterns would seem as insidious if females had more power in designing video games and game characters. Not surprisingly, women have not flocked to video games. Female gamers represent about 20% of video game players (Kaplan 1983; Kubey & Larson 1990), with over 50% of the girls surveyed by Lin and Lepper (1987) playing home games once a month or less.

In an effort to uncover what video game designers can do to make video games more accessible to females, Cassell and Jenkins (1998a) edited a volume: *From Barbie to Mortal Kombat: Gender and Video Games*. Focusing on the unprecedented success of Barbie: Fashion Designer, which sold more than 500,000 copies, Subrahmanyam and Greenfield (1998) argue that video games focus too heavily on violence and competition and not enough on story, character development and collaboration in order to attract girls. Predictably, a group of "grrrl gamers" interviewed in this volume (Jenkins, 1998) finds this focus on traditional female characteristics offensive, if not repulsive, and argues that aggressiveness and competitiveness are worthwhile qualities that girls should be encouraged to develop through playing video games. As Herz (1999) argues in her review of

From Barbie to Mortal Combat, the most interesting and worthwhile implications for video game designers come from the authors in the volume who are trying to create quality, creative games with broad appeal. Designers such as Duncan and Gesue (1998) are writing games that capture the user with rich, interactive narrative and deep characters development. Educators can look to these authors's games, such as *Chop Suey* or *Smarty* for models of games that push game themes beyond the traditional "shoot 'em up" and into the realm of interactive fiction. As Murray argues (1998) interactive digital storytelling should emerge as a legitimate art form in the upcoming years, and video games seem to be paving the way. Educators can study this emerging for new ways to engage learners in digital environments. For example, interactive storytelling might be one way of "anchoring instruction" (Cognition and Technology Group at Vanderbilt 1993).

From rugged individualism to collaboration

The image of the "lone ranger" is as prevalent in video games as it is in any other popular American medium (Herz 1997). Games from Asteroids to Doom capitalize on making gamers feel isolated, taking the world on alone. More recently, however, MUDs (Multi User Dungeons) and MOOs have revolutionized the gaming industry. MUDs are text-based online environments where users can collaborate in groups to complete quests, solve puzzles, or slay villains.[6] In Avatar, for example, game difficulty and variables are manipulated so that gamers are forced to quickly collaborate with other players and create the bonds that can sustain an online gaming community. Consistent with the Role Playing Game genre, characters are given unique strengths and weaknesses, and no character can survive without collaborating with others. Gaming communities like Avatar have a wealth of experience designing challenges which foster community building. With the development of graphical online RPGs like *Everquest*, which has thousands of players online at any given time, and the next generation of console systems coming equipped with modems, online gaming appears to be an increasingly important part of the gaming environment. Given recent pedagogical interest in communities of practice (Barab & Duffy 2000; Lave & Wenger 1991), MUDs may offer designers guidance on how to foster community in online environments.

At the Media Lab at M.I.T., educators have begun designing online environments specifically to foster learning (Bruckman & De Bonte 1997). In MOOSE, a text-based virtual reality environment designed to support constructionist learning, Bruckman (1993a; 1998) found that the community supports for learning were much more important than the environment itself. In current iterations of the design experiment, MOOSE has been redesigned to better foster collaboration and explicitly address collaboration. The resulting product, *Pet Park*, reflects a different kind of thinking. De Bonte (1998) recognizes that "every aspect of the design should be evaluated to see what kind of an effect it might have on the developing community." Bruckman (1993b; 1994) has examined some of the social interworkings of MUDs, such as how communities handle deviant behavior or how cultural boundaries are tested through MUDs. As educators continue to design online environments to support community, further study of MUDs and MOOs, can uncover the mechanisms that designers use to foster collaboration and contribute to community building.

From video game consumers to creators

Provenzo's (1991) last critique of video games is that they place children in consumer roles, where they enter other designers' worlds instead of creating their own through play. In an argument that closely mirrors those made against television, he argues that children are losing opportunities to develop their creativity by playing video games. This argument has seemed compelling to a number of pundits over the years (See MediaScope 1996). However, current research suggests that video games are a form of popular culture very similar to film or television. In all but extreme cases, video game use has no visible negative effects on children (Lin & Lepper 1987). Indeed, the largest evidence contradicting this rationale might be that over the past two decades, where video games have infiltrated American Youth culture, there has been little evidence to suggest that children have grown up without the ability to think creatively. In other words, as the first two generations of "video kids" have grown up, becoming, perhaps more savvy consumers of and creators with digital media (Herz 1997).

Entering another's virtual world is as old as storytelling, and has been a continued tradition through printed literature, television, film, and now interactive digital media. Taken in this historical context, critics' concern with video games seems awfully familiar; critics were concerned that sound and color would ruin film, and later, were concerned that Americans would never leave the comforts of their homes, transfixed by the hypnotizing effects of television. Certainly, one could make persuasive arguments that television has had some negative effects on American culture, but short of killing pop culture, there is not much that can be done to stem any of these cultural patterns. However, when understood in its historical context, there is little reason to believe that video games will taint a generation of youth.

What Provenzo (1991) and likeminded critics fail to consider is that children are not just passive consumers of popular culture, but they reappropriate its symbols and forms and integrate it into their own play, as well. Video game playing occurs in social contexts; video game playing is not only a child (or group) of children in front of a console, it is also children talking about a game on the school bus, acting out scenes from a game on the playground, or discussing games on online bulletin boards. Ellis (1983) argues that like any popular media, video games become the building blocks of children's worlds. They are children's stories, characters, and heroes. Children do not play games in isolation. Often, they play in groups, and when they do not, they share their experiences socially. Arcades, for example, have always been about much more than video games; they

30

are a meeting place for adolescents to meet, display skills, and socialize free from parental control (Michaels 1993). And, home video game use is not just about playing a game; it is most often about friends getting together; for example, in order to explore the effects of a video game console system on a family, Mitchell (1985) gave video game consoles to twenty families and measured their effects on family interactions. Mitchell (1985) found that most families used the game systems as a way for the family together, to share play activity. Instead of leading to poor school performance, or strained family interactions, video game were a positive force on family interactions, "reminiscent of days of Monopoly, checkers, card games, and jigsaw puzzles" (Mitchell 1985 p.134). These findings suggest that video game play cannot be properly understood as simply a human-machine interaction; video game playing is situated in social and cultural spheres that are perhaps more important than the game itself.

As authors of digital environments and designers of interactions with technology, instructional technologists can learn from this debate about the social contexts of video games. Video gamers love their pixels, sounds, and hardware, but gaming, fundamentally, is a social phenomena, occurring in social groups distributed both through traditional social networks (work, school, family) and through the internet. In many ways, these groups resemble communities of practice; they have their own practice (game playing), language, and socially acceptable ways of behaving. Educators could benefit by studying these communities that form around gaming, in order to understand what *non-game* elements contribute to the engaging activity that is video game playing. For example, an instructional designer could study a group of video game players playing games together, or socializing outside of game play, such as on the internet, to understand what the social contexts are that help define game play as an activity. At the very least, studying video game players shows us that to take the human-computer relationship as the fundamental unit of analysis in determining what makes video gaming fun is misguided and suggests that a theory of motivation derived from video game playing ought to account for the social activities in which video game playing is embedded.

The future of video games in education

In the 1980s, there was great enthusiasm for harnessing the design knowledge embedded in video games to improve instruction. Educators learned some guidelines about designing engaging environments, most of which have become incorporated into student centered learning environments (Jonassen & Land 2000). Since then, gaming technology has improved dramatically, but very little has been done to study how these improvements might be incorporated into learning environments.

First, many teachers and educators have begun using commercially available "edutainment" products, but there has been very little empirical research into how these environments work. Design experiments (Brown 1992), which examine how instructional programs which employ video games could be useful for instructional technologists. Through such design experiments, instructional technologists might be able to empirically ground the work on instructional-design theory for simulations and games initiated by Reigeluth and Schwartz (1989). Taking a design approach to researching games might provide a useful framework for studying games, which thus far, have lacked a coherent research paradigm (Gredler 1996).

As designers of interactive learning environments, instructional technologists can also learn from current developments in gaming. Interactive fiction and online games are two areas of gaming that have not been studied much at all, and can inform the design of learning environments. Developments in interactive games can produce guidelines on developing socially based microworlds, and character development in interactive environments. Online games offer instructional technologists opportunities to understand how online environments are designed to support community development.

Last, video games, as one of the first, best developed, and most popular truly digital mediums embody a wealth of knowledge about interface, aesthetic, and interactivity issues. Historically, video games have been on the technological cutting edge of technically of what is possible, whether it is building online communities on the Internet, creating rich worlds using 3D graphics cards, or allowing dynamic synchronous interaction play by streaming information over the Internet. Indeed, even a cursory glance at the latest games can leave the designer blown away by what is currently possible with technology and inspired by the sleek interface or production values games contain. In fact, the greatest benefit of studying games may not be as much in generating theoretical understandings of human experience in technology or guidelines for instructional design, but rather, in inspiring us to create new designs.

Appendix I

Pac-Man	Traditional Schooling
Player controls how much she plays and when she plays.	Groups of students learn at one pace, and are given very little freedom to manage the content and pacing of their learning.
Students are actively engaged in quick and varied activity.	Students passively absorb information in routine activities, such as lecture.
Players play and practice until they master the game; players can take all of the time they need to master Pac-Man.	Students must all go at the same pace, regardless of achievement. As Reigeluth (1992) describes, traditional schooling holds time constant, allowing achievement to vary, instead of holding achievement constant (ensuring that all students master material) and allowing time to vary.
Players have feeling of mastering the environment, becoming more powerful, knowledgeable and skillful in the environment.	Students learn knowledge abstracted by teachers and regurgitate this knowledge on pencil and paper tests, rarely applying it in any dynamic context.

Video game players work together, sharing tips and trading secrets.	Students perform in isolation, and cannot use one another as resources.
Performance is criterion based; each student competes against his/her ability to master the game, to reach new goals. Every student can reach a state of "mastery" over the game.	Students are graded normatively, graded against one another's performance and encouraged to compete against one another.
Games are played for the intrinsic reward of playing them, for the emotional state they produce (Herz, 1997).	Schools are structured around extrinsic rewards, such as good grades or a fear of failure (flunking).

Contrasting "Pac-Man" with Traditional Schooling

Notes

1 There may be distinctions between the technical features and cultural significance of computer and video games that are worth exploring when discussing games in education, but for the purposes of this paper, they will both be treated as "video games" to simplify matters.
2 These principles, sound as they may be, are not new to education. Simulations and games are a long standing part of educational technology traditions and a good deal is known about how to use them in learning environments (Heinich, Molenda, Russell, & Smoldino, 1996; Gredler, 1996).
3 I deliberately use the word education rather than training to discuss the potentials of games. Many of these issues have direct analogs in training, although they are not discussed here. For a good discussion of training programs using game-based technology, see Prenksy, 2000.
4 Hi fidelity simulations need not be digital, however, as a "dress rehearsal" of an event or procedure might be considered a simulation.
5 Although these simulations use powerful computer technology, they are considered low fidelity because it is obvious to the player that he/she is using a model of the system, and not the controlling the Earth's weather. A high fidelity simulation would place more emphasis on actually reproducing weather conditions.
6 Some MUDs focus less on collaboration than others. For the purposes of this discussion, I will focus on those that specifically foster collaboration.

References

Anderson, C.A. & Ford, C.M. 1986. Affect of the game player: Short-term effects of highly and mildly aggressive video games. *Personality and Social Psychology Bulletin*, 12(4), 290–402.

Appleman, R. & Goldsworthy, R. 1999. The Juncture of Games & Instructional Design: Can Fun be Learning? Presentation made at the 1999 annual meeting of the Association of Educational Communications and Technology, Houston, TX.

Barab, S.A., Hay, K.E., & Duffy, T.M. 1999. Grounded constructions and how technology can help. *Tech Trends, 43 (2)*, 15–23.

Barnett, M., Barab, S. A., & Hay, K. E. in review. The virtual solar system project: Student modeling of the Solar System. Submitted to the Journal of College Science Teaching.

Bowman, R.F. 1982. A Pac-Man theory of motivation. Tactical implications for classroom instruction. *Educational Technology 22(9)*, 14–17.

Bracey, G.W. 1992. The bright future of integrated learning systems. *Educational Technology*, 32(9), 60–62.

Brown, A. L. 1992. Design experiments: Theoretical and methodological challenges in creating complex interventions in classroom settings. *The Journal of The Learning Sciences, 2*(2), 141–178.

Bruckman, A. 1993a. Community support for constructionist learning. *Computer Supported Cooperative Work.* 7, 47–86. Available online at *http://www.cc.gatech.edu/fac/Amy. Brocman/papers/index.html.*

Bruckman, A. 1993b. Gender Swapping on the Internet. Proceedings of INET, 93. Reston, VA: The Internet Society, 1993. Presented at the Internet Society (INET '93) in San Francisco, CA. Available online at http://www.cc.gatech.edu/fac/Amy.Brocman/papers/index.html

Bruckman, A. 1994. Approaches to managing deviant behavior in virtual communities. Proceedings of CHI New York: Assocation for Computing Machinery. Available online at http://www.cc.gatech.edu/fac/Amy.Brocman/papers/index.html.

Bruckman, A. 1997. MOOSE goes to school: A comparison of three classrooms using a CSCL environment. Proceedings of the Computer Supported Collaborative Learning Conference, Toronto, CA. Available online at http://www.cc.gatech.edu/fac/Amy. Brocman/papers/index.html.

Calvert, S.L., & Tan, S. 1994. Impact of virtual reality on young adults' physiological arousal and aggressive thoughts: Interaction versus observation. Special Issue: Effects of interactive entertainment technologies on development. *Journal of Applied Developmental Psychology, 15(1)*, 125–139.

Cassell, J & Jenkins, H. 1998. *From Barbie to Mortal Kombat: Gender and Computer Games*. Cambridge, MA: MIT Press.

Cassel, J. & Jenkins, H. 1998b. Chess for girls? Feminism and computer games. In Cassell, J & Jenkins, H. (Ed.), *From Barbie to Mortal Kombat: Gender and Computer Games*. Cambridge, MA: MIT Press.

Clark, R. E. 1983. Reconsidering research on learning from media. *Review of Educational Research 53(4)*, 445–459.

Cooper, J., & Mackie, D. 1986. Video games and aggression in children. *Journal of Applied Social Psychology, 16(8)*, 726–744.

Cordova, D. I., & Lepper, M. R. 1996. Intrinsic motivation and the process of learning: Beneficial effects of contextualization, personalization, and choice. *Journal of Educational Psychology, 88*, 715–730.

Csikszentmihalyi, M. 1990. *Flow: The Psychology of Optical Experience*. New York: Harper Perennial.

Csikszentmihalyi, M. & Larson, R. 1980. Intrinsic rewards in school crime. In M. Verble (Ed.), *Dealing in Discipline*, Omaha: University of Mid-America, 1980.

Dominick, J.R. 1984. Videogames, television violence, and aggression in teenagers. *Journal of Communication, 34(2)*, 136–147.

Driskell, J.E. & Dwyer, D.J. 1984. Microcomputer videogame based training. *Educational Technology, 24(2)*, 11–15.

Dunanc, T. & Gesue, M. 1998. Interviews with Theresa Duncan and Monica Gesue (Chop Suey). In Cassell, J. & Jenkins, (Ed.), *From Barbie to Mortal Combat: Gender and Computer Games*. Cambridge, MA: MIT Press.

Ellis, G.J. 1983. Youth in the electronic environment: An introduction. *Youth and Society, 15*, 3–12.

Graybill, D., Kirsch, J.R., & Esselman, E.D. 1985. Effects of playing violent versus nonviolent video games on the aggressive ideation of aggressive and nonaggressive children. *Child Study Journal 15(3)*, 299–205.

Graybill, D., Strawniak, M., Hunter, T., & O'Leary, M. 1987. Effects of playing versus observing violent versus nonviolent video games on children's aggression. *Psychology: A Quarterly Journal of Human Behavior, 24(3)*, 1–8.

Gredler, M.E. 1996. Educational games and simulations: A technology in search of a research paradigm. In In Jonassen, D.H. (Ed.), *Handbook of research for educational communications and technology*, p. 521–539. New York: MacMillan.

Hawley, C. Lloyd, P., Mikulecky, L., & Duffy, T. 1997. Workplace simulations in the classroom: The teacher's role in supporting learning. Paper presented at the annual meeting of the American Educational Research Association. Chicago, IL.

Hay, K.E. 1999. The digital weather station: A study of learning with 5D visualization. Paper presented at the Annual meeting of the American Educational Research Association, Montreal, Canada.

Heinich, R., Molenda, M., Russell, J.D., & Smaldino, S.E. 1996. *Instructional media and technologies for learning. (5th Ed.)*. Englewood Cliffs, NJ: Prentice Hall.

Herman, L. 1997. *Phoenix: The Fall & Rise of Videogames*. Union, NJ: Rolenda Press.

Herz, J.C. 1997. *Joystick Nation. How videogames ate our quarters, won our hearts, and rewired our minds*. Princeton, NJ: Little Brown & Company.

Jenkins, H. 1998. Voices from the combat zone: Game grrlz talk back. In Cassell, J. & Jenkins, (Ed.), *From Barbie to Mortal Combat: Gender and Computer Games*. Cambridge, MA: MIT Press.

Jonassen, D.H. 1988. Integrating learning strategies into courseware to facilitate deeper processing. In David H. Jonassen (Ed.), *Instructional Designs for Microcomputer Courseware (*pp. 151–181). Hillsdale, New Jersey: Erlbaum.

Jonassen, D.H. & Land, S. 2000. *The theoretical foundations of learning environments*. Mahwah, NJ: Erlbaum.

Kafai, Y.B. 1998. Video game designs by girls and boys: Variability and consistency of gender differences. In Cassell, J. & Jenkins, (Ed.), *From Barbie to Mortal Combat: Gender and Computer Games*. Cambridge, MA: MIT Press.

Kaplan, S.J. 1983. The image of amusement arcades and differences in male and female video game playing. *Journal of Popular Culture, 16*, 93–98.

Klein, M.H. 1984. The bite of Pac-Man. *Journal of Psychohistory, 11(3)*, 395–401.

Kubey, R. & Larson, R. 1990. The use and experience of the new video media among children and young adolescents. Special Issue: Children in a changing media environment. *Communication Research, 17(1)*, 107–130.

Malone, T.W. 1980. What makes things fun to learn? A study of intrinsically motivating computer games. (Report CIS-7). Palo Altao, CA: Xerox Palo Alto Research Center.

Malone, T. W. 1981. Toward a theory of intrinsically motivating instruction. *Cognitive Science, (4)*, 333–369.

MediaScope, 1996. The Social effects of electronic interactive games. An annotated bibliography. Studio City, CA: MediaScope.

Michaels, J.W. 1993. Patterns of video game play in parlors as a function of endogenous and exogenous factors. *Youth and Society 25(2)*, 272–289.

Mitchell, E. 1985. The dynamics of family interaction around home video games. Special Issue: Personal computers and the family. *Marriage and Family Review 8(1–2)*, 121–135.

Murray, J. H. 1997. *Hamlet on the Holodeck: The Future of Narrative in Cyperspace*. New York: The Free Press.

Papert, S. 1981. *Mindstorms: Children, computers and powerful ideas*. Brighton: Harvester Press.

Prensky, M. 2000. Digital Game-Based Learning. New York: McGraw Hill.

Provenzo, E.F. 1991. *Video kids: Making sense of Nintendo*. Cambridge, MA: Harvard.

Provenzo, E.F. 1992. What do video games teach? *Education Digest, 58(4)*, 56–58.

Reigeluth, C.M. (Ed.) 1999. *Instructional–design theories and models: A new paradigm of instructional theory Volume II*. Mahwah, NJ: Erlbaum.

Reigeluth, C.M. & Squire, K.D. 1998. Emerging work on the new paradigm of instructional theories. *Educational Technology,38(4)*, 41–47.

Reigeluth, C.M. & Schwartz, E. 1989. An instructional theory for the design of computer-based simulations. *Journal of Computer–Based Instruction, 16(1)*, 1–10.

Saltzman, M. (Ed.) 1999. *Game design: Secrets of the sages*. Indianapolis: Brady.

Savery, J.R., & Duffy, T.M. 1995. Problem based learning: An instructional model and its constructivist framework. *Educational Technology, 35(5)*, 31–37.

Schutte, N.S., Malouff, J.M., Post-Gorden, J.C., & Rodasta, A.L. 1988. Effects of playing videogames on children's aggressive and other behaviors. *Journal of Applied Social Psychology, 18(5)*, 454–460.

Sheff, D. 1999. *Game Over: Press Start to Continue*. Wilton, CT: GamePress.

Silvern, S.B., & Williamson, P.A. 1987. The effects of game play on young children's aggression, fantasy, and prosocial behavior. *Journal of Applied Social Psychology, 8(4)*, 453–462.

Sony Corporate website, 2000. *http://www.sony.com/*

Subrahmanyam K. & Greenfield, P.M. 1998. Computer games for girls: What makes them play? In Cassell, J. & Jenkins, (Ed.), *From Barbie to Mortal Combat: Gender and Computer Games*. Cambridge, MA: MIT Press

Thiagarajan, S. 1998. The myths and realities of simulations in performance technology. *Educational Technology, 38(5)*, 35–41.

Thiagarajan, S. & Thiagarajan, R. 1999. *Interactive experiential training: 19 strategies*. Bloomington, IN: Workshops by Thiagi, Inc.

74

FROM CONTENT TO CONTEXT

Videogames as designed experience

Kurt Squire

Source: *Educational Researcher*, 35(8), November 2006, 19–29.

Abstract

Interactive immersive entertainment, or videogame playing, has emerged as a major entertainment and educational medium. As research and development initiatives proliferate, educational researchers might benefit by developing more grounded theories about them. This article argues for framing game play as a *designed experience*. Players' understandings are developed through cycles of performance within the gameworlds, which instantiate particular theories of the world (ideological worlds). Players develop new identities both through game play and through the gaming communities in which these identities are enacted. Thus research that examines game-based learning needs to account for both kinds of interactions within the game-world and in broader social contexts. Examples from curriculum developed for *Civilization III* and *Supercharged!* show how games can communicate powerful ideas and open new identity trajectories for learners.

Although beneath the radar of many educators, November 9, 2004, was the largest-grossing media day in world history. No, the occasion was not the release of *Spiderman 2* or the latest *Star Wars* movie. The $125 million grossed on November 9 was for *Halo 2*, the anticipated sequel to the hit Xbox game *Halo*. Immersive interactive digital entertainment, or videogame playing, has emerged as an important medium exerting tremendous economic, cultural, and social influence. Many of today's youth spend more time playing in digital worlds than they do watching television, reading, or watching films (Funk, Hagen, & Schimming, 1999; Williams, 2003). How is all this time that is spent living in virtual worlds affecting people, schools, and our society? How will students react to the "grammar" of traditional schooling when they can buy entire "worlds in a box" for $50 (Gee, 2004; Squire, 2002)? The importance of gaming for education might best be summarized by the rhetorical question an elementary school student raised at the Game Developer's Conference: "Why read about ancient Rome when I can build it?" (Moulder, 2004). Survey studies suggest that game experiences are changing a generation's attitudes toward work and learning. However, these studies are largely overlooked by educators (Beck & Wade, 2004).

Games are an important site of a shift toward a *culture of simulation*, whereby digital technologies make it possible to construct, investigate, and interrogate hypothetical worlds that are increasingly a part of how we work and play (Turkle, 1995). Simulations play an increasingly important role in everything from conducting scientific inquiry to predicting the weather, to debating the future of Social Security (Casti, 1997; Starr, 1994; Wolfram, 2002). For the lay public, however, the medium of videogames is most often our first entrée into the culture of simulation (Starr). Videogame players can lead civilizations, fly aircraft, lead squadrons of urban warriors in foreign countries, or participate in virtual societies with their own languages, cultures, and economies (Squire, 2002; Steinkuehler, in press b). Consider *Full Spectrum Warrior*, a game designed by the U.S. Army in conjunction with the University of Southern California, which is both an urban warfare training tool and a commercial entertainment videogame where ordinary citizens can lead squadrons in urban environments. But games are not just static code; rather, they are sociotechnical networks. For example, *America's Army* is the $8 million game developed by the U.S. Army to attract new recruits. Not only does *America's Army* encode the Army's values into the game play, but it is also designed so that veterans, military personnel, and civilians can play together, creating an Army-owned space to interact with the public (Li, 2004).

America's Army and *Full Spectrum Warrior* are obvious, if not controversial, examples of the experiences that games can provide. However, a deeper look into gaming reveals a plethora of experiences available for children (and adults) that are more or less unknown in school. Farming and town simulators such as *Animal Crossing* and *Harvest Moon*, games aimed at younger children and available on the Nintendo *GameBoy*, make it possible to plan and plant crops, pay off mortgages, and essentially run a farm. Disney's *Toontown* allows kids from around the world to interact in a realtime 3D world where they meet and chat with other kids, engage in collaborative quests, and outfit their own furnishings (Mine, Shocet, & Hughston, 2003). For an even more dramatic example, consider a Chinese 16-year-old playing the Korean-based game *Lineage*, in which she becomes an international financier, trading raw materials, buying and selling goods, and speculating on currencies bought up by players in Europe and North America (Steinkuehler, 2004b). While videogames can be thought of as an extension of earlier media, clearly today's Internet connectivity, computational power, and 3D rendering ability make whole new kinds of experiences available outside school.

In this article, I argue that educators (especially curriculum designers) ought to pay closer attention to videogames because they offer *designed experiences*, in which participants learn through a grammar of *doing* and *being*. Until recently, there has been little study of the medium or of the implications of its attendant social structures for formal education (see Gee, 2003; McFarlane, Sparrowhawk, & Heald, 2002; Squire, 2004; Steinkuehler, in press a). However, "serious" games, or games used for purposes other than entertainment, are entering most public spheres and are estimated to be a $75 million annual industry, growing to perhaps $1 billion by the end of the decade (Erwin, 2005). Groups as diverse as the U.S. military, the National Association of Home Builders, and the National Alliance (a neo-Nazi organization) invest in games that represent their ideological views; but traditional educational interests are much slower to respond and less well represented within the serious games movement. Corporations, the military, and nonprofits are turning to games to express their ideologies; the challenge for K–1 2 educators is not just how to respond, but also how to mobilize and make available their own ideological views.

To date, educational research that treats videogames seriously has been slim, with the bulk of existing work examining representations in games. However, a mature body of educational games scholarship should address three interrelated areas: the critical study of games as participation in ideological systems, "learning as performance," and educational games as designed experiences. Central to the serious study of games are questions of how players make sense of these digitally mediated experiences: If games are "possibility spaces," then researchers need to account for how players inhabit them and the mechanisms by which meanings become interpreted from these experiences. For educators designing games, this shifts the question from one of "delivering content" to one of "designing experience." Many important questions persist—such as how games create and mobilize hybrid identities for players, and how these identities are enacted across contexts. However, given the contradictions between the grammar of games and the grammar of schooling, a bigger question looms: How will students react to the "designed experience of schooling" with its attending potential identities? Right now, it appears that corporations, the military, and private interests are ready to capitalize on this mismatch between the compelling learning potentials of educational media and schools' slowness to react to the changes. As these other groups leverage games toward their political agendas, the question is how the public sector will respond.

Games as participation in ideological worlds

In a 2002 Missouri court decision on the legality of restricting access to violent videogames (*Interactive Digital Software Association V. St. Louis County*, 2002), Senior U.S. District Judge Stephen N. Limbaugh wrote:

> This court reviewed four different video games and found no conveyance of ideas, expression, or anything else that could possibly amount to speech. The court finds that video games have more in common with board games and sports than they do with motion pictures.

Eventually, the 8th Circuit Court overturned Limbaugh's decision, with Judge Morris S. Arnold writing that videogames "are as much entitled to the protection of free speech as the best of literature'" (*Interactive Digital Software Association v. St. Louis County*, 2003, p. 5). Indeed, most games communities and the games press picked up on the logical contradiction behind Limbaugh's decision: If games cannot represent a point of view, then why care who plays them? (See Figure 1.) The notion that *Grand Theft Auto: San Andreas* or *Deus Ex 2* might communicate ideas is becoming increasingly accepted, but research and theory on how to make sense of games as interactive texts lags behind. Contemporary criticism of games—from a multiplicity of perspectives—assumes that the *presence of* violence or misogyny in a game world is necessarily equated with *advocating* violence or misogyny and thus creates violent or misogynist attitudes in players.

To illustrate the problem with this view, it is worth examining *Grand Theft Auto: San Andreas*, a controversial game representing aspects of 1990s Los Angeles urban culture, as an interactive text. The player inhabits the character of Carl Johnson, a Black man who is returning to the city of San Andreas to attend his slain mother's funeral. The player is handed a bicycle, which he is told to ride home, but after the first mission the player is more or less free to do as he or she pleases. The game does not require players to run over, shoot, or harm a player character in the game; these are choices that players might make. To be sure, there

Figure 1 A Penny-Arcade cartoon mocking Judge Limbaugh's ruling. The cartoon was quite popular and represented typical gamer discourse surrounding the decision. From http://www. penny-arcade.com/view.php3?date=2002-04-26&res=l, reproduced with permission of publisher

is a particular ideology at work in the game. The violent streets of San Andreas are rife with gang warfare, and certain actions are rewarded in ways, while others are not even possible. Thus we can talk about *San Andreas* as a *world*, and it is a world with particular rules that give consequence to actions. To survive in this world, players need to learn the underlying rule systems and how they interact.

Of course, *San Andreas* is not "any old world" but a stylized rendition of 1990s California, containing a mixture of authentic and fictitious California landmarks and neighborhoods, mostly in the Los Angeles area. And the "Los Angeles" depicted in *San Andreas* is not "any old Los Angeles," but one created by a team of developers from Dundee, Scotland, most of whom first visited California during preproduction for the game and were a little surprised that it was not as described in popular media. Thus *San Andreas* is a curiously global artifact, the product of a team of Scottish developers who, having been raised with the fictitious Los Angeles of N.W.A.'s music and Spike Lee's films, now export that culture back to Americans. Players are invited to try on the persona of an inner-city Black gangster, experiencing in stylized form *some* of what it means to live in a 1990s hip-hop world. For some players, inhabiting Carl Johnson may be an empowering experience, enabling them to understand America's fear of and fascination with the urban African American male. Other players might ponder the limited choices and identities presented to African American males or representations of African Americans in popular media, or America's fetishization and marginalization of hip-hop culture.

Among game players, the *Grand Theft Auto* series is most noted for the free form play it allows. It is common knowledge that most players never complete a majority of the missions, instead using the game as a driving- or chase-scene simulator of sorts. For players, part of what makes *San Andreas* interesting is the material that it provides for creating interesting interactions—whether in driving into the countryside in a "pimped-out" 1970s-style sedan or stealing a hot dog truck and driving it through a recreation of a 1990s Compton neighborhood. It is critical that researchers examine what players actually do with games, rather than assuming that there is any one "game itself" as it is meant to be played.

If a hallmark of games is their *interactivity*, their ability to grant players *agency* within the narrative fiction of the gameworld and its rules, then theoretical models need to account for players' actions in creating the experience. Indeed, because play is instantiated only through players' actions, tensions arise over who exactly is the "author" of the game experience. As noted game designer Doug Church (2000) describes, "Our desire to create traditional narrative and exercise authorial control over the gaming world often inhibits the players' ability to involve themselves in the game world" (cited in Kreimeier, 2000). Many designers have come to see games as vehicles for player expression, thinking of game design as choreographing the rules, representations, and roles for players, in other words the contexts, in which players can generate meaning (LeBlanc, 2005). As such, game designers "write" the *parameters* for players' experience, and the game experience as such is best described as an interaction between the game designer and player (Robison, 2004).

If player agency is central to the medium, then we can only understand games' meanings by understanding what players *do* with them and the meanings that players construct through these actions (Malone, 1981; Murray, 1997). Too often, past analyses have focused on representations in the games or on the games' surface features, without examining gaming practices or experiences, or the games' meanings for their players (Jenkins, 1992; Jenkins, in press; Provenzo, 1991). Whereas traditional critiques of games have focused solely on the text, images, and animations, the fact that games can be enacted only through the player requires theoretical models that span the game and its contexts of consumption. As the case of *San Andreas* suggests, understanding a game's context of production may also be important for understanding the layers of meaning in a text.

For an example closer to education, take *Civilization III* (the third installment of the top selling *Civilization* franchise), a strategy game where the player rules a civilization from 4000 B.C. to the present. The game is based on a geographical-materialist game system where players build cities to gather resources (food, natural resources, and commerce; Friedman, 1999). Players also build cities, engage in trade, and of course wage war, giving rise to situations such as civilizations negotiating (and perhaps warring) over scarce resources such as oil. The central features of the game system present an argument for the fates of civilizations as largely governed by geographical and materialist processes, an argument also made by Jared Diamond (1999) in his Pulitzer Prize-winning *Guns, Germs, and Steel*. A single game requires about 20 hours to play, and achieving mastery requires one hundred hours or more (Squire, in press a).

A number of educators and critics have raised valid concerns that what players learn from games is not the properties of complex systems but simple heuristics (e.g., one learns the strategic necessity of always keeping two spearmen in every city). The fear is that without access to the underlying model, students will fail to recognize simulation bias or the "hidden curriculum" of what is left out (see Starr, 1994; Turkle, 2003). In a dissertation study of poor African American ninth-graders playing *Civilization III*, Squire (2004) found that most students turned the game into a simulation of European colonization, asking, Why is it that Europeans colonized the Americas, and why did Africans and Asians not colonize America or Europe? In school, most of these students were given a historical narrative of the steady march of Western liberty, democracy, and rationality (see Dunn, 2000; Manning, 2003). In contrast, *Civilization III* can offer a story of advantageous geographical conditions that provides access to global trade networks, resources, technologies, and limited opportunities for population expansion. In the words of one student, the game shows "how geography and gold (i.e., materialist goods) determine how history plays out" (Squire, in press a). Thus *Civilization III* enlisted students' identities as gamers and created a space where they could bring their own experiences to the study of world history.

Although *Civilization III* was designed more as entertainment than as a political statement, many contemporary videogames *are* designed with politics in mind. *Deus Ex* is a popular science fiction game series full of government-sponsored terrorists, powerful corporations, and duplicitous leaders. The goal behind the original game, according to designer Warren Spector, is to give the player moral choices between trusting organizations and trusting individuals, and to let the player rethink who is considered an "enemy" of the state. In *Deus Ex 2*, the player must continuously decide whether to ally with multiple competing organizations (governments, corporations, family loyalties) in a world where every choice involves moral ambiguity and no decision is ethically "right." Personal politics aside, it is clear that games are introducing players to powerful ideas, some of which may align with school, some of which may not.

Games provide high graphic, dynamic "worlds in a box," but these worlds are not full representations of reality; they are stripped-down worlds, with limited opportunities for interaction. A *Civilization III* player cannot invent a new religion, and a *Deus Ex 2* player cannot (really) make love to an NPC (nonplayable or computer character). Thus games focus our attention and mold our experience of what is important in a world and what is to be ignored. The game designers' choices, particularly of what to strip away from a world, can be read as ideological when considered in relation to other systems (Starr, 1994). We are only beginning to understand how these games are interpreted and understood by their players. Building from work on other media (see Black, 2005; Jenkins, 1992), we can predict that some of this interpretive work occurs through *interpretive communities* where meanings are produced, negotiated, and given legitimacy (Dewey, 1938; Scardamalia & Bereiter, 1996).

Knowledge as performance

To date, there are few studies of learning through game play, although games are rich sites for studying learning, for both practical and theoretical reasons: Practically, it is important to know what players are taking away from games such as *Grand Theft Auto, Civilization III,* and *Deus Ex 2*, as well as such games' potential as educational media, given recent interest in games in e-learning (Aldrich, 2005). Theoretically, games are interesting in that they are sites of naturally occurring, intrinsically motivated learning. Early studies of games showed how they use challenge, curiosity, control, and fantasy (as well as opportunities for social interaction, competition, and collaborative play) to engage players (Malone, 1981; Malone & Lepper, 1987). These same design features have been used to increase learning on pre-post gains in controlled studies using mathematics software (Cordova & Lepper, 1996). Such studies suggest the promise of deriving learning principles from studies of games but are focused on a relatively general level of abstraction and do not account for innovations from the last two generations of games, such as *interactive narratives, collaborative problem solving*, and *game players as producers* (Squire, 2003).

Digital games as microcosms for 21st-century learning environments

Today's generation of games contain a whole new set of features, making them intriguing suites of learning. Specifically, they are sites where we can look at learning both as (a) interaction in the social and material world, where learners participate in open and closed problem solving; and (b) participation in distributed social organizations such as self-organizing learning communities, which are "microcosms for studying the emergence, maintenance, transformation, and even collapse of online affinity groups" (Steinkuehler, in press a). In short, just as previous generations of psychologists studied expert chess players, Vai tailors in West Africa, or the navigators of destroyer warships as examples of "cognition in the wild," we might study games as sites of digitally mediated learning (Chase & Simon, 1973; Hutchins, 1995; Lave & Wenger, 1991). James Paul Gee (2003, 2004, 2005) argues that videogames are an ideal laboratory for studying learning principles because, as the games increase in complexity, game designers embed structures to help players learn them. Examining these features may provide insights into the design of other learning environments— particularly educational software. Virtual worlds, in particular, might help us understand how to design distributed communities of practice, or affinity groups stretched across physical space and linked by telecommunications technologies such as the cell phone and Internet.

Learning by doing

A core characteristic of games is that they are organized around *doing*. They are uniquely organized for a *functional* epistemology, where one learns through doing, through performance (Squire, in press a). Cognition in digital worlds is thoroughly mediated by players' capacities for action: The player's actions are his or her interface with the world (Clinton, 2004; Young, 2004). Legendary game designer Shigeru Miyamoto claims to design games around the verbs that players enact, and these verbs—the running, jumping, diving, punching, kicking, and swinging through enemies and obstacles—are the building blocks by which players *become* action heroes, civilization leaders, or L.A. gangsters (Clinton, 2004; Sheff, 1993; Squire, 2005a). It is no coincidence that players new to a game start by picking up a controller and seeing what they can do, as figuring out "what the body can *do* in the world is figuring out who you *are* in that world" (Clinton, 2004, p. 3). Of course, game players aren't doing just anything in these worlds, they are motivated by challenges set up by designers (or constructed by the players themselves), and are limited by the constraints of the game system.

    Perception of the game world is the other half of the perception/action system. Games' graphics are more than pretty pictures; they are signs that the player must learn to read. As players interact with the world to ascertain possibilities for action, they develop a *professional vision* for the affordances of the world (Gee, 2005; Goodwin, 1994; Jenkins & Squire, 2004). This vision is shaped by the strategic significance of the world's signs; a *Viewtiful Joe* player, for example, learns to read the signs of the system in terms of his or her goals and needs in the space (the first being to stay alive), pointing to the importance of *intentionality* in cognition and understandings (Barab et al., 1999; Squire, in press b). Critically, games require players to learn to read the game space under what Dewey might call "the threat of extinction." The game is quite literally over for the player who fails to "read" *Viewtiful Joe*.

Through recursive cycles of perceiving and acting, thinking and doing within the game system, a player begins to adopt a particular perceptivity of an avatar within the game world; the player becomes a hybrid version of himself or herself playing as Carl Johnson in *San Andreas* or the leader of a civilization (Gee, 2005). Examining games from a socially situated linguistics framework, Gee (2003) argues that games set up *projective identities* for players, spaces where they develop unique hybrid characters, which Gee calls the "Jim Gee playing as Lara Croft" hybrid. The resultant game actions are a synthesis between the character and the affordances—capacities for action of the avatar. Critically, players learn not just facts or procedures but how to "be" in the world as the game character, developing the appreciative systems of the avatar as well. This problem—how to set up transformative identity spaces—is also a core enterprise for educators, who want to help students become scientists, doctors, or global activists (Shaffer, Squire, Halverson, & Gee, 2005). Educators in general, and educational technologists in particular, might benefit by thinking of videogames as a "research and development lab" for educational theory and practice.

Participating in social worlds

Given the technical sophistication and visual appeal of videogames, it is tempting to focus on the properties of games-as-objects; however, videogames and their use are mediated by social structures, such as families, peer groups, affinity groups, or classrooms (Crawford, 1982; Hakkarainen, 1999; Mitchell, 1985; Salen & Zimmerman, 2004; Squire, 2002, 2003). Indeed, if we observe them, most children playing games will be talking, sharing strategies, downloading FAQs from the Internet, or participating in online forums (to say nothing about the media—drawings and stories—that they create about games). Game play, as an activity, frequently spans multiple media (Squire & Steinkuehler, in press). Most gamers describe their play as a social experience, a way to connect with friends, and rare is the player who truly games "alone" in any meaningful sense (Kuo, 2004; Johnson, 2005a).

The most intense social learning is found in massively multiplayer games, games where players interact with thousands of other players in real time over the Internet. Unique to these games is the *persistent game world*. The game world itself is online 24 hours a day, 7 days a week, across sessions, so that if my character on *Star Wars Galaxies* owns a house, it is in the world whether I log in or not. Players' avatars also persist across sessions, so that their online avatar becomes another identity that they inhabit. Psychologist Sherry Turkle (1995) calls this unique state *pseudonymity*. Players have a degree of anonymity, but it is mediated through avatars' histories and roles within the community. The most noted example of these spaces has been the way that they allow players to explore new identities, particularly ones where they inhabit worlds through different genders (Bruckman, 1999; Steinkuehler & Chmiel, 2005). Already, a number of legal scholars, economists, and sociologists are using them as laboratories to gain fundamental insights about their fields (Castronova, 2001; Ondrejka, 2004). A growing number of educators are doing the same (Lemke, 2004; Steinkuehler, in press a).

Once the domain of "computer nerds and hackers," persistent online game worlds are now entering the mainstream. Disney's *ToonTown*, a massively multiplayer online role-playing game (MMORPG) aimed at elementary-school-aged kids, now reaches more than a hundred thousand subscribers and is rising (Woodcock, 2005). In *ToonTown*, players create cartoon avatars and band together in teams to play pranks on "cogs," evil cartoon villains who want to turn *ToonTown* into a drab office environment (Mine et al., 2003). *World of Warcrafit*, the current king of MMORPGs, boasts 6 million global subscribers as of this writing (Woodcock, 2005). Aimed at a general gaming market, *World of Warcraft* (somewhat like *Everquest* before it) is also attracting a large number of school-age children (Squire, 2005b). The social pressure of such games, where players literally live second lives in virtual worlds, has yet to become much of a mainstream issue in the United States, although China and Korea both have experienced social friction from online gaming (British Broadcasting Corporation, 2005). In China, legislation has been passed limiting youth access to online games, affecting *World of Warcraft* (with over 2 million Chinese subscribers), among others. As global gaming cultures continue to grow, everyday American game players are beginning to experience the kind of social, economic, and cultural issues (virtual sweatshops, virtual racism) that arise from a global gaming market where virtual currencies and labor flow freely across national boundaries (Loftus, 2005; Steinkuehler, 2004a; Thompson, 2005).

As designed cultures, persistent world games function more like digital nations than like traditional games, making them intriguing sites for studying how people reciprocally inhabit and create culture (Barde, 1996; Squire & Steinkuehler, in press). At a minimum, to be an expert player means not just learning a specialized language—knowing the difference between "kiting" and "trolling," "beta vets" and "n00bs," "twinking" and "nerfing"—but also participating in practices in socially valued ways. "Being" a competent druid, princess, droid maker, architect, or speculator in an online world demands learning new geographies, literacies, rule systems, and ways of expressing oneself (Leander & Lovvorn, 2004; Steinkuehler, 2003; Squire & Steinkuehler). One productive tract for inquiry is studying such environments as laboratories for how societies function (Steinkuehler, 2005). A second may be to examine the disconnect between the kinds of identities made available for players in games (e.g., international money trader), and those available to students in school (passive recipient of knowledge).

In popular media, videogames are frequently blamed for a decline in literacy, intellectual life, and even civic engagement (Solomon, 2004). Despite the many "literacy" scares based on fear that games will replace text, Steinkuehler (in press a, in press b) finds that participation in Massively Multiplayer Online (MMO) Discourses *is itself* a literacy activity. Facility with written language is central in the community as players use text to negotiate activities, enact identities, and apprentice others into the community. Using discourse analysis, Steinkuehler (2004b) describes a defining feature of apprenticeships as *joint participation in mutually valued practices*, wherein an expert, modeling expert behavior, guides practice by focusing attention on important environmental features and gradually entrusts control to the apprentice. All of these practices occur within legitimate game play and with all information given just-in-time. As Steinkuehler emphasizes, players are "socialize[d] into certain ways of being and understanding the virtual world, ways that are tied to particular values" (pp. 6-7). In short, participation in MMOs constitutes participation in social practices with real consequences for its members.

To date, there are still relatively few studies of what players do in these environments or what the consequences are for participation outside the game context. Participation in online gaming— much like high-end participation in any part of today's popular culture (i.e., Pokemon, fan fiction), demands a range of (primarily written) social practices, eliciting an enormous amount of reading, writing, research, analysis, and argumentation (Black, 2005; Jenkins, in press; Johnson, 2005a; Leander & Lovvorn, 2004; Steinkuehler, 2004a; Steinkuehler, Black, & Clinton, 2005). Typical game practices—including mentoring, writing FAQs, participating in message boards, developing fictional back-stories, and creating mathematical models of game systems are quite similar to many practices valued in school (Steinkuehler & Chmiel, 2006). As such, they could be *leading activities*, activities that orient learners to academically valued practices and their underlying purposes, both of which are critical for academic success (Brown & Cole, 2002). Given contemporary theories of transfer as preparation for future learning, whereby "good learning" is that which prepares one for future success, games and other forms of popular culture could be educationally important, raising important equity issues about who has access to such communities (Johnson, 2005a, 2005b). Outside school, in *games such as Star Wars Galaxies*, students have opportunities to become architects, shopkeepers, designers, warriors, Jedi, financial traders, or dancers, and can make real world wages while playing a game. Will we provide students similarly diverse opportunities for experience in schools?

Games as designed experience

Given the complexity of games such as *Sim City* and the ability of gaming technologies to support interaction among thousands of users in photorealistic worlds and in real time, it is no wonder that games are attracting attention as a medium for learning (Aldrich, 2005; Games-to-Teach Team, 2003). On the one hand, given that nearly every other medium has been used for learning, it seems self-evident that games eventually will become a part of our educational system. On the other hand, games embody values (collaborative learning, learning through failure, personalized learning) that are at odds with the grammar of formal schooling (Beck & Wade, 2004). The history of educational media suggests that media that do not conform to the values of the broader system will not be taken up (Cuban, 1986). Although drill and practice games and relatively simple simulation activities have long been used in formal learning environments, today's contemporary games, which frequently last for 40 hours or more, operate under different assumptions (see Table 1). The game provides a set of experiences, with the assumption being that learners are active constructors of meaning with their own drives, goals, and motivations. Most good games afford multiple trajectories of participation and meaning making. Content is delivered just-in-time and on demand to solve problems. An emerging model of games suggests that they excel by providing learners with situated experiences of activities, whereby they develop new ways of thinking, knowing, and being in worlds (Shaffer, Squire, Halverson, & Gee, 2005).

Entertainment games used for learning

Many in the current generation of students first experience history, urban planning, or business not through school, television, or movies but through videogames. The *Sim City, Civilization*, and various *Tycoon* simulation games are now about 15 years old, and for about as long, educators have hypothesized that they could be effective learning tools (e.g. Berson, 1996; Hope, 1996; Kolson, 1996; Prensky, 2001; Teague & Teague, 1995). Although teachers around the country use or have used *Sim City, Civilization*, and *Rollercoaster Tycoon* in urban planning, world history, or physics classes, there has been little academic study of how learning occurs through such programs or how conceptions of history or urban planning change as they are represented through digital media.

Emerging studies of educators using videogames suggest that the videogames are much more complex than earlier game- based media. For example, turning *Civilization III* into a colonial simulation affected the kinds of questions students asked as well as the observations and interpretations they made about history. For the most part, students interpreted their game events in terms of preexisting notions of colonization or geography but expanded and modified their understandings of colonization in the process of playing. As players managed natural resources, they learned not only where oil, coal, or sugar cane is located but how these resources affect the growth of civilizations. Ross Dunn (2000) called this approach to world history the "patterns of change" model, wherein world history consists of patterns of human activity across broad time-scales, as opposed to the traditional national or "Western civilization" approach.

Table 1 Contrasting game types

Aspects	Exogenous Games[a]	Endogenous Games[b]
Learner is . . .	An empty receptacle. An example is *Math Blaster*, where the learner is "motivated" to learn a prescribed set of skills and facts.	An active, sense-making, social organism. An example is *Grand Theft Auto*, where the learner brings existing identities and experiences that color interpretations of the game experience.
Knowledge is . . .	Knowledge of discrete facts. The facts are "true" by authority (generally the authority of the game designer).	Tool set used to solve problems. The right answer in *Civilization* is that which is efficacious for solving problems in the game world.
Learning is . . .	Memorizing. Learners reproduce a set of prescribed facts, such as mathematics tables.	Doing, experimenting, discovering for the purposes of action in the world. Players learn in role-playing games for the purposes of acting within an identity.
Instruction is . . .	Transmission. The goal of a drill and practice game is to transmit information effectively and to "train" a set of desired responses.	Making meaning/construction, discovery, social negotiation process. Instruction in *Supercharged*! involves creating a set of well-designed experiences that elicit identities and encourage learners to confront existing beliefs, perform skills in context, and reflect on their understandings.
Social model is . . .	"Claustrophobic." Players are expected to solve problems alone; using outside resources is generally "cheating."	Fundamentally group oriented. Games are designed to be played collectively, in affinity groups, and distributed across multiple media. They are designed with complexity to spawn affinity groups and communities that support game play.
Pre-knowledge is . . .	Set of facts, knowledge, and skills to be assessed for proper pacing. In *Math Blaster*, players' self-efficacy in mathematics is not addressed.	Knowledge to be leveraged, played upon. Pre-knowledge is expected to color perception, ideas, and strategies. In *Environmental Detectives*, challenges are structured so that players become increasingly competent and learn to see the value of mathematics.
Identity is . . .	Something to be cajoled. If players are not "motivated" to do math, the game developer's job is to create an "exciting" context for the learner.	Something to be recruited, managed, built over time. In *Environmental Detectives*, learners develop identities as scientists.
Context is . . .	A motivational wrapper. The context in *Math Blaster* is something to make learning more palatable.	The "content" of the experience. In *Civilization*, the geographical-materialist game model is the argument that situates activity and drives learning.

a Games in which the context is extrinsic to the game play.
b Games in which the context and game play are inextricably linked. (These terms are from Rieber, 1996).

Students used these game experiences to think about why civilizations grow, flourish, and fade, and how wars, revolutions, and civilizations evolve as the products of interweaving geographical, social, economic, and political forces. Many students who rejected traditional school-based curricula as "heritage" or cultural myths of "Western progress" found that *Civilization III* allowed them to "replay history" and learn history through geographical materialist lenses rather than the ideology of Western progress. In one discussion (reported in Squire & Barab, 2004), students explain what they learned through playing *Civilization III*:

Tony: Luxuries buys you money and money buys you everything. The right location gives you luxuries gives you income more income gives you technology which affects your politics. It all connects.

Kent: Geography affects your diplomacy because it gets you more resources and affects how they treat you.

Tony: Geography can affect the growth of your civilization.

Dwayne: It affects your war.

As students interacted with the game and discussed it in class, they began to understand its ideological bias and at times, took it up as a framework for explaining world history. But simulation games also remediate games in ways that educators ought to consider more deeply. When asked to describe what he learned from this unit, Tony commented, "I learned that no matter how it plays out, history plays by the same set of rules."

Games as new educational media

If we take McLuhan's "the medium is the message" seriously, then it is interesting to think about how representing ideas through games remediates how we experience those phenomena (Holland, Jenkins, & Squire, 2003). Conceptualizing domains through the medium of games means taking content and rethinking it in terms of designed experience, as represented through challenges, goals, and practices (Games-to-Teach Team, 2003). Such an approach might allow educators to go beyond traditional notions of education as "exposure to content" and reimagine it, along progressive lines, as enrichment of experience (Dewey, 1938; Gee, 2004). Contemporary games function in ways very different from traditional "educational" games; whereas traditional educational games use context as a motivational wrapper for the game experience, contemporary games literally put players *inside* game systems. Expanding on Rieber's (1996) distinction between endogenous and exogenous games, we can contrast games where the context *is* the game play with games where the context is irrelevant to game play (see Table 1).

As an example of what a game-based pedagogy might look like, consider the physics game *Supercharged!* that was developed at MIT to help students learn basic concepts in electrostatics (Jenkins, Squire, & Tan, 2004). Studies of physicists in labs show that, in order to understand physics phenomena, the physicists frequently put themselves *into* problem spaces. Ochs, Gonzales, and Jacoby (1996) write that "scientists express their subjective involvement . . . by taking the perspective of (and empathizing with) some object being analyzed and by involving themselves in graphic (re)enactment of physical events." Electrostatics, a foundational area in physics, is particularly difficult for students to grasp because—although they may use electricity or even play around with magnets—they have no *direct experience* of charged particles interacting or moving through magnetic fields. Given that one of the affordances of games is the way that they place players within systems, the designers of *Supercharged!* hoped to give students the experience of entering the arena of physics problems just as physicists do, an instructional strategy common to the qualitative physics approach (diSessa, 1998; Forbus, 1997; Jenkins, Squire, &Tan).

In *Supercharged!*, players enter a world of electrostatic charges and must lead a group of virtual classmates through levels that are matched to classic physics thought experiments. Building on diSessa's notion of intuitive physics, game levels are designed to confront players' understandings of physics phenomena and to help them develop more robust intuitions of electrostatic physics through a playful rethinking of traditional physics curricula. Figure 2, for example, shows a level designed to build players' intuitions about electrostatic forces and distance; players, attempting to go straight through the level and toward the goal frequently hypothesize that the forces generated from each charge will negate one another or create a balance of forces. In reality, because the strength of a force diminishes over distance by the square of the distance (Coulomb's Law, $F = kqQ/r^2$), the player quickly moves toward the charge that is closest to his or her position (the point of view of the camera). As players confront a variety of levels designed to elucidate this mathematical principle, they begin to intuit how electrostatic forces interact.

In a study of *Supercharged!* *in* a middle school classroom, Barnett, Squire, Higgenbotham, and Grant (2004) found that students who participated in a unit based on playing *Supercharged!* outperformed students in learning physics through hands-on experiments, demonstrations, and viewing simulations. In an interview following the game, one student described how he learned the meaning of field lines (a scientific visualization technique) in the game. "The electric goes from the positive charge to the negative charge like this [drawing a curved line from a positive charge to a negative charge]. I know this because this is what it looked like in the game . . . . " The most dramatic results, in fact, came from students who were unsuccessful in school, suggesting that game-based formats may make complex science thinking accessible to a broader range of students.

Supercharged!, originally designed to help MIT students in physics, does not include many other aspects of science learning that would be critical for less science-minded populations, such as coming to see, think, act, and be in the world as a physicist might—coming to inhabit the identity of a physicist. One can imagine games that provide students with experiences as scientists, environmental engineers, or doctors, much as role-playing games offer experiences as government agents, urban gang members, or leaders of civilizations. However, videogames that are designed to provide experiences of inhabiting identities within ideological worlds are much more complex to make. They must provide objects, characters, and interactions that are believable. They need to immerse players so that they experience the world as scientists, replete with perceptions, actions, conversations, and modes of expression where they participate in social practice as scientists. The possibility of creating such games in fully digitized media is now visible on the horizon; with appropriate funding it can be done (Holland, Jenkins, & Squire, 2003; Shaffer, Squire, Halverson, & Gee, 2005).

Such models are being prototyped with emerging technologies such as augmented reality simulation games (Klopfer & Squire, in press). Klopfer and colleagues have been using augmented reality simulations, simulations that span real and virtual worlds, to incorporate the world around them into gameboards. Augmented reality simulations attempt to place students in roles as investigators, scientists, or activists, leveraging players' emotional connections to physical locations. Players begin with a challenge, such as investigating a friend's death that might be tied to environmental poisoning. Using handheld technologies, players take readings from simulated stations to measure toxins (such as trichloroethene flowing through groundwater) or to interview virtual characters. Working in teams, players must identify problems, pose data-gathering strategies, draw conclusions, and reframe their hypotheses as they work.

A core feature underlying such simulations is that they give students the experience of being competent, independently thinking problem solvers, enabling them to develop identities in relation to an established community of practice. Thus these augmented reality simulation games share much in common with professional practice simulations, where students learn as doctors, architects, or journalists (Shaffer, 2004). Shaffer argues that participating in such simulations, particularly when built on ethnographies of practice, allows students to develop *epistemic frames*, or coherent ways of thinking that they can bring to new situations. Students with experience in "being" environmental engineers gain a way of thinking that they can draw from in other academic areas. Thus it is important that role-playing games such as *Environmental Detectives* give players access to ways of *thinking* and *being* in the world, as opposed to just asking them to memorize facts.

Role-playing games such as *Environmental Detectives* try to draw on the engaging features of *Deus Ex, Grand Theft Auto*, or *Civilization* by providing players with designed experiences in a world constructed by a particular set of rules where they can learn through performing a certain kind of role, a certain way of being in the world. Hopefully, the ideological nature of such pedagogies is clear; educators using game-based pedagogies are designing experiences for students that privilege certain worldviews and ways of being in the world over others. Therefore, serious consideration needs to be given to what kinds of experiences our students ought to have. At a minimum, such experiences, which are based on participation in ideological systems and which draw on learning as performance, include a hidden curriculum of active participation in problem solving, as opposed to docile reception of school-sanctioned content (Apple, 1992; Gee, 2004; Squire, in press a).

Conclusions

Although digital games have largely been ignored by educational researchers, they are a powerful new medium with potential implications for schooling. In videogames, knowing is at its essence a kind of performance, as learners learn by doing, but within powerful constraints instantiated through software and social systems. The focus is on experience that enables students to develop situated understandings, to learn through failure, and to develop identities as expert problem solvers (Gee, 2003; Squire, in press a). In this article I argue that educators might profit by studying these *designed experiences*, experiences resulting from the intersection of design constraints and players' intentions.

Possibly more important, videogame cultures represent tacit assumptions about knowledge, learning, expertise, and formal institutions that may be at odds with those of schools (Beck & Wade, 2004; Gee, 2004; Lankshear & Knobel, 2003). Videogames epitomize a potentially destabilizing wave of technologies whereby students can access information and social networks at any time, anywhere. As students confront more sophisticated digital worlds outside school, educators

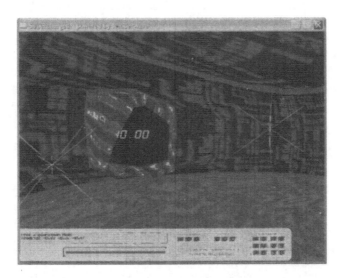

Figure 2 Screen shot from Supercharged! The player's position is represented by the camera position. The black hole is the goal and the numbers indicate the distance to the goal. The stars indicate negative electric charges; the lines are field lines showing the force of the charge. Copyright 2006 by Massachusetts Institute of Technology. Reproduced with permission

are challenged to react: Do we present and expect students to pursue print-based literacies, ignoring the visual culture and computer mediated worlds they inhabit out of school? And, perhaps most important, what identities do we make available to students in school? Our schools ask students to learn all at the same rate, in the same way, and at the same time; but games make a variety of learning paths available. Schools ask students to inhabit a limited and very particular set of identities as recipients of ideas and agendas prescribed for them; in contrast, games require players to be active participants in co-constructing their worlds and identities with designers. Games and their associated technologies may not render schools obsolete, but the educational community should pay attention to the kinds of learning that occur through games and digital worlds.

As videogames mature as a medium, the question becomes not whether they will be used for learning but for whom and in what contexts. If games have the dramatic potential to immerse players in complex systems, allowing them to learn the points of view of those systems and perhaps even develop identities within the systems, it is not surprising that the military, "advergaming" advertisers, and private groups have begun using games to support their agendas (Squire, 2005b). Perhaps it is also not surprising that games have been taken up most stridently in the military, which is largely charged with training those who have fallen through the cracks of the American educational system. As the military, private businesses, and nonprofit groups use games to spread their ideologies, it is crucial that educators with an interest in democracy and K–12 education examine the medium's potential to spread their influence. With the U.S. Navy and Air Force planning similar games, and middle-class parents playing *Pokemon* or *Civilization* with their children, we need to ask, What will happen to families that cannot afford such technologies? And what will become of formal schools if they are the last to recognize the potential of this powerful medium?

References

Aldrich, C. (2003). *Learning by doing: A comprehensive guide to simulations, computer games, and pedagogy in e-learning and other educational experiences.* New York: Wiley.

Apple, M. W. (1992). *Ideology and curriculum.* New York: Routledge.

Barab, S. A., Cherkes-Julkowski, M., Swenson, R., Garrett., S., Shaw, R. E., & Young, M. (1999). Principles of self-organization: Ecologizing the learner-facilitator system. *Journal of the Learning Sciences,* 8(3–4), 349–390.

Barnett, M., Squire, K., Higgenbotham, T., & Grant, J. (2004). *Electromagnetism supercharged!* In Y. Kafai, W. Sandoval, N. Enyedy, A. Dixon, & F. Herrera (Eds.), *Proceedings of the 2004 International Conference of the Learning Sciences* (pp. 513–520). Mahwah, NJ: Lawrence Erlbaum.

Bartle, R. (1996). Hearts, clubs, diamonds, spades: Players who suit MUDs. *Journal of MUD Research,* 7(1). Retrieved November 3, 2003, from *http:/www. mud.co.uk/ richard/hcds.htm*

Beck, J., & Wade, (2004). *Got game: How the gamer generation is reshaping business forever.* Cambridge, MA: Harvard Business School Press.

Berson, M. J. (1996). Effectiveness of computer technology in the social studies: A review of the literature. *Journal of Research on Computing in Education, 28*(4), 486–499.

Black, R. W. (2005). Access and affiliation: The literacy and composition practices of English language learners in an online fanfiction community. *Journal of Adolescent & Adult Literacy, 49*(2), 118–128.

British Broadcasting Corporation. (2005, August 25). China imposes online gaming curbs. *BBC News Online.* Retrieved January 26, 2006, from *http://news.bbc.co.uk/1/hi/technology/4183340.stm*

Brown K., & Cole, M. (2002). *Cultural historical activity theory and the expansion of opportunities for learning after school.* La Jolla, CA: Laboratory of Comparative Human Cognition, San Diego State University. Retrieved November 16, 2006, from *http://lchc.ucsd.edu/People/MCole/browncole. html*

Bruckman, A. S. (1999). Gender swapping on the Internet. In V. J. Vitanza (Ed.), *CyberReader* (2nd ed., pp. 418–423). Needham Heights, MA: Allyn & Bacon.

Casti, J. L. (1997). *Would-be worlds: How simulation is changing the frontiers of science.* New York: Wiley.

Castronova, E. (2001). *Virtual worlds: A first-hand account of market and society on the cyberian frontier* (CESifo Working Paper Series No. 618). Fullerton, CA: Center for Economic Studies and Institute for Economic Research, California State University. Retrieved November 16, 2006, from *http://ssrn.com/abstract=294828*

Chase, W. G., & Simon, H. A. (1973). The mind's eye in chess. In W. G. Chase (Ed.), *Visual information processing (pp.* 215–281). New York: Academic Press.

Church, D. (2000, March). *Abdicating authorship.* Talk presented at the annual meeting of the Game Developer's Conference, San Jose, CA.

Clinton, K. A. (2004, April). *Embodiment in digital worlds: What being a videogame player has to teach us about learning.* Paper presented at the annual meeting of the American Educational Research Association, San Diego.

Cordova, D. L., & Lepper, M. R. (1996). Intrinsic motivation and the process of learning: Beneficial effects of contextualization, personalization, and choice. *Journal of Educational Psychology, 88,* 715–730.

Crawford, C. (1982). *The art of computer game design.* Vancouver, WA: Washington State University. Available at *http://www.vancouver.wsu. Edu/fac/Peabody/game-book/Coverpage.html*

Cuban, L. (1986). *Teachers and machines.* New York: Teacher's College Press.

Dewey, J. (1938). *Experience and education.* New York: Collier Books.

Diamond, J. (1999). *Guns, germs, and steel: The fates of human societies.* New York: Norton.

diSessa, A. (1998). *Changing minds.* Cambridge, MA: MIT Press.

Dunn, R. E., (2000). Constructing world history in the classroom? In P. N. Stearns, P. Seixas, & S. Wineburg (Eds.), *Knowing teaching and learning history.* New York: New York University Press.

Erwin, S. (2005, December). Games are gaining ground, but how far can they go? *National Defense Magazine.* Available at http://*www.nationaldefensemagazine.org/issues/2005/dec1/games_are.htm*

Forbus, K. (1997). Using qualitative physics to create articulate educational software. *IEEE Expert* (May/June), 32–41.

Friedman, T. (1999). Civilization and its discontents: Simulation, subjectivity, and space. In G. Smith (Ed.), *Discovering discs: Transforming space and place on CD-ROM.* New York: New York University Press.

Funk, J. B., Hagen, J. D., & Schimming, J. L. (1999). Children and electronic games: A comparison of parent and child perceptions of children's habits and preferences in a United States sample. *Psychological Reports, 85*, 883–888.

Games-to-Teach Team. (2003). Design principles of next-generation digital gaming for education. *Educational Technology, 43*(5), 17–33.

Gee, J. P. (2003). *What video games have to teach us about learning and literacy.* New York: Palgrave/St. Martin's.

Gee, J. P. (2004). *Language, learning, and gaming: A critique of traditional schooling.* New York: Routledge.

Gee, J. P. (2005). *Why video games are good for your soul: Pleasure and learning.* Melbourne, Australia: Common Ground.

Goodwin, C. (1994). Professional vision. *American Anthropologist, 96*(3), 606–633.

Hakkarainen, P. (1999). Play and motivation. In Y. Engström, R. Miettinen, & R.-L. Punamäki (Eds.), *Aspects of activity theory.* Cambridge, UK: Cambridge University Press.

Holland, W., Jenkins, H., & Squire, K. (2003). Theory by design. In B. Perron & M. Wolf (Eds.), *Video game theory.* New York: Routledge.

Hope, W. C. (1996). It's time to transform social studies teaching. *Social Studies, 87*(4), 149–151.

Hutchins, E. (1995). *Cognition in the wild.* Cambridge, MA: MIT Press.

Interactive Digital Software Association v. St. Louis County, 200 F. Supp. 2d 1126 (E.D. Mo. 2002).

Interactive Digital Software Association v. St. Louis County, No. 023010 (June 3, 2003).

Jenkins, H. (1992). *Textual poachers.* New York: Routledge.

Jenkins, H. (in press). *Convergence cultures.* New York: New York University Press.

Jenkins, H., & Squire, K. D. (2004). Harnessing the power of games in education. *Insight, 3*(1), 5–33.

Jenkins, H., Squire, K., & Tan, P. (2004). You can't bring that game to school! Designing *Supercharged!* In B. Laurel (Ed.), *Design Research* (pp. 244–252). Cambridge, MA: MIT Press.

Johnson, S. (2005a). *Why everything bad is good for you.* New York: Riverhead.

Johnson, S. (2005b). Your brain on video games: Could they actually be good for you? *Discover, 26*(7). Retrieved November 17, 2006, from *http://www.discover.com/issues/jul-05/features/brain-on-video-games/*

Klopfer, E., & Squire, K. (in press). Environmental detectives: The development of an augmented reality platform for environmental simulations. *Educational Research Technology & Development.*

Kolson, K. (1996, March). The politics of *Sim City. Political Science and Politics, 29*(1), 43–46.

Kreimeier, B. (2000, April 13). Puzzled at GDC 2000: A peek into puzzle design. *Gamasutra.* Retrieved October 31, 2006, from *http://www.gamasutra.com/features/20000413lkreimeier_01.htm*

Kuo, J. (2004, May). *Online video games in mental health.* Paper presented at the annual meeting of the American Psychiatry Association, New York.

Lankshear, C., & Knobel, M. (2003). *New literacies.* London: Open University Press.

Lave, J., & Wenger, E. (1991). *Situated learning: Legitimate peripheral participation.* New York: Cambridge University Press.

Leander, K. M., & Lovvorn, J. (2004, April). *Literacy networks: Following the circulation of texts and identities in the school-related and computer gaming-related literacies of one youth.* Paper presented at the annual meeting of the American Educational Research Association, San Diego.

LeBlanc, M. (2005). Tools for creating dramatic game dynamics. In K. Salen & E. Zimmerman (Eds.), *The game design reader: A rules of play anthology* (pp. 438–459). Cambridge, MA: MIT Press.

Lemke, J. (2004). *Why study digital gameworlds? Notes toward a basic research agenda for learning technologies.* Retrieved December 11, 2004, from *http://www-personal. umich.edu/~jaylemke/games.htm*

Li, Z. (2004). *The potential* of America's Army *as civilian public sphere.* Unpublished master's thesis. Cambridge, MA: MIT.

Loftus, T. (2005, February 7). Virtual worlds wind up in real world's courts: Online games intended as escape face legal headaches. *MSNBC.com.* Retrieved November 11, 2006, from *http://www.msnbc.msn.com/id/6870901/*

Malone, T. W. (1981). Toward a theory of intrinsically motivating instruction. *Cognitive Science,* 5(4), 333–369.

Malone, T. W., & Lepper, M. R. (1987). Making learning fun: A taxonomy of intrinsic motivations for learning. In R. E. Snow & M. J. Farr (Eds.), *Aptitude, learning and instruction: Vol. 3. Conative and affective process analysis* (pp. 223–253). Hillsdale, NJ: Lawrence Erlbaum.

Manning, P. (2003). *Navigating world history: Historians create a global past.* New York: Palgrave Macmillan.

McFarlane, A., Sparrowhawk, A., & Heald, Y. (2002). *Report on the educational use of games: An exploration by TEEM of the contribution which games can make to the education process.* Cambridge, UK: Futurelab. Retrieved June 29, 2005, from *www. teem.org.uk/publications/teem_gamesined_full.pdf*

Mine, M. R., Shochet, J., & Hughston, R. (2003). Building a massively multiplayer game for the million: Disney's *Toontown* Online. *Computers in Entertainment, 1*(1), 15.

Mitchell, E. (1985). The dynamics of family interaction around home video games [Special issue: Personal computers and the family]. *Marriage and Family Review* 8(1–2), 121–135.

Moulder, S. (2004, March). *Fun with a purpose.* Presentation at the Serious Games Summit, San Jose, CA.

Murray, J. H. (1997). *Hamlet on the holodeck: The future of narrative in cyberspace.* New York: Free Press.

Ochs, E., Gonzales, P., & Jacoby, S. (1996). When I come down I'm in a domain state: Talk, gesture, and graphic representation in the interpretive activity of physicists. In E. Ochs, E. Schegloff, & S. Thompson (Eds.), *Interaction and grammar* (pp. 328–369). Cambridge, UK: Cambridge University Press.

Ondrejka, C. R. (2004). *Living on the edge: Digital worlds which embrace the real world.* Social Science Research Network. Retrieved on June 5, 2006, from *http://ssrn.com/ abstract=555661*

Prensky, M. (2001). *Digital game-based learning.* New York: McGraw Hill.

Provenzo, E. F. (1991). *Video kids: Making sense of Nintendo.* Cambridge, MA: Harvard University Press.

Reiber, L. (1996). Seriously considering play: Designing interactive learning environments based on the blending of microworlds, simulations, and games. *Education and Technology Research & Development, 44,* 42–58.

Robison, A. (2004, April). *The "internal design grammar" of video games.* Paper presented at the annual meeting of the American Educational Research Association, San Diego, CA.

Salen, K., & Zimmerman, E. (2004). *The rules of play*. Cambridge, MA: MIT Press.

Scardamalia, M., & Bereiter, C. (1996). Computer support for knowledge-building communities. In T. Koschmann (Ed.), *CSCL: Theory and practice of an emerging paradigm*. Mahwah, NJ: Lawrence Erlbaum.

Shaffer, D. W. (2004). Pedagogical praxis: The professions as models for post-industrial education. *Teachers College Record, 106*(7), 1401–1421.

Shaffer, D. W., Squire, K. D., Halverson, R., & Gee J. P. (2005). Video games and the future of learning. *Phi Delta Kappan, 87*(2), 104–111.

Sheff, D. (1993). *Game over: How Nintendo zapped an American industry, captured your dollars and enslaved your children*. New York: Random House.

Solomon, A. (2004, July 10). The closing of the American book. *New York Times*. Retrieved October 2, 2004, from *http://www.nytimes.com*

Squire, K. D. (2002). Cultural framing of computer/video games. *Game Studies: The International Journal of Computer Game Research, 1*(2). Retrieved November 3, 2003, from *http://www.gamestudies.org/0102/squire!*

Squire, K. D. (2003). Video games in education. *International Journal of Intelligent Games & Simulation, 2*(1). Retrieved November 1, 2003, from *http://www.scit.wlv. ac.uk/~cm1822/ijkurt.pdf*

Squire, K. D. (2004). *Replaying history*. Unpublished dissertation, Indiana University, Bloomington.

Squire, K. D. (2005a). Educating the fighter. *On the Horizon, 13*(2), 73–88.

Squire, K. D. (2005b). Toward a theory of games literacy. *Telemedium, 52*(1–2), 9–15.

Squire, K. D. (in press a). *Civilization III as* a world history sandbox. In M. Bittanti (Eds.), *Civilization and its discontents: Virtual history: Real fantasies*. Milan, Italy: Ludilogica Press.

Squire, K. D. (in press b). Educating the fighter. *On the Horizon*.

Squire, K. D., & Barab, S. A. (2004). Replaying history. In Y. Kafai, W. Sandoval, N. Enyedy, A. Dixon, & F. Herrera (Eds.), *Proceedings of the 2004 International Conference of the Learning Sciences* (pp. 505–512). Mahwah, NJ: Lawrence Erlbaum.

Squire, K. D., & Steinkuehler, C. A. (in press). The genesis of "CyberCulture": The case of Star Wars Galaxies. In D. Gibbs & L. Krause (Eds.), *Cyberlines: Languages and cultures of the Internet* (2nd ed.). Albert Park, Australia: James Nicholas Publishers.

Starr, P. (1994). Seductions of sim. *The American Prospect, 5*(17). Retrieved October 31, 2006, from *http://www.prospect.org/print/V5/17/starr-p.html*

Steinkuehler, C. A. (2003, March). *Videogaming as participation in a Discourse*. Paper presented at the annual conference of the American Association for Applied Linguistics (AAAL), Arlington, VA.

Steinkuehler, C. A. (2004a, October). *Emergent play*. Paper presented at the State of Play Conference, New York University Law School, New York. Retrieved June 29, 2005, from *https://mywebspace.wisc.edu/steinkuehler/web/papers/SteinkuehlerSoP2004.pdf*

Steinkuehler, C. A. (2004b, April). *The literacy practices of massively multiplayer online gaming*. Paper presented at the 2004 annual meeting of the American Educational Research Association, San Diego, CA.

Steinkuehler, C. A. (in press a). Learning in massively multiplayer online games. *Mind, Culture, and Activity*.

Steinkuehler, C. A. (in press b). The new third place: Massively multiplayer online gaming in American youth culture. *Tidskrift Journal of Research in Education*.

Steinkuehler, C. A., Black, R. W., & Clinton, K. A. (2005) Researching literacy as tool, place, and way of being. *Reading Research Quarterly, 40*(1), 7–12.

Steinkuehler, C. A., & Chmiel, M. (2005, July). *Gendered talk in massively multiplayer online games*. Paper presented at the 14th World Congress of Applied Linguistics, Madison, WI.

Steinkuehler, C. A., & Chmiel, M. (2006, June). *Fostering scientific habits of mind in the context of online play*. Paper presented at the 7th International Conference of the Learning Sciences, Bloomington, IN.

Teague, M., & Teague, G. (1995). *Learning and leading with technology, 23*(1), 20–22.

Thompson, T. (2005, March 13). They play games for 10 hours—and earn £2.80 in a "virtual sweatshop." *The Observer*. Retrieved January 26, 2006, from *http://observer. guardian.co.uk/international/story/0,6903, 1436411,00.html*

Turkle, S. (1995). *Life on the screen: Identity in the age of the Internet*. New York: Touchstone.

Turkle, S. (2003). From powerful ideas to PowerPoint. *Convergence: The Journal of Research into New Media Technologies, 9*(2), 19–28.

Williams, D. (2003). The video game lightning rod. *Information, Communication & Society, 6*(4), 523–550.

Wolfram, S. (2002). *A new kind of science*. Champaign, IL: Wolfram Media.

Woodcock, B. S. (2005). *An analysis of MMOG subscription growth—Version 10.0*. Retrieved October 2, 2005, from *http://pwl.netcom.com.nyud.net:8090/~sirbruce/ Subscriptions.html*

Young, M. (2004, July). *Games in education: Learning in formal and informal ways from role playing and arcade video games*. Paper presented at the 2004 International Conference of Education and Information Systems Conference, Orlando, FL.

75

GAME DESIGN AND LEARNING

A conjectural analysis of how massively multiple online role-playing games (MMORPGs) foster intrinsic motivation

Michele D. Dickey

Source: *Educational Technology Research and Development*, 55(3), June 2007, 253–273.

Abstract

During the past two decades, the popularity of computer and video games has prompted games to become a source of study for educational researchers and instructional designers investigating how various aspects of game design might be appropriated, borrowed, and re-purposed for the design of educational materials. The purpose of this paper is to present an analysis of how the structure in massively multiple online role-playing games (MMORPGs) might inform the design of interactive learning and game-based learning environments by looking at the elements which support intrinsic motivation. Specifically, this analysis presents (a) an overview of the two primary elements in MMORPGs game design: character design and narrative environment, (b) a discussion of intrinsic motivation in character role-playing, (c) a discussion of intrinsic motivational supports and cognitive support of the narrative structure of small quests, and (d) a discussion of how the narrative structure of MMORPGs might foster learning in various types of knowledge.

Introduction

During the past two decades, the advent of new technologies and media has precipitated many changes in the field of instructional design. According to Winn (2002), the current movement within the field is toward the cultivation and development of interactive learning environments. The emergence of learning environments has been in part fueled by the epistemological shift towards constructivism and in part fueled by the impact and integration of technology and learning (Hannafin & Land, 1997; Hannafin, Land, & Oliver, 1999; Jonassen,

1999; Jonassen & Rohrer-Murphy, 1999; Land & Hannafin, 1996, 1997; Wilson, 1996; Winn, 2002). The theoretical assumption underlying interactive learning environments is that learners construct understandings by interacting with information, tools, and materials as well as by collaborating with other learners. Yet, these environments must also help scaffold the learning process. Although much research has been devoted to the design of learning environments (Hannafin, Hall, Land, & Hill, 1994; Hannafin et al., 1999; Jonassen, 1999; Land & Hannafin, 1997), the emergence of new tools and technology is continually challenging the field of instructional design to find models and methods for developing engaging interactive learning environments. One source of inspiration for potential models, strategies, and techniques is the design of popular video and computer games. Certainly, the purpose of video and computer games is to entertain, however, in order to engage players, game designers have become well versed in creating activities and environments which foster intrinsic motivation. The identification and appropriation of many of these techniques may be of great relevance for the creation of interactive learning environments.

There are many genres of video and computer games such as strategy games, adventure games, role-playing games, action games, and others. Although each genre can inform instructional designers and educators about engagement (Dickey, 2005), the new game genre, massively multiple online role-playing games (MMORPG), may be of great relevance in the design of interactive learning environments because it provides a flexible environmental design which provides scaffolding for problem-solving along with elements which foster intrinsic motivation. An MMORPG is a persistent, networked, interactive, narrative environment in which players collaborate, strategize, plan, and interact with objects, resources, and other players within a multimodal environment. Instructional designers and educators continually seek methods for fostering collaboration and critical thinking in rich learning environments. Collaboration and critical thinking are activities central to the MMORPG gameplay experience.

Although digital games offer potential for the field of instructional design, it is important to note that digital games have also traditionally been considered a male leisure pastime (Bryce & Rutter, 2002, 2003; Cassell & Jenkins, 1998, Dickey, 2006a). However, more recently there has been a noted influx of female players in the gameplay market and the demographics are now shifting (ESA, 2004; Yee, 2001). This may be due in part to the inclusion of such elements as engaging narratives, self-selection of roles, interactive challenges, exploration, collaboration, and community which are elements that have been associated with female-oriented design (AAUW, 2000; Cassell & Jenkins, 1998; de Castell & Bryson, 1998; Dickey, 2006a; Kafai, 1994, 1998; Miller, Chaika, & Groppe, 1996; Murray & Kliman, 1999; Rubin, Murray, O'Neil, & Ashley, 1997; Slaton, 1998; Taylor, 2003).

Within a learning environment, it is important for learners to have opportunities for exploration and manipulation in order to foster the construction of knowledge (Cognition and Technology Group at Vanderbilt, 1990, 1993; Jonassen, 1999). MMORPGs are increasingly constructed as representations of 3D spaces allowing players to move and interact in simulated realistic or fantasy environments. Additionally, conversation and discourse are important features of learning environments. Conversation and collaboration support social negotiation in learning (Lave & Wenger, 1991; Vygotsky, 1978). This in turn allows learners to share information, test understandings, and reflect on learning (Duffy & Cunningham, 1996; Jonassen, 1999). Most MMORPGs are social environments in which players communicate, collaborate, plan, strategize, and socialize with other players. Finally, learning environments should include opportunities for interactive challenges, which require players to synthesize, analyze, and evaluate multiple modes of information and use critical thinking skills to form strategies and problem-solve. MMORPGs include many of these same opportunities which educators attempt to foster in learning environments. Although much more research needs to be conducted about the design of interactive learning environments, certainly looking at game genres such as MMORPGs which engage both male and female participation may provide techniques and strategies for fostering intrinsic motivation in learning environments which are inclusive for both male and female learners.

The purpose of this paper is to present a conjectural analysis of how the structure in MMORPGs might inform the design of interactive learning and game-based learning environments by looking at the elements that support intrinsic motivation. Specifically, this analysis presents (a) an overview of the two primary elements in MMORPGs game design: character design and narrative environment, (b) a discussion of intrinsic motivation in character role-playing, (c) a discussion of intrinsic motivational supports and cognitive support of the narrative structure of small quests, and (d) a discussion of how the narrative structure of MMORPGs might foster learning in various types of knowledge. The goal of this investigation is to suggest how the narrative design of MMORPGs might aid in the instructional design of interactive and game-based learning environments.

This analysis is conjectural in as much as it is interpretive, but not conducted within the confines of a formal study. This analysis will draw upon both qualitative and quantitative research as well as cognitive and constructivist- based perspectives of learning. There are obvious parallels between game design and constructivist-based models (i.e., open learning environments and constructivist learning environments), however, there is much informative research about the design and use of game elements for learning from a cognitive perspective. Therefore, this analysis will draw on both constructivist and cognitive research. Similarly, both qualitative and quantitative research often reveals different aspects of a phenomenon or activity being studied (Lincoln & Guba, 1985, pp. 70–91).

Literature review

During the past two decades, the design of computer and video games has become a source of study for educational researchers and instructional designers investigating how various aspects of game design support intrinsic motivation and how aspects of game design might be appropriated for educational materials

(Bowman, 1982; Dickey, 2005, 2006b; Gee, 2003; Malone, 1981; Prensky, 2001; Provenzo, 1991; Rieber, 1996; Squire, 2003). Bowman's (1982), Malone's (1981), Provenzo's (1991) and Rieber's (1996) respective research focused on the motivational supports in popular game design of their eras. Bowman applied Csikszentmihalyi and Lawson's (1980) *flow state interaction* to help explain motivation of extrinsic supports found in the game *Pac-Man*. Malone (1981) investigated a series of games and identified the elements of challenge, fantasy, and curiosity as being key aspects of design that fostered engagement. Provenzo (1991) applied Malone's elements of challenge, fantasy, and curiosity to deconstruct and explain the intrinsic motivational support of *Super Mario Bros. 2*. Bowman (1982), Malone (1981), and Provenzo (1991) each contemplated how game design elements might be integrated into education. Whereas Bowman's (1982) study focused primarily upon the feedback cycle and motivation, Provenzo's (1991) addressed aspects of intrinsic motivation. Rieber's (1996) research into the psychological and sociological benefits of play reveals that games support intrinsic motivation by providing feedback, fantasy, and challenge (Rieber, 1996). Rieber's work also addresses how narrative/fantasy can foster both intrinsic motivation and potentially be an aid to learning when it is integral to the gameplay experience.

Bowman's (1982), Provenzo's (1991), Rieber's (1996), and Malone's (1981) respective studies reveal commonalities of game design that include clear goals and tasks, reinforcing feedback, and increasing challenge. Each study also reveals aspects of design that foster intrinsic motivation, however, the games Bowman, Malone, and Provenzo reviewed are nearly two decades old. Games have grown increasingly sophisticated in design. The simple one screen mazes of *Pac-Man* have evolved into three-dimensional online multi-playing gaming environments with a full cast of both player and non-player characters. The arguments both Bowman (1982) and Provenzo (1991) presented for recasting game design elements into classroom instruction are revealing for the then current level of game design, however, game design has evolved and now incorporates narrative, role-playing, multi-player environments, representations of three-dimensional spaces, and interactive elements beyond the limits of games represented in the previous studies.

MMORPG game design: character and narrative environment

With the advent of high-speed networks and more sophisticated graphics capacity for computers, MMORPGs have become one of the most popular game genres. An MMORPG is a networked game which enables thousands of players to simultaneously interact in an online gameplay environment. Among the more popular MMORPGs are *EverQuest, Lineage, World of Warcraft*, and *ToonTown*. The roots of MMORPGs can be found in digital single-player role-playing games and table-top games such as *Dungeons and Dragons*. Among the first of the online digital games were *Multi-User Dungeons or Domains* (MUDs) which are text-based games played on a computer network. Like table-top games and single-player computer games, MMORPGs are a game genre in which players adopt a character role and play the game as that character. Within the design MMORPGs are two main elements: the character design and the narrative environment. Both support intrinsic motivation in various ways.

Character design

Within the MMORPG genre, players begin by creating a character they will play. Typically players are presented with a variety of base-characters from which to select. Players customize their character by choosing from a limited number of traits, skills, adornments and attributes. These limits force players to make decisions about the types of characteristics in which to endow their characters. The individual combination of attributes, adornments, skills, and traits are what make each character unique. Throughout gameplay, players continually enhance their character's skills and attributes by participating in the narrative environment.

A key aspect within the MMORPG environment is character management. In the course of gameplay, players have opportunities to enhance their characters attributes, skills and adornments. Players continually make choices about the types of enhancements to develop characters skills, primary and secondary attributes and appearance. Skill enhancements might include such actions as combat skills, healing powers, and spell casting abilities. Primary attributes might include such features as strength, agility, intelligence, and stamina. Players typically also have the option of adding various adornments to alter or enhance their characters appearance as they progress in the game. Adornments might include clothing, armor, shields, and protection spells. Secondary attributes are often predicated on the combination of traits, skills, primary attributes and adornments. For example, depending upon the game, *the healing powers* (the amount of healing a character can provide for self or other characters) might be determined by such elements as armor and protective spells, along with a character's intelligence. The choice of skills, attributes, and adornments impacts how a player's character advances in the game. When collaborating with others, a player's skills, attributes, and adornments often indicate the potential contribution a player may provide when participating in collaborative events, which in turn may impact the type and amount of invitations to collaborate with other players.

Intrinsic motivation and character role-playing

Character development in MMORPGs is one element which fosters intrinsic motivation in the course of gameplay. There are no final victory or loss conditions in MMORPGs, therefore, the game continues to evolve. In turn, players continue to evolve their character (and/or develop new characters to play). Players may invest hundreds of hours advancing their character and interacting in the gameplay environment. Because they have great input into the development of their characters, players often feel an emotional proximity to their character. The character becomes a type of avatar of the player in the gameplay environment. Much research has been conducted about both the use of digital-based avatars and the emotional proximity that players or users develop for their characters or avatars. Individual works by such diverse researchers as Stone (1995), Turkle (1995), Curtis (1992), Reid (1994) Jakobsson (2002) and Jakobsson and Taylor (2003) have investigated how role-playing in digital environments fosters personal and social reflexivity. Turkle's (1995) investigation into Multi-User Dungeons (MUDs), a predecessor of MMORPGs, revealed that virtual environments allow users to experiment in a safe, non-threatening environment and to expand, explore, and reflect on different aspects of themselves. Dibbell's (1994) landmark article, *A Rape in Cyberspace*, illustrates the depth of emotional connection that can develop as a result of the emotional proximity users have towards their character or avatar. Jakobsson (2002) argues that users invest a great deal of time and energy into their characters or avatars and as a result these alternative identities or roles become a form of social capital or status. Social capital is the networks, norms, and trust gained by participating in community spaces (Putnam, 1995, 2000). MMORPGs are community spaces. Social capital in MMORPG gameplay is the result of a player's character's assets, and the network of affiliations accrued with the playing of one or more characters (Herz, 2001). The attributes, adornments, skills and traits of a character along with the player's actions enhance a player/character's status. Social capital that results from a player-created-character can be very instrumental in an MMORPG environment because it may assist or hinder players in advancing in gameplay. Often social connections are necessary for completing tasks which require group collaboration (Jakobsson & Taylor, 2003). Players form contacts and develop relationships of trust and accountability based on their characters' actions, profile, and affiliations.

As players develop their character, they are in a sense, taking on a role. Role-playing has long been an established technique used for educational activities. Fields such as medicine, social studies, and language learning routinely use role-playing as a teaching and learning technique. Educational researchers have also investigated how role-playing in a digital environment fosters intrinsic motivation. Resnick and Wilensky (1997) integrated roleplaying activities into science and math classes and argue that role-playing can help students understand complex systems and relationships. Riner's (1996) and Riner and Clodius' (1995) research of educational multi-user domains object oriented (MOOs) reveals that role-playing fosters opportunities for collaboration across time and space, both within and across classrooms. Similarly, Dede (1996) argues that the safety of role-playing with a character/ avatar may be even greater in a digital learning environment than in a traditional setting and may foster more risk-taking. While there has been persuasive research into role-playing in both traditional classroom and digital environments, one of the more compelling studies into how character/avatar creations can be motivational is Bruckman's (1997) qualitative study of two adolescent girls' interactions in *MOOSE Crossing*, an online text-based virtual world.

Bruckman's ethnographic "thick description" provides unique insight into how character development and alternate personae within a loosely structured learning environment can be intrinsically motivating. Bruckman's research reveals that role-playing provides new and interesting outcomes for learning including role-reversal and peer mentoring.

Narrative environment

The core of MMORPG design is a narrative interactive environment. In various computer and video genres such as single player role-playing games and adventure games, the game centers around the narrative of a single storyline which is usually linear in nature. In adventure games and single player role-playing games, the focus of gameplay is on uncovering the narrative storyline during the advent of gameplay. In both of these genres the storyline stops when the player stops playing and resumes when the player begins again. In contrast, MMORPGs are networked, persistant, communal environments. Because they are multi-player, networked environments, gameplay continues even when a player logs off. Within the MMORPG genre, there is no one-single storyline for players to uncover, but rather the gameplay experience is an environment. Embedded within the environment are thousands of short narrative storylines. These short narratives are usually embedded in the environment in the form of a non-player character posing a short narrative tale in which they request the aid or assistance of the player's character. These short narrative tales provide players with opportunities for interaction. As players move through the environment, they encounter these various non-player characters requesting their aid or assistance. The request for assistance is usually framed as a small quest (e.g., deliver a package, find a lost book, and escort an ally). Players may opt to select and complete or reject the small quest. Typically within the environment are many small quests from which players may select. Upon the successful completion of a small quest, a player's character is rewarded. This allows players to continually enhance their character's attributes and skills. Rather than the focus of gameplay being on uncovering one major narrative storyline, the environment is a network of narrative spaces (Jenkins, 2002) in which the player interacts and even in limited ways, helps shape.

Most MMORPGs have a very loose over-arching narrative and one central conflict (e.g., in *World of Warcraft*, two groups are fighting for control over a kingdom and in *ToonTown*, the humorless enemies are taking over *Toon-Town* and displacing its citizens). The player's character determines which type of role the player will have in this over-arching narrative. Typically in most game genres the player is often cast in the lead role of the protagonist who must save a town, kingdom, world, universe, or some other domain from some impending threat. In contrast, players in MMORPGs typically begin the game as low-level members of "rank and file." During gameplay, one of the goals is to help advance the character through adding or enhancing skills and attributes (Rollings & Adams, 2003).

Although small quests are usually encountered by non-player characters (NPCs) requesting help, small quests may also be found in other ways such as encountering an object (a "magic" book or a strange bottle of liquid) and yet others may be offered through a wanted poster or during the process of completing another small quest. Some small quests may be accomplished by individual players while other quests require the organized efforts of several groups of players. Depending upon the extent of the narrative, these small quests may be a simple one stage quest (defeat five enemies) or they may be more complex and require the player to complete several small quests to completely uncover the narrative (e.g., collect several herbs, then find an herbalist to mix herbs and create a poltice to cure an illness). Both the selection of the small quests and the successful completion advances gameplay and reinforces the player's role in the overarching narrative and narrative space.

Because MMORPGs are persistent, networked narrative spaces, other players also contribute to a player's narrative. Typically a chat tool allows players to communicate during the gameplay experience. This allows players to request help, strategize on group quests, and socialize. Alliances with other players (clans, guilds, friends' lists) allow players to complete small quests which require assistance. Naturally friendships emerge, as do animosities. Stories of other players intrigue, assistance, or betrayals are part of this ongoing player narrative. Additionally, player created websites often emerge where players offer advice or recount the strategies they employed in completing a small quest. Narratives emerge which are parallel and embedded in the narrative landscape of the interactive gameplay environment, but are player contributions and not those of the game designers.

The narrative design of an MMORPG design is a design model which fosters exploration. Players continually explore various regions to find both quest givers and characters and objects related to completing a small quest. There is often no "one way" to complete a small quest, but rather players must balance the skills and attributes of their character against the demands of the quest and plan strategically to accomplish most quests. Additionally, players must make critical choices about whether the rewards are worth the investment required to complete a small quest. Because MMORPGs are narrative environments, the environments are often vast and it may take players a great deal of time to "travel" from region to region. Players often make critical choices about the most economical way to complete a variety of small quests in the most travel-efficient way.

Although small quests are typically framed as small narratives, there are categories of small quests based upon the types of actions players must perform in completing the quests. Common types of small quests include: *bounty quests, Fed Ex quests, collection quests, escort quests, goodwill quests, and messenger quests*. Each quest type requires different actions from the player. The bounty quest requires players to defeat a character or number of characters. Often players must explore new regions to find the "bounty" characters. The benefit of this quest is that players may have to fully explore a region and in turn be exposed to new areas and resources. Additionally, bounty quests often require players to defeat a non-player character of a higher level and players may have to collaborate with other players to complete the quest. This fosters community as players build contact lists of other players providing mutual support during gameplay. This collaboration also allows players to look at how combining unique differences between player characters can be used to overcome an obstacle. For example in *World of Warcraft*, characters have unique combinations of strengths and weaknesses (see Figure 1). One character may be able to heal other characters, but may not be able to use projectiles; whereas another character may be able to use projectiles (i.e., bow and arrows and guns), but cannot heal. A group of players often strategize on what each player will do during a bounty quest to ensure the success of the entire group.

The Fed Ex quest is similar to a bounty quest, but requires players to collect a package or object from one character or place and deliver it to another. The purpose and benefit of this quest is to move the player into new regions and expose them to new areas of the gameplay environment. For example in *ToonTown*, players are often required to perform both bounty quests and Fed Ex quests by either defeating an NPC or collecting a packet from a store on a street in a particular neighborhood (see Figure 2). *ToonTown* is divided into various neighborhoods, each of which have different resources and activities. If players were not prompted to move into different neighborhoods, many players would miss the various resources and activities. Fed Ex quests move players through different neighborhoods and expose them to a wider variety of resources. These resources are often necessary and relevant for problem-solving in later stages of the game.

Figure 1 World of Warcraft: A *Paladin* healing another character

68

The collection quest is a quest in which players must collect a variety of objects in order to progress in the game. In the example of *ToonTown*, players must often collect a number of designated items to help build experience points and to build resources. The purpose and benefit of the collection quest is to help the player progress in the game by requiring players to gain higher levels of skills by "leveling up". In turn, this scaffolds players in advancing to more difficult levels and performing more difficult tasks.

The escort quest is a quest which requires a player to escort an NPC from one area to another. This often involves strategic planning by coordinating timing, navigation, and even collaboration with other players. Often, key information about the game may be conveyed during this experience. For example, in *World of Warcraft*, there are several small quests in which a player may escort an NPC from one place to another. Typically, the player must protect the character, yet often intrigue or a twist in the storyline such as a traitor in the midst is relayed during that experience. This in turn fosters engagement as players may only receive incomplete pieces of information. Additionally, a player may be required to develop new skills in order to defeat a character.

Goodwill quests are quests which require a higher-level player to assist a lower-level player. For example, in *ToonTown*, more advanced players are sometimes required to assist lower-level players in completing a quest. This provides scaffolding to beginning players and helps initiate them into the gameplay environment. Finally, the messenger quest is a quest in which a player must find a NPC and talk with them. The benefit of the messenger quest is that the NPC may

Figure 2 ToonTown: A *Toon* encountering a *Cog* in ToonTown

be offering some key advice, information, or directions which will help guide and mentor the player in problem-solving.

Intrinsic motivation and narrative environment

It may initially seem incongruent to look at MMORPG game design as a model for instructional design because the purpose of a MMORPG is to entertain, whereas the purpose of instructional design is to foster learning. However, it is important to note that interactive learning environments are often multi-modal environments requiring learners to access and integrate various forms of information and to formulate plans of action. MMORPGs are multi-modal environments which require players to access and integrate various forms of information and to act upon that knowledge. What is most noteworthy about the design of an MMORPG is that it is an open-ended environment. There is no one penultimate end to the game which players strive to achieve and there is no one way to the play the game. It is a flexible design which allows players choice, collaboration, challenge, and achievement, while at the same time it is a design which provides scaffolding for players to progress and learn.

The design of narrative environment small quests in MMORPGs may provide a model of how to design learning tasks within an interactive learning environment. Small quests within MMORPG promote gameplay by supporting three functions. First, participation in small quests exposes players to various resources thereby insuring that players have been exposed to key resources. Second, small quests provide experience to advance the player's character. Third, small quests foster collaboration and strategic planning by supplying quests, which require multiple players to complete. Not only do small quests advance gameplay, but they advance gameplay by fostering intrinsic motivation. Typically within MMORPGs, players are presented with a *choice* of many quests and they choose the quests they would like to complete. Successful completion of smaller quests allows player's charac-ters to gain points and attain advanced levels which, in turn, provide players with a choice of increasingly more difficult tasks. Malone and Lepper (1987) argue that choice is a significant variable in fostering motivation when learners are given a range of choice and provided with a sufficient structure with which to make choices. It is interesting to note that many MMORPGs limit the amount of quests players can work on at one time. Research conducted by Iyengar and Lepper (1999, 2000) examined not only the motivating aspects of choice, but also the demotivat-ing aspects of choice when participants are presented with too wide of an array of choices. Although MMORPGs are a relatively recent model of game design, more recent games such as *World of Warcraft* and *ToonTown* seem to recognize the importance of fostering a balance of choice in order to maintain motivation among players while avoiding overwhelming or demotivating others. Within the small quest structure of MMORPGs, players typically have a choice of their selection of small quests, and also have *control* of how they plan to complete each small quest and the order in which they complete them. Malone and Lepper (1987) also argue that control is a key aspect for fostering intrinsic motivation. According to

Malone and Lepper, control is dependent upon affordances and constraints of the environments and how players react to those affordances and constraints. Within the small quest structure of MMORPGs, players typically have control over which small quests to select and the order and strategies for completing small quests. Typically players are presented with small quests which match their gameplay level. In other words, an advanced-level small quest is not available to a beginning level player and beginning level quests offer relatively insignificant rewards for an advanced player. Within research of cognition and control, Cordova and Lepper (1996) found that providing students with control, within a personalized and contextualized environment led to increased motivation and learning.

The small quest structure of MMORPGs also fosters *collaboration* among players. Typically MMORPGs have some type of chat feature which allows players to communicate. Often more difficult quests require several players to collaborate to complete. The chat features allow players to chat with other players to request help and plan strategies. This fosters a sense of community as players develop a contact list of other players and use the chat feature to provide instructions, advice, and encouragement to one another. Studies of similar environments such as education multi-user domains object-oriented (MOOs) and 3D virtual worlds note the importance of collaboration in fostering motivation since collaboration allows for the emergence of peer role models and an appreciative audience (Bruckman, 1997; Dickey, 2003; Riner, 1996). Malone and Lepper (1987) also note that cooperation may foster interpersonal motivation.

In addition to collaboration, the small quest structure in MMORPGs also fosters a sense of *achievement* during ongoing gameplay. Because MMORPGs are ongoing experiences (much like the process of learning) there is need to mark progress. Within MMORPGs, small quests provide a type of accountability, as consequences for actions determine the success or failure at various tasks. Both challenge and uncertainty are key elements in the MMORPG gameplay experience. Because players are provided with continually more difficult small quests as they progress through the gameplay experience, players must continually strive to complete each one. This challenge and uncertainty of outcome fosters a sense of achievement when small quests are completed. Both Malone (1981) and later Malone and Lepper (1987) note the importance of challenge and uncertainty in fostering motivation in gameplay.

MMORPGs provide a model for a flexible design which allows players choice, control, collaboration, challenge, and achievement. Yet, at the same time, there are elements within the design of a narrative environment which help scaffold players in the gameplay experience by providing a cognitive framework for problem-solving and by fostering metacognitive skills. The game setting (i.e. the environment and the backstory) establishes boundaries and provides a context for players to construct causal patterns which integrate what is known with that which is conjectural, yet plausible, within the context of the environment. In turn, the environment provides affordances or possibilities for action (Gibson, 1977). Players combine known information (setting, backstory, conflict, etc.) with affordances encountered in the environment and form conjectures about what combinations and processes might assist them in overcoming an obstacle and accomplishing a task. Players are put in a position of having to make conjectures about causal relationships based on the type of information they have encountered while exploring and participating in previous small quests. The various types of small quests expose players to the affordances of the environment. For example, during the process of completing a bounty quest, players are often required to travel into new areas of the gameplay environment. While traveling to their destination, players are exposed to new resources. These new resources may be necessary or helpful in completing subsequent small quests. Plausibility is established through the use of the narrative and supported with the affordances of the environment. As Winn and Snyder (1996) noted, research in situated learning reveals that cognition is more likely to be dependent upon context and affordances of a place and situation than to be determined by formal reasoning (Brown, Collins, & Duguid, 1989; Lave & Wenger, 1991; Suchman, 1987). The actions required through participating in small quests may foster a type of metacognition or perhaps more precisely a type of meta-inferencing (Collins, 1978) and possibly a type of meta-indexing by exposing players to resources and information in initial small quests and then later providing subsequent quests which rely on resources encountered previously.

In summary, the narrative environment of MMORPGs provides choice, control, collaboration, and achievement, yet also provides scaffolding for problem-solving. Table 1 elements of intrinsic motivation and MMORPG design. Malone's (1981) landmark research into the design and application of game design strategies for educational design identified three primary characteristics of computer games which fostered intrinsic motivation: challenge, fantasy, and curiosity. Malone and Lepper (1987) further expanded this framework to add the elements of choice and control to support intrinsic motivation. Although Malone's (1981) and Malone and Lepper's (1987) studies are still relevant and informative, game design has evolved since the era in which these studies were conducted. Within contemporary games, *fantasy* has developed into complex narrative structures. Game environments such as MMORPGs are narrative spaces with opportunities for exploration, collaboration, and challenge. The narrative environment fosters motivation and serves as the organizational framework for the interactive environment. Within the MMORPG genre, Malone's (1981) element of fantasy in game design is now full-fledged narrative environment. The narrative of small quests provides a cognitive framework for problem-solving and fosters metacognitive skills while simultaneously supporting intrinsic motivation by providing opportunities for choice, control, collaboration, and achievement.

Small quests and knowledge domains

The elements of character design and the narrative environment of MMORPGs may prove useful for the design of interactive and game-based learning environments. MMORPG game design is a flexible structure in which players

Table 1 Summary of intrinsic motivation and MMORPG design

Intrinsic motivation	MMORPG design
Choice	Character design Traits, skills, attributes, and adornment Narrative environment Choice of small quests (with limits place on the amount of small quests a player can adopt Option to drop or delete small quest selected
Control	Narrative environment Quest selection Order of completion Strategies employed
Collaboration	Character design Social capital associated with player's character Narrative environment Chat and communication tools Collaborative quests
Challenge	Character design and narrative environment Quests equivalent to current level of skills combined with attributes
Achievement	Character design and narrative environment Marked progress indications Elevated status Advanced skills Enhanced attributes Bounty

are afforded opportunities for choice, control, collaboration, challenge, and achievement, yet with scaffolding for problem-solving. The question for instructional designers and educators is how they might annex those elements for learning. Certainly, there are innumerable studies which have looked at incorporating choice, control, collaboration, challenge, and achievement in a learning context, however, what the design of MMORPGs provides is a model for how all of these elements can be combined in a rich, interactive learning environment and ways to think about how to provide scaffolding in complex, interactive learning environments.

Goal-based Scenarios (Schank, Berman, & Macpherson, 1999), WebQuests (Dodge, 1995), and Case-based Learning (Eisner, 1998; Ertmer & Quinn, 1999; Julian, Larson, & Kinzie, 1999; Shulman, 1992) are some of the existing models of learning environments which, to varying degrees, incorporate elements such as role-playing, narrative, and tasks somewhat similar to small quests. Both the use of character development and use of small quests foster intrinsic motion. Character development allows players (and potential learners) opportunities to self define and refine personas in a learning environment. The benefit of

Table 2 Categorizing small quest-types by knowledge domains

Knowledge domains	Small quests
Declarative knowledge	• Collection quests • Goodwill quests
Procedural knowledge	• Fed Ex quests • Messenger quests
Strategic knowledge	• Bounty quests • Escort quests
Metacognitive knowledge	• Bounty quests • Escort quests • Goodwill quests

integrating a narrative environment is to foster intrinsic motivation; however, it is important to note that each type of small quests within the MMORPG narrative environment serves a different purpose. In order for the small quest narratives to be used effectively in a learning environment, it would be beneficial to look at how the various small quests might support various types of knowledge and suggest how they might function in a learning environment by looking at how various types of knowledge might correspond with the various types of small quests.

Diverse researchers from cognitive psychology, knowledge management, learning theory, and instructional design have identified and characterized four types of knowledge: (a) declarative knowledge, (b) procedural knowledge, (c) strategic knowledge, and (d) metacognitive knowledge (Ackerman, 1986; Anderson, 1983; Bloom, 1956; Bransford, Brown, & Cocking, 2000; Brown, 1978; Gagne, 1985; Jonassen, 1996; Kraiger, Ford, & Salas, 1993; Smith & Ragan, 1993; Wagner, 1987). Declarative knowledge consists of facts, data, concepts, and principles. Procedural knowledge consists of knowledge of how to perform a task, action, or process. Strategic knowledge refers to the awareness of how to apply knowledge, principles, and experiences to various and new situations. It is the foundation of problem-solving. Metacognitive knowledge involves the reflection and regulation of one's thinking during an activity (Brown, 1978). The following taxonomy is an attempt to characterize how various quests might foster learning in various knowledge types (see Table 2). Because the natures of the quests are flexible and determined by the context of the narrative, different types of quests might be relevant for several knowledge-types. It is important to note that this conjectural analysis and taxonomy is far from comprehensive and not intended to serve as a formula, but rather is meant to suggest how the narrative structure of small quests might be used to foster different types of knowledge in interactive and game- based learning environments.

Declarative knowledge

A collection quest is a quest in which players must collect a variety of objects or perform an activity a certain number of times. The purpose and benefit of the collection quest is to help the player progress in the game by accumulating points.

This type of quest might be useful for fostering and reinforcing declarative knowledge because declarative knowledge indicates knowledge of facts and data. For example, students might be required to complete a quest in which they must label, identify, or define something. They may have to complete the act several times in different combinations or ways to complete the task. Similarly goodwill quests are quests which require a player to help another lower-level player. Teaching or assisting a peer is a way to reinforce knowledge. This type of quest may be useful in fostering declarative knowledge by having one student peer mentor or assist another learner.

Procedural knowledge

The Fed Ex quests and messenger quests are quests which move players through the environment and expose them to new areas and resources. They are also procedural in nature. The Fed Ex quest is procedural in that it may involve going to various places to collect items and manipulate items and then finally deliver them. Procedural knowledge focuses on knowledge about how to perform a task. In a learning environment, this type of task might be useful in fostering procedural knowledge by simulating how something is done. The learner might be required to find various objects or to complete actions in a particular order with the goal of demonstrating a process. Similarly, the messenger quest is also often procedural in nature in which players often are required to pass information along from one source to another. In turn, this might be used by a learner to first simulate or learn a process then to recount that process to another learner or to a narrative character.

Strategic knowledge

The bounty quest requires players to defeat a character or number of characters, while the escort quest requires players escort a NPC from one location to another. Both quests-types are often challenging and require players to plan and strategize. Strategic knowledge refers to knowledge of how to apply knowledge, principles, and experiences to various and new situations. Both bounty quests and escort quests require players to analyze their character's strengths and weaknesses and to balance those against the environmental factors they may encounter and the type of challenge. These types of small quests might be useful for assisting learners in integrating and fostering knowledge gained from exploration, interaction, and various procedures and applying that knowledge in a new or unique situation.

Metacognitive knowledge

Both bounty quests and escort quests also require players to explore, observe, speculate, and make conjectures. Players make conjectures by gauging the demands of the quests while reflecting on their past experiences. In goodwill quests, players may articulate their experiences while assisting lower-level players. In turn players may model, scaffold, and coach lower-level players. These types of quests might be helpful in helping learners foster and apply "adaptive expertise" in problem-solving (Bransford et al., 2000; Hatano & Inagaki, 1986) by exposing learners to resources and processes and then providing a challenge in which they must make conjectures about combining resources, processes, and skills.

Conclusion

The purpose of this paper is to discuss how the structure in MMORPGs might inform the design of interactive learning and game-based learning environments by looking at the elements that support intrinsic motivation. Specifically, the focus of this analysis is on intrinsic motivation of both the character development and role-playing and the small quest design in the narrative environment. It is important to acknowledge that games are designed primarily for entertainment, whereas the purpose of learning environments is to educate and foster learning. Despite these differences, there are elements within the design of MMORPGs which foster intrinsic motivation while requiring players to think, plan, and act critically and strategically. The elements of character development and the narrative environment are already present in varying degrees in various instructional design models, however, what the design of MMORPGs offer is a way to frame different types of learning domains within a compelling, individualized, collaborative environment.

Although popular game design has much to offer the field of instructional design, it should be acknowledged that there is content in many popular games, which is controversial on many levels. It is not the purpose of this analysis to suggest that all elements of MMORPGs be adopted for educational use. MMORPGs are combative in nature. Additionally, the aspect of character design and development is problematic in some MMORPGs. Issues of race, gender, and culture should always be taken into consideration during the instructional design process. It is, however, the intent of this analysis to suggest that MMORPG design may provide a flexible model for creating engaging interactive learning environments which foster intrinsic motivation by providing choice, control, collaboration, challenge, and achievement. There is much in contemporary game design to be explored and annexed to support different types of learning. The design of MMORPGs is a potential flexible model that may be of use to instructional designers and educators looking at how to develop interactive and game-based learning environments which are engaging for all students.

Acknowledgements

Thanks to the ETR&D Development Editor, J. Michael Spector, and the reviewers for their insightful comments and suggestions.

References

AAUW Educational Foundation Commission on Technology, Gender, and Teacher Education (2000). Tech-savvy: Educating girls in the new computer age. Retrieved June 14, 2004 from http://www.aauw.org/member_center/publications/TechSavvy/TechSavvy.pdf.

Ackerman, P. L. (1986). Individual differences in information processing: an investigation of intellectual abilities and task performance during practice. *Intelligence, 10,* 109–139.

Anderson, J. R. (1983). *The architecture of cognition.* Cambridge, MA: Harvard University Press.

Bloom, B. (1956). *Taxonomy of educational objectives: The cognitive domain.* New York: McKay.

Bowman, R. F. (1982). A "Pac–Man" theory of motivation: Tactile implications for classroom instruction. *Educational Technology, 22*(9), 14–17.

Bransford, J. D., Brown, A. L., & Cocking, R. L. (2000). *How people learn: Brain, mind, experience, and school committee on developments in the science of learning.* Washington, D.C.: National Academy Press.

Brown, A. L. (1978). Knowing when, where, and how to remember: A problem of metacognition. In R. Glaser (Ed.), *Advances in instructional psychology* (pp. 77–165). Hillsdale, NJ: Erlbaum.

Brown, J., Collins, A., & Duguid, P. (1989). Situated cognition and the culture of learning. *Educational Researcher, 18*(1), 32–A2.

Bruckman, A. (1997). *MOOSE Crossing: Construction, community, and learning in a networked virtual world for kids.* Doctoral dissertation, MIT.

Bryce, J., & Rutter, J. (2002). Killing like a girl: Gendered gaming and girl gamers visibility. CGDC Conference Proceedings. University of Tampere Press. Finland, 243–255. Retrieved May 5, 2004 from http://www.digiplay.org.uk/media/cgdc.pdf.

Bryce, J., & Rutter, J. (2003). Gender dynamics and the social and spatial organization of computer gaming. *Leisure Studies, 22,* 1–15.

Cassell, J., & Jenkins, H. (1998). Chess for girls? Feminism and computer games. In: G. Cassell & H. Jenkins (Eds.), *From Barbie to Mortal Kombat: Gender and computer games* (pp. 2–45). Cambridge, MA: MIT.

Cognition and Technology Group at Vanderbilt (1990). Anchored instruction and its relationship to situated cognition. *Educational Researcher, 19*(6), 2–10.

Cognition and Technology Group at Vanderbilt (1993). Anchored instruction and situated cognition revisited. *Educational Technology, 33*(3), 52–70.

Collins, A. (1978). *Fragments of a theory of human plausible reasoning.* Proceedings of the 39th conference on Theoretical Issues in Natural Language Processing–2 (TINLAP–2), (194–201). New York: ACM.

Cordova, D. I., & Lepper, M. R. (1996). Intrinsic motivation and the process of learning: Beneficial effects of contextualization, personalization, and choice. *Journal of Educational Psychology, 88*(4), 715–730.

Csikszentmihalyi, M., & Lawson, R. (1980). Intrinsic rewards in school crime. In M. Verble (Ed.), *Dealing in discipline.* Omaha: University of Mid-America.

Curtis, P. (1992). Mudding: Social phenomena in text-based virtual realities. Berkeley, CA. Retrieved January 5, 1999 from: ftp://parcftp.xerox.com in pub/MOO/papers/DIAC92.

de Castell, S., & Bryson, M. (1998). Retooling play: Dystopia, disphoria, and difference. In G. Cassell & H. Jenkins (Eds.), *From Barbie to Mortal Kombat: Gender and computer games* (pp. 231–261). Cambridge, MA: MIT.

Dede, C. (1996). The evolution of constructivist learning environments: Immersion in distributed, virtual worlds. In B. G. Wilson (Ed.), *Constructivist learning environments: Case studies in instructional design* (pp. 165–175). Edgewood Cliffs: Educational Technology Publications.

Dibbell, J. (1994). A rape of cyberspace; or how an evil clown, a Haitian trickster spirit, two wizards, and a cast of dozens turned a database into a society. In M. Dery (Ed.), *Flame wars: Discourse of cyberculture.* Duke: Duke University Press.

Dickey, M. D. (2003). Teaching in 3D: Pedagogical affordances and constraints of 3D virtual worlds for synchronous distance learning. *Distance Education, 24*(1), 105–121.

Dickey, M. D. (2005). Engaging by design: How engagement strategies in popular computer and video games can inform instructional design. *Educational Technology Research and Development, 53*(2), 67–83.

Dickey, M. D. (2006a). Girl gamers: The controversy and relevance of female- oriented design for instructional design. *British Journal of Educational Technology, 35*(5), 785–793.

Dickey, M. D. (2006b). Game design narrative for learning: Appropriating adventure game design narrative devices and techniques for the design of interactive learning environments. *Educational Technology Research and Development,* 54(3), 245–263.

Dodge, B. J. (1995). WebQuests: A structure for active learning on the world wide web. *The Distance Educator, 1*(2).

Duffy, T. M., & Cunningham, D. J. (1996). Constructivism: Implications for the design and delivery of instruction. In D. Jonassen (Ed.), *Handbook of research for educational communications and technology* (pp. 170–198). New York: Macmillan.

Eisner, E. W. (1998). *The enlightened eye: Qualitative inquiry and the enhancement of educational practice.* New Jersey: Prentice Hall.

Ertmer, P. A., & Quinn, J. (1999). *The ID casebook: Case studies in instructional design.* Columbus, OH: Merrill.

Entertainment Software Association (ESA) (2004). Essential facts about the computer and video game industry. Retrieved October 12, 2004, from http://www.theesa.com/EFBrochure.pdf.

EverQuest. (1999). Verant Interactive. 989 Studios. EverQuest Website: http://everquest.station.sony.com/.

Gagné, R. M. (1985). *The conditions of learning and theory of instruction* (4th ed.). New York: Holt, Rinehart, and Winston. Z.

Gee, J. P. (2003). *What video games have to teach us about learning and literacy.* New York: Palgrave.

Gee, J. P. (2005). *Learning, literacy, and good video games.* Montreal, CA: Paper presented at the annual meeting of the American Educational Research Association.

Gibson, J. J. (1977). The theory of affordances. In R. Shaw & J. Bransford (Eds.), *Perceiving, acting, and knowing: Toward an ecological psychology* (pp. 67–82). Hillsdale, New Jersey: Erlbaum Associates.

Hannafin, M. J., & Land, S. (1997). The foundations and assumptions of technology-enhanced, student-centered learning environments. *Instructional Science, 25,* 167–202.

Hannafin, M. J., Land, S., & Oliver, K. (1999). Open learning environments: Foundations, methods, and models. In C. M. Reigeluth (Ed.), *Instructional-design theories and models: A new paradigm of instructional theory. vol. II* (pp. 115–140). Hillsdale, NJ: Lawrence Erlbaum Associates.

Hatano, G., & Inagaki, K. (1986). Two courses of expertise. In H. Stevenson, H. Azuma, & K. Hakuta (Eds.), *Child development and education in Japan* (pp. 262–272). San Francisco: Freeman.

Herz, C. J. (2001). Gaming the system: What higher education can learn from multiplayer online worlds. *The Internet and the University, Educause Forum on the Future of Higher Education*. Retrieved February 15, 2004 from http://www.educause.edu/ir/library/pdf/ffpiuol9.pdf.

Iyengar, S. S., & Lepper, M. R. (1999). Rethinking the value of choice: A cultural perspective on intrinsic motivation. *Journal of Personality and Social Psychology, 76*, 349–366.

Iyengar, S. S., & Lepper, M. R. (2000). When choice is demotivating: Can one desire too much of a good thing? *Journal of Personality and Social Psychology, 76*, 995–1006.

Jakobsson, M. (2002). Rest in peace, Bill the bot. Death and life in virtual worlds. In R. Schroeder (Ed.), *The social life of avatars: Culture and communication in virtual environments*. London: Springer-Verlag.

Jakobsson, M., & Taylor, T. L. (2003). *The Sopranos meets Ever quest: Social networking in massively multiuser networking games*. MelbourneDAC, the 5th International Digital Arts and Culture Conference. Melbourne, Australia.

Jenkins, H. (2002). Game design as narrative architecture. Retrieved September 10, 2004, from: http://web.mit.edu/21fms/www/faculty/henry3/games&narrative.html#l.

Jonassen, D. H. (1996). *Computers in the classroom: A Mindtools for critical thinking*. Englewood Cliffs, NJ: Prentice-Hall.

Jonassen, D. H. (1999). Designing constructivist learning environments. In C. M. Reigeluth (Ed.), *Instructional-design theories and models: A new paradigm of instructional theory. Vol. II* (pp. 215–240). Hillsdale, NJ: Lawrence Erlbaum Associates.

Jonassen, D. H., & Rohrer-Murphy, L. (1999). Activity theory as a framework for designing constructivist learning environments. *Educational Technology Research and Development, 47*(1), 61–79.

Julian, M. F., Larson, V. A., & Kinzie, M. B. (1999). *Compelling case experiences: Challenges for emerging instructional designers*. Houston, TX: Paper presented at the annual meeting of the Association for Educational Communications & Technology (AECT).

Kafai, Y. B. (1994). *Minds in play: Computer game design as a context for children's learning*. Hillsdale, N.J.: Lawrence Erlbaum Associates.

Kafai, Y. B. (1998). Video game designs by girls and boys: Variability and consistency of gender differences. In G. Cassell & H. Jenkins (Eds.), *From Barbie to Mortal Kombat: Gender and computer games* (pp. 90–114). Cambridge, MA: MIT.

Kraiger, K., Ford, J. K., & Salas, E. (1993). Integration of cognitive, behavioral, and affective theories of learning into new methods of training evaluation [Monograph]. *Journal of Applied Psychology, 78*, 311–328.

Land, S. M., & Hannafin, M. J., (1996). A conceptual framework for the development of theories-in-action with open-ended learning environments. *Educational Technology Research & Development, 44*(3), 37–53.

Land, S. M., & Hannafin, M. J. (1997). Patterns of understanding with open-ended learning environments: A qualitative study. *Educational Technology Research & Development, 45*(2), 47–73.

Lave, J., & Wenger, E. (1991). *Situated learning*. New York: Cambridge University Press.

Lincoln, Y. S., & Guba, E. G. (1985). *Naturalistic inquiry*. Beverly Hills, CA: Sage.

Lineage. (1998). NCsoft™. Lineage Website: http://www.lineage.com/.

Malone, T. W. (1981). Toward a theory of intrinsically motivating instruction. *Cognitive Science*, *4*, 333–369.

Malone, T. W., & Lepper, M. R. (1987). Making learning fun: A taxonomy of intrinsic motivations for learning. In R. E. Snow & M. J. Farr (Eds.), *Aptitude, learning and instruction, Vol. 3: Conative and affective process analyses* (pp. 223–253). Hillsdale, NJ: Erlbaum.

Miller, L., Chaika, M., & Groppe, L. (1996). Girls preferences in software design. Insights from a focus group. *Technology and Electronic Journal the 21st Century*, *4*(2), 1–6. Retrieved October 10, 2004, from http://www.helsinki.fi/science/optek/1996/n2/miller.txt.

MOOSE Crossing. (1996). MOOSE Crossing Website: http://www- static.cc.gatech.edu/elc/moose- crossing/.

Murray, M., & Kliman, M. (1999). Beyond point and click: The search for gender equity in computer games. *ENC Focus*, *6*(3), 23–27.

Pac-Man. (1983) Atari.

Putnam, R. D. (1995). Bowling alone: America's declining social capital. *Journal of Democracy*, *6*(1), 65–78.

Putnam, R. D. (2000). *Bowling alone: the collapse and revival of American community*. New York: Simon & Schuster.

Prensky, M. (2001). *Digital game-based learning*. New York: McGraw-Hill.

Provenzo, E. F. (1991). *Video kids: Making sense of Nintendo*. Cambridge, MA: Harvard University Press.

Resnick, M., & Wilensky, U. (1997). Diving into complexity: Developing probabilistic decentralized thinking through role-playing activities. *Journal of the Learning Sciences*, *7*(2), 153–172.

Rieber, L. P. (1996). Seriously considering play: Designing interactive learning environments based on the blending of microworlds, simulations, and games. *Educational Technology Research & Development*, *44*(2), 43–58.

Reid, E. (1994). *Cultural formations in text-based virtual realities*: M.A. thesis, University of Melbourne.

Riner, R. D. (1996). Virtual ethics ← Virtual reality. *Futures Research Quarterly*, *12*(1), 57–70.

Riner, R. D., & Clodius, J. A. (1995). Simulating future histories: The NAU solar system simulation & mars settlement. *Anthropology & Education Quarterly*, *21*(2), 121–127.

Rollings, A., & Adams, E. (2003). *Game design*. Indianapolis, IN: New Riders.

Rubin, A., Murray, M., O'Neil, K., & Ashley, J. (1997). What kinds of educational computer games would girls like? Paper presented at the American Educational Research Association annual meeting, Boston, April 1997. Retrieved June 12, 2004, from http://www.terc.edu/mathequity/gw/html/MITpaper.html.

Schank, R. C., Berman, T. R., & Macpherson, K. A. (1999). Learning by doing. In C. M. Reigeluth (Ed.), *Instructional-design theories and models: A new paradigm of instructional theory. Vol. II* (pp.161–182). Hillsdale, NJ: Lawrence Erlbaum Associates.

Schank, R. C., Fano, A., Bell, B., & Jona, M. (1993). The design of goal-based scenarios. *The Journal of the Learning Sciences*, *3*(4), 305–345.

Sfard, A. (1998). On two metaphors for learning and the dangers of choosing just one. *Educational Researcher*, *27*(2), 4–13.

Shulman, L. S. (1992). Toward a pedagogy of cases. In J. Shulman (Ed.), *Case methods in teacher education*. New York: Teachers College Press.

Slaton, J. (1998). The games girls play: Who says girls are afraid of mice? *GameSpot, Inc.* Retrieved June 12, 2004, from http://www.gamespot.com/features/girlgames/index. html.

Smith, P., & Ragan, T. (1993). *Instructional design.* New York, NY: Merrill.

Stone, A. R. (1995). *The war of desire and technology at the close of the mechanical age.* Cambridge: The MIT Press.

Squire, K. (2003). Video games in education. *International Journal of Intelligent Simulations and Gaming, 2*(1). Retrieved August 2, 2004 from http://cms.mit.edu/ games/education/pubs/IJIS.doc.

Suchman, L. A. (1987). *Plans and situated actions: The problem of human-machine communications.* Cambridge, UK: Cambridge University Press.

Super Mario Bros II. (1988). Nintendo.

Taylor, T. L. (2003). Multiple pleasures: Women and online gaming. *Convergence, 9*(1), 21–46.

Turkle, S. (1995). *Life on the screen: Identity in the age of the internet.* New York: Simon and Schuster.

ToonTown (2004). Disney Interactive. ToonTown Online Website: http://www.toontown.com.

Vygotsky, L. S. (1978). *Mind in society: The development of higher psychological processes.* Boston, MA: Harvard University Press.

Wagner, R. K. (1987). Tacit knowledge in everyday intelligent behavior. *Journal of Personality and Social Psychology, 52,* 1236–1241.

Wilson, B. G. (1996). *Constructivist learning environments: case studies in instructional design.* Englewood Cliffs, NJ: Educational Technology Publications.

Winn, W., & Snyder, D. (1996). Cognitive perspectives in psychology. In D. Jonassen (Ed.), *Handbook for research in educational communications and technology* (pp. 117–123). New York, NY: Simon & Schuster Macmillan.

Winn, W. (2002). Current trends in educational technology research: The study of learning environments. *Educational Psychology Review, 14*(3), 331–351.

World of Warcraft. (2004). Blizzard. Wow Website: http://www.worldofwarcraft.com.

Yee, N. (2001). The Norrathian Scrolls: A study of EverQuest (version 2.5). Retrieved on May 4, 2004 from http://www.nickyee.com/eqt/report.html.

76

VIDEO GAMES AND THE FUTURE OF LEARNING

David Williamson Shaffer, Kurt R. Squire, Richard Halverson, and James P. Gee

Source: *The Phi Delta Kappan*, 87(2), October 2005, 104–111.

Abstract

Most educators are dismissive of video games. But corporations, the government, and the military have already recognized and harnessed their tremendous educative power. Schools have to catch up, the authors argue.

Computers are changing our world: how we work, how we shop, how we entertain ourselves, how we communicate, how we engage in politics, how we care for our health. The list goes on and on. But will computers change the way we learn? The short answer is yes. Computers are already changing the way we learn—and if you want to understand how, just look at video games. Not because the games that are currently available are going to replace schools as we know them any time soon, but because they give a glimpse into how we might create new and more powerful ways to learn in schools, communities, and workplaces—new ways to learn for a new Information Age. Look at video games because, while they are wildly popular with adolescents and young adults, they are more than just toys. Look at video games because they create new social and cultural worlds—worlds that help us learn by integrating thinking, social interaction, and technology, all in service of doing things we care about.

We want to be clear from the start that video games are no panacea. Like books and movies, they can be used in antisocial ways. Games are inherently simplifications of reality, and today's games often incorporate—or are based on—violent and sometimes misogynistic themes. Critics suggest that the lessons people learn from playing video games as they currently exist are not always desirable. But even the harshest critics agree that we learn *something* from playing video games. The question is, How can we use the power of video games as a constructive force in schools, homes, and workplaces?

In answer to that question, we argue here for a particular view of games—and of learning—as activities that are most powerful when they are personally meaningful, experiential, social, and epistemological all at the same time. From this perspective, we describe an approach to the design of learning environments that builds on the educational properties of games but grounds them deeply within a theory of learning appropriate to an age marked by the power of new technologies.

Virtual worlds for learning

The first step toward understanding how video games can—and, we argue, will—transform education is changing the widely shared perspective that games are "mere entertainment." More than a multibillion-dollar industry, more than a compelling toy for both children and adults, more than a route to computer literacy, video games are important because they let people participate in new worlds. They let players think, talk, and act in new ways. Indeed, players come to *inhabit* roles that are otherwise inaccessible to them. A 16-year-old in Korea playing Lineage can become an international financier, trading raw materials, buying and selling goods in different parts of the virtual world, and speculating on currencies.[1] A Deus Ex player can experience life as a government special agent, operating in a world where the lines between terrorism and state-sponsored violence are called into question.

These rich virtual worlds are what make video games such powerful contexts for learning. In game worlds, learning no longer means confronting words and symbols that are separated from the things those words and symbols refer to. The inverse square law of gravitational attraction is no longer something to be understood solely through an equation. Instead, students can gain virtual experience walking in a world with a mass smaller than that of Earth, or they can plan manned space flights—a task that requires understanding the changing effects of gravitational forces in different parts of the solar system. In virtual worlds, learners experience the concrete realities that words and symbols describe. Through these and similar experiences in multiple contexts, learners can understand complex concepts without losing the connection between abstract ideas and the real problems they can be used to solve. In other words, the virtual worlds of games are powerful because they make it possible to develop *situated understanding*.

Although the stereotypical gamer is a lone teenager seated in front of a computer, game playing can also be a thoroughly social phenomenon. The clearest examples are the "massively multiplayer" online games, in which thousands of players are simultaneously online at any given time, participating in virtual worlds with their own economies, political systems, and cultures. Moreover, careful study shows that most games—from console action games to PC strategy games—have robust game-playing communities. Whereas schools largely sequester students from one another and from the outside world, games bring players together—competitively and cooperatively—in the virtual world of the game and in the social community of its players. In schools, students largely work alone, with school-sanctioned materials; avid gamers seek out news sites, read and write FAQs, participate in discussion forums, and become critical consumers of information.[2] Classroom work rarely has an impact outside the classroom; its only real audience is the teacher. Game players, in contrast, develop reputations in online communities, cultivate audiences by contributing to discussion forums, and occasionally even take up careers as professional gamers, traders of online commodities,[3] or game designers and modders (players who use programming tools to modify games). The virtual worlds of games are powerful, in other words, because playing games means developing a set of *effective social practices*.

By participating in these social practices, game players have an opportunity to explore new identities. In one well-publicized case, a heated political contest erupted for the presidency of Alphaville, one of the towns in The Sims Online. Arthur Baynes, the 21-year-old incumbent, was running against Laura McKnight, a 14-year-old. The muckraking, accusations of voter fraud, and political jockeying taught young Laura about the realities of politics. The election also gained national attention on National Public Radio, as pundits debated the significance of games that allowed teens not only to argue and debate politics but also to run a political system in which the virtual lives of thousands of real players were at stake. The complexity of Laura's campaign, political alliances, and platform—a platform that called for a stronger police force and a significant restructuring of the judicial system—shows how deep the disconnect has become between the kinds of experiences made available in schools and those available in online worlds. The virtual worlds of games are rich contexts for learning because they make it possible for players to experiment with new and *powerful identities*.[4]

The communities that game players form similarly organize meaningful learning experiences outside of school contexts. In the various websites devoted to the game Civilization, for example, players organize themselves around the shared goal of developing the skills, habits, and understandings that are necessary to become experts in the game. At Apolyton.net, one such site, players post news feeds, participate in discussion forums, and trade screenshots of the game. But they also run a radio station, exchange saved game files in order to collaborate and compete, create custom modifications, and, perhaps most unusually, run their own university to teach other players to play the game at deeper levels. Apolyton University shows us how part of expert gaming is developing a set of values— values that highlight enlightened risk taking, entrepreneurship, and expertise rather than the formal accreditation emphasized by institutional education.[5]

If we look at the development of game communities, we see that part of the power of games for learning is the way they *develop shared values*. In other words, by creating virtual worlds, games integrate knowing and doing. But not just knowing and doing. Games bring together ways of knowing, ways of doing, ways of being, and ways of caring: the situated understandings, effective social practices, powerful identities, and shared values that make someone an expert. The expertise might be that of a modern soldier in Full Spectrum Warrior, a zoo operator in Zoo Tycoon, or a world leader in Civilization III. Or it might be expertise in the sophisticated practices of gaming communities, such as those built around Age of Mythology or Civilization III.

There is a lot being learned in these games. But for some educators, it is hard to see the educational potential of the games because these virtual worlds aren't about memorizing words or definitions or facts. But video games are about a whole lot more.

From fact fetish to ways of thinking

A century ago, John Dewey argued that schools were built on a fact fetish, and the argument is still valid today. The fact fetish views any area of learning—whether physics, mathematics, or history—as a body of facts or information. The measure of good teaching and learning is the extent to which students can answer questions about these facts on tests.

But *to know* is a verb before it becomes a noun in *knowledge*. We learn by doing—not just by doing any old thing, but by doing something as part of a larger community of people who share common goals and ways of achieving those goals. We learn by becoming part of a community of practice and thus developing that community's ways of knowing, acting, being, and caring—the community's situated understandings, effective social practices, powerful identities, and shared values.[6]

Of course, different communities of practice have different ways of thinking and acting. Take, for example, lawyers. Lawyers act like lawyers. They identify themselves as lawyers. They are interested in legal issues. And they know about the law. These skills, habits, and understandings are made possible by looking at the world in a particular way—by thinking like a lawyer. Doctors think and act in their own ways, as do architects, plumbers, steelworkers, and waiters or physicists, historians, and mathematicians.

The way of thinking—the epistemology—of a practice determines how someone in the community decides what questions are worth answering, how to go about answering them, and how to decide when an answer is sufficient. The epistemology of a practice thus organizes (and is organized by) the situated understandings, effective social practices, powerful identities, and shared values of the community. In communities of practice, knowledge, skills, identities, and values are shaped by a particular way of thinking into a coherent *epistemic frame*.[7] If a community of practice is a group with a local culture, then the epistemic frame is the grammar of the culture: the ways of thinking and acting that individuals learn when they become part of that culture.

Let's look at an example of how this might play out in the virtual world of a video game. Full Spectrum Warrior (Pandemic Studios, for PC and Xbox) is a video game based on a U.S. Army training simulation.[8] But Full Spectrum Warrior is not a mere first-person shooter in which the player blows up everything on the screen. To survive and win the game, the player has to learn to think and act like a modern professional soldier.

85

In Full Spectrum Warrior, the player uses the buttons on the controller to give orders to two squads of soldiers, as well as to consult a GPS device, radio for support, and communicate with commanders in the rear. The instruction manual that comes with the game makes it clear from the outset that players must take on the values, identities, and ways of thinking of a professional soldier if they are to play the game successfully. "Everything about your squad," the manual explains, "is the result of careful planning and years of experience on the battlefield. Respect that experience, soldier, since it's what will keep your soldiers alive."[9]

In the game, that experience—the skills and knowledge of professional military expertise—is distributed between the virtual soldiers and the real-world player. The soldiers in a player's squads have been trained in movement formations; the role of the player is to select the best position for them on the field. The virtual characters (the soldiers) know part of the task (various movement formations), and the player knows another part (when and where to engage in such formations). This kind of distribution holds for every aspect of military knowledge in the game. However, the knowledge that is distributed between virtual soldiers and real-world player is not a set of inert facts; what is distributed are the values, skills, practices, and (yes) facts that constitute authentic military professional practice. This simulation of the social context of knowing allows players to act as if in concert with (artificially intelligent) others, even with-in the single-player context of the game.

In so doing, Full Spectrum Warrior shows how games take advantage of situated learning environments. In games as in real life, people must be able to build meanings on the spot as they navigate their contexts. In Full Spectrum Warrior, players learn about suppression fire through the concrete experiences they have while playing. These experiences give a working definition of suppression fire, to be sure. But they also let a player come to understand how the idea applies in different contexts, what it has to do with solving particular kinds of problems, and how it relates to other practices in the domain, such as the injunction against shooting while moving.

Video games thus make it possible to "learn by doing" on a grand scale—but not just by wandering around in a rich computer environment to learn without any guidance. Asking learners to act without explicit guidance—a form of learning often associated with a loose interpretation of progressive pedagogy—reflects a bad theory of learning. Learners are novices. Leaving them to float in rich experiences with no support triggers the very real human penchant for finding creative but spurious patterns and generalizations. The fruitful patterns or generalizations in any domain are the ones that are evident to those who already know how to look at the domain and know how complex variables in the domain interrelate. And this is precisely what the learner does not yet know. In Full Spectrum Warrior, the player is immersed in activity, values, and ways of seeing but is guided and supported by the knowledge built into the virtual soldiers and the weapons, equipment, and environments in the game. Players are not free to invent everything for themselves. To succeed in the game, they must live by—and ultimately come to master—the epistemic frame of military doctrine. Full Spectrum Warrior is an example of what we suggest is the promise of video games and the future of learning: the development of epistemic games.[10]

Epistemic games for initiation and transformation

We have argued that video games are powerful contexts for learning because they make it possible to create virtual worlds and because acting in such worlds makes it possible to develop the situated understandings, effective social practices, powerful identities, shared values, and ways of thinking of important communities of practice. To build such worlds, one has to understand how the epistemic frames of those communities are developed, sustained, and changed. Some parts of practice are more central to the creation and development of an epistemic frame than others, so analyzing the epistemic frame tells you, in effect, what might be safe to leave out in a re-creation of the practice. The result is a video game that preserves the connections between knowing and doing that are central to an epistemic frame and so becomes an epistemic game. Such epistemic games let players participate in valued communities of practice to develop a new epistemic frame or to develop a better and more richly elaborated version of an already mastered epistemic frame.

Initiation

Developing games such as Full Spectrum Warrior that simultaneously build situated understandings, effective social practices, powerful identities, shared values, and ways of thinking is clearly no small task. But the good news is that in many cases existing communities of practice have already done a lot of that work. Doctors know how to create more doctors; lawyers know how to create more lawyers; the same is true for a host of other socially valued communities of practice. Thus we can imagine epistemic games in which players learn biology by working as a surgeon, history by writing as a journalist, mathematics by designing buildings as an architect or engineer, geography by fighting as a soldier, or French by opening a restaurant. More precisely, these players learn by inhabiting virtual worlds based on the way surgeons, journalists, architects, soldiers, and restaurateurs develop their epistemic frames.

To build such games requires understanding how practitioners develop their ways of thinking and acting. Such understanding is uncovered through *epistemographies* of practice: detailed ethnographic studies of how the epistemic frame of a community of practice is developed by new members. Gathering this information requires more work than is currently invested in most "educational" video games. But the payoff is that such work can become the basis for an alternative educational model. Video games based on the training of socially valued practitioners let us begin to build an education system in which students learn to work (and thus to think) as doctors, lawyers, architects, engineers, journalists, and other important members of the community. The purpose of building such education systems is not to train students for these pursuits in the traditional sense of vocational education. Rather, we develop such epistemic frames because they can provide students with an opportunity to see the world in a variety of ways that are fundamentally grounded in meaningful activity and well aligned with the core skills, habits, and understandings of a postindustrial society.[11]

One early example of such a game is Madison 2200, an epistemic game based on the practices of urban planning.[12] In Madison 2200, players learn about urban ecology by working as urban planners who are redesigning a downtown pedestrian mall popular with local teenagers. Players get a project directive from the mayor, addressed to them as city planners, including a city budget plan and letters from concerned citizens about crime, revenue, jobs, waste, traffic, and affordable housing. A video features interviews about these issues with local residents, business-people, and community leaders. Players conduct a site assessment of the street and work in teams to develop a land use plan, which they present at the end of the game to a representative of the city planning office.

Not surprisingly, along the way players learn a good deal about urban planning and its practices. But something very interesting happens in an epistemic game like Madison 2200. When knowledge is first and foremost a form of activity and experience—of doing something in the world within a community of practice—the facts and information eventually come for free. A large body of facts that resists out-of-context memorization and rote learning comes easily if learners are immersed in activities and experiences that use these facts for plans, goals, and purposes within a coherent domain of knowledge. Data show that, in Madison 2200, players start to form an epistemic frame of urban planning. But they also develop their understanding of ecology and are able to apply it to urban issues. As one player commented, "I really noticed how urban planners have to think about building things. Urban planners also have to think about how the crime rate might go up or the pollution or waste, depending on choices." Another said about walking on the same streets she had traversed before the workshop, "You notice things, like that's why they build a house there, or that's why they build a park there."

The players in Madison 2200 do enjoy their work. But more important is that the experience lets them inhabit an imaginary world in which they are urban planners. The world of Madison 2200 recruits these players to new ways of thinking and acting as part of a new way of seeing the world. Urban planners have a particular way of addressing urban issues. By participating in an epistemic game based on urban planning, players begin to take on that way of seeing the world. As a result, it is fun, too.

Transformation

Games like Full Spectrum Warrior and Madison 2200 expose novices to the ways professionals make sense of typical problems. But other games are designed for those who are already members of a professional community, with the intention of transforming the ways they think by focusing on atypical problems: cases in which established ways of knowing break down in the face of a new or challenging situation.

Just as games that initiate players into an epistemic frame depend on epistemographic study of the training practices of a community, games designed to transform an epistemic frame depend on detailed examination of how the mature epistemic frame of a practice is organized and maintained—and on when and how the frame becomes problematic. These critical moments of "expectation failure" are the points of entry for reorganizing experienced practitioners' ways of thinking.[13] Building the common assumptions of an existing epistemic frame into a game allows experienced professionals to cut right to the key learning moments.

For example, work on military leadership simulations has used *goal-based scenarios* to build training simulations based on the choices military leaders face when setting up a base of operations.[14] In the business world, systems like RootMap (Root Learning, www.rootlearning.com) create graphical representations of professional knowledge, offering suggestions for new practice by highlighting breakdowns in conventional understanding.[15] Studies of school leaders similarly suggest that the way professionals frame problems has a strong impact on the possible solutions they are willing and able to explore.[16] This ability to successfully frame problems in complex systems is difficult to cultivate, but Richard Halverson and Yeonjai Rah have shown that a multimedia representation of successful problem-framing strategies—such as how a principal reorganized her school to serve disadvantaged students—can help school leaders reexamine the critical junctures where their professional understanding is incomplete or ineffective for dealing with new or problematic situations.[17]

Epistemic games and the future of schooling

Epistemic games give players freedom to act within the norms of a valued community of practice—norms that are embedded in nonplayer characters like the virtual soldiers in Full Spectrum Warrior or the real urban planners and planning board members in Madison 2200. To work successfully within the norms of a community, players necessarily learn to think as members of the community. Think for a moment about the student who, after playing Madison 2200, walked down the same streets she had been on the day before and noticed things she had never seen. This is situated learning at its most profound—a transfer of ideas from one context to another that is elusive, rare, and powerful. It happened not because the student learned more information but because she learned it in the context of a new way of thinking—an epistemic frame—that let her see the world in a new way.

Although there are not yet any complete epistemic games in wide circulation, there already exist many games that provide similar opportunities for deeply situated learning. Rise of Nations and Civilization III offer rich, interactive environments in which to explore counterfactual historical claims and help players understand the operation of complex historical modeling. Railroad Tycoon lets players engage in design activities that draw on the same economic and geographic issues faced by railroad engineers in the 1800s. Madison 2200, of course, shows the pedagogical potential of bringing students the experience of being city planners, and we are in the process of developing projects that similarly let players work as biomechanical engineers,[18] journalists,[19] professional mediators,[20] and graphic designers.[21] Other epistemic games might allow a player to experience the world as an evolutionary biologist or as a tailor in colonial Williamsburg.[22]

But even if we had the world's best educational games produced and ready for parents, teachers, and students to buy and play, it's not clear that most educators or schools would know what to do with them. Although the majority of students play video games, the majority of teachers do not. Games, with their anti-authoritarian aesthetics and inherently anti-Puritanical values, can be seen as challenging institutional education. Even if we strip away the blood and guts that characterize some video games, the reality is that, as a form, games encourage exploration, personalized meaning-making, individual expression, and playful experimentation with social boundaries—all of which cut against the grain of the social mores valued in school. In other words, even if we sanitize games, the theories of learning embedded in them run counter to the current social organization of schooling. The next challenges for game and school designers alike is to understand how to shape learning and learning environments to take advantage of the power and potential of games and how to integrate games and game-based learning environments into the predominant arena for learning: schools.

How might school leaders and teachers bring more extended experiments with epistemic games into the culture of the school? The first step will be for superintendents and spokespersons for schools to move beyond the rhetoric of games as violent-serial-killer-inspiring time-wasters and address the range of learning opportunities that games present. Understanding how games can provide powerful learning environments might go a long way toward shifting the current anti-gaming rhetoric. Although epistemic games of the kind we describe here are not yet on the radar of most educators, they are already being used by corporations, the government, the military, and even by political groups to express ideas and teach facts, principles, and world views. Schools and school systems must soon follow suit or risk being swept aside.

A new model of learning

The past century has seen an increasing identification of learning with schooling. But new information technologies challenge this union in fundamental ways. Today's technologies make the world's libraries accessible to anyone with a wireless PDA. A vast social network is literally at the fingertips of anyone with a cell phone. As a result, people have unprecedented freedom to bring resources together to create their own learning trajectories.

But classrooms have not adapted. Theories of learning and instruction embodied in school systems designed to teach large numbers of students a standardized curriculum are dinosaurs in this new world. Good teachers and good school leaders fight for new technologies and new practices. But mavericks grow frustrated by the fundamental mismatch between the social organization of schooling and the realities of life in a postindustrial, global, high-tech society. In the push for standardized instruction, the general public and some policy makers may not have recognized this mismatch, but our students have. School is increasingly seen as irrelevant by many students who are past the primary grades.

Thus we argue that, to understand the future of learning, we should be looking beyond schools to the emerging arena of video games. We suggest that video games matter because they present players with simulated worlds—worlds that, if well constructed, are not just about facts or isolated skills but embody particular social practices. And we argue that video games thus make it possible for players to participate in valued communities of practice and so develop the ways of thinking that organize those practices.

Our students will learn from video games. The questions we must ask and answer are: Who will create these games, and will they be based on sound theories of learning and socially conscious educational practices? The U.S. Army, a longtime leader in simulations, is building games like Full Spectrum Warrior and America's Army—games that introduce civilians to a military world view. Several homeland security games are under development, as are a range of games for health education, from games to help kids with cancer take better care of themselves to simulations to help doctors perform surgery more effectively. Companies are developing games for learning history (Making History), engineering (Time Engineers), and the mathematics of design (Homes of Our Own).[23]

This interest in games is encouraging, but most educational games to date have been produced in the absence of any coherent theory of learning or underlying body of research. We need to ask and answer important questions about this relatively new medium. We need to understand how the conventions of good commercial games create compelling virtual worlds. We need to understand how inhabiting a virtual world develops situated knowledge—how playing a game like Civilization III, for example, mediates players' conceptions of world history. We need to understand how spending thousands of hours participating in the social, political, and economic systems of a virtual world develops powerful identities and shared values.[24] We need to understand how game players develop effective social practices and skills in navigating complex systems and how those skills can support learning in other complex domains. And most of all, we need to leverage these understandings to build games that develop for players the epistemic frames of scientists, engineers, lawyers, political activists, and members of other valued communities of practice—as well as games that can help transform those ways of thinking for experienced professionals.

Video games have the potential to change the landscape of education as we know it. The answers to the fundamental questions raised here will make it possible to use video games to move our system of education beyond the traditional academic disciplines—derived from medieval scholarship and constituted within schools developed in the Industrial Revolution—and toward a new model of learning through meaningful activity in virtual worlds. And that learning experience will serve as preparation for meaningful activity in our postindustrial, technology-rich, real world.

Notes

1 Constance A. Steinkuehler, "Emergent Play" paper presented at the State of Play Conference, New York University Law School, New York City, October 2004.

2 Kurt R. Squire, "Game Cultures, School Cultures," *Innovate*, in press.

3 As Julian Dibbell, a journalist for *Wired* and *Rolling Stone*, has shown, it is possible to make a better living by trading online currencies than by working as a freelance journalist!

4 Constance A. Steinkuehler, "Learning in Massively Multiplayer Online Games," in Yasmin Kafai et al., eds., *Proceedings of the Sixth International Conference of the Learning Sciences* (Mahwah, N.J.: Erlbaum, 2004), pp. 521–28.

5 Kurt R. Squire and Levi Giovanetto, "The Higher Education of Gaming," *eLearning*, in press.

6 Jean Lave and Etienne Wenger, *Situated Learning: Legitimate Peripheral Participation* (Cambridge: Cambridge University Press, 1991).

7 David Williamson Shaffer, "Epistemic Frames and Islands of Expertise: Learning from Infusion Experiences," in Kafai et al., pp. 473–80.

8 The commercial game retains about 15% of what was in the Army's original simulation. For more on this game as a learning environment, see James P. Gee, "What Will a State of the Art Video Game Look Like?," *Innovate*, in press.

9 *Manual for Full Spectrum Warrior* (Los Angeles: Pandemic Studios, 2004), p. 2.

10 David Williamson Shaffer, "Epistemic Games," *Innovate*, in press.

11 David Williamson Shaffer, "Pedagogical Praxis: The Professions as Models for Postindustrial Education," *Teachers College Record*, July 2004, pp. 1401–21.

12 Kelly L. Beckett and David Williamson Shaffer, "Augmented by Reality: The Pedagogical Praxis of Urban Planning as a Pathway to Ecological Thinking," *Journal of Educational Computing Research*, in press; and Shaffer, "Epistemic Games."

13 Roger C. Schank, *Virtual Learning: A Revolutionary Approach to Building a Highly Skilled Work Force* (New York: McGraw-Hill, 1997).

14 Roger C. Schank et al., "The Design of Goal-Based Scenarios," *Journal of the Learning Sciences*, vol. 3, 1994, pp. 305–45; and A. S. Gordon, "Authoring Branching Storylines for Training Applications," in Kafai et al., pp. 230–38.

15 Kurt R. Squire, "Game-Based Learning: Present and Future State of the Field," e-Learning Consortium, an X-Learn Perspective Paper, Masie Center, February 2005, available at www.masie.com/xlearn/game-based_learning.pdf, 2005.

16 Richard Halverson, "Systems of Practice: How Leaders Use Artifacts to Create Professional Community in Schools," *Education Policy Analysis Archives*, vol. 11, 2003, p. 37; and idem, "Accessing, Documenting and Communicating Practical Wisdom: The Phronesis of School Leadership Practice," *American Journal of Education*, vol. 111, 2004, pp. 90–121.

17 Richard Halverson and Yeonjai Rah, "Representing Leadership for Social Justice: The Case of Franklin School," *Journal of Cases in Educational Leadership*, Spring 2005.

18 Gina Svarovsky and David Williamson Shaffer, "SodaConstructing Knowledge Through Exploratoids," *Journal of Research in Science Teaching*, in press.

19 Shaffer, "Pedagogical Praxis."

20 David Williamson Shaffer, "When Computer-Supported Collaboration Means Computer-Supported Competition: Professional Mediation as a Model for Collaborative Learning," *Journal of Interactive Learning Research*, vol. 15, 2004, pp. 101–15.

21 David Williamson Shaffer, "Learning Mathematics Through Design: The Anatomy of Escher's World," *Journal of Mathematical Behavior*, vol. 16, 1997, pp. 95–112.
22 Kurt R. Squire and Henry Jenkins, "Harnessing the Power of Games in Education," *Insight*, vol. 3, 2004, pp. 5–33.
23 Ibid.
24 Kurt R. Squire, "Sid Meier's Civilization III," *Simulations and Gaming*, vol. 35, 2004, pp. 135–40.

Part 10

VIDEO GAMES AND CULTURE

77

WHAT IS VIDEO GAME CULTURE?

Cultural studies and game studies

Adrienne Shaw

Source: *Games and Culture*, 5(4), 2010, 403–424. Originally published online May 7.

Abstract

What is video game culture, however? What does it mean to have a culture defined by the consumption of a particular medium? Moreover, what are the implications of defining this culture in a particular way? While there has been a great deal of ink spilt on video game culture, the actual definition of the term is often treated as common sense. Unpacking the discourses surrounding "video game culture" allows us to see the power dynamics involved in attributing certain characteristics to it, as well as naming it "video game culture" as such. This has implications for how video games are studied and is connected with how culture is studied more broadly. By critically examining how video game culture has been defined in both press and academic articles, this paper illuminates how this definition has limited the study of video games and where it can move.

From books that look at *Gaming as Culture* (Williams, Hendricks, & Winkler, 2006) to journals such as *Games and Culture* (SAGE), there is a great deal of academic buzz about video game culture.[1] There has been a great deal of "cultural" work done around video games, particularly in the past 10 years. Authors look at video games in relation to thinking (S. Johnson, 2005a), learning (Gee, 2003), gender (Cassell & Jenkins, 2000), children (Kinder, 1991), war (Halter, 2006), and so on. The great majority of recent work on video game culture centers on massively multiplayer online games (MMOGs) like *Everquest, World of Warcraft*, or *SecondLife* (Castronova, 2005; Chee, Vieta, & Smith, 2006; Ondrejka, 2006; Taylor, 2006; D. Williams, Yee, & Caplan, 2008; Yee, 2001). In these areas, authors look at video games with regard to knowledge acquisition, identity and performance, representation, and the relationship between media and audiences. Throughout this research, there is a pervasive sense of video game culture as separate from a constructed mainstream culture, as something new, different, and more importantly definable.

What is video game culture, however? What does it mean to have a culture defined by the consumption of a particular medium? Moreover, what are the implications of defining this culture in a particular way? Although there has been a great deal of ink spilt on the subject of video game culture, writers usually treat the actual definition of the term as common sense. As King and Krzywinska point out, however, "[t]he most potent ideologies achieve precisely this status, being taken for granted as part of the 'commonsense' understanding of particular regimes, rather than recognized *as* ideology" (2006, p. 188). This article unpacks this common sense and interrogates how video game culture is defined in the mainstream U.S. press as well as the academe. I do this not to argue that all video game studies must approach games as culture, but that those scholars that do approach video games through the lens of culture should adopt the same critical and reflexive approaches to culture that cultural studies has. Herein I argue for a critical cultural study of games, rather than a study of game culture as such.

"Game culture" is often defined via descriptions of gamers. The point of this article is not to outline the gamer stereotype yet again. Instead, it begins with the categories from which the stereotype stems. These categories include (a) who plays video games, (b) how they play, and (c) what they play. Starting with these categories and not looking for a prototypical definition of a gamer identity allows us to see that popular discourses actually offer a much more diverse view of what gaming is than they are generally given credit for. They still define "video game culture" as something very distinct and very different from mainstream U.S. culture. This othering of games, whether done in a positive or negative manner, shapes how video games are studied. Unpacking the discourses surrounding "video game culture" allows us to see the power dynamics involved in attributing certain characteristics to it, as well as naming it "video game culture" as such. Definitions of gaming culture have implications for how video games are studied and are connected with how culture is studied more broadly. By critically examining how video game culture has been defined in both press and academic articles, this article illuminates how this definition has limited the study of video games and where culturally based game studies can move.

Conceptualizing video game culture

I begin with the assertion that although much has been written about video game culture, little work in this area has actually looked at games from the perspective of cultural studies. Without delving too deeply into the long and complicated history of cultural studies, "we can picture cultural studies as a distinctive approach to culture that results when we stop thinking about culture as particular valued texts and think about it as a broader process in which each person has a equal right to be heard, and each person's voice and reflections about culture are valuable" (Couldry, 2000, p. 2). That is to say, "culture, from the cultural studies view, is a process" (Carey, 1997 [1992], p. 272). Moreover, cultural studies is in a state of constant debate and flux, as it is "a tendency across disciplines, rather than a discipline itself" (Miller, 2006, p. 1). As outlined in various texts, cultural studies is a field of approaches which is under constant tension and conflict over definitions, methods, theories, and even the fundamental goals and existence of cultural studies (a few texts in this debate include Bennett, 1998; Grossberg, 1994; R. Johnson, 1986–1987). I am not arguing that game studies must look at games as culture or that it has yet to look at games as culture. Rather, I assert that if video game studies are going to look at games as culture, it must adopt the conflicts and struggles of cultural studies, not just the terms and foci.

Much like cultural studies, the study of video games has relied on borrowing techniques from other disciplines, including anthropology, economics, philosophy, psychology, film studies, and so on (Boellstorff, 2006; Loftus & Loftus, 1983; Mortensen, 2007; Myers, 2003). Although they are both interdisciplinary fields, however, game studies has not drawn deeply as it might from cultural studies, particularly its critical and reflexive tendencies though notable exceptions do exist (see Kline, Dyer-Witheford, & De Peuter, 2003; Mayra, 2008). This is problematic as cultural studies could help video game studies approach the field in very productive ways.

How one defines culture, for example, has been a persistent debate in cultural studies as it should be in the analysis of video game culture. Raymond Williams (1998) outlines three ways in which culture has been defined. The first follows from Matthew Arnold's famous quote that culture is "the best that has been thought and said in the world" (Arnold, 1998, p. 7). The second is culture defined as a form of criticism, "the body of intellectual and imaginative work, in which, in a detailed way, human thought and experience are variously recorded" (R. Williams, 1998, p. 48). The third, defines culture as a way of life: "[i]n contemporary parlance, culture consists of four sorts of elements: norms, values, beliefs, and expressive symbols" (Peterson, 1979, p. 137). Geertz (1973) conceptualizes culture as a web of meanings. Hall (1998) asserts that culture is studied both as ideas and as social practices. As culture can be defined in so many different ways, it is of little surprise that the definition of video game culture is so difficult to pin down.

The study of video games as cultural texts or the culture of video games relies on many of the differing understandings of culture outlined above. Video game culture has been defined as a subculture marked by certain tastes (Winkler, 2006, p. 147) and as an art form (Jenkins, 2005). Some look at games as social practice. T. L. Taylor's (2006) ethnography on the MMOG *Everquest*, for example, describes an "online gaming culture," which she defines in terms of its social practices and a shared identity/community created in the gamespace. Analyses of the video game industry are also used to define game culture (Kerr, 2006; Kline, Dyer-Witheford, & De Peuter, 2003). Dovey and Kennedy (2006), for instance, define video game culture by way of the major discourses used by members of the video game development industry. "Games culture is . . . a critical site where discourses around technology, technological innovation, and technological competence converge with dominant conceptions of gender and race" (p. 131). They describe how these discourses shape who is allowed into the industry (as acculturation is a requirement for entry into the field) and the effect this has on the products.

These examples demonstrate how video game culture has been defined in the academe. Video game scholars, however, tend to write about the culture from the inside, as many of them identify as gamers. Journalists, however, tend to write about video gaming from this outside. Game studies academics often try to describe video game culture against the mainstream discourse. Likewise, journalists often quote, or misquote, game scholars. To get a sense of what is meant by games culture, we must take account of how it has been described in the popular press as well as the academe.

As Steven Johnson describes there is "an experiential gap between people who have immersed themselves in games, and people who have only heard secondhand reports, because the gap makes it difficult to discuss the meaning of games in a coherent way" (2005a, p. 25). Often in academic accounts this gap is addressed by adding the "gamer's side" to the story. Yet rarely do scholars look closely at precisely what these "secondhand reports" are saying about gaming culture. One exception to this is Dimitri Williams' (2003) frame-based analysis of news magazine coverage of video games from 1970 to 2000. Although a very useful analysis, and in fact many of the frames found in the study are still seen in current news coverage, the task in this essay is a different one. The question is not how are video games discussed in print media but rather how video game play is framed as a culture in the popular press as well as the academe.

Looking for gaming culture

In this discourse analysis, I used a ground theory (Glaser & Strauss, 2006 [1967]) approach to popular and academic descriptions of video game culture. It would be a worthwhile project to talk with people who do play and make video games and ask how they define video game culture. The aim of this project, however, is to understand how more widely available discourses discuss video game culture, which does not preclude the perspective of those who play video games. Moreover, in my interviews with gamers and observations of message boards, those that play video games often draw on news and academic sources in discussing aspects of video game culture.

I used LexisNexis to compile articles for this analysis. A search on the terms: "video game culture," "gamer culture," "gaming culture," and "games culture" was run on major U.S. and world publications for all available dates.[2] Articles with these terms specifically, and not more general discussions of video games, were selected because the focus of this analysis is not how video games are discussed in the press, but how video game play/texts/practices are described as a culture. To limit the sample, only U.S.-based publications were chosen and of those only papers in the top six on the available list of newspapers by circulation (as listed in Wikipedia, 2007). Only four of the top six papers had results in the

LexisNexis search: *USA Today* ($N = 4$), *The New York Times* ($N = 16$), *Los Angeles Times* ($N = 4$), and *The Washington Post* ($N = 8$).[3] As described earlier, academic studies of video games are often in dialogue with the popular discourse about video games. Thus, this analysis is contextualized with a review of literature on video game culture. Although not a particularly large discourse is available to be analyzed here, it provides a good grounding for a critique of how "video game culture" has been described and what a cultural studies approach to game culture might look like.

Who plays

The issue of who "counts" as a member of video game culture is central to studying games within a cultural studies framework. "[C]ultural studies thinks of culture in relation to issues of power; the power relations . . . which affect who is represented and how, who speaks and who is silent, what counts as 'culture' and what does not" (Couldry, 2000, p. 2). This is a question we must ask of all new media, as Carolyn Marvin discusses.

> [T]he early history of electronic media is less the evolution of technical efficiencies in communication than a series of arenas for negotiating issues crucial to the conduct of social life; among them, who is inside and outside, who may speak, who may not, and who has authority and may be believed. (1988, p. 4)

These questions are important ones in the study of gamers.

There is a tendency for the newspaper articles to point out that video gamers are not necessarily who we think they are. As one article asserts, "the stereotype of the gamer as a glazed, incoherent teenage boy is wrong" (Copeland, 2000). One article even emphasizes that gamers are more charitable than is often presumed (Freire, 2006). Articles acknowledge that video games, particularly thanks to Nintendo's Wii, have become mainstream entertainment (Schiesel, 2007a). This may prove Williams' (2003) prediction that media coverage of a diverse gaming audience would result in a more diverse gaming audience has come true. Even as the game audience is described as more diverse than typically presumed, however, there is still the underlying assertion that there is a truth-based stereotype of gamer identity that is being changed, not challenged.

> [F]or most of the last two decades gaming has been considered an odd, insular subculture, the territory of teenage boys and those who never outgrew their teens. But now, as the first generation of gamers flirts with middle age, and as family friendly game systems like Nintendo's Wii infiltrate living rooms around the country, video games are beginning to venture beyond geekdom into a region approaching the mainstream. (Schiesel, 2007b)

New definitions of game culture are never used to question the constructed past of video game culture's insularity, maleness, and youthfulness.

When articles point out that not all gamers are young U.S. males, it is generally done in a way that reasserts the expectation. So yes, women play video games, but video game culture is not necessarily a welcoming space for them (Pham, 2007). Sure not everyone is a hardcore gamer but South Korea where competitive video game stars are heroes is the model of video game culture to emulate (Schiesel, 2006a). Perhaps, gamers, as geeks, are not expected to throw good parties, but violent media, scantily clad women, and lewd behavior are to be expected at the parties they do throw (Verini, 2006). Although video games may be played by soccer moms and retirees, the hardcore, quick-fingered gamer market is still something very different and the site of traditional gaming culture (Schiesel, 2007a). Furthermore, the expansion of "gamer culture" involves some negotiation of that culture. As one article points out, when (Columbia Broadcasting System) televises gaming matches they plan on excluding certain games because of violence and "tweaking games' rules to make them more viewer-friendly" (Schiesel, 2007b). Even as game play expands, knowledge of the subcultural capital of video game play is still required to understand more "advanced" types of play.

Acknowledging broader types of gaming seems to be mainly the province of marketers, for whom having a wider range of gamers is more profitable (Elliott, 2005). Similarly, *World of Warcraft's* popularity is tied to its appeal to both hardcore and casual players (Schiesel, 2006b). This is interesting in relation to Ang's (1991) analysis that often academics look at audiences as defined by the industry. In the case of video games, however, the industry seems more interested in a broader range of gamers than academics, which focus almost exclusively on dedicated video game fans, though counter examples, like the article by Williams et al. (2008), which debunks "the stereotypical gamer profile," offer impetus to question this focus.

The implication of narrowly defining video game culture, even while simultaneously acknowledging the expansion of this category, is that game studies scholars who study the "others" to this dominant definition are forced to talk about their subject in relation to the perceived center. This is often the case with studies of women gamers (Cassell & Jenkins, 2000; Schott & Horrell, 2000). Most studies of gender and video games take it for granted that "girls" and "boys" play differently and that finding ways of dealing with that can help make video game culture more accessible to female players (Cassell & Jenkins, 2000). Gender is certainly a factor in media consumption, as Bird (1992) describes in her study of tabloid newspaper readers. Butsch too describes the gendered nature of media consumption as, "some thought passive radio listening was de-masculinizing" (2000, p. 180). Essentializing gendered media practices, however, is problematic. "The essentializing moment is weak because it naturalizes and dehistoricizes difference, mistaking what is historical and cultural for what is natural, biological, and genetic" (Hall, 1993, p. 111). More productive work looks at how cyberculture in general has been gendered as male, largely through the exclusion of women's voices from texts, which serve as the cultural substance and points of reference within that subculture (Flanagan & Booth, 2002). As Dovey and Kennedy (2007) describe, "star" biographies on the "founding fathers" of gaming help promote a culture where technical proficiency, "geek" cultural capital, maleness, and Whiteness have defined gamer identity.

The answer to this, however, is not to shift a focus to female gaming groups, as many academics, journalists, and marketers have done. What is necessary is a critical reexamination of the place of women and girls in those spaces of gaming culture that have been traditionally defined as male as McRobbie (1980) argues for subcultures more generally. In my own research, a review of the literature on Arab video games demonstrated this tendency to make "other" anyone who did not fit the dominant U.S. gamer identity. In interviews, however, Arab gamers did not position themselves outside the "traditional" gamer culture. Neither did lesbian, gay, bisexual, and transgender gamers in another project. That is not to say that the ways in which their identities differed from the main gamer stereotype had no impact on their consumption of video games. If they do not place themselves outside what is often called video game culture, however, why should researchers? To do so privileges the dominant gamer identity while marginalizing all others.

What they play

Beyond studying games culture, Steinkuehler (2006) argues that games can also be studied as cultural artifacts. It is logical then, that the second category used to define video game culture in the press is the textual products the culture produces. The news articles emphasize a predilection for violent fare (Snider, 1999), elaborately created fantasy worlds (Memmott, 2005), fast-paced high action games (Robbins, 2002), and MMOGs (Schiesel, 2006a, 2006b). Sports games are mentioned but largely in the context of games changing "real sport" culture, rather than being part of video game culture (Velin, 2003; Walker, 2004). This is important, as the texts we use to define video game culture affects what we deem worthy of study (Dovey & Kennedy, 2007). The edited volume *Gaming as Culture*, for example, focuses exclusively on tabletop and electronic role-playing games. Similarly, the more journalistic book *Dungeons and Dreamers: The Rise of Computer Game Culture from Geek to Chic* relies on a very specific history and definition of this culture (B. King & Borland, 2003). Press discourses about video games further affect the study of games as video game academics tend to study the games that are most controversial, like a recent edited volume on *Grand Theft Auto* (Garrelts, 2006), or that get the most news coverage, like *World of Warcraft* and *SecondLife*.

The work of journalists and scholars has also helped construct a history of video games in which particular game texts, like *Pong, Space Invaders*, and so on, have been canonized (Gaudiosi, 2007; Kent, 2001; Schiesel, 2006b). What is important here is not that particular game texts and images have become exemplars for what gets defined as video game culture. The problem is the lack of reflection on which objects earn that status. Early games like *Space Invaders* and *Pong* did not just emerge out of the ether, nor did *SecondLife* or *World of Warcraft*. The complex interweaving of social networks, mainstream and video game press coverage, marketing, economics, and so on, all go into what makes a game popular. Moreover, "[a] considerable part of how games mean as cultural artifacts depends on how agent/reviewers apply a variety of influential forces in the work they do of evaluating titles for agent/consumers" (McAllister, 2004, p. 139). Pinckard (2003), for example, demonstrates how the marketing for the game *Tomb Raider* limited the potential feminist readings of Lara Croft and anchored her image as a pinup rather than a hero.

Beyond the games, a certain geek style has also been correlated with video game culture. Articles mention the pervasiveness of symbols of video game culture in the "rest" of culture, like pixilated characters from early video games or digital music (Has Anybody Here Seen My Old Friend Martin, 2005; Wilson, 2005). Such assertions ignore the intertextuality of most media and the interrelationship between different media industries, like film, television, video games, toys, and so on. Winkler (2006) offers a very specific definition of gamer culture as "marked by modes of dress, specific linguistic jargon, and a sense of solidarity. Gamers often wear clothing that references specific games, comics, television shows, or movies that are not widely known outside of a small following" (p. 147). Describing video games as a subculture on the basis of style and taste markers is not wrong per se. However, it only tells part of the story. It also often results in not looking at this subculture as part of a larger culture.

Cultural studies offer a rich history on which game studies could build in this regard. In his book *Subculture, the Meaning of Style*, Dick Hebdige (1979) moves beyond just the fashions and musical tastes that mark youth punk subculture by tracing these expressions of culture to class identities and tensions. Placing video games within larger cultural discourses is important, as video games themselves are the product of larger cultural contexts. King and Krzywinska (2006) assert, for instance, that although game play in some ways is a subculture of subcultures, it is also a part of mainstream culture. "If game playing has an array of niche cultures, and the broader subculture of self-identified 'gamers,' it has also established a place in the much wider landscape of popular culture and entertainment in recent decades" (p. 222).

Assumptions about what gamers play influence how researchers approach the field. Similarly, what researchers play affects their investigations as they often study the types of games they enjoy. Dovey and Kennedy caution game studies academics against this, however. "As reflexive critical thinkers, it is essential that we also pay attention to our own internalized technicities and tastes and to the way in which they inflect and determine the choices we make about which games to study and how to study them" (Dovey & Kennedy, 2007, p. 151). Too much attention to defining what gamers play without reflecting on why certain types of texts and styles are codified is problematic. Taking a cultural studies approach, with "its openness and theoretical versatility, its reflexive even self-conscious mood, and, especially, the importance of critique" (R. Johnson, 1986-1987, p. 38), would be more productive. Cultural studies have been subject to much internal debate and critique, and although game studies have come to draw on the concepts and subjects of cultural studies, it has not taken on the conflicts.

How they play

Much as we can study culture in terms of social practices, gaming can be, and has been, studied in terms of play practices. Generally speaking, however, play practices are very narrowly understood in dominant discourses about video games. Video game play is unquestionably assumed to encourage flow, "the state in which people are so involved in an activity that nothing else seems to matter; the experience itself is so enjoyable that people will do it even at great cost for the sheer sake of doing it" (Csikszentmihalyi, 1990). The implications of claiming that our object of study becomes such an all encompassing aspect of players' lives, however, are rarely considered. This type of description also discredits a great many other types of interactions with video games as cultural objects. Turning to the press, the relationship between the definition of gamer culture and how people play encompasses many issues, which fall into two main categories, negative connotations and positive connotations.

The negative connotations include correlating video game playing with childhood obesity (Perez-Pena, 2003) and obsessive play (Faiola, 2006). Video game culture is also defined in terms of the amount of time people spend doing it, obsessively or not, of which South Korea is used as an exemplar (Schiesel, 2006a, 2007b). Video game culture is often defined in terms of the social interaction it engenders or negates. It is either a culture of people in isolation (bad) or a culture of obsessed people playing across the Internet into the dawn (better, but still bad). The positive connotations include the claim that video games enhance learning (S. Johnson, 2005b). A great deal of research on digital games has focused on this issue. Some researchers have suggested that games can encourage problem solving skills and logical thinking (Higgins, 2000; Inkpen, Booth, Gribble, & Klawe, 1995; Whitebread, 1997). Along similar lines, a review of literature by Sandford and Williamson states that "computer games are designed 'to be learned' and therefore provide models of goods learning principles" (2005, p. 2). Similar definitions are present in discourses about game culture. Academic studies of video games often attempt to disprove these negative assessments but rarely question the positive ones (Fromme, 2003; Jenkins).

Many of the articles, as well as academics, define game culture in terms of interaction and immersion. "We are about to enter an intensification of the mediation of our everyday lives. An intensification in which we learn how to flow seamlessly between the virtual and the actual, with our experiences in one being just as affecting as those in the other" (Dovey & Kennedy, 2006, p. 2). There is a heavy emphasis on the interactivity between audience and text, as one press article states, "there's something more going on here than passive, mindless escapism:

105

it's active, complex, multilayered escapism" (Walker, 2004). It involves using complex, high action, face-paced media, "Now we have an industry that makes its money by doing . . . rather than watching, listening, reading" (Copeland, 2000). It is also about thinking, learning on the go (S. Johnson, 2005b). Video game culture is about interacting with media, participating, and convergence (Jenkins, 2006). A great deal of attention is paid to "home brew," or modification, applications programming savvy players make on existing games (Musgrove, 2006). In this regard, a great deal of game scholarship emphasizes that video game consumption is definitively different from all other mediums. "[T]hough we may refer to film spectatorship as 'active,' due to the viewer's ongoing attempt to make sense of the film, the video game player is even more active, making sense of the game as well as causing and reacting to the events depicted" (Wolf, 2001, p. 3). Jenkins (2002) too describes interactive audiences as a largely modern phenomenon. This might not actually be the case, however.

Butsch (2000) demonstrates that the notion of the interactive or productive audiences is not necessarily new. In the 1840s, "b'hoys" existed as a very masculine, rowdy, and knowledgeable theater audience. Critiques of their interactive behavior had strong class overtones, as the wealthier patrons who also used the theater as part of their cultural capital did not appreciate the intrusion of working class manners (p. 56). Similarly, early radio, like early video game design, was dominated by amateurs. As radio's popularity rose however, amateurs had to share their field with the masses. While audience interaction and production were discouraged in Butsch's examples, in the current discourse, both are highly valued. This is not properly analyzed in studies that focus too closely on valorizing gamer agency. In fact what "counts" as a location of production may tell us more about power dynamics of a particular time/place than it does about audience practices per se. Some early critiques of mass culture for instance put greater value on "folk art", user-generated content (like player-made gaming modifications), than on mass culture (MacDonald, 1957). Curiously, the situations in which user-generated content and agency is celebrated are the very instances in which it is exploitable by media corporations. *SecondLife*, for example, exists almost entirely as user-generated content.

Beyond being historically myopic, there are both methodological and political ramifications to emphasizing the interactive nature of video games. "The activity of the players is essential to the realization of much of what unfolds in the playing of games, even where the parameters are clearly established in advance. As a consequence, the player can seem more directly implicated than traditional media consumers in the meanings that result" (G. King & Krzywinska, 2006, p. 169). Violent games can teach children to kill because they are interactive (Grossman & DeGaetano, 1999). Likewise, the educational benefits of games, whether or not the games are designed for that purpose, are correlated to the audience activity they require (Gee, 2003; Greenfield, 1984; S. Johnson, 2005a). The very appeal of video games is posited to be their interactivity (Klimmt, 2003). The focus on games as highly interactive and audience-dependent texts can lead us to ignore that they are in fact encoded with ideological positions just as any other medium (G. King & Krzywinska, 2006; Leonard, 2006). That is not to say we should ignore the activity of the audience but that we should also look at the dominant meanings encoded in the texts they are playing. As Toby Miller (2005) asserts, media must be studied both in terms of active audiences and dominant ideology, rather than one or the other. There is movement in the game studies in this direction, with an emphasis on platform studies and investigating the interactions between culture, technological design, and user interfaces (Bogost & Montford, 2007). More work, however, should be done.

Both journalists and academics also assert that gaming is highly social. This is often set against the stereotype of the solitary gamer (Schiesel, 2006a), assumed on both sides to be a negative caricature. Dmitri Williams (2006), for example, argues that studying gamers is important as "gamers don't bowl alone;" here, Williams is playing on the title of Robert Putnam's book *Bowling Alone* (2000), which asserts that U.S. society is becoming increasingly isolating. Who has led us to think video game play is a solitary act, when both academics and journalists are constantly telling us it is a myth, is unclear. Some players' experiences are solitary, others' purely social, and most likely many fit somewhere in-between. One might argue that, perhaps, the only way academics can create a "culture" around games is by making games social, but the site and context of consumption has never wholly defined cultural analyses of other media.

Furthermore, there is reason to think that video game play is not as simple as a solitary/social dichotomy.

[A]s suggested more generally in Huizinga's definition of play, which includes the tendency for play to generate particular play-communities on the basis of 'the feeling of being 'apart together' in an exceptional situation, of sharing something important, or mutually withdrawing from the rest of the world' – a quality similar to that invoked in more recent studies of subcultural forms. (G. King & Krzywinska, 2006, p. 219)

The simultaneously isolating and social aspects of video game play need more investigation. Games, for example, can be played alone or with others. They can also be played alone with others, that is, playing an MMOG while sitting alone in your apartment. Similarly, they can be played together alone if two partners sit in the same room playing on their respective computers, handheld devices, or on separate televisions (and obviously mixtures of all three types of devices). The types of sociality in gaming, and I would argue all media consumption, are extremely complicated and worthy of more research.

The negative connotation to playing alone, moreover, is rarely critiqued. As seen in the example of interactive and productive audiences, however, game studies academics miss an important opportunity by not interrogating why solitary play is so disparaged. Butsch (2000), for example, describes how early radio moved from being communal to familial. Even later it became an individual activity. This shift to private listening "provided grounds for critics to decry 'hypnotic,' 'narcotic,' effects of broadcasting on individuals" (p. 207). There is a social and political function to valuing certain types of consumption and play over others, something cultural analyses of video games should interrogate.

Finally, there is an increasing emphasis in digital studies on the importance of the body in video game play, which ties together both the interactive and social aspects of video game play. This is a rhetoric, which has historical roots. "The enormous range of discussion about electricity, nature, and the body attempted to locate electricity, a force of unknown dimensions, by means of the most familiar of all human landmarks, the human body" (Marvin, 1988, p. 151). Similarly, discourses about video games and even new game technologies, which are necessarily not that new, seek to make it more acceptable by more firmly locating it with the body (motion sensitive controllers, vibrating controllers, Dance Dance Revolution mats, etc.). As it has a long history of analyzing bodies, cultural studies is a valuable resource for game studies in this regard. Indeed, cultural studies theorists have already sounded off on the matter: "[T]he most powerful effects of video games may be determined less by ideological dimensions than by certain forms of embodiment, by the way in which the player controls/produces the sounds and lights that engulf, produce, and define a 'rhythmic body'" (Grossberg, 1988, p. 383)

Video game culture as other

Video game culture, in both press and academic discourses, is framed by descriptions of who plays, what they play, and how they play. Starting with these three categories and not looking for a prototypical definition of a gamer identity allows us to see that popular discourses actually offer a much more diverse view of what gaming is than they are generally given credit. Video games are played by the young and old, males and females, and across the world. People play violent games, sports games, puzzle games, and action games. Games help players think, force audiences to be active, are social, and engage the body. These articles still, however, define "video game culture" as something very distinct, as separate from the rest of some constructed mainstream culture. This is done primarily by discussing the "effect" video games have had on culture, including national culture, media culture, sports culture, and so on. "Gaming is changing us: our technology, our art, how we learn, and what we expect from the world" (Copeland, 2000). Video game culture is thus often seen as something on the fringes of, but which nevertheless influences, popular culture. This has ideological and political ramifications as it allows for video games to be dismissed both as a form of entertainment or the culture of an "other."

When looking at "the world's most advanced video game culture," South Korea, emphasis is placed on the ways in which this country is different from the United States (Schiesel, 2006a). It is stressed, for example, that Koreans are very different from Americans because they treat pro-gamers as heroes, unlike

U.S. sports culture that values athletes, though both, arguably, treat individuals as idols for their ability to play games. This is done in an ambiguous way, however, as the article attempts to demonstrate that this is not disastrous for Korean society, yet it is still spoken of as markedly "other" from U.S. culture.

The "othering" of video games is not only done by journalists. Much of the introduction of *The Medium of the Video Game* is spent explaining why games are so different from other media (Wolf, 2001). The function of defining video game culture as separate could be a required step in defining this area of study by academics. It may be, as Hall (1993) asserts, "that what replaces invisibility is a kind of carefully regulated, segregated visibility" (p. 107). That is to say, in an effort to make video games visible and have them taken seriously as cultural products, video game culture has to be defined as something specific. Looking at previous models of studying media as culture, however, can demonstrate where game studies could move instead.

The books *Comic Book Culture* (Pustz, 1999) and *Television Culture* (Fiske, 1989) provide two different versions of discussing media culture. The first, like video game studies, relies on a conception of fan culture as a singular entity defined by its own language, rituals, and tastes. The essence of the book is an effort to make respectable an often undervalued medium and readers. This is a valuable goal but perhaps, like video game studies, a bit too reactionary. Putz's focus is on what others have said about the author's in-group, rather than critically reflecting on the ways in which the comic book culture has been structured. This is particularly reflected in the erasure of women and queer comics' histories from his historical overview. Fiske's book, however, situates the codes and representations of television within larger social and cultural ideological structures. Fiske discusses the specific qualities of television in relation to broader issues like gender and class. He also offers a much broader analysis of different types of television programming, something game studies does only cursorily.

Huizinga (1955) argues that play is an intrinsic part of culture, not something separate from it. Indeed, Henry Jenkins' (2006) work attempts to situate video games in a larger convergence culture. Only one press article, however, describes video games in relation to a broader national culture (Schiesel, 2006b). In doing so, it affirms an East/West distinction between games that are produced and popular in North America and those in Asia. Thankfully some academic articles look at video games as either national or transnational products (Consalvo, 2006; Kerr & Flynn, 2003; Machin & Suleiman, 2006; Sisler, 2006). One particularly useful article looks at the technological, cultural, and social relationship between the video game industry and other creative and technological industries in Japan (Aoyama & Izushi, 2003). There is, however, much more work to be done in this respect.

Defining video game culture serves to separate it from "the regular" culture, much as mass culture was separated from high culture in earlier critiques (MacDonald, 1957). One dichotomy set up in both academic and press discourses, as seen in cultural critiques more generally, is a distinction between video games as popular and video games as art. Much of the effort to get video games "taken seriously" has relied on arguing for their aesthetic or moral value (i.e., serious games). This is done by showing the video games are worthy of academic study (Schiesel, 2005) or can encourage social justice (Gorman, 2007). To be relevant then, video games must mean something outside of their entertainment medium niche. If game studies are to learn anything from cultural studies, however, it should not take for granted the ways in which certain types of games, modes of play, and types of players are used to validate this field of study.

Conclusion

Culture is not the only way to study games of course. Like any text, medium, or phenomenon there are a diversity of approaches and perspectives one might take. If we *are* going to study games within a framework of culture, however, we as scholars must draw on the concepts as well as the conflicts of cultural studies. We must be reflexive and critical of both our object of study and our methodologies. Defining gaming culture as something distinct and separate from a constructed mainstream culture encourages us to only study those who identify as gamers, rather than more dispersed gaming. That is, we should look at video games in culture rather than games as culture. Video games permeate education, mobile technologies, museum displays, social functions, family interactions, and workplaces. They are played by many if not all ages, genders, sexualities, races, religions, and nationalities. Not all of these types of play and players can be encompassed in a study of an isolated gamer community. Moreover, the reification of certain types of game texts over others limits the field of study. Finally, the concerted effort of game academics to disprove the negative connotations of video game play and not the positive ones is problematic.

Interestingly, the term "video game culture," at least based on the search conducted for this analysis, is a relatively new expression. The earliest occurrence retrieved was from 1996 (Amdur, 1996), and most are from the past 4 years. While there are certainly articles on video games predating this, and there are limits to the LexisNexis database, that the term game culture arose around the same time as video game studies began to coalesce is interesting. It may indicate that, regardless of "ivory tower" rhetoric, game academics are defining their field of study as much as they are studying it. This is precisely why game studies should adopt the reflexivity of cultural studies in its analyses.

Academics and journalists generally express a tension between the stereotype and the "reality" of gaming, but only with the negatively charged values assigned to each category. The violence, the "boys only," the isolated, and the obsessed are all stereotypes that are willingly challenged. The complexity of thought, however, is rarely rethought. Moreover, the claim that video game play demonstrates a departure from previous forms of media studies is problematic. The assertion of a medium's revolutionary quality is neither a new nor an inconsequential tendency of new media.

A useful strategy for stripping social phenomena of the power to endanger the status quo is to anchor them to safely established notions while presenting them for public consumption as revolutionary . . . . The introduction of electricity was seen to have *no* political consequences, no winners or losers of power, or winners called to account for abuses of power, since politics would exist no more. (Marvin, 1988, p. 206)

By allowing us to be anyone, by making audiences active and productive, by making us smarter and better thinkers, video games are supposed to fix a lot of "problems" with media. As many game studies authors point out, however, video games have their own ideological baggage (Consalvo, 2003; G. King & Krzywinska, 2006; Leonard, 2006). Although game studies have drawn on cultural studies' history of analyzing ideology, active audiences, encoding and decoding, not enough effort has been made to question how video game culture itself has been defined, with perhaps the exception of analyses of gendered game spaces (Fullerton, Ford Morie, & Peasrce, 2007; Kline, Dyer-Witheford, & De Peuter, 2003).

Many of the themes seen in press and academic discourses about play map onto the "Seven Rhetorics" of play Sutton-Smith (1997) outlines. "In general, each rhetoric has a historical source, a particular function, a distinctive ludic form, and specialized players and advocates, and is the context for particular academic disciplines" (p. 214). The rhetoric used to describe play shapes the study of play, it narrows what we think is valuable for study. Along these lines, one lesson video game studies should learn from cultural studies is that beyond just labeling culture, it is important to unpack why culture has been labeled in certain ways. Hall's recommendations for the study of Black culture can be extended to video game culture studies in this regard, "[t]here is, of course, a very profound set of distinctive, historically defined Black experiences that contribute to those alternative repertoires, I spoke about earlier. But it is to the diversity, not the homogeneity, of the Black experience that we must now give our undivided creative attention" (1993, pp. 111–112). As cultural studies "works with an inclusive definition of culture" (Storey, 1996, p. 2), it is best for video game studies to look at video game culture as inclusively and diversely as possible.

One example of this critical cultural approach to video games is the study of older gamers by Quandt, Grueninger, and Wimmer (2009). In this article, the authors take some popular assumptions about who games and why and critically reassess the popular descriptions of these players by looking at the experience of actual players. Another option is to look at games as a media practice, "[c]onsidering video games as a media practice . . . would imply not only attending to video game consumption (or the practice of playing games), but also to how the gaming practice is related to other media practices and how it is socially organized" (Roig, San Cornelio, Ardevol, Alsina, & Pages, 2009, p. 91). This type of perspective looks at video games culturally rather than video games as culture. Game studies have largely focused on validating video game consumption, video game texts, and video game players. Video game studies, however, should be reflexive, not reactive. The legacy of cultural studies on which video game studies should draw is not to study culture in games, though that is useful as well, but to investigate how video game culture is constructed. This is a critical, not descriptive practice.

Acknowledgement

The author would like to thank Professor Barbie Zelizer and an anonymous reviewer for their comments on earlier drafts of this article.

Declaration of conflicting interests

The author(s) declared no conflicts of interest with respect to the authorship and/or publication of this article.

Funding

The author is a fully funded graduate student at the Annenberg School for Communication at the University of Pennsylvania.

Notes

1 For the purposes of this article, the broadest possible understanding of video games, including all forms of digital games, is being considered.
2 The original search was run on October 15, 2007, and rerun on November 17, 2007, to retrieve additional articles.
3 Other articles from these papers that came up in the results were eliminated because they referred to a sports game culture not video game culture.

References

Amdur, D. (1996, October 30). Earth Quake. *The Washington Post*, p. R19.
Ang, I. (1991). *Desperately seeking the audience*. London: Routledge.
Aoyama, Y., & Izushi, H. (2003). Hardware gimmick or cultural innovation? Technological, cultural, and social foundations of the Japanese video game industry. *Research Policy*, 32, 423–444.
Arnold, M. (1998). Culture and anarchy. In J. Storey (Ed.), *Cultural theory and popular culture* (2nd ed.). Athens, Georgia: Prentice Hall.
Bennett, T. (1998). *Culture: A reformer's science*. Thousand Oaks, CA: SAGE.
Bird, S. E. (1992). Gendered readings. In *For Enquiring Minds: A cultural study of supermarket tabloids*: University of Tennessee Press.
Boellstorff, T. (2006). A ludicrous discipline? Ethnography and game studies. *Games and Culture*, 1, 29–35.
Bogost, I., & Montford, N. (2007). Platform studies. Retrieved December 5, 2007, from http://platformstudies.com/
Butsch, R. (2000). *The making of American audiences: From stage to television* (pp. 1750–1990). New York: Cambridge University Press.

Carey, J. (1997 [1992]). Political correctness and cultural studies. In E. Stryker Munson & C. A. Warren (Eds.), *James Carey: A critical reader.* Minneapolis: University of Minnesota Press.

Cassell, J., & Jenkins, H. (2000). *From Barbie to Mortal Kombat: Gender and computer games.* Cambridge, MA: The MIT Press.

Castronova, E. (2005). *Synthetic worlds: The business and culture of online games.* University of Chicago Press.

Chee, F., Vieta, M., & Smith, R. (2006). Online gaming and the interactional self. In J. P. Williams, S. Q. Hendricks & W. K. Winkler (Eds.), *Gaming as culture: Essays on reality, identity, and experience in fantasy games.* Jefferson, NC: McFarland and Company.

Consalvo, M. (2003). Hot dates and fairy-tale romances: Studying sexuality in video games. In M. J. P. Wolf & B. Perron (Eds.), *The video game theory reader* (pp. 171–194). New York: Routledge.

Consalvo, M. (2006). Console video games and global corporations: Creating a hybrid culture. *New Media & Society,* 8, 117–137.

Copeland, L. (2000, April 13). Games people play; Is interactive entertainment a fantasy come true or a bad dream? *The Washington Post,* p. C01.

Couldry, N. (2000). *Inside culture: Re–imagining the method of cultural studies.* London: SAGE.

Csikszentmihalyi, M. (1990). *Flow: The psychology of optimal experience.* New York: Harper & Row.

Dovey, J., & Kennedy, H. W. (2006). *Game cultures: Computer games as new media.* New York: Open University Press.

Dovey, J., & Kennedy, H. W. (2007). From margin to center: Biographies of technicity and the construction of hegemonic games culture. In J. P. Williams & J. H. Smith (Eds.), *The players' realm: Studies on the culture of video games and gaming.* Jefferson, NC: McFarland and Company.

Elliott, S. (2005, October 17). Madison Avenue's full-court pitch to video gamers. *The New York Times,* p. C7.

Faiola, A. (2006, May 27). When escape seems just a mouse click-away. *The Washington Post,* p. A01.

Fiske, J. (1989). *Television culture.* New York: Routledge.

Flanagan, M., & Booth, A. (2002). *Reload: Rethinking women + cyberculture.* Cambridge, MA: MIT Press.

Freire, P. (2006, December 27). From far and wide, video gamers join in a child charity. The *New York Times,* p. A20.

Fromme, J. (2003). Computer games as a part of children's culture. *Game Studies,* 3, 91.

Fullerton, T., Ford Morie, J., & Peasrce, C. (2007). *A game of one's own: Towards a new gendered poetics of digital space.* Paper presented at the perthDAC 2007: The 7th Annual Digital Arts and Culture Conference – The Future of Digital Media Culture, Perth, Australia.

Garrelts, N. (2006). *The meaning and culture of Grand theft auto: Critical essays.* Jefferson, NC: McFarland & Co.

Gaudiosi, J. (2007, January 19). A game that keeps it all in the family. *The Washington Post,* p. T51.

Gee, J. P. (2003). *What video games have to teach us about learning and literacy* (1st ed.). New York: Palgrave Macmillan.

Geertz, C. (1973). *Interpretation of cultures.* New York: Basic Books.

Glaser, B., & Strauss, A. (2006 [1967]). *The discovery of grounded theory: Strategies for qualitative research*. New Brunswick: Aldune Transaction.

Gorman, A. (2007, July 9). Immigration debate finds itself in play; Advocacy groups are using video and board games to advance their agendas and influence public opinion. *Los Angeles Times*, p. A11.

Greenfield, P. M. (1984). *Mind and media: The effects of television, video games, and computers*. Cambridge, MA: Harvard University Press.

Grossberg, L. (1988). Wandering audiences, nomadic critics. *Cultural Studies*, 2, 377–391.

Grossberg, L. (1994). Can cultural studies find true happiness in communication? In M. R. Levy & M. Gurevitch (Eds.), *Defining media studies: Reflections on the future of the field*. Oxford University Press.

Grossman, D., & DeGaetano, G. (1999). *Stop teaching our kids to kill: A call to action against TV, movie & video game violence* (1st ed.). New York: Crown Publishers.

Hall, S. (1993). What is this "black" in black popular culture. *Social Justice*, 20, 104–111.

Hall, S. (1998). Cultural studies: Two paradigms. In J. Storey (Ed.), *What is cultural studies?* New York: St. Martin's Press.

Halter, E. (2006). *From Sun Tzu to XBox: War and video games*. New York: Thunder's Mouth Press.

Has Anybody Here Seen My Old Friend Martin. (2005). *The New York Times*, p. T148.

Hebdige, D. (1979). *Subculture, the meaning of style*. London: Methuen.

Higgins, S. (2000). The logical zoombinis. *Teaching thinking*, 1, 12–15.

Huizinga, J. (1955). *Homo ludens; a study of the play-element in culture*. Boston: Beacon Press.

Inkpen, K., Booth, K., Gribble, S., & Klawe, M. (1995). *Give and take: Children collaborating on one computer*. Paper presented at the CHI 95: Human Factors in Computing Systems, Denver, CO.

Jenkins, H. *Eight myths about video games debunked*. Retrieved August 2007, from http:// www.pbs.org/kcts/videogamerevolution/impact/myths.html

Jenkins, H. (2002). Interactive audiences? In D. Harries (Ed.), *The new media book*. London: British Film Institute.

Jenkins, H. (2005). Games, the new lively art. In J. Raessens & J. Goldstein (Eds.), *Handbook of computer game studies*. Cambridge, MA: MIT Press.

Jenkins, H. (2006). *Convergence culture: Where old and new media collide*. New York University Press.

Johnson, R. (1986–1987). What is cultural studies anyway? *Social Text*, 16, 38–80.

Johnson, S. (2005a). *Everything bad is good for you: How popular culture is making us smarter*. London: Allen Lane/Penguin.

Johnson, S. (2005b, April 24). Watching TV makes you smarter. *The New York Times*, p. 55 Section 56.

Kent, S. L. (2001). *The ultimate history of video games*. New York: Prima Publishing.

Kerr, A. (2006). *The business and culture of digital games: Gamework/gameplay*. London: SAGE.

Kerr, A., & Flynn, R. (2003). Revisiting globalisation through the movie and digital games industries. *Convergence*, 9, 91–113.

Kinder, M. (1991). *Playing with power in movies, television, and video games: From Muppet babies to teenage mutant Ninja turtles*. Berkeley, CA: University of California Press.

King, B., & Borland, B. (2003). *Dungeons and dreamers: The rise of computer game culture, from Geek to Chic*. Emeryville, CA: McGraw-Hill.

King, G., & Krzywinska, T. (2006). *Tomb raiders & space invaders: Videogame forms & contexts*. New York: I.B. Tauris.

Klimmt, C. (2003). Media psychology "is not yet there:" Introducing theories on media entertainment to the presence debate. *Presence*, 12, 346–359.

Kline, S., Dyer-Witheford, N., & De Peuter, G. (2003). *Digital play: The interaction of technology, culture and marketing*. Montréal London: McGill-Queen's University Press.

Leonard, D. J. (2006). Not a hater, just keepin' it real: The importance of race-and gender based game studies. *Games and Culture*, 1, 83–88.

Loftus, G. R., & Loftus, E. F. (1983). *Mind at play: The psychology of video games*. New York: Basic Books.

MacDonald, D. (1957). A theory of mass culture. In B. Rosenberg & D. Manning White (Eds.), *Mass culture: The popular arts in America*. New York: Free Press/ MacMillan.

Machin, D., & Suleiman, U. (2006). Arab and American computer war games: The influence of global technology on discourse. *Critical Discourse Studies*, 3, 1–22.

Marvin, C. (1988). *When old technologies were new: Thinking about communications in the late nineteenth century*. New York: Oxford University Press.

Mayra, F. (2008). *An Introduction to Game Studies: Game in Culture*. London: SAGE.

McAllister, K. S. (2004). *Game Work: Language, Power and Computer Game Culture*. Tuscaloosa: The University of Alabama Press.

McRobbie, A. (1980). Settling Accounts with Subcultures: A Feminist Critique. *Screen Education*, 34, 37–49.

Memmott, C. (2005, July 11). Harry Potter and the phenomenal fascination. *USA Today*, p. 1D.

Miller, T. (2005). Introduction. In A. Abbas & J. N. Erni (Eds.), *Internationalizing cultural studies*. Malden, MA: Blackwell.

Miller, T. (2006). What it is and what it isn't: Introducing . . . Cultural Studies. In T. Miller (Ed.), *A companion to cultural studies*. Malden, MA: Blackwell Publishers.

Mortensen, T. E. (2007, 15–18 September). *"The real truth about what games researchers do all day"* – methods strategies and ethics of multi-user games research. Paper presented at the perthDAC 2007: The 7th International Digital Arts and Culture Conference – The Future of Digital Media Culture, Perth, Australia.

Musgrove, M. (2006, July 6). Routine upgrades are the bane of 'homebrew' enthusiasts. *The Washington Post*, p. D04.

Myers, D. (2003). *The nature of computer games: Play as semiosis*. (Vol. 16). New York: Peter Lang.

Ondrejka, C. (2006). Finding common ground in new worlds. *Games and Culture*, 1, 111–115.

Perez-Pena, R. (2003, July 9). Obesity on rise in New York public schools. *The New York Times*, p. B1.

Peterson, R. A. (1979). Revitalizing the culture concept. *Annual Review of Sociology*, 5, 137–166.

Pham, A. (2007, September 3). A refuge for women in a hostile game space. *Los Angeles Times*, p. C1.

Pinckard, J. (2003). Gender play: Successes and failures in character designs for videogames. Retrieved April 16, 2005, from http://www.gamegirladvance.com/archives/2003/04/16/genderplay_successes_and_failures_in_character_designs_for_videogames.html

Pustz, M. J. (1999). *Comic book culture: Fanboys and true believers*. Jackson: University Press of Mississippi.

Putnam, R. D. (2000). *Bowling alone: The collapse and revival of American community*. New York: Simon & Schuster.

Quandt, T., Grueninger, H., & Wimmer, J. (2009). The gray haired gaming generation: Findings from an explorative interview study on older computer gamers. *Games and Culture*, 4, 27–46.

Robbins, L. (2002, July 31). Bouncing to extremes: Introducing SlamBall. *The New York Times*, p. D4.

Roig, A., San Cornelio, G., Ardevol, E., Alsina, P., & Pages, R. (2009). Videogame as Media Practice: An exploration of the intersections between play and audiovisual culture. *Convergence*, *15*, 89–103.

Sandford, R., & Williamson, B. (2005). *Games and learning: A handbook from Futurelab.* Bristol, UK: Futurelab.

Schiesel, S. (2005, November 22). Video games are their major, so don't call them slackers. *The New York Times*, p. A1.

Schiesel, S. (2006a, October 8). Land of the video geek. *The New York Times*. Retrieved November 17, 2007, from http://www.nytimes.com/2006/10/08/arts/08schi.html?

Schiesel, S. (2006b, September 5). An Online Game, made in America, Seizes the Globe. *The New York Times*, p. A1.

Schiesel, S. (2007a, July 14). Can Sony revitalize its games? Yes, maybe. *The New York Times*, p. B7.

Schiesel, S. (2007b, July 28). Video game matches to be televised on CBS. *The New York Times*, p. B7.

Schott, G. R., & Horrell, K. R. (2000). Girl gamers and their relationship with the gaming culture. *The International Journal of Research into New Media Technologies*, 6, 36–53.

Sisler, V. (2006). Representation and self-representation: Arabs and Muslims in digital games. In M. Santoineous & N. Dimitriadi (Eds.), *Gaming realities: A challenge for digital culture* (pp. 85–92). Athens: Fournos.

Snider, M. (1999, May 14). Games are no problem in this crowd. *USA Today*, p. 12A.

Steinkuehler, C. A. (2006). Why game (culture) studies now? *Games and Culture, 1,* 97–102.

Storey, J. (1996). *Cultural studies and the study of popular culture: Theories and methods.* Athens: University of Georgia Press.

Sutton-Smith, B. (1997). *The ambiguity of play*. Cambridge, MA: Harvard University Press.

Taylor, T. L. (2006). *Play between worlds: Exploring online game culture*. Cambridge, MA: MIT Press.

Velin, B. (2003, August 29). 21st-century status symbol. *USA Today*, p. 1C.

Verini, J. (2006, May 12). The E3 scene: Yeah, they're game, boy; White, hot nights after a day of thumb twiddling. *Los Angeles Times*, p. E1.

Walker, R. (2004, September 12). Maddening. *The New York Times*, pp. 32, Section 36.

Whitebread, D. (1997). Developing children's problem solving: The educational uses of adventure games. In A. McFarlane (Ed.), *Information technology and authentic learning*. London: Routledge.

Wikipedia. (2007). List of newspapers in the United States by Circulation. Retrieved October 15, 2007, from http://en.wikipedia.org/wiki/List_of_newspapers_in_the_United_States_by_circulation

Williams, D. (2003). The video game lighting rod. *Information, Communication & Society*, 6, 523–550.

Williams, D. (2006). Why game studies now? Gamers don't bowl alone. *Games and Culture, 1,* 13–16.

Williams, D., Yee, N., & Caplan, S. E. (2008). Who plays, how much, and why? Debunking the stereotypical gamer profile. *Journal of Computer-Mediated Communication, 13,* 993–1018.

Williams, J. P., Hendricks, S. Q., & Winkler, W. K. (2006). *Gaming as culture: Essays on reality, identity and experience in fantasy games.* Jefferson, NC: McFarland & Company.

Williams, R. (1998). The analysis of culture. In J. Storey (Ed.), *Cultural theory and popular culture* (2nd ed.). Athens, Georgia: Prentice Hall.

Wilson, E. (2005, December 22). A sense of fashion is lost in transit. *The New York Times,* p. G12.

Winkler, W. K. (2006). The business and culture of gaming. In J. P. Williams, S. Q. Hendricks & W. K. Winkler (Eds.), *Gaming as culture: Essays on reality, identity, and experience in fantasy games.* Jefferson, NC: McFarland and Company.

Wolf, M. J. P. (2001). Introduction. In M. J. P. Wolf (Ed.), *The medium of the video game.* Austin: University of Texas Press.

Yee, N. (2001). The Norranthian scrolls: A study of EverQuest. Retrieved November 15, 2007, from http://www.nickyee.com/eqt/report.html

78

PRODUCTIVE PLAY

Game culture from the bottom up

Celia Pearce*

Source: *Games and Culture*, 1(1), January 2006, 17–24.

Abstract

In this article, the author argues against the assertion, originating with "canonical" game studies texts such as *HomoLudens* and *Man, Play, and Games*, that inherent in the definition of games is that they are "unproductive." Instead, she makes a case for the notion of productive play, in which creative production for its own sake (as opposed to production for hire) is an active and integral part of play activities, particularly those enabled by networks. Citing from her recent ethnographic research studying intergame immigration between massively multiplayer online games (MMOGs), the author describes some case in which players ejected from the MMOG Uru: Ages Beyond Myst became highly productive, creating artifacts from Uru in other virtual worlds like There and Second Life. Over time, the Uru Diaspora expanded the game's culture, eventually creating their own original Uru- and Myst-inspired artifacts, including an entirely new game.

Productive play: an oxymoron?

Most of game studies has inherited from the two canonical texts of play, Huizinga's (1955) *Homo Ludens* and Callois's (1961/2001) *Man, Play, and Games*, the axiomatic assumption that games are by definition "unproductive." This position is shared by the majority of game taxonomies in recent years, although thankfully, we seem to be moving out of the phase of taxonomania and into a more mature cycle of investigation. The "mass media" at large also shares the view that games, to invoke Monty Python's forgotten classic, are a "complete waste of time"—or worse. As with chess in the Middle Ages (Yalom, 2004), theatre in Shakespeare's day, and film during the McCarthy era, some sectors of the U.S. government are trying to protect the masses from perceived dangers of games, as if the medium has some mysterious property that made it a particularly insidious way to take one's daily dose of media violence.

Even for people who regard games as a high cultural form—including those of us who make a living playing, writing, talking about, and making them—the general consensus is that games are not productive. Game developers themselves are sometimes puzzled by the academic interest in games—after all, they say, it's "only entertainment."

I would like to argue that in fact neither play nor games is inherently unproductive and furthermore, that the boundaries between play and production, between work and leisure, and between media consumption and media production are increasingly blurring. In the process, the sacred "magic circle," which appears in various forms from Turner (1982) to Salen and Zimmerman (2004), is also beginning to blur.

The play revolution

In an earlier article on emergent authorship (Pearce, 2002), I began to examine the notion of play as an act of production, identifying a new hybrid entertainment form in which players were paying to produce their own entertainment media. I believe that this fundamental shift in the media production schema has profound cultural implications that transcend merely the "questionable" pursuit of "game studies."

First, the trend in consumer-production represents a fundamental inversion of the capitalist/industrial media production/broadcast model that has dominated Western culture for at least a century—it is the media snake eating its own head. Enabling people to their own entertainment experience has become a viable business model, as evidenced by the thousands of Sims skins (player-created characters) that have perpetuated that brand's longevity to historical levels (Poremba, 2003). What new business opportunities are emerging around these new autoludic practices? What happens when we empower players to "play with themselves?"

Second, in an ironic reversal, the malleability, discursive quality, and networked infrastructure of the Internet returns us to a preindustrial culture of play, a time when games were not products that were owned, published, and distributed by a corporatized "hegemony of play" but were made up, changed, and reconfigured by groups of ordinary people in site-specific, socially and culturally specific contexts. "Pre-digital" thinkers—such as Bernie DeKoven (1978) and Iona and Peter Opie (1969)—give us insight into these analog cultures of play. As Henry Jenkins (1998) so eloquently pointed out, for many children in Western culture, as wide-open natural spaces, like those portrayed in books like *Huckleberry Finn*, have given way to pavement and apartment complexes, children have expanded inward, into cyberspace. Yet all too often, these overmediated virtual playgrounds have not had the flexibility of a piece of chalk, a tree branch, or an upside-down cardboard box.

Third, this confluence emerges out of a prevailing postmodern sensibility in popular culture and across all media in which appropriation is not only allowed, it is exalted. Players feel emboldened not only to borrow but to reformulate and remediate their gaming experience, creating still more breaches in the magic circle, as well as breaches between magic circles—machinima films made in game engines being perhaps the best instance of this. Furthermore, those who do this well are both respected by their peers and in isolated but growing cases, empowered by the game companies themselves, who see player production as a way to mitigate spiraling game development costs. But there's more. Not only do player-producers simulate simulations, they propel them out into the real world so that reality becomes the playground of the virtual. And, as we've seen in the case of earlier fan culture forms, such as the *Star Trek* fan Trekkie phenomenon (Jenkins, 1992), they also expand the game narrative and eventually begin to take it over. The preponderance and increasing legitimacy of blogs, zines, and "open-source" content-production frameworks, such as Wikipedia (www.wikipedia.org), demonstrate that self-created content is not just an isolated phenomenon within game culture but a widespread, transmedial, and international zeitgeist.

These trends fly in the face of the status quo of centralized, hegemonic, broadcast, and distribution models of media creation. Like the Vatican of the Middle Ages, the Western media hegemony (including the game industry) has enjoyed total control over content for at least a century, probably longer if you go back as far as the printing press. This power elite has maintained total control and economic domination through technologies that by their very nature are nondiscursive. A dynamic, two-way medium in which the "audience" has just as much power to create content as the "producer" threatens to upend this power structure.

More important, productive play also challenges traditional capitalistic notions of "productivity" versus "leisure." We need only look at the history of hobby culture in the United States and elsewhere to see that for many, productive leisure is a welcome escape from the regimen of being productive at someone else's behest. Furthermore, as we have tended to relegate play to the realm of childhood, also a period of "supposed" unproductivity, the notion that play is not only productive but an adult-worthy activity represents a major shift in cultural perception.

A case study: the Myst/Uru Diaspora

To illustrate some of these points, I'd like to draw some examples from my recent research that demonstrate the many facets of productive play.

Over the past 14 months, I have been conducting an ethnographic study of what I have come to refer to as the Uru Diaspora—a group of players who were made refugees by the closure of the Myst-based massively multiplayer online game (MMOG) Uru in February of 2004.[1] There were about 10,000 Uru players in total online, and although the game ran for a relatively short period of time and had a relatively small subscribership, it inspired a passionate response from its player community. The closure of the game server compounded this by subjecting the players to a collective trauma that formed a bond that, as of this date, has out-lived the original game by a time factor of about 2 to 1.

The core of the study focused on one particular group that immigrated and formed an "ethnic" community in There, an online virtual world that has allow-ances for player asset creation. Players combined the existing culture of There with that of Uru to create a hybrid culture that is comparable to a Chinatown or Little Italy in the United States. Like a real-world group of immigrant refugees, the Gathering of Uruz met much initial resistance from the There community. Because the group was so large (about 300 people), they wielded a significant amount of power in the relatively new virtual world. This was only exacerbated by their demographics. These longtime Myst fans were mostly professional people in their 40s and 50s, most with children, and about half women. They were competent, articulate, and their traumatic experience in Uru made them somewhat demanding of There management, wishing to avert the mistreatment they felt they had experienced in being cast out of Uru. The community became extremely influential, both socially and politically, and eventually "assimilated" so that they now feel as much Therians as Uruvians. Concurrently, they also explored ways of creating their own self-contained re-creation of Uru using first text-based MUD technology and later, the Adobe Atmosphere virtual world crea-tion tool. In the summer of 2004, along with a number of other Uru groups that were still active, they were able to negotiate a deal with publisher Cyan to release the server software to allow for player-run servers. The Uru Diaspora literally took over the game, and now all Uru servers are run by players. Surprisingly, the Uru immigrants in There did not return to Uru as their main home world; rather, they meet there once a week to experience their homeland and meet up with other members of the group who do not make their virtual homes in places other than There.

Even from the beginning, there were controversies regarding how to bring the Uru culture into There. Some wanted to try to re-create Ages (the Myst/Uru term for game levels), but others had a philosophical objection to this based in the narrative of the original game. In all Myst games, Ages are created by writ-ing books, each of which is a distinct world and complex, elaborate puzzle unto itself. It would seem that the storyline supports the idea that one could "write" new Ages. However, according to the Myst mythology, only the D'Ni, the lost society at the center of the game series, had the ability to write Ages. This some-what talmudic theological argument led to some interesting outcomes. At first, players created artifacts that were directly derived from the original Uru game. Over time, players who emerged as the artisans of the group began creating new Uruesque objects, using the aesthetics, symbols, imagery, and in some cases, back story of the game. One of the top artisans of the group, Damanji[2] proposed building an entirely new Uru Age in There, but this was met with intense resist-ance from the There community, reinforcing their anxiety that the Uru refugees were trying to take over their world. Damanji then formulated a new approach to what I would call emergent Age creation, although he did not characterize it as such. His idea was to create new Uru-like objects in the style of There and put them on sale for the general There public. (There has an auction mechanism for player-created items.) He created an octagonal cone house, inspired by but distinctly different from one that appears in Uru. As a result, Thereians who were not Uruvians and knew nothing of the game or its immigrant population in There began to purchase cone house components, and over time, these structures became ubiquitous throughout There. In addition, one of his Uru comrades, one of many Uru refugees who became influential citizens in There, founded the University of There. Most of the buildings on the campus are constructed from Damanji's cone houses.

From a methodological perspective, tracking a digital Diaspora is a challenging task. I have been able to keep track of some other trajectories of the Uru Diaspora and continue to find new instantiations of it in various contexts. A large community of Uru/Myst players has settled in Second Life, which also has affordances for player creation that are much more versatile but harder to use than those of There. A small builder's group created an exact replica of major portions of the Uru game in Second Life, an example of what was referenced earlier as a simulation of a simulation. This area is so like the original Uru game, down to the most minute detail, including scripting features such as swarms of fireflies that follow you around and linking books that take you between Ages, it is a stupendous achievement by anyone's reckoning. Another group of combined Uru and Myst players in Second Life finally did the inevitable and designed their own entire Age. Rendered with equal craftsmanship and attention to detail, it is a completely new game in the Myst tradition, with the same type of puzzle structure, including notebooks and poems with clues hidden throughout, strange machines that have to be reactivated, and unusual combinations of things that must be done to enter a new area. Both areas are popular with non–Myst/Uru players, who admire the elaborate craftsmanship of the buildings and furnishings, fantastical natural settings, intricate narratives, and complex scripting. As with There, Uru players are among some of the top creators in the larger Second Life community.

Numerous other examples of Uru fan culture abound, some resembling more traditional forms such as fan art and stories, dictionaries of the D'Ni language, T-shirts and mugs, and so on. But there are also some unusual offerings. One woman makes Uruthemed quilts. The Welcomers (see Note 2) whose mission in Uru was to greet newcomers, now have a similarly charged branch in The Matrix Online.

The Uru group, though only one example, is of particular interest because the game itself is no more. Players have quite literally taken it over and made it their own, carrying it forward to a new level. Eighteen months after the game was closed, we still see a vibrant, creative, and highly productive community, dispersed throughout other games and reinforced by their shared traumatic experience. As games begin to integrate increasing affordances for player creativity, I anticipate the growth of an entirely new form of autoludic culture in which players will feel more and more empowered to make the game their own.

Conclusion

As more and more players engage in productive activity in and around play, we may want to question the assumption that games and play are unproductive. These trends show that play has its own productive character, which can also be seen as a form of cultural production and perhaps could be defined as a form of folk art. Studying emergent forms of player production can also inform game design. How can player production be promoted within the game structure? Can we find new models for production in partnership with players? It seems from these examples that players are more than willing to pay for this service, and given the increasing costs and complexity of commercial game production, it may turn out that in the long run, we have no choice but to let players take over their play experience completely.

Notes

* The author wishes to acknowledge her research avatar, Artemesia.

1 The detailed ethnographic study will be published as a doctoral dissertation in summer of 2006.
2 All avatar and group names have been changed to protect subjects' anonymity.

References

Callois, R. (2001). *Man, play, and games*. Chicago: University of Illinois Press. (Original work published 1961)

DeKoven, B. (1978). *The well-played game: A player's philosophy*. New York: Anchor.

Huizinga, J. (1955). *Homo ludens: A study of the play-element in culture*. Boston: Beacon.

Jenkins, H. (1992). *Textual poachers: Television fans and participatory culture*. New York: Routledge.

Jenkins, H. (1998). "Complete freedom of movement": Video games as gendered play spaces. In H. Jenkins & J. Cassel (Eds.), *From Barbie to Mortal Kombat: Gender and computer games* (pp. 262–297). Cambridge, MA: MIT Press.

Opie, I., & Opie, P. (1969). *Children's games in street and playground*. Oxford, UK: Clarendon.

Pearce, C. (2002). Emergent authorship: The next interactive revolution. *Computers & Graphics, 26*, 21–29.

Poremba, C. (2003). *Player as author: Digital games and agency*. Unpublished master's thesis, Simon Frasier University, Vancouver, Canada.

Salen, K., & Zimmerman, E. (2004). *Rules of play: Game design fundamentals*. Cambridge, MA: MIT Press.

Turner, V. (1982). *From ritual to theatre: The human seriousness of play*. New York: PAJ Publications.

Yalom, M. (2004). *The birth of the chess queen*. New York: Harper Collins.

79

MATERIAL CULTURE AND ANGRY BIRDS

Heikki Tyni and Olli Sotamaa

Source: *Proceedings of Nordic DiGRA 2014 Conference*, Digital Games Research Association DiGRA, 2014.

Abstract

The article examines different ways in which the research of material culture is relevant for digital games. It is argued that despite the wide adoption of digital distribution, material culture still registers as a significant component of the overall gaming culture. The paper compiles a collection of different research areas relevant for the study of games and materiality. In order to better contextualize the different research approaches, the framework is applied to Angry Birds (Rovio 2009). The different approaches, ranging from platform studies and political economy to merchandizing and collecting, highlight how a seemingly small, digitally distributed mobile game still manages to connect with multiple facets of material culture in significant ways.

Introduction

The last decade has seen the rise of digital services, the cloud, and immaterial content. Relevant especially in vulnerable sectors such as newspaper industry, critical research focused on game industry, too, needs to pose the question: what are the consequences of this development to the material culture of digital gaming and its players? Digital games are increasingly distributed in a completely digital form. From smart phone games to free-to-play games to MMOs, digital games are available more often than not as services that sidestep physical game boxes and retail stores. However, instead of disappearing, materiality of digital games can now be discovered in new places. Peteri et al. (2013) point out how materiality of media artifacts is rarely addressed and heavily understudied. The recent dematerialization of cultural artifacts is accompanied by rhetorics that foreground techno-futuristic perspectives, hiding the mundane aspects of media production and use. Still, dematerialization does not inevitably mean less importance for materiality. Instead, new technologies also actively stimulate new material practices.

The new wave of hybrid playful products like Skylanders (Activision 2011) expands digital experiences into material realm (Tyni et al. 2013). In addition, empirical studies show that people can still have deep appreciation towards game boxes, cover art and collector's edition figurines in a time when digital games are turning to digital-only distribution (Toivonen & Sotamaa 2011). Research focused on the materiality of game culture is not restricted only to research dealing directly with games. Study on materiality in general can be in many instances extrapolated on game culture, for example in considering questions of identity and how we relate to our physical belongings.

This paper highlights several ways in which the research of material culture is relevant for digital games. Often, it is precisely because of the perceived immateriality that the research has begun to see the actual materiality of games in more revealing light. The paper first goes over multiple strands of research on material culture. Second, a collection of different research approaches relevant for the study of games and materiality is compiled. Finally, the paper looks at Angry Birds (Rovio 2009) as a case study in order to better contextualize the different research approaches, at the same time illustrating the surprisingly material nature of this digital hit game. Thus, we aim the paper to serve as an outline that will hopefully spark further discussion and more advanced models from future research.

Researching material culture

Recent years have seen researchers among and on the borders of game studies cast renewed interest on the materiality of game culture. Apperley and Jayemane (2012) go over the central threads of the so called "material turn". They identify three research areas that focus on the materiality of game culture in different ways. First, the *ethnographic line of research* examines player-users using games as content for their social and participatory media behavior. Offline affects online gaming in many ways and material elements are used for example to help digital gameplay in various manners. MMO communities might produce loads of out-of-game material that is referenced and serves to support the feeling of community. The physical place of play affects the game experience depending on whether it happens in a net-café or at home. Access to gaming is restricted by the expenses of hardware, online connection and electricity as well as access to a credit card.

Second, *platform studies* (Montfort & Bogost 2009) focuses on how the materiality of the gaming platform affects the design and the play of games. The research shifts away from peoples' relationship with software, towards the relationship of software and platform. While people can tamper with this relationship, it remains as the constant for the study. Thus, the focus can be on how the manufacturing of particular microchips (possible assembly line difficulties; gambling on a lucrative deal, etc.) might spell the end or success of an entire game console. This way platform studies form a flexible method, a bridge of sorts, for examining the connections between corporate leadership and game design. Platform studies can also be combined for example with media archeology (Huhtamo & Parikka ed. 2011), as researching the intricacies of past console productions can offer insight on larger industry trajectories. The third research trend focuses on the *political economy of game industry* (for example Kline et al. 2003; Kücklich 2005; Dyer-Witheford & De Peuter 2009). The focus is turned on the real-world relationships of work and play in the contemporary society. Fan labour, for example, is seen as a problematized area, i.e. whether game modding is work or fun in circumstances where fans do not keep any IP rights, despite carrying all the risks. The excruciating crunch times in game development fall on the same line of critical examination.

The tripartite review of Apperley & Jaymane nicely highlights the many linkages between digital games and materiality. At the same time, we feel that the rich tradition of material culture studies is still not utilized to its full potential. While the advantages of applying science and technology studies (STS) or actor-network theory (ANT) in revealing the socio-technological basis of digital games have been discussed to some extent (Giddings 2005; Kerr 2006; Taylor 2006), the conceptualizations within the study of material culture that can help us unfold the everyday function and meanings associated with digital games remain heavily underused.

Russell W. Belk (1988), who has studied the many meanings of possession for decades, describes thoroughly how we unknowingly feel our belongings to be a part of our 'selves'. His central concept is the 'extended self' by which he means five categories, or layers, of the things we consider to be a part of ourselves. The layers start from our body, continue to our internal processes, ideas and experiences, finally stopping to 'the people, places, and things' towards which we hold a special relationship. Thus we feel everything that we describe as 'mine' to be part of us (my car, my dad, my name, etc.). Belk (1988) also goes over 'special cases' such as collections, which allow us to achieve a self-defined uniqueness within set boundaries. Both the things themselves and the order that is imposed on them reflect the collector's identity. Controlling the miniature world of the collection feels good, as filling the holes in it means "completing" areas of the collector herself. Belk's ideas have an immediate connection to game collections and other fan materials. Storing, organizing, and putting games on display can have an important role in creating a particular gamer identity, gathering subcultural capital, and ensuring the opportunity for reminiscing past gaming experiences (Toivonen & Sotamaa 2011).

Perhaps most importantly, though, Belk's conception reminds us how media in general and digital games in particular should not be reduced to "'mere' contents but manifest themselves also as artefacts that can be owned, collected and placed in the home" (Peteri et al. 2013). Concentrating on the material aspects and the "performance" of gaming at home, Enevold (2012) argues that situating computers and consoles at home is revealed relating to parenting, sharing among siblings and everyday life in nuanced ways. The time-space of gaming "is regulated in an automatic and routinized way, and motivated and ruled by a range of norms, explicit and implicit" (ibid., pp.4). Such regulations and norms intertwine with sleep, work and family-life, and concern now both gaming children and parents.

Anthropologist Daniel Miller (2010) asserts that our fundamental materiality is the best way to understand us. Our relationship to objects is dialectic: we make objects and objects make us. Miller argues that we are constructed out of objects and appearances, such as our clothing. Objects are not important because they are everywhere to be seen or because they physically enable or restrict us. They are important precisely because we do not see them, notice them. As objects are taken more and more for granted, they increase in their power to control our behavior through setting various frames for us. Furthermore, at this taken-for-granted phase they are not open for contestation. If something is present everywhere – Miller uses blue jeans as an example –, they become *less* interesting to us, not more, while at the same time we are increasingly blinded to their characteristics in setting a certain kind of culture. Applying these perspectives to the study of games challenges us to explore how games are not only raw material for identity building but also actively impose their own dynamics on their players.

Bart Simon (2007) points out how gaming experience is crucially connected to the material pleasures of embodied practice. While the futuristic game industry rhetorics may foreground the processes of dematerialization and virtualization, for the players the very machines that enable and facilitate playful behaviors become "material instantiations or enhancements of the gaming experience" (ibid., p. 188). Similarly, an earlier study conducted by one of the authors showed that game cartridges, discs, and boxes can operate as important carriers and mediators that provide game cultural value that surpasses the passing gaming instances (Toivonen & Sotamaa 2011).

Different research approaches

In the following, we introduce a selected collection of research approaches that we find most relevant for the study of games and materiality. Similar to a handful of prior studies (Kline et al. 2003; Consalvo & Dutton 2006; Sotamaa 2009), we call for radically multiperspectival research approaches. Our aim is not to list all possible research approaches or make a timeless classification of potential objects of study. Instead, the applicability of different approaches needs always to be evaluated in connection to the particular cases. We see the following as an outline that will hopefully give way to more sophisticated models and approaches in the years to come.

Platform

Platform studies focus on the hardware and the software of a gaming device. These are seen as central factors in shaping the look, sound and feel of the gaming device, the games designed on the system, the culture that subsequently forms around the system and reaching all the way to the business that can be conducted on it. Thus, for platform studies, both the cultures surrounding Atari 2600 (1977) and the iPhone (2006) follow same kind of principles in how the game development is dictated most of all by the hardware and the code that makes it run.

Conditions of game production

Political economy of games looks critically at the production of games and how this relates to the games, players and developers. In relation to the material aspects of digital games, it considers the actual physical consequences of manufacturing digital games, such as the conditions in which games are developed – whether this include for example overt "crunch time" – and the conditions in which the game related production materials are made, such as copper mines and cheap labour silicon factories.

Game stores and physical advertising

Even as digital distribution is becoming more and more common, marketing of digital games includes a wide variety material advertising in physical spaces. It is paramount for the game companies to consider where their product is located in larger stores in terms of electronics department, toy department, etc. or if a special section, a "store within a store", can be created (Sheff 1993). Major game launches are often accompanied by material advertising "stunts" – such as the giant mech robot at Berlin Central Station promoting *Titanfall* (Respawn Entertainment 2014) – which are aimed to create a viral Internet sensation.

Merchandising

The digital game is now one of the central components in cross-media franchising and marketing. Hit games are tried to turn into cultural phenomena that should be seen everywhere. Depending on the franchise this means everything from action figures, collectibles and plush toys to licensed soda, sweaters, backpacks and even theme parks. Following the threat of digital distribution, brick-and-mortar game stores like Gamestop have widened their product categories to include as many game related physical toys and merchandising as possible. Even if the games exist solely in the cloud, game related physical objects constantly advertise them on the streets, desks and car windows.

Collectibles and collecting

One important sector of physical game merchandising are the special collector's editions that persuade players both to buy a physical copy of the game but also to build and showcase identity. Expensive special edition figure on the desk communicates gamer identity to self and to others. Further, physical game collections are important to many gamers who consider them both more reliable and more "owned" compared to digital copies or see game shelves as interior decoration, among various other meanings.

Fan practices outside the games

Besides using the official game materials to communicate meanings, fans recreate, remediate, transform and move digital play into new physical contexts. This might include for example cosplaying game characters, building LEGO versions of game locales, creating game related everyday objects such as knitting Space Invaders cardigans, baking game themed cakes, and so on. This is especially relevant in the age of the Internet when numerous sites and blogs are quick to spread any such fan practices that are sufficiently well made and presented.

Physical environment of play

Research on the actual physical environments in which various kinds of play happens consists of a variety of different research approaches, from architecture to anthropology. The physical play situations, be it at home, in school, or on the train, each come with their specific contexts, limitations and possibilities. Arcade, for example, was a very specific kind of environment with its possibly dark atmosphere, blinking lights and historical associations to bars and gambling. Nowadays, mapping the different smart phone play situations alone would form a formidable research data; we might for example ask where is it now appropriate to play mobile games and what kind of clashes does this cause.

Oscillation between material play and digital play

As play on many fronts seems to be becoming more digital now, it is important to examine the transition of physical play into digital with special vigor. How for example different historical forms of material play find their equivalent in modern culture: how construction toys compare to games like *SimCity* (Maxis 1989), doll houses to *The Sims* (Maxis 2000), or toy car play to *Micro Machines* games (Codemasters and others 1991–2006). Many physics based games simulate real world physics very convincingly, letting players experience games like Jenga in virtual form, whereas some action games simulate gun recoil, ricochet and bullet penetration to high fidelity.

Games combining physical and digital play

One way modern play culture tries to reconcile the chasm between traditional physical play and new modes of digital play are games that create a unified play experience out of both digital and physical elements. This could mean hybrid games like the mega franchise *Skylanders* with its RFID toyline or app toys, such as *YetYet* (Totoya Creatures 2012), where a smart device is inserted into a plush toy to turn it into a talking, reacting smart toy that can be updated. It could also mean "appcessories", apps that complement a physical play product or physical play products that complement an app.

These modern "hybrid games" are not of course the first examples of games fluctuating between material and digital play. CD-ROM and DVD board games of the 1990s were already preceded by the VCR games of the 1980s and motion based games of the mid 2000s were preceded by Nintendo's Power Glove (1987) and *Skylanders* by *R.O.B.* the robot (1986). Furthermore, various digital pets and "demanding robots" (Turkle 2011) such as Tamagochi (1996) and Furby (1998) have been hugely popular at their time.

Altogether, it appears that many popular forms of play have already for quite some time existed in the crossing point of digital and physical entertainment. In order to evaluate and contextualize the different research approaches we now move on to examine the hit game Angry Birds (Rovio 2009). This highly successful combination of mobile media and easily approachable game design provides a timely case study for analyzing the diverse materialities connected to contemporary digital games.

Angry Birds in material culture

First released in 2009 as an iOS game, Angry Birds (AB) is now available in almost every current digital game platform including Android, Windows Phone, PC, DS, 3DS, Wii, PS3 and Xbox 360, and many others. Instead of one game, AB can now be seen as family of thematically interrelated games consists of ten different titles including *Angry Birds Seasons* (2010), *Angry Birds Rio* (2011) and *Angry Birds Star Wars* (2012), each an iteration of the original game, *Angry Birds Go!* (2013), a kart racing game, and *Angry Birds Epic* (2014), a turn based RPG battle game.

The perfect platform

While we take into account the special qualities of the various versions and platforms, it is clear that the success story of AB is near inseparable from the success of the iPhone. AB was launched during iPhone 3GS, the third generation iPhone, when Apple's high end smart phone was still new to the wide majority of consumers. Wilson et al. (2011) draw comparisons between AB and *Snake* which came pre-loaded on the early Nokia phones onwards from 1998 and how each game helped us familiarize ourselves with their respective platforms. For Wilson et al. playing AB allowed the user to "refine" her interactions with the iOS touch screen in a satisfying manner. Through play, in noticing how a small difference in aiming the sling shot equals into a big difference in the flight path of the bird, user cultivated a feel as to how sensitive the touch screen actually is. Though Steve Jobs famously did not like the iPhone to be seen as a gaming device, Wilson et al. (ibid.) posit that the precision of the touch screen controls in AB most certainly helped iOS to become a platform for games.

AB has had a key role in the process where high profile gaming on mobile phones has become a cultural phenomenon. Many smart phone games, AB included, are created in a way that they are playable in quick downtime moments in various real world environments. As Giddings (2014) writes, "[i]ts virtual time-space has evolved to nest within the crannies and hollows of players' actual time and space: in empty moments at the bus-stop, the waiting room." In turn, the demands from these new 'casual' situations and environments have meant new design restrictions, such as constructing the gameplay experience from short play bursts that keep players coming back and designing games in a way that they are playable with the sound turned off.

Downloaded roughly two billion times, AB has been one of the key products in establishing the low pricing of the game apps and a major attraction for visiting Apple's App Store. In harnessing Apple's 'Game Centre', AB helped in establishing the now-common social play networks on smart phones (Wilson et al. 2011). iOS in particular is important in how Apple retained much greater control over the software-hardware whole compared to its main competitors. "The Angry Birds game is an extremely successful example of the synthesis of personal mobile media and videogame culture", Giddings (2014) writes. "If this is the immediate environment of the Angry Bird, then its hypermediate domain is the new communication networks and ludic experiences of the smart phone, the app store, the touch screen" (ibid.). Here, the logic of platform studies as described by Montfort and Bogost (2009) comes full circle; the design of the iPhone hardware and software spiral around each other and emerge as chief factors in setting a particular kind of landscape of affordances for new modes of design, business and play.

The material conditions and consequences of games production

Once you enter the headquarters in Rovio in Espoo, Finland, the first thing you notice is the multitude of plush toys and other AB merchandise that decorate the office space. Visit the board rooms and meeting spaces and you will find more birds and pigs painted on walls. The laidback and hip atmosphere is finished with trendy furnishing and other playful elements, including for example a large real-life slingshot. This is nothing new as such. Creating and nurturing an innovative, fun and trendy atmosphere is a life-line for many of the successful businesses in creative industries. According to Fleming (2005), the attempts to foster "cultures of fun" in workplaces began already in the 1980s. Since then things like flexible hours, relaxed dress code and funky décor have been associated with facilitating co-operation and creativity.

One of the identified pleasures of game development is the work as play ethos that is supported by playful working environments and visible for example in open attitude towards "rebellious" and quirky behavior (de Peuter & Dyer-Witheford 2005). While this management approach, grounded in actively blurring the boundaries between work and play, can both improve efficiency and contribute to work wellbeing, it also appears to fuel some cynicism. Sometimes flexibility and seemingly laidback corporate culture appears to lead to extreme hours, extended "crunch time" and very precarious positions (ibid.). While the Finnish game development scene is rarely associated with extreme working conditions, developers surely recognize the crunch promoting attitude typical of the industry (Roininen 2013).

The carefully designed studio environments are often actively displayed in company marketing materials and feature articles. At the same time, we know very little of the conditions in which for example AB merchandising products are created. While the social corporate responsibility agendas provided by publicly traded game companies provide at least some information on relationships with their suppliers (Jones, Comfort & Hillier 2013), Rovio is a privately owned company and no public documentation of its commitments is available.

One of the pros often associated with digital distribution of games is that moving away from physical discs and game cartridges automatically means a smaller ecological footprint. This claim does not take into account how the current video game industry not only relies on constantly changing hardware based on minerals mined in developing countries and produced in undesirable working conditions by cheap labour but also generates remarkable amounts of electronic waste. Added to this, contemporary mobile games rely heavily on cloud computing. While celebrated for its immaterial advantages, cloud computing still relies on bricks-and-mortar data centers. These data storage infrastructures consume a tremendous amount of energy, often lack transparency and provide very limited metrics for measuring the actual environmental impact.

Retail stores and the physical marketing of digital games

For some years now, toy industry has been under great pressure by digital children's entertainment, whereas digital distribution of games has equally threatened physical game retail stores. Thus, retail welcomes brands with both material and digital presence as a shared ground, while digital business benefits from the traditional and safe appeal of physical merchandise. Its origin as a digitally distributed download-only game meant that AB did not initially have any kind of presence in traditional gaming stores (physical advertising, stands, kiosks, and so on). This immaterial nature of the new economy might have very well contributed to the studio's resolve to come up with alternative ways of entering the traditional retail stores.

Marketing research on products and brands sees product manufacturers actually branding us, us carrying different product brands much in the same way cattle carries the brand of its owner. Much of the postmodern research on customer behavior and identity posits that one of the central ways customers construct their identity is through products (Belk 1988) and branded products in particular. Echoing Miller (2010), the products – to a degree – make us; products and brands allow us to communicate to others how we are 'gamers', 'from the streets', 'alternative'

132

or 'rich'. One of the first major AB product categories outside the digital game were the AB plush toys. Plush toys soon became one of central ways to associate with the game, the characters and the brand in general. For many, AB plush toys became a banner of identification, a tool through which one was able to communicate the identity of an Angry Birds fan, the identity of a gamer, but also – at least first – the identity of somebody who has a smart phone.

Interestingly, AB plush toys started to come out in increasingly larger sizes, as if to reflect the ballooning size of the game phenomenon. In every turn, the smallness of the smart phone – the screen size, the length of the play sessions, the simplicity of the gameplay – was contrasted by the huge plush toys Rovio used in its official marketing situations. Further, by offering multiple sizes of the plush toys, Rovio actually facilitated a situation where fans could compete who had the biggest plush bird. This competition was only fueled by celebrities such as Conan O'Brien participating by shooting giant pigs with a giant sling in his talk show and private people creating ever more new AB themed objects. Thus, from one perspective, the studio had managed to create a situation where creating an identity was turned into a game. Subsequently its digital hit game had colonized also the physical realm.

Licensing and merchandising

Since its launch in 2009, AB has become a global merchandising phenomenon. There is an extremely wide variety of toy variants available within the AB brand, including figurines, squishy toys, board games, physical action games, and yard games. A huge number of licensees sell AB branded plush toys, soda, candy, shower gel, coffee, and backpacks, to name but a few examples. There are branded theme parks – Angry Birds Lands – located in Finland and UK, while two AB themed Space Encounter centers can be found in the United States. The birds have also been featured on F1 cars, airliner jets and as the official hockey world championship mascots. Rovio reported that in 2012 45% of its revenue came from "consumer products", a section separated from paid games, virtual goods and advertising, basically referring to merchandising and licensed goods.

The success of AB and the subsequent merchandising has led Rovio to expand its licensing efforts to ever new product lines. It now regards itself as an "entertainment company" rather than a game studio, backed by its spreading out to animation via *Angry Birds Toons* (2013) and its plans to release a feature film based on the characters in 2016. AB has been featured in various TV shows and movies both by being referenced in talk and by physical "stunts". An Israeli TV-show parodied Israeli-Palestinian peace negotiations through puppeteers moving arguing birds and pigs, while talk show host Jon Stewart echoed Conan O'Brien by hurling toy birds at piggies in his show. While it is unclear whether Rovio participated in organizing these numbers, they certainly worked in generating viral items that were shared on popular sites. This kind of 'virality' seems to be one of the key factors for a phenomenon such as AB.

As Rovio's licencing efforts keep new AB product categories coming, sites are more and more probable to report them, gasping "where does it end" and "what do they come up with next". The amount of product categories Angry Birds has been licensed to seem to be, in itself, news worth reporting. Rovio's intention seems to be to create advertising buzz precisely by licensing Angry Birds to as many product categories as possible, in as extravagant contexts as possible. Similar to *Pokémon* in the 1990s and Disney in previous decades (Buckingham & Shefton-Green 2004), the situation allows Rovio to harness an economy of scale with its merchandising: the more there is, the harder it is to avoid, and the more compelled or indulged one is to pursue it.

Further, and again similar to *Pokémon* (ibid.), it has become harder and harder to draw lines around the AB "source text" in terms of audience: *Angry Birds* the game was there first, yes, but by now it is easy to imagine there being new generations and segments of AB enthusiasts who have never actually played the game but nevertheless consider themselves fans. On the other hand, the exploding popularity has also meant that AB has become a very pirated brand. In a recent lawsuit Rovio was awarded 500 000€ in damages for copyright violation in regards to AB toys (GamePolitics 2014). In 2011, there was even an illegal AB theme park opened in Changsta, China.

Collectibles and fan-made artifacts

Given the downloadable and casual nature of AB, it may not to lend itself to similar extensive collector's editions as the popular AAA console titles. Nevertheless, Angry Birds Trilogy (Rovio/Housemarque 2012), a console version of the first three AB games that is available as a physical copy for various platforms, was depicted as "the ultimate collector's edition", containing "cinematics, extras and other entertaining content" (Miller 2012). A quick view on Ebay still indicates that AB collecting is mostly focused on merchandising. For example K'Nex, the provider of popular construction toy sets, offers a large series of AB figurines and items. The figures come in sealed packages which don't reveal the contents from the outside, adding a bit of mystery and excitement to the act of collecting. The collectibles exhibit the all-around marketing logic of Rovio: while the company aims at making the birds and pigs an instantly recognized and mundane part of the global media environment, they at the same time build exclusivity by providing hard-to-obtain artifacts for "true fans". In addition, as the HockeyBird collaboration with the National Hockey League (NHL) shows, the birds are also customized to particular audiences in order to push more merchandizing and collectibles to the market.

The case of Angry Birds nicely highlights the interplay between manufactured objects and fan-made artifacts that often envelopes popular media phenomena. Side by side with the official apparel we witness home-made products like knitted AB skiing caps. The recipes of the official AB cookbook are challenged by a multitude of parents-turned-into-confectioners who prepare AB birthday cakes and other delicacies in most meticulous fashion. Various custom-made bird outfits are used in marketing the game, but still the most innovative AB-inspired costumes are found among the cosplayers. In this respect, AB illustrates how the current participatory popular culture is defined by increasingly complex relations between top-down and bottom-up approaches (Jenkins 2006), importantly including the material aspects of game culture.

The physical environment of play

The most downloaded game ever and playable on almost every imaginable digital platform, AB could be attached to a huge variety of differing play situations. Everyone who owns a smart phone owns a platform for games, and game content is now targeted equally for toddlers, moms and grandmothers. Paradoxically, games like AB allow one to be always socially connected, but also work very efficiently to draw the attention of the user to these games, away from the user's surroundings.

For Parikka & Suominen (2006), the development of personal, mobile entertainment started with the railroads of the 1800s. As many were now travelling with strangers for the first time, personal media such as pocket books allowed passengers to immerse themselves, be "transported away" from the monotony and the awkwardness (ibid.). Similarly, for many, the Sony Walkman redefined both the spatial experience of the city and the sense of privacy (Bull 2000). Isolated from their surroundings by the headphones users could give new meanings to their surroundings, all the while acting as if an invisible wall was covering them (ibid.). Being immersed in the smart phone, be it talking into the phone or playing a game, continues this tradition in what Östergren & Juhlin (2006) and Belk (2013) call "accompanied solitude". Contrary to portable game consoles, the smart phone is practically always with the user. An internal game industry study on the play habits of mobile gamers, conducted by Information Solutions Group (2012), reported that mobile games are now played in various situations in everyday life. Situations like commuting on public transport, and waiting for an appointment were mentioned by over one half of the respondents, whereas 'work breaks', 'at restaurant or café', 'in class', 'at work during a meeting or conference call' and 'in a place of worship' were among listed. The most typical place for play however was at home on the couch, while over one half also reported playing in bed.

Thus, as smart phone games are now played even at church, it becomes relevant to ask in what ways the smart phone has changed the place for play. The designers of Walkman were surprised to find out that many users wanted to get as big headphones as possible – for the Japanese designers being discreet was paramount (Bull 2000) –, and in the same way we are surprised to find out that many play mobile games at home lying on couch, despite the seeming mobility of the device. The results from Information Solutions Group seem to support the view that the same kind of development is happening also with mobile gaming. It also seems that gaming in these new environments has shaped the design of the game in ways discussed in the platform section: gameplay mechanic of simple swipes with one finger allows discreet play and games need to be playable in short bursts. On the other hand, these quick sessions can pile up into long play streaks on the couch, similar to so-called hardcore games. And while many consider AB play a solitary affair, the game is played also in competitions, such as when Rovio organized an AB contest on an intercontinental Finnair flight (Mahtani 2011), demonstrating how a mobile game like AB, played on small phone screens with online connection, is still able to bring crowds of people together in various physical conditions.

The oscillation between material play and digital play

Children start to use touch devices at a younger and younger age and for many, AB is now one of the earliest games they play. Suoninen (2014) reports that AB is the most played game for all Finnish children aged 0–8 (n = 921 households) and that one child out of five, aged 0–2, plays digital games at least sometimes – a significant increase in numbers compared to 2010. The study also points out that the youngest children played almost exclusively on touch devices (ibid.). Generally speaking, AB offers a great case example on the ways the touch screen is so intuitive to use and how children first learn to use these devices. It is also interesting to consider the ways this first contact "sets a tone" on further technological (and non-technological) encounters, meaning, in what ways do the special qualities of AB build children's understanding of pictures, moving pictures, touch screen devices and a particular kind of interactivity. Should we for example consider how physical puzzle games, board games etc. are continued in tablet play and gaming? How do these kinds of fine-motoric skills (swipes, drawing on the screen, etc.) compare to earlier forms of child's play?

Lauwaert (2009) has written extensively about the development of play from the late 1800s to modern day and how old construction toy play continues in games like *SimCity* (Maxis 1989), while *The Sims* (Maxis 2000) is a digital version of a doll house. In the very core of AB are carefully modeled physics, and it could be argued that the distinct "demolish a built construction" form that AB takes has long roots in the history of play. Children have always constructed play things such as pinecone cows and sand castles, and one essential part of this kind of development through play is also demolishing things, tearing down what has been built (to examine the innards, the test one's strength, to examine one's responsibilities and the consequences of own actions, and so on). It is interesting to wonder, then, whether the gameplay mechanic of collapsing block structures captures some kind of archetypal, universal mode of play that is particularly pleasant for us. And if smart phone games help us to familiarize ourselves with these devices, do the pigs' collapsing structures teach children about physics and gravity?

Since the "casual revolution" of the early 2000s, many digital game players have changed their play habits to embrace more physical ways to play (motion and gesture control games such as Wii and Kinect) (Juul 2010). One explanation for the success of these games are their intuitive controls, understandable also to infants and elderly, and touch screen controls such as the two finger pinch have only continued this trend. Illustrating this deepening mix of the physical and digital, it is now a common occurrence to see young children trying to 'swipe' the pictures in a traditional book. On the other hand, many have also moved back to physical board gaming, as the scene has become more and more popular with a huge selection of games. It might not be such a surprise then that there is now also a physical AB game, *Angry Birds Action Game* (Tactic 2012), in which players toss birds in order to collapse wooden block structures.

Games combining physical and digital play

In September 2012, Rovio collaborated with Mattel in launching an Angry Birds 'Apptivity' toy for the AB tablet game. By placing it on the tablet screen, the toy – King Pig from AB – allows the player to open up new game modes, such as 'Material Mix-Up' in which two level materials are switched to something else, and 'Total Destruction' where players have a short period of time to use the King Pig toy to demolish the level. The Apptivity toy is a typical 'appcessory', a toy that utilizes different smart device features and affordances such as cameras, image recognition, capacitive ink and gyro sensors to facilitate play with physical pawns on and around the touch screen device.

One year later, Rovio partnered with Hasbro in creating the Telepods. Available for the tablet version of the game, Telepods are physical AB character toys which can be read by the device's camera in order to 'transport' them into the game. That is, the game recognizes the physical toy via a QR code embedded into the toy and a virtual version of the corresponding character opens up for play. Telepods are game specific and have so far been released for *Angry Birds Star Wars II* and *Angry Birds GO!*, while upcoming *Angry Birds Stella* is reported to also support the toys. The logic of Telepods can be seen following both the other appcessory games and the extremely successful toy-game hybrid franchise *Skylanders* (2011), which popularized a similar transport mechanism with its ever-expanding roster of toy characters. Player-customer who wants to get the complete set needs to collect over 30 Telepods counting *Angry Birds Star Wars II* alone. Rovio is also actively expanding its character roster through new games and re-branding mechanisms, such as with *Angry Birds Star Wars*. While Telepods might not necessitate collecting a sizeable selection of characters as an integral part of its game design to a same degree as *Skylanders* and *Pokémon* do, it is important to notice that, similar to *Skylanders,* Telepod toys open up new stages for play, thus acting as a sort of physical correspondent for digital add-on content.

Discussions with Rovio indicate that Telepods are merely the first step in a longer process of refining the hybrid play experience for smart devices. The question for Rovio, too, is what the 'right kind' of hybridity is, and how could the longevity of the hybrid experience be maximized. Some researchers, like

Van Campenhout et al. (2013), have argued for stepping back from the excessive dematerialization of objects and services and looking for a balanced middle way of incorporating the best of both worlds into design. Proposing new, hybrid designs for everyday objects like an MP3 player, Van Campenhout et al. (2013) see flexibility and availability as the best features of the digital world, whereas material objects are thanked for their "rich interaction", i.e. the affordances of physical manipulation and the cognitive clarity they offer. Meanwhile, Tyni et al. (2013) argue that the experience of a hybrid product consists of both digital and material characteristics. Their evaluation model builds on two axes to determine, first, how dependent the two sides of the hybrid play product, the material and the digital are of each other, and second, how synchronous or asynchronous they are.

Conclusions

In the introduction we promised to compile different research approaches relevant for the study of games and materiality. Through the exploration of Angry Birds we have tried to exemplify how these perspectives can importantly inform our understanding of how the AB phenomenon is constructed, also in very material ways. Symptomatically, Rovio's desire to highlight the Big Physical (giant plushies, the championship contest in an aeroplane etc.) seems to communicate that half of the appeal is still in the physical space, outside the screen and online networks. The diversity of Rovio's operations also effectively contests any simple conception of a modern game studio as mere software developer. The marketing logic of tying the physical toys into the larger ecosystem of hybrid media, composed of equally important elements of physical and digital components, is in the center of both the hybrid AB toys and the multimodal AB phenomenon as a whole. Discussions with Rovio employees confirm this: the company sees digital games, animation and physical merchandising as the three equally important corner stones of its enterprise. This kind of three-fold strategy helps to bring sustainability and predictability, as business is not at the mercy of the fluctuating economic situation of only one entertainment sector. In conclusion, it has to be acknowledged that a lot of the play experiences now available to us, are more or less hybrid experiences, combinations of physical and digital elements.

Bibliography

Apperley, T.H. and D. Jaymane. Game Studies' Material Turn. *Westminster Papers* 9, no.1, 2012: 5–25.

Belk, R.W. Possession and the Extended Self. *The Journal of Consumer Research* 15, no 2, 1988: 139–168.

Belk, R.W. Extended Self in a Digital World. *The Journal of Consumer Research* 40, no 3, 2013: 477–500.

Bull, M. *Sounding Out the City: Personal Stereos and the Management of Everyday Life.* Oxford & New York: Berg Publishers, 2000.

Buckingham, D. & J. Shefton-Green. Structure, Agency, and Pedagogy in Children's Media Culture. In Tobin, J. (ed.) *Pikachu's Global Adventure: The Rise and Fall of Pokémon*. Durham & London: Duke University Press, 2004: 12–33.

Consalvo, M. and N. Dutton. Game Analysis: Developing a Methodological Toolkit for The Qualitative Study of Games. *Game Studies* 6, no 1, 2006.

Dyer-Witheford, N. and G. de Peuter. *Games of Empire: Global Capitalism and Video Games*. Minneapolis: University of Minnesota Press, 2009.

Enevold, J. Domesticating Play, Designing Everyday Life: The Practice and Performance of Family, Gender, and Gaming. In *Proceedings of DiGRA Nordic 2012 Conference: Local and Global Games in Culture and Society*. Tampere: University of Tampere, 2012. Retrieved from: http://www.digra.org/wp-content/uploads/digital-library/12168.15073.pdf

Fleming, P. Workers' Playtime?: Boundaries and Cynicism in a "Culture of Fun" Program. *Journal of Applied Behavioral Science* 41, no. 3, 2005: 285–303.

GamePolitics. 'Rovio Wins Counterfeit Toy Lawsuit. Awarded $700K in Damages.' *Game-Politics*, Mar 24. 2014. Retrieved from: http://www.gamepolitics.com/2014/03/24/rovio-wins-counterfeit-toy-lawsuit-awarded-700k-damages

Giddings, S. Playing with Non-humans: Digital Games as Techno-cultural Form. In *Proceedings of DiGRA 2005 Conference: Changing Views - Worlds in Play*. Vancouver: University of Vancouver, 2005. Retrieved from http://www.digra.org/dl/db/06278.24323.pdf

Giddings S. Towards The Phenomenology of Angry Birds, 2014. Retrieved from: http://www.microethology.net/towards-the-phenomenology-of-angry-birds/

Huhtamo, E. and J. Parikka (eds.). *Media Archaeology: Approaches, Applications, and Implications*. Berkeley, Los Angeles & London: University of California Press, 2011.

Information Solutions Group. *2012 PopCap Games Mobile Gaming Research – Where People Play Mobile Games*, 2012. Retrieved from: http://www.infosolutionsgroup.com/2012_PopCap_Where_People_Play_Mobile _Games.pdf

Jenkins, H. *Convergence Culture: Where Old and New Media Collide*. New York: New York University Press, 2006.

Jones, P., D. Comfort & D. Hillier. Playing The Game: Corporate Social Responsibility and The Games Industry. *Journal of Public Affairs* 13, no. 3, 2013: 335–344.

Juul, J. *A Casual Revolution: Reinventing Video Games and Their Players*. Cambridge (Mass.) & London: MIT Press, 2010.

Kerr, A. *The Business and Culture of Digital Games: Gamework and Gameplay*. London, Thousand Oaks & New Delhi: Sage Publications, 2006.

Kline, S., N. Dyer-Witheford, and G. de Peuter. *Digital Play: The Interaction of Technology, Culture, and Marketing*. Montreal & Kingston: McGill-Queen's University Press, 2003.

Kücklich, J. Precarious Playbour: Modders and the Digital Games Industry. *Fibreculture* 5, 2005. Retrieved from: http://www.journal.fibreculture.org/issue5/kucklich.html

Lauwaert, M. *The Place of Play: Toys and Digital Cultures*. Amsterdam: Amsterdam University Press, 2009.

Mahtani, S. 'Angry Birds Descend Upon Singapore'. *The Wall Street Journal Southeast Asia*, Sep 21. 2011. Retrieved from: http://blogs.wsj.com/searealtime/2011/09/21/angry-birds-descend-upon-singapore/

Miller, D. *Stuff*. Cambridge & Malden: Polity, 2010.

Miller, G. 'Angry Birds Trilogy Coming to PS3, 360 and 3DS'. *IGN*, Sep 25. 2012. Retrieved from: http://www.ign.com/articles/2012/07/10/angry-birds-trilogy-coming-to-ps3-360-and-3ds

Montfort, N. and I. Bogost. *Racing the Beam: The Atari Video Computer System*. Cambridge (Mass.) & London: MIT Press, 2009.

Parikka, J. & Suominen, J. Victorian Snakes? Towards A Cultural History of Mobile Games and the Experience of Movement. *Game Studies* 6, no 1, 2006.

Peteri V., J. Luomanen and P. Alasuutari. Materiality of Digital Environments. *Widerscreen*, 1/2013. Retrieved from http://widerscreen.fi/numerot/2013-1/materiality-of-digital-environments/

de Peuter, G & N. Dyer-Witheford. "EA Spouse" and the Crisis of Video Game Labour: Enjoyment, Exclusion, Exploitation, Exodus. *Canadian Journal of Communication* 31, no 3, 2006. Retrieved from: http://www.cjconline.ca/index.php/journal/article/view/1771/1893

Roininen, T. *The Quality of Life in The Finnish Game Industry*. Master's Thesis. Jyväskylä: University of Jyväskylä, 2013. Retrieved from: https://jyx.jyu.fi/dspace/handle/123456789/42687

Sheff, D. *Game Over: How Nintendo Conquered The World*. New York: Random House, 1993.

Simon, B. Geek Chic: Machine Aesthetics, Digital Gaming, and the Cultural Politics of the Case Mod. *Games and Culture* 2, no. 3, 2007: 175–193.

Sotamaa, O. *The Player's Game: Towards Understanding Player Production Among Computer Game Cultures*. Tampere: University of Tampere, 2009.

Suoninen, A. (2014) *Lasten mediabarometri 2013: 0–8-vuotiaiden mediankäyttö ja sen muutokset vuodesta 2010*. Helsinki: Nuorisotutkimusverkoston julkaisut, 2014. Retrieved from: http://www.nuorisotutkimusseura.fi/julkaisuja/lastenmediabarometri2013.pdf

Taylor, T. L. *Play Between Worlds: Exploring Online Game Culture*. Cambridge (Mass.) & London: MIT Press, 2006.

Toivonen, S. and O. Sotamaa. Of Discs, Boxes and Cartridges: The Material Life of Digital Games. In *Proceedings of DiGRA 2011 Conference: Think Design Play*. Hilversum: Utrecht School of the Arts, 2011. Retrieved from http://www.digra.org/dl/db/11312.23263.pdf

Turkle, S. *Alone Together: Why We Expect More from Technology and Less from Each Other*. New York: Basic Books, 2011.

Tyni, H., A. Kultima and F. Mäyrä. Dimensions of Hybrid in Playful Products. In *Proceedings of Academic Mindtrek 2013*. New York: ACM, 2013: 237–244.

Van Campenhout, L. D. E., J. W. Frens, C. J. Overbeeke, A. Standaert & H. Peremans. Physical Interaction in A Dematerialized World. *International Journal of Design* 7, no 1, 2013: 1–18.

Wilson, J., C. Chesher, L. Hjorth and I. Richardson. Distractedly Engaged: Mobile Gaming and Convergent Mobile Media. *Convergence: The International Journal of Research into New Media Technologies* 17, no. 4, 2011: 351–355.

Östergren M. & Juhlin, O. Car Drivers Using Sound Pryer – Field Trials on Shared Music Listening in Traffic Encounters. In O'Hara, K. & B. Brown (eds.) *Consuming Music Together: Social and Collaborative Aspects of Music Consumption*. Dordrecht: Springer, 2006: 173–190.

80

NINTENDO® AND NEW WORLD TRAVEL WRITING

A dialogue

Mary Fuller and Henry Jenkins

Source: Steven G. Jones (ed.), *Cybersociety: Computer-Mediated Communication and Community* (Thousand Oaks, CA: Sage Publications, 1995), pp. 57–72.

Mary Fuller: We want to start by telling you two stories.

Henry Jenkins: Here's the first. Princess Toadstool is kidnapped by the savage King Koopa. Two brave brothers, Mario and Luigi, depart on a series of adventures to rescue her. Mario and Luigi, simple men of humble beginnings (in fact, Italian American plumbers), cross a vast unexplored space, encountering strange creatures, struggling against an inhospitable landscape. Finally, they confront and best the monarch and his minions in a life and death struggle. In the process, the Super Mario Brothers not only restore the princess to her people but also exert control over this strange new world and its curious resources.

MF: My story is really a collection of stories, which I can probably evoke for you in some form just by mentioning a few key words: Walter Raleigh, Roanoke, the Lost Colony, Virginia Dare. Or Jamestown, John Smith, Pocahontas, John Rolfe. I want to draw for the moment not on the complexities and particularities of these stories but on what is simple and popular, what can be evoked as an indistinct impression: the saleable, inaccurate, recurrent myth of the captive princess and her rescuers (Virginia Dare, the first child born in what was to become the "Lost Colony"; Pocahontas, a genuine princess who became a candidate for rescue—or kidnapping—thanks to her own gesture of rescuing John Smith; Smith himself, both a hero of humble origins and a kind of princess in drag who represented his entire career as a repeated experience of captivity and rescue by women; or, for that matter, Virginia itself, personified by English apologists for colonization as a virgin to be rescued from savages). Nintendo®'s Princess Toadstool and Mario Brothers is a cognate version of this story.

141

What we want to get at is not these alluring narratives of Princess Toadstool, Pocahontas, and Virginia Dare (or of Mario, Luigi, and John Smith) but another shared concern in our material that seems to underlie these more memorable fictions in a constitutive way. Both terms of our title evoke explorations and colonizations of space: the physical space navigated, mapped, and mastered by European voyagers and travelers in the 16th and 17th centuries and the fictional, digitally projected space traversed, mapped, and mastered by players of Nintendo® video games. Simply put, we want to argue that the movement in space that the rescue plot seems to motivate is itself the point, the topic, and the goal and that this shift in emphasis from narrativity to geography produces features that make Nintendo® and New World narratives in some ways strikingly similar to each other and different from many other kinds of texts.

HJ: This chapter is the result of a series of conversations we've been having over the past four years. Our conversations began with hesitant efforts by each of us to understand the other's area of specialization but have grown in frequency and intensity as we began to locate points of contact between our work. We hope that what follows will reflect the process of that exchange, opening questions for future discussion rather than providing answers for immediate consumption.

MF: This work is a confessedly exploratory attempt at charting some possibilities of dialogue and communication between the disparate professional spaces we inhabit. Yet the association between computer software and the Renaissance "discovery" of America is not exactly new. A computer software firm in Boston claims in its advertisement, "Sir Francis Drake was knighted for what we do every day . . . The spirit of exploration is alive at **The Computer Merchant**" *(Boston Computer Currents*, September 1990, p. 34). More generally, discussions of virtual reality have widely adopted a language borrowed from this earlier era: One headline reads, "THE RUSH IS ON ! COLONIZING CYBERSPACE" *(Mondo2000*, Summer 1990, no. 2, cover).

HJ: The description and analysis of virtual reality technologies as the opening up of a new frontier, a movement from known to unknown space, responds to our contemporary sense of America as oversettled, overly familiar, and overpopulated. Howard Rheingold's (1991) *Virtual Reality* unselfconsciously mimics the rhetoric of earlier promoters and settlers when he promises to share with his readers the account of "my own odyssey to the outposts of a new scientific frontier . . . and an advanced glimpse of a possible new world in which reality itself might become a manufactured and metered commodity" (p. 17). Or consider Timothy Leary's proclamation in that same book: "We live in a cyber-culture surrounded by limitless deposits of information which can be digitalized and tapped by the individual equipped with cybergear . . . . There are no limits on virtual reality" (Rheingold, 1991, p. 378). Virtual reality opens new spaces for exploration, colonization, and exploitation, returning to a mythic time when there were worlds without limits and resources beyond imagining. Technologists speak of the "navigational systems" necessary to guide us through this uncharted realm. The advent of this new technological sphere meets the needs of a national culture which, as Brenda Laurel suggests, finds contemporary reality "too small for the human imagination" (quoted in Rheingold, 1991, p. 391). Few of us have donned goggles and power gloves to become settlers of this new cyberspace, although both heroic and nightmarish accounts of virtual reality proliferate in popular culture. Many of us have, however, interacted with digitalized space through Nintendo® games. We felt it might be productive to take seriously for a moment these metaphors of "new worlds" and "colonization" as we look more closely at the spatial logic and "cognitive mapping" of video games.

MF: One has to wonder why these heroic metaphors of discovery have been adopted by popularizers of the new technologies just as these metaphors are undergoing sustained critique in other areas of the culture, a critique that hardly anyone can be unaware of in the year after the quincentenary of Columbus's first American landfall. When John Barlow (1990) writes that "Columbus was probably the last person to behold so much usable and unclaimed real estate (or unreal estate) as these cybernauts have discovered" (p. 37), the comparison to cyberspace drains out the materiality of the place Columbus discovered, and the nonvirtual bodies of the pre-Columbian inhabitants who did, in fact, claim it, however unsuccessfully. I would speculate that part of the drive behind the rhetoric of virtual reality as a New World or new frontier is the desire to recreate the Renaissance encounter with America without guilt: This time, if there are others present, they really won't be human (in the case of Nintendo® characters), or if they are, they will be other players like ourselves, whose bodies are not jeopardized by the virtual weapons we wield. The prospect of seeing VR as a revisionary reenactment of earlier history raises issues that we address only in passing: One would be the ethics and consequences of such a historical revision; another would be to ask whether it *is* accurate to say that VR is unlike Renaissance discovery in having no victims, that at no point does it register harmfully on real bodies that are not the bodies of its users. These kinds of questions frame our discussion, which has a narrower focus on the specificities of Nintendo® games and voyage narratives as rhetorical and cultural artifacts. If the simple celebration of expansiveness borrowed from the age of discovery for virtual reality no longer seems adequate to the texts and experiences it once described, it seems no less important to map the narrative and rhetorical configurations of these texts themselves, which have provided model and metaphor for so much later experience, their authors', in Derek Walcott's (1986) words, "ancestral murderers and poets" (p. 79).

The kinds of New World documents I have in mind are ones like Columbus's *Diario* (1492–1493) or Walter Raleigh's *Discoverie of the large, rich and beautiful empire of Guiana* (1596) or John Smith's *True Relation of such occurrences and accident sof noate as hath hapned in Virginia* (1608)—that is, chronologically structured narratives of voyage and exploration, from ships' logs to more elaborate texts. At the outset, one might expect these narratives of travel to and return from what was at least conceptually another world to assume a different kind of structure than, in fact, they do: a romance or quest motif, the ironic contrasts of utopian fiction, or at least an overt "theme." Such expectations are largely disappointed. One literary critic complains that the travel journal underwent no sustained development as a literary form but conforms more or less consistently to a formulaic pattern: "The abstract reads, we sailed, did and saw this and this, suffered and were saved or lost, made such and such encounters with the savages, hungered, thirsted, and were storm worn, but some among us came home" (Page, 1973, p. 37). Part of the problem lies outside the texts, in that practical strategies embedded in the material diverge from the demands of narrative coherence: the same critic complains that the carefully prepared climax of Jacques Cartier's *Brief Reedit is* spoiled when Cartier decides to sail for home instead of waiting for a long anticipated Indian attack. Reading the voyage narratives from the perspective of conventional narrative expectations is an experience of almost unremitting frustration. Yet these texts, if they are not conventional narratives, are equally clearly not transparent records of an experience that itself demands no commentary. On the contrary.

And so one wants first to find a way of characterizing their structure and its shaping imperatives on its own terms and second, to account for their reception, their uses and pleasures for audiences then and now. This is material that was produced and printed in extraordinary quantity. Richard Hakluyt, one of the founding members of the Virginia Company, made a lasting name for himself by collecting and publishing documents of voyages by his contemporaries, documents ranging the gamut of possibilities from ethnographic survey to narrative poem to navigational instructions. Hakluyt's first collection appeared in 1582 as a slim quarto volume. By 1601, the third and final collection, *The Principal Navigations . . . of the English Nation*, took up three large folio volumes totaling almost 900 pages (12 volumes in the modern edition). Hakluyt's work was continued by Samuel Purchas, whose *Hakluytus Posthumus*, appearing in 1625, had expanded to 4,262 pages. Simply on the basis of volume, these documents would impose themselves on our attention, whatever their narrative shape.

HJ: Nintendo®, similarly, plays an increasingly visible role with the American imagination. By the end of 1990, one of three homes in the United States owned a Nintendo® system. My household was one of them, and I wanted to know more about how we might discuss these phenomenally popular games as cultural artifacts, as popular narratives, and as a new media for mass communication. As I discovered when asked to review two recent books on Nintendo® (Kinder, 1991;

Provenzo, 1991; see Jenkins, 1993), current accounts lack any serious discussion of the particularity of Nintendo® as a means of organizing cultural experience; the writers fail to address what it meant to be playing the games rather than watching or reading them. Both books seemed interested in talking about Nintendo® for other reasons: in one case in terms of issues of pedagogy, in the other in terms of issues of intertextuality but both offered accounts that presuppose that traditional narrative theory (be it literary or film theory) can account for our experience of Nintendo® in terms of plots and characters.

This application of conventional models to an emergent form seemed unsatisfying because it ignores the way that game players discuss the experience of play and the ways that the games are marketed to their consumers. Plot is not a central feature of Nintendo®"s sales pitch. Ads talked about interactivity rather than characterization ("Nintendo® gives you power to choose") and about atmospheres rather than story lines ("awesome graphics"). Nintendo®, a 100-year-old playing card company little known outside Japan, revitalized the declining American video game market by moving from the simple, abstracted spaces of Pong or Pac-Man(TM) to create an ever changing and visually fascinating arena for play.

Nintendo®'s central feature is its constant presentation of spectacular spaces (or "worlds," to use the game parlance). Its landscapes dwarf characters who serve, in turn, primarily as vehicles for players to move through these remarkable places. Once immersed in playing, we don't really care whether we rescue Princess Toadstool or not; all that matters is staying alive long enough to move between levels, to see what spectacle awaits us on the next screen. Mario's journey may take him by raft across a river of red hot molten lava, may require him to jump from platform to platform across a suspended city, or may ask him to make his way through a subterranean cavern as its ceiling collapses around him. The protagonist of a sword and sorcery game may struggle against a stormy sea, battle a massive serpent, confront a pack of wolves who rule a frozen wasteland, or combat an army of the dead that erupt from the trembling earth, all in search of lost fortunes and buried gold. A game like *Lemmings* puts us in charge of an army of tiny creatures, willing slaves who live and die at our bidding and who dig tunnels or construct bridges to allow us to continue to venture deeper into the game space. For the most part, the technological limitations of the game systems mean that we move left to right through this space, but designers may simulate other kinds of movement, such as an elevator in the *Ninja Turtles* game that allows us to battle our way higher and higher into Shredder's command center or racing games that allow us to skim forward along a winding racetrack getting closer and closer to the glistening city that looms on the horizon. The more sophisticated Super Nintendo® system allows for multiple levels of graphics that interact with each other in ever more complex fashions. The art of game design comes in constructing a multitude of different ways we can interact with these visually remarkable spaces.

Most of the criteria by which we might judge a classically constructed narrative fall by the wayside when we look at these games as storytelling systems. In Nintendo®'s narratives, characters play a minimal role, displaying traits that are largely capacities for action: fighting skills, modes of transportation, preestablished goals. The game's dependence on characters (Ninja Turtles, Bart Simpson, etc.) borrowed from other media allows them to simply evoke those characters rather than to fully develop them. The character is little more than a cursor that mediates the player's relationship to the story world. Activity drains away the characters' strength, as measured by an ever shifting graph at the top of the screen, but it cannot build character, since these figures lack even the most minimal interiority. Similarly, plot is transformed into a generic atmosphere—a haunted house, a subterranean cavern, a futuristic cityscape, an icy wilderness—that the player can explore. This process becomes most visible when we look at games adapted from existing films or television programs; here, moments in the narrative trajectory become places in the player's itinerary, laid out as a succession of worlds we must travel through in order to reach our goals. Playing time unfolds in a fixed and arbitrary fashion with no responsiveness to the psychological time of the characters, sometimes flowing too slow to facilitate player interest and blocking the advance of the plot action, other times moving so fast that we can't react quickly enough to new situations or the clock runs out before we complete our goals. Exposition occurs primarily at the introduction and closing of games: For instance, the opening of Super Mario World reminds us that the Princess has once again been kidnapped. The game's conclusion displays the reunion of Princess and champion and a kind of victory tour over the lands that Mario has conquered. But these sequences are "canned": Players cannot control or intervene in them. Often, a player simply flashes past this exposition to get into the heart of the action. These framing stories with their often arbitrary narrative goals play little role in the actual experience of the games, as plot gives way quickly to a more flexible period of spatial exploration. Although plot structures (kidnapping and rescue, pursuit and capture, street fighting, invasion and defense) are highly repetitive (repeated from game to game and over and over within the game, with little variety), what never loses its interest is the promise of moving into the next space, of mastering these worlds and making them your own playground. So although the child's play is framed by narrative logic, it remains largely uncontrolled by plot dictates.

The pleasure of spatial spectacle may be most visible in games that do not seem to require anything more than the most rudimentary spaces. *Street Fighter II* (TM), one of the most popular Nintendo® games in recent years, basically centers around a kickboxing tournament that could have been staged in any arena. The game, however, offers players a global array of possible spaces where the individual competitions can occur: a Brazilian dock, an Indian temple, a Chinese street market, a Soviet factory, a Las Vegas show palace. In the Indian sequence, elephants sway their trunks in the background. Water drips from the ceiling into a Japanese reflecting pool. In Spain, flamenco dancers strut and crowds cheer as the combatants struggle for dominance. All of these details constitute a form of visual excess ("eye candy," as computer enthusiasts call it), a conspicuous consumption of space. Such spectacular visions are difficult to program, unnecessary to the competition, yet seem central to the game's marketing success.

MF: It sounds to me as if not only space but culture is being consumed, used and also used up as local cultures from India to Las Vegas shrink into a procession of ornamental images. Each is "colorful," yet none is really alien. Certainly, the ability to register local differences varied among Renaissance travel narratives: The same image might begin its career as close observation at first hand and reappear in progressively more stylized and ornamental forms detached from its original reference, as John White's drawings of North Carolina Algonquians reappeared on the engraved frontispiece to Theodor de Bry's *America* and were, in turn, reproduced as illustrations for John Smith's adventures in Virginia. One might also think of the famous Rouen entry of Henri II, where an entire Tupi village was recreated, employed for a day or so as a place for the performance of Brazilian life, and then burned.

If Nintendo® feeds the appetite for encountering a succession of new spaces (as well as helping to create such an appetite), that same appetite was, of course, central to these New World narratives. In turn, there were pressures on texts to conform to a locodescriptive form, the equivalent in writing of Nintendo®'s scrolling succession of spaces. One precursor of the travel narrative would be the logbook, in which a grid divides the page into spaces for date, time, compass bearing, wind, speed, and, finally, notes. The logbook presents a succession of indexed spaces on the page that correspond to a succession of days and places. Implicitly, each of these spaces is of equal importance: The grid predisposes its user to make *some* notes in each space but not too many. Although the logbook was a technical tool of long-distance navigation, its form strongly influenced landbased narratives that followed arrival.

As an instance of a locodescriptive project both in action and writing, John Smith's strategy of successively exploring and mapping all the rivers around Jamestown contrasted with the Virginia Company's desire to impose grander, more recognizable, and more goal-oriented trajectories on the travels of the colonists: to find a gold mine, a passage to China, or Raleigh's Lost Colony. These ultimate objectives, held as in suspension, enabled Smith's presence in Virginia and his day-by-day progress through the natural and human geography of the Chesapeake. This configuration, of "story" as pretext for narratives of space, is (as we suggested at the outset) a common one in this material. Voyages and narratives that set out in search of a significant, motivating goal had a strong tendency to defer it, replacing arrival at that goal (and the consequent shift to another kind of activity) with a particularized account of the travel itself and what was seen and done. Hernan Cortes (1986) walked into Tenochtitlan in 1534, becoming master of its gold and other resources; yet the bulk of his Second and Third Letters concerns not this period of achieved conquest and consumption but the survey of points on the way there and then a second survey of points passed through on the drive to reconquer the city through more conventional military means. Even goal-driven narratives like those of Raleigh or Columbus at best offered only dubious signs of proximity in place of arrival—at China, El Dorado, the town of the Amazons—phenomena that, interpreted, erroneously suggested it was just over the horizon, to be deferred to some later date.

Rhetorical as well as documentary goals bear on the narratives, which aim not only to describe but to persuade. That is, Walter Raleigh wanted to find El Dorado, and he also wanted to produce a narrative that would stimulate interest in Guiana and persuade Elizabeth to restore him to favor. The imperative that operates on his text in consequence is less that of coherence than of completeness, a (doubtless, loaded) inventory of what was done and seen, one that provided at once both an alternate, more diffuse kind of justification for the discovery and motives and informational resources for a repeat performance. Ralph Lane, one of the Roanoke Colony's governors, noted that the particularity of his account is "to the end it may appear to you . . . that there wanted no great good will . . . to have perfected this discovery" – of a rumored mine the company never set out towards (Lane, 1979, p. 309). Even in the *Discoverie of Guiana*, a text whose teleology is announced in the title, the actual search for Guiana, the narrative concomitants of searching for something, get lost in a welter of details, of events and places that have little to do with El Dorado but that occupied the days of the voyage. The sequenced inventories of places and events replace, defer, and attest to an authentic and exculpating desire for goals the voyages almost invariably failed to reach.

Given the inconclusiveness I've described, it was the ability to move in space (rather than to arrive) that generated and structured narrative; John Smith wrote primarily about the times he was in motion, not the times he was sitting in Jamestown. The resulting narratives were, in turn, organized by elapsed time (sequences of dates) but also determined by it. Henry mentioned that "characters" in Nintendo® can be described less in terms of learning and transformation than in terms of resources gradually expended in the course of the game. This sense of a trajectory dictated not by change or crisis but by expenditure, the gradual running out of a fixed quantity of time or resources, is an almost universal feature of the narratives I study because it was an equally frequent phenomenon in the voyages and colonial experiments they document. Many documents record the consequences of poorly managing resources—the season for sailing passing as one sits windbound in an English harbor, a crew mutinying at the idea of sailing beyond Ireland, food running out in the middle of the winter or the middle of the ocean (this one over and over), having to write home hypothetical accounts of the treasures you would discover if you had better boats or more food or it were not so late in the year. These documents end not because some resolution or conclusion has been achieved but because something has run out. To give another example, John Smith's ability to trade for corn to feed a starving colony was unarguably more critical than the story about the rescue of the Lost Colony that the Virginia Company tried to impose on him or the story about Pocahontas that he recounted 16 years after the event and 6 years after her death.

HJ: Although we've noted the experimental nature of this chapter's juxtapositions, there is, in fact, a precedent for them in Michel De Certeau's work in successive books on New World discourse *(Heterologies,* 1984a) and on the politics of consumption in contemporary popular culture *(The Practice of Everyday Life,* 1984b). While we are claiming space as the organizing principle for two kinds of narrative, as what makes them different from novels, for example, De Certeau (1984b) lays out a grand claim for spatial relations as the central organizing principle of all narratives: "Every story is a travel story—a spatial practice" (p. 115). Our cultural need for narrative can be linked to our search for believable, memorable, and primitive spaces, and stories are told to account for our current possession or desire for territory.

De Certeau's analysis of "spatial stories" provides tools for talking about classes of narratives that have proven difficult to discuss in terms of traditional notions of plot or character. Consider, for example, the emergence of science fiction in the late 19th and early 20th century as a means of creating imaginary spaces for our intellectual exploration. The adventure stories of Jules Verne drew upon centuries of travel writing as they recounted a variety of trips to the moon, under the sea, into the center of the earth, or around the globe. The technological utopian writers often created static plots (a man from our present goes to the future) that allowed them simply to describe the landscape of tomorrow; one can draw a direct line from the moment in Edward Bellamy's *Looking Backward,* where the book's protagonist stands on his balcony and surveys Boston's future, to the train cars that allowed visitors to the 1939 New York World's Fair to ride above and look down upon Futurama. Hugo Gernsback's *Amazing Stories* magazine was full of chronicles of "odysseys" across the uncharted wilderness of Mars or Venus and encounters along the way with strange flora and fauna. Writers often modeled these aliens' worlds after the American West so that they could cross-market their stories to both western and science fiction pulps. A focus on plot and characterization was slow to develop in this genre that seemed so obsessed with going "where no one has gone before."

A similar claim could be made for various forms of fantasy writing. Trips to Oz or Narnia or through the looking glass, adventures in Middle Earth, or quests for the Grail all seem to center as much on the movement of characters through space as on the larger plot goals that motivate and give shape to those movements. Maps appear in fantasy novels with the same frequency and function that genealogies appear in the great 19th-century novels, suggesting the relative stress the two forms give to spatial relations and character relations. It is not surprising that science fiction, fantasy, and sword- and-sorcery stories provide much of the iconography of the Nintendo® games.

Nintendo® may also be linked to another class of spatial stories, the amusement park rides that as early as turn-of-the-century Coney Island adopted popular fictions into spaces we can visit and explore. Walt Disney's *Peter Pan* becomes a ride by flying ship across the landscape of London and Never-Never-Land, *Snow White* turns into a runaway mine car tour, and *20,000 Leagues Under the Sea is* remade into a submarine ride. The introduction of virtual reality technology to the Orlando, Florida, amusement parks results in a succession of ever more intense "tours" of the stars, the oceans, the human body, the World of Hanna-Barbera, and the dawn of time. Nintendo®'s constant adaptation of plot-centered contemporary films into spatial narratives represents a miniaturization of this same process. The tamed frontier of the virtual new world has, from the first, been sold to us as a playground for our world-weary imagination, as a site of tourism and recreation rather than labor and production. Public interest in virtual reality is directly linked to the amusement park's long history of satisfying popular demand for spatial difference, spectacular attractions, affective stimulation, and sensual simulation. De Certeau's description of Jules Verne's stories as focused around the related images of the *Nautilus*'s porthole (a windowpane that "allows us to see") and the iron rail (that allows us to "move through" fantastic realms) has its obvious parallels in these amusement park attractions that invite us to look upon and travel through but not to touch these spectacular spaces (De Certeau, 1984b, p. 112). What is a spectacle at the amusement park ("Keep your hands in the car at all times") becomes a site of more immediate interaction in the Nintendo® game that asks us to act upon and transform the places it opens to our vision.

MF: Voyage narratives were almost never presented as recreative texts, whatever they might become for later readers. Two exceptions are Richard Willes's *Historie of travel* (London, 1577) and Andre Thevet's *Les singularitez de la France antarctique* (Paris, 1558). Although a narrative like Thomas Harriot's *Brief and True Report of the New Found Land of Virginia* (London, 1588) might offer a catalogue of America's abundant flora and fauna, the items of the catalogue were presented not as strange things to wonder at but as "marchantable commodities," goods for use and sale, the potential for industrious activity. Leisure in the New World was pejoratively characterized as idleness, associated with disease, mendacity, and social disorder. In most places the English settled, colonists had to do some work to feed and shelter themselves; when a company shipwrecked on the uninhabited Bermudas and found an Edenic land of temperate weather and dreamlike abundance, its leaders found means to take the company back to starvation in Jamestown. The project of colonizing itself was, in the English case, less a matter of acquiring a native workforce than of finding work for what contemporaries envisioned as the teeming masses of England's unemployed. Virginia's colonists were there (at least in theory) to labor, not to look, and labor was directed to activating the commercial potentials of the land.

HJ: For De Certeau (1984b), narrative involves the transformation of place into space (pp. 117–118). Places exist only in the abstract, as potential sites for narrative action, as locations that have not yet been colonized. Place may be understood here in terms of the potential contained as bytes in the Nintendo® game cartridge or the potential resources coveted but not yet possessed in the American New World. Places constitute a "stability" which must be disrupted in order for stories to unfold. Places are there but do not yet matter, much as the New World existed, was geographically present, and culturally functioning well before it became the center of European ambitions or the site of New World narratives. Places become meaningful only as they come into contact with narrative agents (and in the construction of the New World in Mary's Renaissance stories, only Europeans are understood as narrative agents). Spaces, on the other hand, are places that have been acted upon, explored, colonized. Spaces become the location of narrative events. As I play a Nintendo® game and master it level by level, I realize the potentials encoded in the software design and turn it into the landscape of my own saga.

The place-space distinction is closely linked to De Certeau's discussion of the differences between "maps" and "tours" as means of representing real-world geographies. Maps are abstracted accounts of spatial relations ("the girl's room is next to the kitchen"), whereas tours are told from the point of view of the traveler/ narrator ("You turn right and come into the living room") (De Certeau, 1984b, pp. 118–122). Maps document places; tours describe movements through spaces. The rhetoric of the tour thus contains within it attention to the effects of the tour, its goals and potentials, its limitations and obligations. A door is a feature of a place, or it may be a potential threshold between two spaces. One of my favorite games, *A Boy and His Blob*, places the resources of its imaginary world fully at our disposal. The blob can be transformed into everything from a blowtorch to a stepladder depending on what flavored jellybean we feed him, and as a result, the mutating blob contains endless possibilities for acting upon and transforming the virtual playing space. The pleasure of the game lies in creating our own paths, tunneling down deeper and deeper into its cavernous world. The blob, the various levels, the jellybeans exist as potentials that only become narratively meaningful when we act upon them and bring them into our control.

De Certeau is thus interested in analyzing and documenting the process by which we "mark off boundaries" within the narrative world, by which characters map, act upon, and gain control over narrative spaces. Just as narratives involve movement from stability through instability and back again, narratives also involve a constant transformation of unfamiliar places into familiar spaces. Stories, he argues, are centrally concerned with "the relationship between the frontier and the bridge, that is, between a (legitimate) space and its (alien) exteriority" (De Certeau, 1984b, p. 126). He continues: "The story endlessly marks out frontiers. It multiplies them, but in terms of interactions among characters—things, animals, human beings" (De Certeau, 1984b, p. 126). Plot actions, he argues, involve the process of appropriation and displacement of space, a struggle for possession and control over the frontier or journeys across the bridges that link two spaces together. Such terms will, of course, be familiar to anyone who has thought about the discovery and colonization of America. Yet Nintendo® also enacts a constant struggle along the lines that separate known and unknown spaces—the line of the frontier—which is where the player encounters dangerous creatures and brutal savages, where we fight for possession and control over the story world. As De Certeau (1984b) notes, the central narrative question posed by a frontier is "to whom does it belong?" (p. 127). The frontier here is apt to be technological and urban rather than primitive and pastoral (or, as in the Mario Brothers games, a strange mix of the two) but then Mary's settlers were also mapping their adventures on spaces already occupied by someone else's culture. The frontier line is literalized through the breakdown of story space into a series of screens. The narrative space is not all visible at once. One must push toward the edge of the screen to bring more space into view.

The games also often create a series of goalposts that not only marks our progress through the game space but also determines our dominance over it. Once you've mastered a particular space, moved past its goalpost, you can reassume play at that point no matter the outcome of a particular round. These mechanisms help us to map our growing mastery over the game world, our conquest of its virtual real estate. Even in the absence of such a mechanism, increased understanding of the geography, biology, and physics of the different worlds makes it easy to return quickly to the same spot and move further into the frontier.

A related feature of the games are warp zones—secret passages that, like De Certeau's bridges, accelerate one's movement through the narrative geography and bring two or more worlds together. Knowledge about warp zones, passwords, and other game secrets are key items of social exchange between game players. More to the point, they have become important aspects of the economic exchange between game companies and players. Nintendo® engages in a playful yet lucrative form of "insider trading," selling secret tips about traversing the game space to consumers either through 1-900 hotlines or through subscriptions to *Nintendo® Power* magazine, which markets detailed maps of the many worlds and levels of popular games and tips for coping with the local flora and fauna or crossing difficult terrain.

The maps and charts that Nintendo® Power publishes are curious documents. Strictly speaking, they are not maps at all, not abstract representations of geographic places. The magazine simply unfolds the information contained on many different screens as a continuous image that shows us the narrative space from the player's point of view, more or less as it will be experienced in the game. (The closest analogy would be something like Japanese scroll painting.) Surrounding these successive representations of the screen space is a narration or "tour" that identifies features of the landscape and their potentials for narrative action, as in this text from a discussion of *Adventure Island 3*: "Lush jungle regions dominate Stage 2. However, a remote island to the southwest appears to be snowed under.

How unusual! One of the largest waterfalls known to mankind will be encountered in Stage 2. Its cascading torrents may be too much for the loin-clothed island hero. To the south, Higgins will be lost in the mist". The text may also suggest possible ways of acting upon this space and point toward the forms of resources and knowledge needed to survive there: "The Spiders shouldn't give Higgins too much trouble. Some move up and down and some of them don't. There may be hidden Eggs in places such as this." At times, the text may also focus our attention back onto the larger narrative context, onto character disputes or goals that frame the game action: "The volcanos are erupting! Higgins had better act fast so he can rescue his girlfriend and get out of there. Because of the tremendous heat, the supply of fruit is shrinking. There won't be much time for decision making. The aliens, astonished that Higgins made it this far, will be waiting!" ("Adventure Island 3," *Nintendo® Power*, October 1992, no. 41, pp. 8–13)

Such representations of virtual space bear close resemblance to De Certeau's description of early maps that "included only the rectilinear marking out of itineraries (performative indications chiefly concerning pilgrimages), along with the stops one was to make (cities which one was to pass through, spend the night in, pray at, etc.) and distances calculated in hours or in days, that is, in terms of the time it would take to cover them on foot. Each of these maps is a memorandum prescribing actions" (De Certeau, 1984b, p. 120). Much like these earlier maps, the Nintendo® documentation focuses on the specific narrative actions to be performed upon these spaces, purposes to be pursued and sites to be visited, rather than a universalized account of the possible places that exist independent of the reader's goals and desires. In most cases, however, the game company withholds crucial information, and the final stage of the game remains unmapped and undocumented. Players must still venture into an unfamiliar and uncharted space to confront unknown perils if they wish to master the game.

MF: As Henry's citation from De Certeau suggests, we might locate Nintendo®'s treatment of space in relation to a history of cartography. The Renaissance was, in fact, the moment when mapmaking shifted from providing locally oriented maps of previous trajectories and observations by coastal navigators (rutters) to the universalized overview of the Mercator projection. Yet the "universalized overview" was still conceptual rather than actual; the information needed to map the globe was still being gathered in arenas of intense competition and secrecy.

I've suggested that the particularized accounts of travel offered by narratives like Smith's or Raleigh's more or less deliberately replaced arrival with the details of travel as a process. These details, of course, were not only substitutive but also served practical purposes of their own, guiding both future voyagers and investors in the voyages. Printed books like Richard Hakluyt's collection of voyage narratives or Smith's General History were routinely carried by ships on voyages of trade and settlement. Observing this weight given to narratives, one might describe a shift in the center of value from things to be discovered to information about the terrain covered en route. When Hakluyt describes the capture of the Portuguese carrack Madre de Dens in 1592, among its spins was a 1590 treatise on China in Latin, found "enclosed in a case of sweet cedar-wood, and lapped up almost an hundred fold in fine calicut-cloth, as though it had been some incomparable jewel" (Hakluyt, 1598–1600, vol. 2, p. 88). Information itself becomes the priceless commodity. J. B. Harley (1988) links the censorship of cartographic information in early modern Europe to the economic transformations that accompanied the beginnings of overseas empires.

> In a period when the foundations of the European world economy and its overseas empires were being laid, absolute monarchs were also "merchant kings," pursuing economic objectives through the trade monopolies opened up by their navigations. As in the case of the nation-state, the essence of empire is control. For such commercial monopolies to survive and for the policies of *mare clausum* to be implemented, there had to be a monopoly of the knowledge that enabled the new lands and the routes to and from them to be mapped. (Harley, 1988, p. 61)

Christopher Columbus and John Smith withheld information on true distance traveled from the rest of their parties; Francis Drake was restrained from making charts or descriptions of his voyage, and his narrative was held back from publication for eight years. Raleigh's (1848) *Discoverie* broods over the impossibility of keeping any new knowledge secret, an impossibility that justifies his decision not to explore a potential gold mine:

> I thought it best not to hover thereabouts, least if the same had been perceived by the company, there would haue bin by this time many barks and ships set out, and perchance other nations would also have gotten of ours for pilots, so as both our selues might haue been prevented, and all our care taken for good vsage of the people been utterly lost. (pp. 59–60)

Information itself became a valued commodity to be accumulated, withheld from circulation, and given out strategically.

HJ: When I watch my son playing Nintendo®, I watch him play the part of an explorer and a colonist, taking a harsh new world and bringing it under his symbolic control, and that story is strangely familiar. De Certeau reminds us that one traditional function of narratives is to define a people's relation to their spaces, to justify their claims upon a certain geography.

Cultures endlessly repeat the narratives of their founding as a way of justifying their occupation of space. What is interesting about Nintendo® is that it allows people to enact through play an older narrative that can no longer be enacted in reality—a constant struggle for possession of desirable spaces, the ever shifting and unstable frontier between controlled and uncontrolled space, the need to venture onto unmapped terrain and to confront its primitive inhabitants. This holds true for all players. For children, Nintendo® further offers the image of personal autonomy and bodily control that contrasts with their own subordinate position in the social formation.

MF: The notion of simulating this early colonial experience was not born with Nintendo®. The Victorian editor Edward Arber (1885) writes in his preface to *The Three Earliest English Books on America* that in them

> One is able . . . to look out on the New world as its Discoverers and first explorers looked upon it. Nowadays, this Globe has but few geographical mysteries; and it is losing its romance as fast as it is losing its wild beasts. In the following texts, however, the Wonderment of its Discovery in all its freshness, is preserved, as in amber, for all time. (p. v)

And if late 19th-century editions of American voyage narratives offered readers like Virginia Woolf a vicarious experience, America in the 16th and 17th centuries famously offered to the unlanded or disenfranchised youth of England an alternate arena of possible advancement and acquisition. But the offered autonomy was ambiguous. Advertised in some documents as a place where a young man's hands could be his lands, offering unique opportunities for social and economic mobility, America at other moments offers to England a place where potentially subversive elements—heterodox ministers or "masterless men"—can be sent, where the backbreaking labor that subdues the body will necessarily lead to a conformity of the exhausted spirit. The theory contemporaneous with the voyage, as well as the writings of colonists, represents America ambiguously as a place of acquiring mastery and of being mastered.

The time-honored representation of the English voyages has been a confident, masculine "thrust outwards" and expansion of, among other things, an enlightened English rule. The prestige that the voyages retrospectively acquired under Victoria was solidified by accounts that linked territorial expansion to the flowering of literary achievement represented, especially, by Shakespeare (also Marlowe, Sidney, and others). In contrast to this celebratory reception, the mastery of children playing Nintendo® is valued only within restricted circles and largely trivialized, if not stigmatized, within the larger culture. But if, as we argue, Nintendo® plays out in virtual space the same narrative of mastering new territory that these earlier texts repeatedly record, it has also been argued that Renaissance England was preoccupied with its own littleness, insularity, and triviality (Knapp, 1993). It also seems to be the case that most of England's early voyages and settlements were characterized less by mastery and success than by forms of incompetence, failure, and incomprehension. It is difficult to locate unambiguously in these narratives either what is masterful, prestigious, and monumental or what is trivial, disgraceful, and subordinate. Although our two subjects have acquired different cultural meanings, they are in important ways fundamentally the same narrative, the same kind of experience, one real, the other simulated.

HJ: Our purpose in talking about Nintendo® next to these older texts is not to make a claim about direct causal links between the two traditions nor to borrow cultural authority for Nintendo® by brushing it against works with a more prestigious status. A comparison against periods minimally allows us to think more creatively about forms of narrative that privilege space over characterization or plot development not as aberrations or failures to conform to aesthetic norms but as part of an alternative tradition of "spatial stories," a different way of organizing narratives that must be examined and evaluated according to their own cultural logic. Because all ways of organizing narratives presuppose ways of organizing social and cultural experience, there are ideological implications as well in seeing Nintendo® games as sharing a logic of spatial exploration and conquest with these earlier works. Nintendo® not only allows players to identify with the founding myths of the American nation but to restage them, to bring them into the sphere of direct social experience. If ideology is at work in Nintendo® games (and rather obviously, it is), ideology works not through character identification but, rather, through role playing. Nintendo® takes children and their own needs to master their social space and turns them into virtual colonists driven by a desire to master and control digital space.

Just as the earlier narratives played a specific role in relation to the economic and cultural imperialism of Renaissance Europe, Nintendo® games must also be positioned against the backdrop of a new and more complicated phase of economic and cultural imperialism. Critical theorists have often oversimplified this issue: American-based multinationals dump their cultural goods on the rest of the world, producing an international culture that erases indigenous cultural traditions. In this scenario, cultural power flows in one direction, from the West to the East—terms that provide a sharp reminder of how present a Renaissance geography still is, reaching Japan by traveling east, locating direction in relationship to the Old World and not the New. Nintendo®s success complicates a unidirectional model, suggesting ways that the appropriation and rewriting of these cultural goods may become an alternative source of cultural and economic power.

Nintendo®'s much disputed bid to purchase the Seattle Mariners represented a public acknowledgment of the increasingly central role of Japanese popular culture in defining how Americans play. Japan's longtime adaption, appropriation, and reconstruction of Western cultural traditions enables it to sell its cultural goods in the American marketplace, much as in another age British pop stars ruled the American music scene. What exactly is the cultural status of a Nintendo® game, based partially on American generic traditions or adopted from specific Western texts, drawing some of its most compelling iconography from Japanese graphic art, licensed by Japanese corporations, manufactured and designed by corporations in both the Americas and Asia, and for sale to both Japanese and American marketplaces? What are the lines of economic and cultural influence when we see Bugs Bunny, Hulk Hogan, and Bart Simpson existing side by side with samurai, sumo wrestlers, and Mecha-men? Does Nintendo®'s recycling of the myth of the American New World, combined with its own indigenous myths of global conquest and empire building, represent Asia's absorption of our national imaginary, or does it participate in a dialogic relationship with the West, an intermixing of different cultural traditions that insures their broader circulation and consumption? In this new rediscovery of the New World, who is the colonizer and who the colonist?

References

Adventure Island 3. (1992). *Nintendo® Power*, 41, pp. 8–13.

Arbor, E. (1885). *The three earliest English books on America*. Birmingham: 1 Montague Road.

Barlow, J. (1990, Summer). Being in nothingness. *Mondo 2000*, pp. 34–43.

Cortes, H. (1986). *Letters from Mexico* (A. Pagden, Trans. & Ed.). New Haven, CT and London: Yale University Press.

De Certeau, M. (1984a). *Heterologies: Discourse on the other* (B. Massumi, Trans.). Minneapolis: University of Minnesota Press.

De Certeau, M. (1984b). *The practice of everyday life*. Berkeley: University of California Press.

Hakluyt, R. (1598–1600). *Principal navigations*. N.p. London.

Harley, I. B. (1988). *Silences and secrecy: The hidden agenda of cartography in early modern Europe*. Imago Mundi, 40, 57–76.

Jenkins, H. (1993). 'x Logic': Repositioning Nintendo in children's lives. *Quarterly Review of Film and Video*, 14, 55–70.

Kinder, M. (1991). *Playing with power in movies, television and video games: From Muppet Babies to Teenage Mutant Ninja Turtles*. Berkeley: University of California Press.

Knapp, J. (1993). *An empire nowhere: England, America, and literature from Utopia to The Tempest*. Berkeley: University of California Press.

Lane, R. (1979). An account of the particularities . . . sent and directed to Sir Walter Ralegh. In D. B. Quinn (Ed.), *New American world* (pp. 84–119). New York: Arno Press and HectorBye.

Page, E. (1973). *American genesis: Pre-colonial writing in the North*. Boston: Gambit.

Provenzo, E. E (1991). *Video kids: Making sense of Nintendo*. Cambridge, MA: Harvard University Press.

Raleigh, Sir Walter. (1848). *The discoverie of Guiana* . . . (Sir Robert Schomburgk, Ed.). London: Hakluyt Society.

Rheingold, H. (1991). *Virtual reality*. New York: Simon & Schuster.

Smith, J. (1624). *The general history of Virginia, New-England, and the Summer Isles*. In P. Barbour, *Works of Captain John Smith* (pp. 214–261). Chapel Hill: University of North Carolina Press.

Walcott, D. (1986). Ruins of a great house. In D. Walcott, *Collected poems, 1948–84* (p. 79). New York: Farrar, Strauss, Giroux.

81

CIVILIZATION AND ITS DISCONTENTS

Simulation, subjectivity, and space

Ted Friedman

Source: Greg M. Smith (ed.), *On a Silver Platter: CD-ROMs and the Promises of a New Technology* (New York, NY: New York University Press, 1999), pp. 132–150.

New paradigms, old lessons

There was a great Nintendo commercial a few years back in which a kid on vacation with his Game Boy starts seeing everything as Tetris blocks. Mount Rushmore, the Rockies, the Grand Canyon all morph into rows of squares, just waiting to drop, rotate, and slide into place. The effect is eerie, but familiar to anyone who's ever played the game. The commercial captures the most remarkable quality of video and computer games: the way they seem to restructure perception, so that even after you've stopped playing, you continue to look at the world a little differently.

This phenomenon can be dangerous—as when I finished up a roll of quarters on Pole Position, walked out to my car, and didn't realize for a half mile or so that I was still driving as if I were in a video game, darting past cars and hewing to the inside lane on curves. More subtly, when the world looks like one big video game, it may become easier to lose track of the human consequences of real-life violence and war.

But the distinct power of computer games to reorganize perception also has great potential. Computer games can be powerful tools for communicating not just specific ideas, but structures of thought—whole ways of making sense of the world. Just as Tetris, on the simple level of spatial geometry, encourages you to discover previously unnoticed patterns in the natural landscape, more sophisticated games can teach you how to recognize more complex interrelationships. The simulation game *Sim City*, for example, immerses you in the dynamics of building and developing a city, from zoning neighborhoods to building roads to managing the police force. In learning how to play the game, you develop an intuitive sense of how each aspect of the city affects and is affected by other aspects of the city— how, for example, the development of a single residential area will affect traffic, pollution, crime, and commerce throughout the city. The result, once the game is over and you step outside, is a new template with which to interpret, understand,

and cognitively map the city around you. You no longer see your neighborhood in isolation, but as one zone influenced by and influencing the many other zones that make up your town.[1]

Any medium, of course, can teach you how to see life in new ways. When you read a book, in a sense you're learning how to think like the author. And as film theorists have long noted, classical Hollywood narrative teaches viewers not just how to look at a screen, but how to gaze at the world. But for the most part, the opportunities for these media to reorient our perceptions today are limited by their stylistic familiarity. A particularly visionary author or director may occasionally confound our expectations and show us new ways to read or watch. But for the most part the codes of literary and film narrative are set. We may learn new things in a great book or movie, but we almost always encounter them in familiar ways.

Computer games, by contrast, are a new medium, still in flux. While game genres have begun to form, they remain fluid, open-ended. The rules and expectations for computer games are not yet set in stone. Each new game must rethink how it should engage the player, and the best games succeed by discovering new structures of interaction, inventing new genres. What would be avant-garde in film or literature—breaking with familiar forms of representation, developing new modes of address—is standard operating procedure in the world of computer games. Every software developer is always looking for the next "killer application"—the newest paradigm-buster.

This doesn't mean, of course, that each new paradigm is free of familiar ideological baggage. Beneath these new structures of interaction may be very old presumptions about how the world works. *Sim City* may help us see cities with new eyes, but the lessons it teaches us about cities—the political and economic premises it rests on—are conventionally capitalist, if somewhat liberal. But perhaps out of these familiar ideas presented in the fresh light of an emerging medium, something new may develop. At the least, as computer games discover new tools for communicating ways of thinking, new opportunities are opened for more radical visions.

A closer look at the semiotics of a specific computer game can help specify in what ways these new texts teach us to look at the world differently, and in what ways they tell the same old stories. In this essay, I will look at one game that typifies the medium today in all its contradictions. *Civilization II*, a "simulation" game that puts the player in the position of a nation's leader building an empire, radically challenges conventional norms of textual interaction in some ways. Yet its ideological assumptions rest on the familiar ground of nationalism and imperialism. Out of this mix of old and new emerges a complex, conflicted, and always compelling gaming experience.

Booting up *Civilization II*

Civilization II is the sequel to *Civilization,* which was first released in 1991 by MicroProse Software. *Civilization II* appeared in 1996. (*Civilization II* adds new features and spices up the graphics from the original *Civilization*, but the basic dynamics of game play remain unchanged. Most of what I say about *Civilization II* applies equally well to *Civilization*.) Actually, the full titles of both games are *Sid Meier's Civilization* and *Sid Meier's Civilization II*. Meier, the cofounder of MicroProse, is the game's inventor and original designer. Meier is known in the computer gaming world for his skill in designing absorbing, detailed simulations. His early games *Pirates* and *Railroad Tycoon* each helped shape the emerging genre in the 1980s. *Civilization* was hailed on its release as one of the greatest computer games ever; *Civilization II* has been similarly honored. In a 1996 survey of the history of computer games, the magazine *Computer Gaming World* named the original *Civilization* the best game of all time ("One Hundred Fifty Best Games" 1996). Rival magazine PC *Gainer* ranked *Civilization II* the fourth best game ever ("Best Ten Games" 1997), and ranked the original *Civilization* one of the fifteen most significant games of all time ("Fifteen Most Significant Games" 1997).

The manual for the original *Civilization* introduces the game this way;

> *Civilization* casts you in the role of the ruler of an entire civilization through many generations, from the founding of the world's first cities 6,000 years in the past to the imminent colonization of space. It combines the forces that shaped history and the evolution of technology in a competitive environment . . . . If you prove an able ruler, your civilization grows larger and even more interesting to manage. Inevitable contact with neighbors opens new doors of opportunity-treaties, embassies, sabotage, trade and war. (Shelley 1991, 7)

What does it feel like to be cast "in the role of ruler of an entire civilization through many generations"? The game follows the conceit that you play the part of a single historical figure. At the beginning of the game you're given a choice of nation and name. From then on, from the wanderings of your first settlers to your final colonization of outer space, the computer will always call you, for example, "Emperor Abraham Lincoln of the United States." Of course, nobody lives for six thousand years, and even the most powerful real-life despots—to say nothing of democratically elected leaders—could never wield the kind of absolute power that *Civilization II* gives even titular presidents and prime ministers. In *Civilization II* you're responsible for directing the military, managing the economy, controlling development in every city of your domain, building wonders of the world, and orchestrating scientific research (with the prescience to know the strategic benefits of each possible discovery, and to schedule accordingly). You make not just the big decisions, but the small ones, too, from deciding where each military unit should move on every turn to choosing which squares of the map grid to develop for resources. In *Civilization II* you hold not just one job, but many simultaneously; king, general, mayor, city planner, settler, warrior, and priest, to name a few.

How does this tangle of roles become the smooth flow of game play? The answer, I think, is that you do not identify with any of these subject positions so much as with *the computer itself*.[2] When you play a simulation game like *Civilization II*, your perspective—the eyes through which you learn to see the game—is not that of any character or set of characters, be they kings, presidents, or even God. The style in which you learn to think doesn't correspond to the way any person usually makes sense of the world. Rather, the pleasures of a simulation game come from inhabiting an unfamiliar, alien mental state: learning to think like a computer.[3]

Cyborg consciousness

The way computer games teach structures of thought—the way they reorganize perception—is by getting you to internalize the logic of the program. To win, you can't just do whatever you want. You have to figure out what will work within the rules of the game. You must learn to predict the consequences of each move, and anticipate the computer's response. Eventually your decisions become intuitive, as smooth and rapid-fire as the computer's own machinations.

In one sense the computer is your opponent. You have to know how to think like the computer because the computer provides the artificial intelligence that determines the moves of your rival civilizations. Like Kasparov playing Deep Blue, you have to figure out how the computer makes decisions in order to beat it. But in this role of opponent, the computer is only a stand-in for a human player. When multiple players compete, either in *Civilization II* or in the online version, *CivNet*, the AI isn't even needed. And in terms of strategy, the Pentium-powered processor is no Deep Blue; its moves are fairly predictable.

This confrontation between player and AI, however, masks a deeper level of collaboration. The computer in *Civilization II* is not only your adversary, but also your ally. In addition to controlling your rivals, it processes the rules of the game. It tells you when to move, who wins each battle, and how quickly your cities can grow. It responds instantly to your every touch of the mouse, so that when you move your hand along the mousepad, it seems as if you're actually physically moving the pointer on the screen, rather than simply sending digital information to the computer. It runs the universe that you inhabit when you play the game. "Thinking like the computer" means thinking *along with* the computer, becoming an extension of the computer's processes.[4]

This helps explain the strange sense of self-dissolution created by computer games, the way games "suck you in." The pleasure of computer games is in entering into a computer-like mental state: responding as automatically as the computer, processing information as effortlessly, replacing sentient cognition with the blank hum of computation. When a game of *Civilization II* really gets rolling, the decisions are effortless, instantaneous, chosen without self-conscious thought. The result is an almost meditative state, in which you aren't just interacting with the computer, but melding with it.

The connection between player and computer in a simulation game is a kind of *cybernetic circuit*, a continual feedback loop. Today the prefix "cyber-" has become so ubiquitous that its use has diffused to mean little more than "computer-related." But the word "cybernetics," from which the prefix was first taken, has a more distinct meaning. Norbert Wiener (1948) coined the term to describe a new general science of information processing and control. (He took it from the Greek word *kybernan*, meaning to steer or govern.) In particular, he was interested in studying, across disciplinary boundaries, processes of *feedback*: the ways in which systems—be they bodies, machines, or combinations of both—control and regulate themselves through circuits of information. As Steve J. Heims writes in his history, *The Cybernetics Group*,

> [The cybernetic] model replaced the traditional cause-and-effect relation of a stimulus leading to a response by a "circular causality" requiring negative feedback: A person reaches for a glass of water to pick it up, and as she extends her arm and hand is continuously informed (negative feedback)—by visual or proprioceptive sensations—how close the hand is to the glass and then guides the action accordingly, so as to achieve the goal of smoothly grabbing the glass. The process is circular because the position of the arm and hand achieved at one moment is part of the input information for the action at the next moment. If the circuit is intact, it regulates the process. To give another stock example, when a man is steering a ship, the person, the compass, the ship's engine, and the rudder are all part of the goal-directed system with feedback. The machine is part of the circuit. (Heims 1991. 15–16)

The constant interactivity in a simulation game—the perpetual feedback between a player's choice, the computer's almost instantaneous response, the player's response to that response, and so on—is a cybernetic loop, in which the line demarcating the end of the player's consciousness and the beginning of the computer's world blurs.

There are drawbacks to this merging of consciousness. When you're connected to the computer, it's easy to imagine you've transcended your physical body, to dismiss your flesh and blood as simply the "meat" your mind must inhabit, as the protagonist of *Neuromancer* puts it (Gibson 1984). This denial is a form of alienation, a refusal to recognize the material basis for your experience. The return of the repressed comes in the form of carpal tunnel syndrome, eyestrain, and other reminders that cyberspace remains rooted in physical existence.

But what the connection between player and computer enables is access to an otherwise unavailable perspective. In the collaboration between you and the computer, self and Other give way, forming what might be called a single *cyborg consciousness*. In her influential "Manifesto for Cyborgs" (1985), Donna Haraway proposed the figure of the cyborg— "a hybrid of machine and organism"—as an image that might help us make sense of the increasing interpenetration of

162

technology and humanity under late capitalism. Haraway's point was that in this hypermechanized world we are all cyborgs. When you drive a car, the unit of driver-and-car becomes a kind of cyborg. When you turn on the TV, the connection of TV-to-viewer is a kind of cybernetic link. The man steering the ship in Heims's example is a cyborg. And most basically, since we all depend on technology to survive this postmodern world—to feed us, to shelter us, to comfort us—in a way we are all as much cyborgs as the Six Million Dollar Man.

Simulation games offer a singular opportunity to think through what it means to be a cyborg. Most of our engagements with technology are distracted, functional affairs—we drive a car to get somewhere; we watch TV to see what's on.[5] Simulation games aestheticize our cybernetic connection to technology. They turn it into a source of enjoyment and an object for contemplation. They give us a chance to luxuriate in the unfamiliar pleasures of rote computation and depersonalized perspective, and grasp the emotional contours of this world-view. To use the language of Clifford Geertz (1973) (borrowing from Flaubert), simulation games are a "sentimental education" in what it means to live among computers. Through the language of play, they teach you what it feels like to be a cyborg.[6]

Narrativizing geography: *Civilization II* as a "spatial story"

So, what are the advantages to life as a cyborg? Why learn to think like a computer? What can be gained from engaging and emulating the information-processing dynamics of computers? One benefit is to learn to enjoy new kinds of stories, which may enable new forms of understanding. Unlike most of the stories we're used to hearing, a simulation doesn't have characters or a plot in the conventional sense. Instead, its primary narrative agent is *geography*. Simulation games tell a story few other media can: the drama of a map changing over time.

You begin *Civilization II* with a single band of prehistoric settlers, represented as a small figure with a shovel at the center of the main map, which takes up most of the computer screen. Terrain is delineated on this map by icons representing woods, rivers, plains, oceans, mountains, and so on. At the beginning of the game, however, almost all of the map is black; you don't get to learn what's out there until one of your units has explored the area. Gradually, as you expand your empire and send out scouting parties, the landscape is revealed. This process of exploration and discovery is one of the fundamental pleasures of *Civilization II*. It's what gives the game a sense of narrative momentum.

In their published dialogue "Nintendo and New World Travel Writing" (1995), Mary Fuller, an English Renaissance scholar, and Henry Jenkins, a cultural studies critic, compare two seemingly disparate genres that share a strikingly similar narrative structure. Nintendo games and New World travel narratives, like simulation games, are structured not by plot or character, but by the process of encountering, transforming, and mastering geography. Fuller writes, "[b]oth terms of our title evoke explorations and colonizations of space:

163

the physical space navigated, mapped and mastered by European voyagers and travelers in the sixteenth and seventeenth centuries and the fictional, digitally projected space traversed, mapped, and mastered by players of Nintendo video games" (1995, 58). Borrowing from the work of Michel de Certeau (1984a, b), Jenkins labels these geographical narratives "spatial stories." He describes the process of geographic transformation as a transition from abstract "place" into concrete "space":

> For de Certeau (1984b), narrative involves the transformation of place into space (117–118). Places exist only in the abstract, as potential sites for narrative action, as locations that have not yet been colonized. Places constitute a "stability" which must be disrupted in order for stories to unfold . . . . Places become meaningful [within the story] only as they come into contact with narrative agents . . . Spaces, on the other hand, are places that have been acted upon, explored, colonized. Spaces become the locations of narrative events. (Fuller and Jenkins 1995, 66)

Likewise, game play in *Civilization II* revolves around the continual transformation of place into space, as the blackness of the unknown gives way to specific terrain icons. As in New World narratives, the process of "colonization" is not simply a metaphor for cultural influence, but involves the literal establishment of new colonies by settlers (occasionally with the assistance of military force). Once cities are established, the surrounding land can be developed. By moving your settlers to the appropriate spot and choosing from

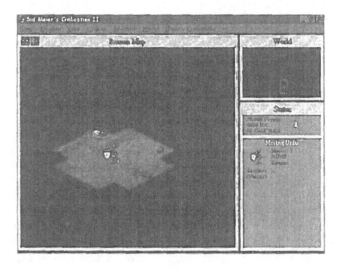

Figure 1 You begin *Civilization II* with a single band of settlers, the unexplored terrain a black void

the menu of "orders," you can build roads, irrigate farmland, drill mines, chop down trees, and eventually, as your civilization gains technology, build bridges and railroads. These transformations are graphically represented right on the map itself by progressively more elaborate icons. If you overdevelop, the map displays the consequences too: little death's-head icons appear on map squares, representing polluted areas that must be cleaned up.

In its focus on the transformation of place into space. *Civilization II* seems like an archetypal "spatial story." However, *Civilization II* differs from the geographic narratives Jenkins and Fuller describe in an important way, one that demonstrates the distinctive qualities of simulation games. In addition to the categories of space and place, Jenkins borrows two other terms from de Certeau, "maps" and "tours": "Maps are abstracted accounts of spatial relations ('the girl's room is next to the kitchen'), whereas tours are told from the point of view of the traveler/narrator ('You turn right and come into the living room') (De Certeau 1984b, 118–122). Maps document places; tours describe movements through spaces" (Fuller and Jenkins 1995, 66). Tours, in other words, are the subjective, personalized experiences of the spaces described abstractly in maps. You start your journey with a map. Then, as you navigate the geography, that abstract knowledge becomes the embodied firsthand experience of a tour. The maze of the Nintendo screen gives way to a familiar, continually retraced path that leads from the entrance to safety. The daunting expanse of the New World is structured by the personal account of one traveler's journey.

In the "spatial stories" Jenkins and Fuller discuss, then, the pleasure comes from two transitions, one involving geographic transformation, the other individual

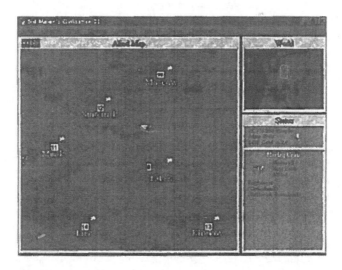

Figure 2 As your civilization grows, you can transform the land with roads, bridges, mines, irrigation, and other "improvements"

subjectivity. *Place* becomes *space* as unfamiliar geography is conquered through exploration and development. And *maps* become *tours* as abstract geography is subjectively situated in personal experience. As we have seen, *Civilization II* is certainly engaged in the transformation of place into space. But in simulation games the map never becomes a tour. The game screen documents the player's changes to the landscape, but these transformations are always represented in the abstract terms of the map. The point of view always remains an overhead, "God's-eye" perspective.

What's the import of this distinction? We might assume that the continued abstraction of the map would indicate a measure of detachment, compared to the ground-level engagement of a tour. But as already noted, simulation games seem singularly skilled at "sucking you in" to their peculiar kind of narrative. The difference is that the pleasure in simulation games comes from *experiencing space as a map*: at once claiming a place and retaining an abstracted sense of it. The spatial stories Fuller and Jenkins discuss respond to the challenge of narrativizing geography by "getting inside" the map—they zoom in from forest level so we can get to know the trees. Character may not be a primary criterion for these stories, but the stories still depend on individual subjective experience as the engine for their geographic narrative. Geography itself is not the protagonist; rather, the protagonist's experience of geography structures the narrative.

But simulation games tell an even more unusual story: the story of the map itself. Drawing a steady bead on the forest, they teach us how to follow, and enjoy, its transformations over time. We need never get distracted by the trees. Because simulation games fix the player in a depersonalized frame of mind, they can tell their story in the abstract, without ever bringing it to the level of individual experience. The map is not merely the environment for the story; it's the hero of the story.

The closest analogues I can think of to the distinct kind of spatial story that simulation games tell are works of "environmental history" such as William Cronon's *Changes in the Land* (1983). Cronon attempts to tell a version of American history from the perspective of the land, turning the earth itself into his protagonist. The limitations of the written word, however, make it difficult to fully treat an abstract entity as a character. You can't easily employ the devices normally used to engage the reader with a human protagonist. As a result, the book—like most works on geography—is still a rather dry read. It may offer a new perspective, but it can't engage the reader enough to give an emotional sense of what this perspective *feels like*.[7]

The clearest way to conceptualize space is not with words, but with images. A map captures the abstract contours of space; any verbal description begins the process of turning that map into a tour. This is why any good work of geography is full of maps; the reader is expected to continually check the words against the images, translating language back into visual understanding. Simulation games are a way to make the maps tell the whole story. As a still frame is to a movie, as a paragraph is to a novel, so is a map to a simulation game. Simulation games are maps-in-time, dramas that teach us how to think about structures of spatial relationships.[8]

Ideology

In one sense, every map is always already a tour. As geographer Denis Wood points out in *The Power of Maps* (1992), a map is the cumulative result of many subjective judgments. Maps always have a point of view. The ideological work of the "scientific," God's-eye view map is to make the traces of those subjective decisions disappear. Critics of computer games worry that the technological aura of computers further heightens this reification, leaving game players with the impression that they have encountered not just one version of the way the world works, but the one and only "objective" version (Brook and Boal 1995; Slouka 1995; Stoll 1995).

This perspective would leave little room to imagine resistance. But the structure of the computer gaming experience does allow for variant interpretations. You can win *Civilization II* in one of two ways. You can win by making war, wiping the other civilizations off the map and taking over the world. Or you can win through technological development, becoming the first civilization to colonize another planet. I haven't emphasized the military aspect of *Civilization II* because I don't like war games all that much myself. They make me anxious. My strategy for winning *Civilization II* is to pour all my efforts into scientific research, so that my nation is the most technologically advanced. This allows me to be the first to build "wonders of the world," which, under the game's rules, force opponents to stay at peace with me. In the ancient world, the Great Wall of China does the trick; by modern times, I have to upgrade to the United Nations.

That's just one strategy for winning. I think it's probably the most effective—I get really high scores—but, judging from online discussions, it doesn't appear

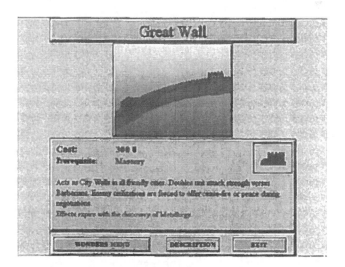

Figure 3 The "Civilopedia" entry for the Great Wall

to be the most popular. Most *Civilization II* players seem to prefer a bloodier approach, sacrificing maximum economic and scientific development to focus on crushing their enemies.

The fact that more than one strategy will work—that there's no one "right" way to win the game—demonstrates the impressive flexibility of *Civilization II*. But there still remain baseline ideological assumptions that determine which strategies will win and which will lose. And underlying the entire structure of the game, of course, is the notion that global coexistence is a matter of winning or losing.

There are disadvantages to never seeing the trees for the forest. *Civilization II*'s dynamic of depersonalization elides the violence of exploration, colonization, and development even more completely than the stories of individual conquest described by Fuller and Jenkins. Military units who fight and die in *Civilization II* disappear in a simple blip; native peoples who defend their homelands are inconveniences, "barbarian hordes" to be quickly disposed of.

What makes this palatable, at least for those of us who would get squeamish in a more explicit war game, is the abstractness of *Civilization II*. Any nation can be the colonizer, depending on who you pick to play. Barbarian hordes are never specific ethnicities; they're just generic natives. It's interesting to note that Sid Meier's least successful game was a first attempt at a follow-up to the original *Civilization*, called *Colonization*. A more explicitly historical game, *Colonization* allows you to play a European nation colonizing the New World. In addressing a more concrete and controversial historical subject, Meier is forced to complicate the Manifest Destiny ethos of *Civilization*. The Native American nations are differentiated, and behave in different ways. You can't win through simple genocide, but must trade and collaborate with at least some Native Americans some of the time. The result of this attempt at political sensitivity, however, is simply to highlight the violence and racism that are more successfully obscured in *Civilization*. There's no getting around the goal of *Colonization:* 10 colonize the New World. And while you have a choice of which European power to play, you can't choose to play a Native American nation.

Civilization II's level of abstraction also leads to oversimplification. The immense time span of *Civilization II* reifies historically specific, continually changing practices into transhistorical categories like "science," "religion," and "nation." Art and religion in *Civilization II* serve a purely functional role: to keep the people pacified. If you pursue faith and beauty at the expense of economic development, you're bound to get run over by less cultivated nations. Scientific research follows a path of rigid determinism; you always know in advance what you're going to discover next, and it pays to plan two or three inventions ahead. You can't play "the Jews" in *Civilization II*, or another diasporic people. The game assumes that "civilization" equals distinct political nation. There's no creolization in *Civilization II*, no hybridity, no forms of geopolitical organization before (or after) the rise of nationalism. Either you conquer your enemy, or your enemy conquers you. You can trade supplies and technology with your neighbors, but it's presumed that your national identities will remain distinct. Playing a single, unchanging entity from the Stone Age to space colonization turns the often slippery formation of nationhood into a kind of immutable racial destiny.

What to do once you've conquered the world

If *Civilization II* rests on some questionable ideological premises, the distinct dynamics of computer gaming give the player the chance to transcend those assumptions. Computer games are designed to be played until they are mastered. You succeed by learning how the software is put together. Unlike a book or film that is engaged only once or twice, a computer game is played over and over until every subtlety is exposed, every hidden choice obvious to the savvy player. The moment the game loses its interest is when all its secrets have been discovered, its boundaries revealed. That's when the game can no longer suck you in. No game feels fresh forever; eventually you run up against the limits of its perspective, and move on to other games.[9] By learning from the limitations of *Civilization II* while exploiting the tools it offers, perhaps the next round of games can go further, challenging players' assumptions and expectations to create an even more compelling and rewarding interactive experience.

Notes

1 I address the semiotics of *Sim City* in much greater detail in "Making Sense of Software: Computer Games and Interactive Textuality" (Friedman 1995)

2 The argument I will be making here is an extension of my discussion of subjectivity in "Making Sense of Software" (Friedman 1995). In that essay I describe the experience of playing *Sim City* as one of identifying with a *process*—with "the simulation itself" (85). In a simulation game, you don't imagine yourself as filling the shoes of a particular character on the screen, but rather, you see yourself as the entire screen, as the sum of all the forces and influences that make up the world of the game. This essay extends that discussion by looking at how this perspective is, in a way, that of the computer itself.

3 I should clarify that in talking about "thinking like a computer," I don't mean to anthropomorphize, or to suggest that machines can "think" the way humans do. As artificial intelligence researchers have learned, often to their chagrin, computers can only systematically, methodically crunch numbers and follow algorithms, while human thinking is less linear, more fluid. My point is that using simulation games can help us intuitively grasp the very alien way computers process information, and so can help us recognize how our relationships with computers affect our own thoughts and feelings.

In describing computers as, in a sense, nonhuman actors with associated states of consciousness, I'm borrowing a technique of Bruno Latour, who in his novelistic history *Aramis, or The Love of Technology*, tells the story of a failed French experimental mass transit program from several perspectives—including that of the train itself Latour writes,

> I have sought to show researchers in the social sciences that sociology is not the science of human beings alone—that it can welcome crowds of nonhumans with open arms, just as it welcomed the working masses in the nineteenth century. Our collective is woven together out of speaking subjects, perhaps, but subjects to which poor objects, our inferior brothers, are attached at all points. By opening up to include objects, the social bond would become less mysterious. (1996, viii)

Latour's conceit is one way to attempt to account for the interpenetration of our lives with technology, to make visible the often unnoticed role of technology in our daily experience and sense of selves.

4 Where, one may ask. in this confrontation between computer and player is the author of the software? In some sense, one could describe playing a computer game as learning to think like the *programmer*, rather than the computer. On the basic level of strategy, this may mean trying to divine Sid Meier's choices and prejudices, to figure out how he put the game together so as to play it more successfully. More generally, one could describe simulation games as an aestheticization of the programming process: a way to interact with and direct the computer, but at a remove. Many aspects of computer game play resemble the work of programming; the play-die-and-start-over rhythm of adventure games, for example, can be seen as a kind of debugging process. Programming, in fact, can often be as absorbing a task as gaming; both suck you into the logic of the computer. The programmer must also learn to "think like the computer" at a more technical level, structuring code in the rigid logic: of binary circuits.

5 Actually one might argue that the pleasure many get out of driving for its own sake and the enjoyment of watching TV no matter what's on (what Raymond Williams [1974] called "flow") are examples of similar aestheticizations of the cybernetic connection between person and machine. We might then say that just as these pleasures aestheticized previous cybernetic connections, simulation games do the same for our relationships with computers.

6 My reference here is to Clifford Geertz's famous essay, "Deep Play: Notes on the Balinese Cockfight" (1973), which discusses how a game can encapsulate and objectify a society's sense of lived social relations:

> Like any art form—for that, finally, is what we are dealing with—the cockfight renders ordinary, everyday experience comprehensible by presenting it in terms of acts and objects which have had their practical consequences removed and been reduced (or, if you prefer, raised) to the level of sheer appearances, where their meaning can be more powerfully articulated and more exactly perceived. (443)

This dynamic is particularly powerful because it is not just an intellectual exercise, but a visceral experience:

> What the cockfight says it says in a vocabulary of sentiment—the thrill of risk, the despair of loss, the pleasure of triumph . . . Attending cock-fights and participating in them is, for the Balinese, a kind of sentimental education. What he learns there is what his culture's ethos and his private sensibility (or, anyway, certain aspects of them) look like when spelled out externally in a collective text. (449)

7 One alternative might be to go ahead and treat an abstract object like a real protagonist, complete with an interior monologue. This is what Bruno Latour does in *Aramis,* as discussed above. But when one is discussing a subject as abstract as geography, even this move would likely remain a compromise with an inhospitable medium. In giving voice to geography, one risks anthropomorphization, falling back into the synecdochical trap of substituting the king for the land.

8 One might also think about how simulations narrativize other abstractions, such as economic relationships. In addition to being maps-in-time, simulations are also charts-in-time. One follows not only the central map in *Civilization II,* but also the various charts, graphs, and status screens that document the current state of each city's trade balance, food supply, productivity, and scientific research. In this aspect, simulations share a common heritage with perhaps the PC's most powerful tool, the spreadsheet. What the spreadsheet allows is precisely for a static object—in this case a chart—to become a dynamic demonstration of interconnections. It's revealing that Dan Bricklin,

170

the inventor of the spreadsheet, first imagined his program as a kind of computer game. Computer industry historian Robert X. Cringely writes. What Bricklin really wanted was . . . a kind of very advanced calculator with a heads-up display similar to the weapons system controls on an F-14 fighter. Like Luke Skywalker jumping into the turret of the Millennium Falcon, Bricklin saw himself blasting out financials, locking onto profit and loss numbers that would appear suspended in space before him. It was to be a business tool cum video game, a Saturday Night Special for M.B.A.s, only the hardware technology didn't exist in those days to make it happen. (1992, 65)

So, of course, Bricklin used the metaphor of a sheet of rows and columns instead of a fighter cockpit, Simulation games, in a way. bring the user's interaction with data closer to Bricklin's original ideal.

9 I make a similar argument in "Making Sense of Software" (Friedman (1995).

Works Cited

The Best Ten Games of All Time. 1997, *PC Gamer*, May, 90–96.

Birkerts, Sven. 1994, *The Gutenberg Elegies: The Fate of Reading in an Electronic Age*. New York: Fawcett Columbine.

Brockman, John. 1996. *Digerati: Encounters with the Cyber Elite*. San Francisco: Hardwired.

Brook, James, and Iain A. Boal. 1995. *Resisting the Virtual Life: The Culture and Politics of Information*. San Francisco: City Lights.

Cringely, Robert X. 1992. *Accidental Empires: How the Boys of Silicon Valley Make Their Millons, Battle Foreign Competition, and Still Can't Get a Date*. New York: Addison Wesley

Cronon, William, 1983. *Changes in the Land*. New York: Hill and Wang

de Certeau, Michel. 1984a. *Heterologies: Discourse on the Other*. Trans. Brian Massumi. Minneapolis: University of Minnesota Press.

———. 1984b. *The Practice of Everyday Life*. Berkeley: University of California Press.

The Fifteen Most Significant Games of All Time. 1997. *PC Gamer*, May, 95.

Friedman, Ted. 1995. Making Sense of Software: Computer Games and Interactive Textuality. In *CyberSociety: Computer-Mediated-Communication and Community*, ed. Steven G. Jones. Thousand Oaks, CA: Sage

Fuller, Mary, and Henry Jenkins. 1995. Nintendo and New World Travel Writing: A Dialogue. In *CyberSociety*: *Computer-Mediated-Communication and Community*, ed. Steven G. Jones. Thousand Oaks, CA: Sage.

Geertz, Clifford. 1973. Deep Play: Notes on the Balinese Cockfight. In *The Interpretation of Cultures*. New York: Basic Books.

Gibson, William. 198–4. *Neuromancer*. New York: Ace Kooks.

Gilder, George. 1990. *Life after Television: The Coming Transformation of media and American Life*. Whittle Direct Books.

Haraway, Donna. 1985. Manifesto for Cyborgs: Science, Technology and Socialist Feminism in the 1980s. *Socialist Review* 80:65–108.

Heims. Steve J. 1991. *The Cybernetics Group*. Cambridge: MIT Tress.

Latour, Bruno, 1996. *Aramis, or The Love of Technology*. Trans. Catherine Porter. Cambridge: Harvard University Press.

Negroponte, Nicholas. 1995. *Being Digital*. New York: Vintage.

The One Hundred Fifty Best Games of All Time. 1996. *Computer Gaming World*, November, 64–80.

Shelley, Bruce. 1991. *Manual for* Sid Meier's Civilization. Hunt Valley, MD: MicroProse Software.

Slouka, Mark. 1995. *War of the Worlds: Cyberspace and the High-Tech Assault on Reality.* New York: Basic Books.

Stoll, Clifford. 1995. *Silicon Snake Oil: Second Thoughts on the Information Super-highway.* New York: Doubleday.

Wiener, Norbert. 1948. *Cybernetics: Or, Control and Communication in the Animal and the Machine.* New York: Wiley.

Williams, Raymond. 1974. *Television: Technology and Cultural Form.* Hanover, NIT. Wesleyan University Press.

Wood, Denis. 1992. *The Power of Maps.* New York: Guilford.

82

SOCIAL PLAY

David Myers

Source: *Play Redux: The Form of Computer Games* (Ann Arbor, MI: University of Michigan Press, 2010), pp. 116–130.

> *The more you tighten your grip,*
> *the more star systems will slip through your fingers.*
> > —Princess Leia, Star Wars (1977)

The most significant development in computer game play over the past quarter century has been the rapid ascension of multiplayer games and game designs, or MMOs. The best-known commercial success story in this genre is, of course, *World of Warcraft* (*WoW*). *WoW* and the rest of the current crop of MMOs remain firmly based on the fundamental mechanics of the paper-and-pencil role-playing game *Dungeons & Dragons*. And as such, these games reflect the same forms and processes of play outlined earlier.[1] Yet it often seems that they claim to offer something more.

In *The Nature of Computer Games*, I emphasized the potential of one of the most popular and long-lived computer role-playing games at that time, *Might and Magic* (*M&M*), to expand its social context.

> As of 2001, there were gathering plans to adapt the *M&M* games to an online, multiplayer environment (*Legends of Might and Magic*). This would involve the creation of a MUD-like context, which would be a natural and congruous expansion of the role-playing genre's basic semiotic form.[2]

Reflecting back, however, that analysis seems naive. For while *Everquest* (1999) and *Ultima Online* (1997) have already been—and continue to be, in their own fashion—successful, the *Might and Magic* franchise had already reached its peak of popularity at the time of my analysis, and it subsequently faded and virtually folded. Nevertheless, the basics of the *M&M* role-playing game design, as carried forth online by Blizzard's *World of Warcraft* and (in planning as of 2009) Bioware's closely analogous *Knights of the Old Republic*, demonstrate that much

173

of the appeal of computer role-playing games remains, broadly put, multiplayer and social. About that, I am not surprised.

I am surprised about some other things. Since I was then—while playing *M&M* in 2001—and am now focused on the nature of play as a cognitive function, I am relatively surprised (and somewhat dismayed) to watch computer game studies and analysis, buoyed by the rise of enormously profitable Internet-based MMOs, increasingly promote the notion that computer game play is most fundamentally a cooperative social activity.[3] This notion is, of course, entirely consonant with similar notions, already discussed, promoting the benefits of good and "functional" play.[4] And based on the analysis here, these paired notions are equally misleading.

> The sociologically-anthropologically oriented tradition of MMORPG and its social aspects is usually related to themes that can be located in what Hakken (1999) calls the microsocial level . . . These studies widely assume that MMORPGs are social spaces . . . As a corollary this tradition usually takes for granted the nature of the individual player as a social being.[5]

WoW—as the now prototypical example of MMOs—offers numerous opportunities for cooperative social play (which usually simply means playing "nice" with others), yet this play, like play in all similar games, might be best attributed either to a game design that forces social grouping in order to accomplish game goals or to what appears to be a common human tendency to establish social relationships without regard to any particular game context or goal or desire to play.

In this inclination toward the social, players of online games might be considered similar to users of MySpace or Facebook or other more generic communications networks, where outside-game relationships dominate and motivate in-game behaviors. Yet games are a special sort of software, and play is a special sort of behavior; and in many instances, neither is explained well with reference to desires for or benefits of group play. Indeed, in *WoW* and its related clones, despite the emphasis on social play, most players play most often alone.[6]

Nevertheless, the inclination to design computer games for social play has been present since very early in video game development and history,[7] although the mechanics that made these designs possible were difficult to achieve without the parallel development of computer-mediated communications networks. Now, with such networks commonplace, it is clearly the intent of many computer game designers to include social play as a meaningful component of computer game play. It is not clear, however, that social play contributes to the experience of computer game play as a unique aesthetic form.

Because computer game play relies so fundamentally on sensory mechanisms and habituated response (i.e., its *interface*), social play within computer games is commonly filtered through some previous realization of locomotor play. This fundamental reliance on bodily mechanics is at least somewhat similar to the experience of reading, insofar as all language systems reference visceral experiences of the human body within three-dimensional space.[8] While playing computer games (unlike reading text/hypertext) may avoid direct reference to language, computer game play cannot avoid reference to these more fundamental schemata or to the cognitive mechanisms that enable and empower them. The presence of other players can refine this reference perhaps, but that presence cannot by itself avoid the interactive and visceral components of computer game play.

For this reason, it seems reasonable to construct an explanation of computer game social play as an extension of computer game individual play, rather than to characterize that individual play as a fragmentary and incomplete version of social play. Indeed, individual computer game play often serves as an antithetical substitute for social play, with video game software often taking the role of (an absent) human opponent.

> Play is older than culture, for culture, however inadequately defined, always presupposes human society, and animals have not waited for man to teach them their playing. We can safely assert, even, that human civilization has added no essential feature to the general idea of play.[9]

In general, the experience of computer game play does not seem to necessarily emerge from social action but, rather, becomes often located within social action through purposeful game design.

Social play contexts

Here, in order to better understand the fundamentals of social play and to better understand the relationship between social and individual play, I would like to examine common characteristics of online social play contexts—particularly those distinguished by cooperative and competitive behaviors in MMOs. These contexts are widely (by players and by designers) represented by the categories of player versus environment (PvE) and player versus player (PvP). While these categories are not mutually exclusive, I will examine them according to the rough configuration in Figure 1.

PvP combat is often described and treated pejoratively within persistent online communities—that is, as "griefing." Community-based analysis then reproduces these values by emphasizing the negative qualities of competitive play and, simultaneously, the positive qualities of cooperative play—for example, its "productiveness"—as does the following statement from a review of Taylor's (2006) study of *EverQuest* players.

> In short, MMOGs have served as avant-garde prototypes for the online social spaces more and more of us are electing to inhabit, and players are the first to understand how integrating with a computer world allows us to subject our social lives to the same efficiencies that govern our work time and make it seem rational and productive.[10]

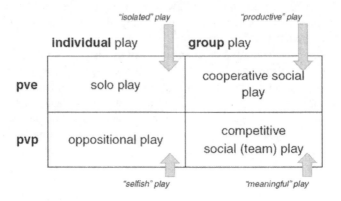

Figure 1 Social contexts of play

This position eventually results in a theoretical denigration of more disruptive and competitive play and distinguishes cooperative play as a more natural and proper extension of individual play. Yet this assumption reflects a disregard—or, perhaps more harmfully, a misrepresentation—of the degree to which competitive play tends to appear and re-appear in a variety of game contexts, regardless of designer intent.

If we position competitive play—among individuals and groups—as a systematic feature of play, then similar formal properties can be observed within cooperative play. And either behavior—cooperative or competitive—can be explained in terms of the systemic manner in which it explores, manipulates, and, over time, transforms the game system.

PvE

"Player versus environment" best describes the play of those single-player games that have been, within the past decades, transformed into today's MMOs. Almost twenty years of *Ultima* single-player games, for instance, preceded the release of *Ultima Online* in 1997. By the time *EverQuest* appeared (in 1999), the computer RPG genre had solidified into a set of design characteristics that could be traced back to early *Dungeons & Dragons* rules sets (1974) and the manipulation of figurines and models within fantasy wargame derivatives such as *Warhammer* (1987).

Under these influences, the computer RPG genre remains marked by two basic components: (1) the creation of a character governed by pre-existing rules and (2) the interactions of that character within a common set of rules. A simplified, linguistic-based model of this process might, for instance, represent a role-playing game as a language system. Playable characters would then be subsets of this rules-based system: grammatically correct sentences. And RPG players are given templates for character structures similar to the basic templates governing sentence structures: a character-creation syntax.

Within the original *Advanced Dungeons & Dragons* (1977) game system, this syntax consisted of seven "basic characteristics": strength, intelligence, wisdom, dexterity, constitution, charisma, and comeliness. All properly constructed characters (well-formed sentences) assigned a bounded value to each of these characteristics. The resulting character array—similar to semantic values chosen during sentence construction—varied slightly from player to player. As a result, each properly constructed character occupied a unique position within the game's multidimensional array of all possible characters. Game play subsequently determined the contextual value of each character in comparison with (or in opposition to) other game characters (or alternative arrays).[11]

Role-playing games remained novel and engaging only to the extent that their play allowed exploration of these character relationships. And in computer games, it is largely immaterial whether these relationships specifically involve other human players. More important, perhaps, is that computer game players assume that they do.

During much of the early history of computer role-playing games, players played in relative social isolation, reacting only to the intricacies of the game system and the variety of character potentials embedded in that system. This sort of play context is then central to the PvE theme and implies an oppositional relationship between game player and game software (or code), with software playing the role of (an imagined) human opponent. Within current MMOs, PvE play now includes groups of players engaged in cooperative attempts to achieve the same or similar game goals.

All PvE play, whether practiced by individuals or groups, remains a meaning-making process that determines values and meanings for game objects; to this end, this process requires an active series of character oppositions during play. The collective history of these oppositions is then used to contextualize each perceptually unique character within an increasingly ordered set of values. These values are continuously weighed and refined with reference to the consequences of in-game interactions, yet they can at times—for example, when narratives are imposed on game play—also include values and meanings imported from external sources. That is, players may assign a low value to a certain character based on game play but may nevertheless highly value that same character for its "aesthetic" value (i.e., as a "concept" character).

In most cases, however, character values and meanings correlate closely with in-game performances, establishing a hierarchy of characters that does not differ greatly from one player to the next. Because this meaning-making process closely parallels the establishment of social hierarchies outside game play, PvE play is formally similar to what appears to be a natural human process: exploring and valuing social relationships. In computer game PvE play, however, this process of assigning contextual values can take place without, strictly speaking, any human contact.

PvP

As technology increasingly has allowed simultaneous and participatory play, the oppositional relationships explored during PvE have become increasingly dependent on other players' presence and choices. Initially, and in parallel with board and card games and most sports, these oppositional relationships result in markedly competitive play. The inclination to design for this competitive tendency among players was present even in early single-player games, where the mechanics of keeping score—or, for instance, hot-seat implementations of turn- based formats—allowed players to value their characters and performances in comparison with the characters and performances of other players.

MMO players distinguish strongly (and emotionally) between these two contexts of play: cooperative and competitive, PvE and PvP. This becomes most obvious in terms of how closely character values come to represent *self* values in these two different play contexts. In general, PvP'ers tend to be much more concerned about the relationship between their in-game characters and their out-of-game selves than are PvE'ers.

There are two clear indications of this exaggerated identification of self with character among PvP players: the tone and topics of in-game communications and, related, the degree to which PvP'ers promote some form of *inequity aversion*.

PvP communications

One of the more obvious and distinguishing characteristics of PvP play—particularly in comparison to PvE play—is the energetic conversation (smack talk) that takes place among players. In comparison to PvE communications, in-game communications among PvP players tends to occur more often as a direct result of the consequences of play, is more predictable as to precisely when during play it will occur, and more often than not concerns the rules of play when it does occur. In contrast, conversations among PvE players commonly exist only as a (often distant) back channel to a more immediate in-game play experience.

When PvP players communicate with their online opponents, that communication plays a significant role in assigning personal character values. Aside from a certain amount of nervous banter and a brief feeling-out process, PvP players talk most often and predictably to their opponents just after they have been defeated in combat and "die."

Because virtually all MMOs determine character oppositions and their consequences according to rules sets that are largely hidden from players, the quantitative meaning of individual combat remains uncertain, leading to necessarily qualitative and social-based interpretations of character values. Therefore, in order to maintain a positive character value, it is vital that players immediately—and publicly—rationalize any indication of weakness or defeat. MMO combat winners occasionally assert their superiority, but these are ritualized and generic comments (e.g., "pwnd!"), without reference to specific elements of game play. MMO combat losers, on the other hand, are much more likely (and much quicker) to point out any inequities that could be attributed to their loss: computer lag, imbalanced game design, and such.

Losing players tend to isolate and criticize specific game elements; winning players tend to generalize their winning performances across broader contexts—often extending the values and meanings derived from in-game play in real-world contexts (e.g., through online forums and message boards). For both winners and losers, these communications establish over time a common and shared set of values based on prioritizing inequity aversion.

PvP values

"Inequity aversion" promotes the assumption that the game is fair and that all PvP combatants have equal opportunities—regardless of characters played—to "win." Any variation in winning outcomes is then attributed to the single aspect of play considered to be uncontrolled and undetermined by the game rules: the game player. This is, of course, a more popular assumption among consistent PvP winners than among consistent PvP losers. However, both winners and losers share this common value. It is just that the winning players, with a higher status granted by their in-game winning characters, are normally louder, more persistent, and more persuasive in its assertion.

With this principle of inequity aversion widely held, there are then two generic arguments presented at the end of any decisive PvP battle. The losers' argument goes something like this: "You killed me in combat only because of game-related factor X." To which the winner replies, "Game-related factor X has little to no significance in the outcome, since that outcome is much more dependent on player skill." Neither of these positions is ever subsequently justified (though the attempt is often made), yet each continues to be supported and promoted by those whose self-valuations would most benefit from its adoption.

These same values and meanings are seldom topics of discussion and debate during PvE play. PvE players are much more willing to allow others to "win" by whatever means (equitable or inequitable)—insofar as that winning does not affect their own self-valuations. As a result, hierarchies of PvE character values are slightly different (i.e., more idiosyncratic) than those constructed solely with reference to PvP activities. Over the course of a long-lived MMO, these values can diverge significantly, resulting in two separate cultures of play. Importantly, however, of the two, PvP value determinations remain more accurate and more indicative of underlying game rules and mechanics, due to their constant testing in game-related competitive contexts.

Based on this realization and on the assumption that an important systemic function of play is to explore the mechanics of the game (or any similarly complex system), PvP play—in which players are put into direct and immediate opposition with one another—provides a quicker, more accurate, and more definitive set of in-game character values and meanings than does PvE play. This determination process is simultaneously a source of satisfaction for individual PvP'ers and a genuine boon for game designers—as an aid in discovering bugs, learning of unintended consequence of complicated rules sets, and so forth.

If, indeed, the values determined and the meanings made during PvP play offer a more complete and thorough analysis of the game system than do the values and meanings resulting from PvE play, it would seem to follow that PvE play can be reasonably conceptualized as a distorted and incomplete version of PvP play—and, further, that much of those supposed dysfunctions associated with strongly individual, competitive, and "grief"- related play are, in fact, positive (and otherwise unachievable) functions when viewed within the context of the game system as a whole.

This is perhaps the most compelling reason to assume that oppositional play *(anti-*play) is a fundamental and default condition of human play—not because computer game players seem to desire it more often (many of them do not), but because it has as an important adaptive function for larger systems. However, simply prioritizing oppositional play over cooperative play does not entirely clarify the relationship between the two. It remains unclear as to whether competition among *groups* or competition among *individuals* is more common and critical to an understanding of competitive play. For, again, just as PvE and cooperative social play are championed within their supportive player communities, there are similarly linked assumptions prioritizing *team-based* PvP.

Social play theory

Clearly, in most play contexts—when observing animal play, for instance—it is relatively easy to distinguish social from individual play. And even in human computer game play, these two forms of play become conceptually intertwined only when computer games also serve as communication devices and, in their communication functions, allow players to share common experiences during play. MMOs currently qualify both as video games and as social communities—though one set of functions may not require and, in fact, may interfere with the other.

Ideally, perhaps, social play within computer role-playing games would extend the liminal qualities of individual play.[12] Turner (1969) has similarly extended his original concept of the liminal—into *communitas.*

> According to Turner, communitas does not engage in active opposition to social structure, but merely appears as "an alternative and more 'liberated' way of being socially human" . . . It is "a loving union of the structurally damned pronouncing judgment on normative structure and providing alternative models for structure" . . . In its most open form, a liminal event reveals a "model of human society as a homogeneous, unstructured communitas, whose boundaries are ideally coterminous with those of the human species."[13]

Communitas, as just defined, is uncommon within MMOs. Online computer games promoting widespread social play generate strict social hierarchies with strong normative guidelines, often only peripherally related to game goals. These hierarchical groups—guilds, fellowships, kinships, and such—tend to restrict computer game object-value relationships much as simulations do. As a result, depending on your point of view, they either protect or prevent individual players from fully accessing a computer game (anti-)aesthetic.

The primary function of computer game social play, then, is to control and deny the experience of self. That is, social play tends to require, as does the simulation, a common set of rules and, correspondingly, a predetermined and fixed set of object-value relationships. This significantly affects game play among members of a social group and becomes most obvious in comparing the consequences of PvE and PvP play.

Social play, in order to maintain a common set of player goals, is more likely to impose sanctions on PvP behavior (e.g., constructing false or "fixed" competitions) than to pursue those competitions without bounds, thus limiting the degree to which individuals can explore the game space, rules, and system. Avoiding the consequences of an anti-play in this fashion requires that social play substitutes social benefits for the more isolated pleasures of individual play and the liminal; accordingly, most currently successful MMO designs manufacture and package the pleasures of play as "loot." In loot-based games, social groups can offer their members information concerning game mechanics, quest walk-throughs, "twinking," and various other boons (depending on the genre and setting of the game) that, in terms of the discussion here, solidify object-value relationships without threat to social cohesion. This means that some members—the majority—of an online social play group are not required to undergo the same habituation process as other members, and for that reason, the former may experience the computer game (anti-)aesthetic solely as a text aesthetic.

This phenomenon, I daresay, also marks much current computer game analysis, which interprets social and cultural strictures on game play as a form of creativity—for example, as a source of "user-created" content.

> There is no culture, there is no game, without the labor of the players. Whether designers want to acknowledge it fully or not, MMOGs *already* *are* participatory sites (if only partially realized) by their very nature as social and cultural spaces.[14] (italics in original)

For those who would observe and record the interpretative practices of players as social activities reflecting shared cultural values, user-created content is an important outcome of play that can be explained and understood with reference to other, similarly located social and cultural phenomena. For those who would locate the phenomenon of play in individual cognition rather than common society, however, user-created content is a largely predetermined feature of a particular game form—that is, a looseness of rules—that allows games to be configured and therein exploited by social groups and pressures. The resulting "user-created" content, like all other rules-based structures within the game, can then engage and empower individual and anti-play only through its opposition and, ultimately, denial.

Summary and implications

Analysis of two well-defined contexts of online social play—PvP and PvE—within the shared game space of MMOs offers at least three potential explanations of the relationship between individual play (particularly individual and competitive play) and social or group play (particularly social and cooperative play).

The first explanation—or hope—might be that these contexts of play could coexist, separate but equal; but this is immediately contradicted by widespread and ongoing conflicts among PvE and PvP players. There are clearly different goals and values associated with PvE and PvP play, despite these two sharing the same game space, rules, and, in many cases, players. One or another, it seems, needs to be assigned precedence in practice and in theory.

Another explanation—the most positive and the most conventional—prioritizes social and cooperative play (primarily within PvE contexts) as a more advanced and mature form of what is initially individual, oppositional, and selfish play. This explanation would eventually subsume all oppositional and individual play within those cooperative groups and game designs that create and maintain social order. It would likewise promote and prioritize teamwork, group coordination, and individual sacrifice over self-reliance, independence, and self-interest.

An immediate difficulty with this second position, however, is that the value and meaning determinations available through supposedly more "mature" and "advanced" forms of play are often less satisfying to players and less useful to designers than those resulting from more "primitive" forms of play. Further, attempting to guide and control oppositional play through social institutions and mechanisms simply doesn't work very well. Self-motivated and solo play is quite common at all levels of MMO play, among beginner and advanced players, in both PvE and PvP contexts. And individual and oppositional play most often occurs without regard to any rules or designs that attempt to limit or channel its effects; individual play appears, for want of a better word, incorrigible.

Cooperative play and tightly knit groups of players may partially distort and sublimate the functions of self-oriented and oppositional play, or social pressures or game designs may temporarily channel player self-interests and activities from direct and immediate oppositions (e.g., 1v1 combat) to other, more complex methods of determining character value (e.g., team-based competitions). However, neither of these factors eliminate the persistence of individual play in MMOs, nor does either significantly alter the self-centered nature of individual play whenever and wherever it occurs.

A third explanation—the most likely—is that individual and competitive play is core and fundamental to an understanding of human play behavior—much more so than cooperative and social play. In other words, human play, regardless of context or group, can be best explained and understood as originating within individual players—in and according to *self*. The most important and revealing consequences of selfish play, however, only become apparent when viewed in the context of larger groups and systems—and, somewhat paradoxically, these larger groups and systems tend to negatively value the motivations and behaviors associated with individual and selfish play. It is not inconceivable, however—or unprecedented—that individual self-interests might be at the core of larger group and system functions, sustenance, and survivability.

In economics, for instance, John Nash came to a similar conclusion regarding the relationship between competitive and cooperative market behaviors. In economic game theory, the so-called Nash program assumes that all market-driven cooperative games can be reduced to a non-cooperative (competitive) form.

> The most important new contribution of Nash (1951) . . . was his argument that this non-cooperative equilibrium concept . . . gives us a complete methodology for analyzing all games.[15]

Since Nash, other economic analyses (e.g., "behavioral finance")[16] have emphasized the degree to which individual, self-determined, and often, as a result, non-rational behaviors explain market outcomes more accurately (and more realistically) than does an assumption of perfect rationality among players.[17] Nevertheless, among theorists most directly concerned with the social outcomes of play—for example, Piaget (1932, 1954)—there is often the implicit assumption that any individual and selfish motives of play are inappropriate and should be subsequently molded into more acceptable social behaviors. Jose Linaza quotes Piaget to make the point that Piaget "at a general level upheld a continuity between all three forms of social behavior (motor, egocentric and cooperative)":

> . . . one must be aware of laying down the law; for things are motor, egocentric, and social all at once . . . . rules of cooperation are in some respects the outcome of rules of coercion and of motor rules.[18]

Clearly, the popularity of social software and social games has been one of the major success stories in the gaming industry over the past decade, and WoW represents an undeniable high point in that trend. Yet many characteristics of WoW—and other similar online games—seem in conflict with an individually located and biologically determined play. In particular, the persistence of online social communities—including those cultural assumptions, rules, and social pressures that sustain play through the indefinite extension of game form— seems counter to an otherwise and elsewhere fragile, fragmented, and fleeting human play.

In promoting group-oriented play behavior, MMO design and analysis tend to denigrate the persistent and incorrigible features of individual play. Yet, despite all their conflicts, PvE and PvP players share the same joys and immediacies of individual play, before and beyond the influence of subsequent player groupings. These shared pleasures are found in common elements of the game that social and cultural analyses often take for granted: the embedded mechanics of the game interface, the analogical sensation of movement through three-dimensional space, and those private and idiosyncratic fantasies evoked during the game's initial process of character creation.

Similarly, there are strongly shared distastes among MMO PvE and PvP players. One of the most telling of these is their mutual desire to avoid "permadeath."[19] For while "death" is, of course, the most common result of a computer game player's inability to achieve game goals, this pseudo-death is entirely representational and primarily serves as a way to limit extended play (e.g., in arcade games) and provide performance-related feedback (in all games). In action-based video games, players bounce back quickly from multiple deaths and, at the end of the game, are none the worse for wear. Within role-playing games, however, the creation of a character is a more involved and more significant portion of the game experience than it is within arcade and action games—and designers greatly extend this process of character creation so that RPG characters slowly change and "level up" over time.

The most repulsive portion of the penalty of permadeath in MMOs is that the dead character, if still valuable in some way, needs to be re-created ("re-rolled") from the beginning of the game. Aside from the great amount of time involved, this is an unacceptable consequence to most players—solo and social—for a common aesthetic reason: enjoyable game play is a meaning-making process based on assigning values to oppositional relationships, including those relationships in which one game object or character is so highly valued over some other that the lower-value character can only "die" as a consequence of that opposition. But if such death-causing oppositions are just as likely, just as informative, and just as valuable (i.e., just as "meaningful" and aesthetically pleasing) as any other, then assigning a particularly onerous consequence to one particular sort of relationship greatly increases the difficulty of determining the proper values for all possible relationships. Indeed, if enjoyable MMO play requires (at least the expectation of) a full exploration of all potential characters and character relationships, then permadeath is overly restrictive to this end. Permadeath therein becomes an incongruous MMO design feature that disrupts the normal and most enjoyable flow and consequences of play within the contexts of both cooperative and competitive play.

Thus, even if we firmly situate PvE as cooperative play and PvP as competitive play, both still involve character creation according to a fixed (and often identical) set of rules. Both involve assigning value and meanings to game characters and game objects based on their in-game relationships and the consequences of interactive play. Both result in a (pseudo-)social hierarchy that arranges and values characters in a manner similar to those values and arrangements found in external social contexts. And both, for all these reasons, find pleasure—and displeasure—in similar game design features, including a mutual abhorrence of character permadeath in MMOs.

"Productive" social play in MMOs would channel individual play into forms that are stable, predictable, and comfortable but also less diverse and less accurate in determining game values based on oppositional relationships. Therefore, currently popular MMO game designs, particularly those promoting cooperative play, operate most fundamentally as a means of social *control*—and this function must be weighed heavily against their more productive outcomes.

Yet, simultaneously, an important distinction between game experiences and literary experiences is the degree to which the latter are essentially personal while the former are always potentially social. To play is to play *with* some idea, object, or person; and as computer game technologies have evolved, it has become not only increasingly common but also increasingly appropriate to incorporate multiplayer components into computer game designs. While computer games may function most fundamentally as private experiences of self-construction, they also have the potential, unrealized by literature during the process of reading, to function as social experiences as well.

Therefore, in order to develop a comprehensive theory of play, analysis of MMOs must more clearly delineate the role of individual play within social game system design and evolution. To this end, social play will need to be re-conceptualized to include its apparently derivative and potentially negative influences on the adaptive functions of individual and oppositional play.

To this end, enter Twixt.

Notes

1 That is, opposition and recursive contextualization—see "The Computer Game Code" in chapter 4.
2 Myers 2003, 121.
3 Rheingold 2000; Taylor 2006.
4 In chapter 1, such notions are discussed in regard to the contrary notion of "bad" play.
5 Salazar 2005, online.
6 Palo Alto Research Center 2005, online.
7 Ali Baba and the Forty Thieves (Quality Software, 1981) displayed most of the basic characteristics of later and more expansive MMOs.
8 Lakoff & Johnson (1999, 2003), for instance, have located the foundations for common language acquisition within image schemata: "conceptual models of human perception and cognition [that] explain how different spatial relationships are used in language" (Rodriguez & Egenhofer 1997, 3). See also chapter 4 in the present study.
9 Huizinga 1955, 1.
10 Horning 2006, online.
11 See also figure 4.1 in chapter 4.
12 See the description of the computer game anti-aesthetic in chapter 5.
13 Spariosu 1989, 47.
14 Taylor 2006, 159.
15 Myerson 1999, available online at [http://home.uchicago.edu/~rmyerson/research/ielnash.pdf].
16 Sent 2004.
17 Shleifer 2000.
18 Linaza 1984, 271, quoting Piaget 1932, 81–82.
19 "Permadeath" occurs when an MMO player-character is defeated ("dies") and, as a result of that defeat ("death"), is permanently removed from the game, with no possibility of resurrection or reuse.

References

Horning, R. 2006. Review of "Play between worlds: Exploring online game culture." July 13. Retrieved January 1, 2009, from Popmatters, [http://www.popmatters.com/pm/review/play-between-worlds/].

Huizinga, J. 1955. *Homo Ludens: A study of the play-element in culture.* Boston: Beacon.

Lakoff, G., & M. Johnson. 1999. *Philosophy in the flesh: The embodied mind and its challenge to Western thought.* New York: Basic Books.

Lakoff, G., & M. Johnson. 2003. *Metaphors we live by.* Chicago: University of Chicago Press.

Linaza, J. 1984. Piaget's marbles: The study of children's games and their knowledge of rules. *Oxford Review of Education* 10 (3): 271–74.

Myers, D. 2003. *The nature of computer games: Play as semiosis.* New York: Peter Lang.

Myerson, R. B. 1999. Nash equilibrium and the history of economic theory. *Journal of Economic Literature* 37 (3): 1067–82.

Palo Alto Research Center. 2005. Grouping ratio by class and level. June 16. Retrieved January 1, 2009, from Play on: Exploring the social dimensions of virtual worlds, [http://blogs.parc.com/playon/archives/2005/06/grouping_ratio.html].

Piaget, J. 1932. *The moral judgment of the child.* London: Routledge & Kegan Paul.

Rheingold, H. 2000. *The virtual community: Homesteading on the electronic frontier.* Cambridge, MA: MIT Press.

Rodriguez, A. M., & M. J. Egenhofer. 1997. Image-schemata-based spatial inferences: The container-surface algebra. In S. Hirtle & A. Frank, eds., *Lecture notes in computer science*, 1329:35–52. Laurel Highlands, PA: Springer-Verlag.

Salazar, J. 2005. On the ontology of MMORPG beings: A theoretical model for research. Retrieved January 1, 2009, from DiGRA 2005, Changing Views: Worlds in Play, [http://www.digra.org/dl/db/06276.36443.pdf].

Sent, E.-M. 2004. Behavioral economics: How psychology made its (limited) way back into economics. *History of Political Economy* 36 (4): 735–60.

Shleifer, A. 2000. *Inefficient markets: An introduction to behavioral finance.* Oxford: Oxford University Press.

Spariosu, M. 1989. *Dionysus reborn: Play and the aesthetic dimension in modern philosophical and scientific discourse.* Ithaca, NY: Cornell University Press.

Taylor, T. L. 2006. *Play between worlds: Exploring online game culture.* Cambridge, MA: MIT Press.

Turner, V. 1969. *The ritual process: Structure and anti-structure.* Chicago: Aldine.

83

GAINING ADVANTAGE

How videogame players define and negotiate cheating

Mia Consalvo

Source: *Cheating: Gaining Advantage in Videogames* (Cambridge, MA: The MIT Press, 2009), pp. 83–105.

> It is all about suspense; it is like someone telling you how an action movie ends. So what is the point in seeing it if you already know how the movie ends?
>
> —*Jake, age twenty-two*

> If a game is good and I am enjoying it, it becomes almost part of my life—I will think about it on the bus home, wake up in the mornings thinking, "Aha! I wonder if I could do that?" And [I] close my eyes at night to find flashes of the game rushing around inside my head.
>
> —*Hope, age thirty*

How do game players play games, and does the experience of gameplay extend beyond direct interaction with the game itself? Beyond thinking about what games do *to* players, there is still a comparatively small amount of research concerning how players themselves organize their gameplay time and space(s), how they make choices about which games to play and why, and what else might be involved in their gameplay experiences, beyond a console, a controller, and a comfy seat.[1] Some researchers have explored how women enjoy games.[2] Others have analyzed the communication and community practices of FPS players.[3] Likewise, T. L. Taylor and Mikael Jakobsson have looked at player dynamics in *EverQuest*, studying how power gamers play the game in ways quite different from more casual gamers, even if they put in the same amount of time.[4]

Still, comparatively little is known about game players' experiences, especially when compared to a field such as television studies, where the audience is still presumed to be more passive than a game player. As players actively engage with games, they don't do so in a vacuum. Players have various ideas and information about games before they begin playing, and they gain further knowledge as

187

they progress. Key components of that information flow include knowledge about supplemental materials such as walkthroughs, strategy guides, and the employment of cheat codes.

One way to contextualize such new knowledge is by thinking about player activities through the lens of gaming capital. As previous chapters have demonstrated, the paratextual industries associated with games, including magazines and enhancement devices, have helped define how players should play games, in addition to how they might evaluate and think about them. Yet such industries can't dictate the terms of use; individuals are active in how they choose to use (or not) such items as well as how they view such things relative to the games they play. Neither side (the player or the industries) has total control, but power differentials do exist. The construction of such industries and elements helps set the terms for debate as well as frames what is debated. And even as paratextual industries have helped to create a thriving system of gaming capital that individual gamers may draw from or contribute to, that very system of capital is sometimes at odds with some of the means of achieving capital.

As we seek greater knowledge about the cultural impacts of videogames, the experiences of players themselves demand attention. This chapter addresses one part of the larger question "How do people play games?" by examining players' uses of supplemental items during gameplay, how they define what is and is not cheating in reference to those items, and then, what actions they ultimately take in accordance with their beliefs and reasoning. In doing so, this chapter offers a more detailed exploration of how gameplay is experienced by a selection of players, and what is involved in that gameplay in terms of the use or rejection of a growing paratextual industry.

Cheating in games: breaking unseen rules or violating the spirit of the game

First, what does it mean to cheat in a videogame? How can one cheat? Asking such questions forces us to consider the issue of just where the rules of a videogame can be found, and then determine how they could be secretly broken or bent for personal gain. Where are the rules? One easy answer is in the instruction manual that comes with a game. The manual often explains the objective of the game, the background of the characters and the situations, how to use the interface (controller) correctly, and what the player needs to do to win the game. It can give pointers for advancing through the game and serves as a (more or less useful) reference to consult during gameplay. But even if instruction manuals describe an objective and detail what characters can do in the game, they don't truly give the player the rules. And many players don't even read the manual and seem to get through the game just fine.

The rules of a videogame are contained within the game itself, in the game code. The game engine contains the rules that state what characters (and thus players) can and cannot do: they can go through certain doors, but not others; they can't walk through walls or step over a boulder (except maybe a special one);

they can kill their enemies, but not their friends; and they must engage in certain activities to trigger the advancement of the story and the game. All of these things are structured into the code of the game itself, and thus the game embodies the rules, *is* the rules, that the player must confront.

Lawrence Lessig writes about the code of the Internet, but his observations also apply to games. He believes that code regulates, and "as the world is now, code writers are increasingly lawmakers."[5] He also maintains that at least in reference to the Internet, our rhetoric about its "essence" hides the truth that this space is constructed, and that real choices have been made about what processes or activities are privileged or discouraged. Although he is correct in assessing current beliefs about the Internet, something different has occurred with games. Here, too, code is law and constructs the rules of the game. But for game players, this rule of law is not a hidden construction, and is also, for some, open to question and even alteration.

There have always been attempts to go beyond the rules in videogames. If we state at the outset that a player must abide by the coded rules in a videogame, what might cheating include? For some, it means going beyond the instruction manual to friends, strategy guides, and gaming magazines for hints or walkthroughs explaining how best to advance through a certain area. Help like this has been around since at least *Nintendo Power* magazine, which as discussed earlier, provided players with extensive guidance to help them play games and find all of the hidden secrets in a game. Cheating might also include the use of cheat codes that when entered into a controller or keyboard, produce a certain (beneficial) effect, such as a complete restoration of health, unlimited ammunition, or more powerful weapons. Cheating might extend to the use of a GameShark, which enters codes electronically to a game system to unlock other features. Cheating might involve altering the code of the game itself, secretly, to gain advantage in multiplayer games. It might also include paying real money for game currency or items, through such sites as the independent International Game Exchange or Sony's Station Exchange. Those aren't the only ways to cheat, and some players would definitely not label them all cheating, but this is at least an idea of what could constitute an advantage for a player.

But how prevalent are certain constructions of cheating? Do all players see cheating in the same way? How do individual game players define cheating for themselves? This chapter investigates those questions, and offers a variety of views and insights into why the definitions vary, and what this can mean for individuals as well as groups of players.

Gamers, game players, gamegrrls, and gamegeeks

As part of this project, I conducted in-depth interviews with twenty-four self-identified game players ranging in age from fourteen to forty-one. Of that group, eleven were girls and women. Two interview methods were employed: half the sample was interviewed face-to-face, with each interview being audiotaped and then transcribed; and the second half of the interviews were conducted over e-mail, with questions initially e-mailed to participants recruited from several sources, and then follow-up e-mail(s) sent for clarification and expansion of certain answers. I also conducted an open-ended survey of fifty game players ranging in age from nineteen to thirty-two who were part of a college-level course on digital games and culture. All subjects from both samples were active game players (with variation in the types of games played, the hours played, and experience levels). Interviewees were recruited through a snowball sampling method, identifying more game players from those first interviewed (initial interviews were with university students who responded to a call for gamers, and others were recruited through Web sites such as womengamers.com and joystick101.org). All interviewees and survey respondents have been assigned pseudonyms, or chose one for themselves, for identification purposes in the study. Interviews and surveys were conducted between May 2001 and May 2004.

This chapter explores several issues, including how respondents chose to define cheating in their own terms, both as an abstract concept and related to game playing; if respondents cheated or not in actual gameplay and why; how this reconciled with their definition(s) of cheating; and what actual material and social elements they used, including such items as walkthroughs, strategy guides, GameSharks, hacks, cheat codes, online sites, help from friends, and any other artifact or source mentioned.

Players' definitions of cheating

This section looks at how peoples' definitions of cheating vary and what the differences could mean to us, and does not take into account subsequent player actions. Here, my interest is in how people define the actions they will or won't take, rather than which they actually choose. The way players talk about cheating appears to fall into three categories, with one overarching theme. It's important to note that players' answers sometimes spanned categories, but when they did, there was always a logical progression in how they did so.

Overarching: cheating gives you an unfair advantage

Running throughout all the definitions was the feeling that cheating creates an unfair advantage for the cheater. Although many times this advantage was in relation to another player in a multiplayer game, it was also mentioned in regard to single-player games as just an unfair advantage in general. And it was mentioned as well by players who thought walkthroughs "were" and "weren't" cheating, and those who felt you could "certainly" or "never" cheat in a single-player game. The common thread appeared to be that cheating was more than just *breaking* a rule or law; it was also those instances of bending or reinterpreting rules to the players' advantage. Players actively made ethical judgments about gameplay that extended beyond the coded rules of the game.

Even as digital games can code in rules for players to follow, there are also "soft rules" that are negotiated. Those rules can be broken more easily than the game code or "hard rules," but to many players they are still important in understanding the bounds of acceptable gameplay and how far one can push those boundaries before an accusation of cheating is made.

The three categories that follow all draw from the unfair advantage conceptualization, but begin to draw distinctions between certain actions and items that when used, can constitute cheating. These categories actually might better be thought of not as separate but as lying on a continuum. That allows for players' more fluid practices to be taken into account as well as to see linkages between concepts.

"Anything other than getting through the game all on your own"

At one end of the continuum or spectrum would be the purist. This player would take the position highlighted above—believing that anything other than a solo effort in completing a game is cheating. Players here define cheating quite broadly, such as "when you use external sources to complete a game" (Tina, twenty-eight). Yet this position quickly becomes qualified, or is a bit of a straw person, as players in this group usually modify their statement along the lines of "anything other than getting through a game all on your own, with the exception of having a friend in the room helping you figure things out" (Mona, thirty-two). Even the most hard-core purists admitted to asking a relative, spouse, or friend, when they got stuck in a game. And for this group, the "ask a friend" lifeline seemed acceptable, but was couched in terms of "but only if you're really stuck," meaning that you had already tried to figure out the situation on your own first.

Along those lines, this group sees commercially published strategy guides, Web site walkthroughs, cheat codes, real-money trade, and everything "beyond" that as all being cheating. For example, one player states that cheating is "using information acquired outside of the game and your head to get items, find shortcuts, etc., that you wouldn't otherwise, while playing earnestly" (Jessica, twenty-five). Likewise, another player explained that "using information from a site, purchased guide, or telephone hotline in order to get around a problem, kill an enemy, solve a riddle, gain a skill, or something like that—without having at least tried to solve the issue yourself—is cheating" (Hope, thirty). While this group sees the use of items like walkthroughs and strategy guides as cheating, even they generally maintain that the use of such things is "acceptable," but in specific situations only—such as when the player has already tried repeatedly to solve the puzzle or kill the boss (or so on), but can't and is thus stuck. At that point, the player might stop playing the game out of sheer frustration and a real inability to progress further. It appears that even if it is labeled as cheating in that instance, it is considered OK.

Likewise, if a player has already beaten or completed a game, and wants to play again to explore new areas or try new things, the use of guides and other items becomes acceptable. A forum on the game magazine *Electronic Gaming Monthly*'s Web site that asked the question "Do you use cheat codes?" was answered by numerous players, the majority of whom responded that the use of such codes and other items was fine, once they had completed the game and were on at least the second round of play.[6]

It's important to keep in mind that the players defining cheating in this grouping are all referring to single-player games. These are not games where a person is opposed to another player—only to the machine (multiplayer cheating is discussed in the third theme). While there is much talk of "only cheating yourself," which may not be serious, these players do still see cheating in games where the player is not competing against anyone but oneself as well as in games that are multiplayer. How can that be, when cheating is normally defined as gaining an unfair advantage over another player?

This particular formulation of cheating can be better understood by referring to Johan Huizinga's concept of the magic circle as well as Espen Aarseth's discussion of aporias and epiphanies in adventure games.[7] For Huizinga, play can only occur in a magic circle that sets the boundaries for the game to be played, where "inside the play-ground an absolute and peculiar order reigns . . . it creates order, is order."[8] What bounds the circle are the rules of the game.

As discussed before, the rules of a digital game are contained within the programming of the game itself. Yet players also acknowledge certain soft rules in defining for themselves how far one could perhaps venture outside the circle for help. This is certainly not the breaking of rules such as the cracking or hacking of codes that form other definitions of cheating but is instead a more complex negotiation of cultural systems of support in gaming culture. How far will players move into that support system? At some point, players must make individual decisions about what they will and won't read, who to ask and for how much information, and so on, in playing a game.

For this group, gameplay is a bounded experience, and the use of almost any external item or resource could be considered cheating. Acceptable gameplay, then, is limited to interacting solely within the game world and cannot include other elements. The more interesting question is what are the implications of doing so? If we can see the benefit of such support (getting past a point where one is hopelessly stuck), is there a drawback as well? If one is only cheating oneself, why would a player be concerned with seeing guides and walkthroughs as wrong in any way?

Just as the magic circle defines the rules of the game, Aarseth's formulation of gaming's aporia-epiphany structure lends clues to this puzzle. Aarseth explains that in digital games such as adventure games, there often arise aporias or gaps that are "local and tangible, usually . . . concrete, localized puzzle[s] whose solution eludes us."[9] We must search for a solution to a puzzle, or the correct strategy to defeat an enemy, to move past the aporia and continue on with the game. The moment when we grasp the logic of the puzzle or determine what attack to employ is our epiphany. "This is the sudden revelation that replaces the aporia, a seeming detail with an unexpected, salvaging effect: the link out."[10]

While Aarseth does not speculate further on the instance of the epiphany for the player, it seems that it is frequently an emotional "aha!" moment, when the player either realizes that she overlooked an important clue or she has painstakingly solved a difficult problem. The greater the struggle is, the more satisfying or bigger the epiphanic moment. Taking this back to the use of guides and walkthroughs, such items will either reduce or eliminate the satisfaction derived from having an epiphany. The player is, essentially, looking up the epiphany in a book. While players themselves admit that such use is acceptable to salvage a failing game or in a second play, they reject the overuse of such items in the first round as cheating. Perhaps they are objecting to being cheated out of the epiphany or the emotional gratification of the epiphany. While they are not breaking any rules, an essential aspect of the gameplay—excitement and satisfaction—is reduced further and further with each glance back through the guide.[11]

Code is law: breaking the rules of the game

Midway across the continuum is a group that doesn't see the use of items like walkthroughs and guides as cheating but draws the line at items such as cheat codes, unlockables, and alterations of the game code itself. Here again, people accept the possibility of cheating in single-player games (as well as in multiplayer games), where the manipulation of code *for its own sake* can be enough to qualify.

For example, one player talks about cheating as "altering the framework that has been set forth, either something like what I understand is done in some online games where the code is actually altered to assist a certain player or using a cheat code" (Roy, twenty-six). Likewise, another player believes that "cheating is when you unfairly take advantage of 'quirks' in the game to further the development of your character in the game or your progress in the game itself" (Sally, twenty-four).

Players make distinctions between using codes that have been created by game developers, and those that players design to hack or alter the game code. Yet for this group, the use of both amounts to the same thing: cheating. There is an echo here of the danger of "epiphany loss" mentioned with the first group; one player said that the use of codes to win a fighting game would be a "hollow win" (Sally). But for this group, there appeared to be a distinction between, on the one hand, asking friends and consulting guides, and on the other, using code to win. The difference here was in the level of interference with the game—a player would have to actively alter the game rules, break the rules, in order to gain the (unfair) advantage.

For this group, as for Lessig, code is law. Players acknowledge that items such as cheat codes are readily available and accepted in some quarters, but the reconfiguration of game code is the central key to what constitutes cheating for them. Here the bending of rules is shifted—lines are drawn more closely around the game itself and further from "outside" elements like walkthroughs, which this group sees as acceptable. While actively hacking the game code is a clear rule breakage, the use of codes to unlock items or benefits not earned through gameplay becomes the bending that is deemed unacceptable. The magic circle bounding play contracts; to push or bend the boundaries involves the use of code, rather than using outside information or items. At this location along the continuum, cheating can involve other players, but can still be a single-player issue.

You can't cheat a gamecube, you can only cheat another player

Finally, a third group of players defined cheating as only existing in relation to another player. These players more closely aligned with J. Barton Bowyer, who characterizes cheating as a social activity: "to cheat, not to play the game that reflected the norm, indicated that there was another world, the world of deception, in which people did not play the game, your game, but their own."[12]

One person described cheating as involving "wrongdoing. Someone has to be worse off because someone else took unfair advantage . . . . You can only cheat another person" (Ralph, twenty-four). Similarly, other players talk about cheating as "breaking the rules or finding a loophole (like a bug in the code) to gain an advantage against someone else who is playing by the rules" (Niles, age not given). It is also implied here that cheaters are using hacks or other enhancements that other players are not—they are hiding their advantage. This should be distinguished from groups of players that, for example, all agree to play a game where player killing (PK) is allowed; in that situation, killing a fellow character would not be cheating, yet playing on a server where it is banned would be.

For this group, cheating is necessarily social (or antisocial), involving others. The use of items such as walkthroughs or code devices in a single-player game is acceptable because, by definition, one cannot cheat a machine or oneself. Those items may further progress, but they do not make another player worse off. Cheating means the introduction of deception and possible chaos into the game world, which is shared with other players. Since players are unaware of who may be cheating, uncertainty and distrust increase, especially as players move from multiplayer games at home with friends and relatives to online games that can feature thousands of unknown colleagues and opponents. Eventually, cheating (or its rumor) can lead to the breakdown of games—such as the problems that have occurred with *Diablo* and *Speed Devils Online Racing*.[13] While some correctives can be attempted (such as the creation of the company Even Balance and its PunkBuster product to stop cheating in online games, discussed in chapter 6), at other times game worlds are simply abandoned due to the rampant cheating.

For this group, the magic circle admits many players, yet the "game" being played differs by player. While deceiving others is the key to cheating, that can include hacking or altering code, exploiting systems, or socially exploiting other players. To cheat is to deceive others, but to make it appear that you are not doing so. The bounds of the magic circle have been cracked in some way, yet only the cheater can perceive the change.

Do what I say, not what I do: cheating as a daily practice

Although players have definite ideas about what does and does not constitute cheating, most of them engage in the practice on a regular basis:

I've cheated in games before because sometimes it is fun to not play by the rules or get that "god mode" feeling. (Abe, twenty-two)

Yes, I find some games far too difficult, and due to my lack of patience I will find a code to make me invulnerable or allow me to skip levels. (Noel, twenty)

Yes, I have cheated, but no one was taking the game seriously anyway! I mean, *everyone* was cheating! We all knew. It was funny. So, my cheating was OK because the rules were redefined. (Cathy, twenty-one)

I have *definitely* cheated in games. I cheated in *Diablo II* online and I had to agree not to cheat before I started playing . . . . I like to have any possible advantage against people who do not necessarily want to play fair with me. (Pete, twenty-two)

As these excerpts demonstrate, players who may define particular actions as cheating have few qualms about actually using that information or resource, at least in specific circumstances. They usually feel the need to justify their actions, however, given the generally negative connotations associated with the term cheating. Notice even in the above examples that players talked of "everyone else cheating" or other players who don't want to play fair to begin with. Likewise, even in single-player games, the activity of cheating is justified—games are too difficult or there is fun in playing god.

When players do decide to cheat, what is it they are using or doing? Most often, it's the benign activities that players engage in—asking friends for help with solving puzzles, going online to consult a Web site or walkthrough with tips on how to beat a specific opponent, or the steps necessary to gain a particular weapon. Clearly the Internet has been a boon to game players, as the availability of what is likely gigabytes of free information makes playing games more fun, more communal, and easier to do.

Almost all players utilize free sources of information—asking friends and family in person and strangers online, and consulting informational sources on the Internet. Next in line are print sources such as strategy guides. Many players do not admit to using such sources or at least to purchasing them on their own. At that stage money is involved, and a greater need must be identified than one simple problem (or the player must have a larger investment in a game, such as being a fan of the series) in gameplay. Following guides would be (legal) technological devices such as the Action Replay and GameShark. While those products are more versatile than a single title guide (being able to hold codes for many games), they also carry with them a greater stigma of cheating and offer one central type of cheating—the entering of codes—that does not appeal to all players.

Finally, coming in last are real-money trade and tip lines. None of the players who I talked with admitted to using real money to buy in-game currency, items, or accounts. That is probably due to the stigma that the practice still carries for many players as well as its violation of most games' terms of service agreements. I'll discuss such dedicated cheaters more in the next chapter, and will offer a more detailed account of real-money trade in chapter 7. I also couldn't find any players who admitted to calling a game tip line for information, although a couple of individuals did mention that someone they knew (a "friend?") had done so. Tip lines seemed to offer the least utility, and especially with the prevalence of information on the Internet, tip lines were seen as a waste of money, and it is questionable how many still exist.

Yet beyond the constraints of money and convenience, which certainly play a certain role in individuals' cheating and noncheating behaviors, why did people cheat? They cheated for different reasons, each of which is discussed in detail next.

To cheat or not to cheat: what made me do it?

There is no one single reason why people will cheat (or "enhance their gameplay experience") in games. After talking with interviewees, game developers, those working in peripheral industries, and monitoring discussion boards for many games over a period of several years, it is apparent there are multiple reasons for player cheating that are not mutually exclusive. Further, these reasons can change for individual players in different situations, on different days, and in different games. Perhaps the only constant is the lack of a constant factor.

That's because cheating isn't just about subverting the (game) system; it's also about augmenting the system. It's a way for individuals to keep playing through:

- boredom
- difficulty
- limited scenarios
- rough patches or just bad games

Cheating, or however such activities might be differently defined, constitutes players asserting agency, taking control of their game experience. It is players going beyond the "expected activity" in the game. Knowledge of how, when, and why people cheat (or refuse to) can help to better understand the gameplay experience.

Because I was stuck

It may seem obvious, but individuals want to play games and succeed in some way at them.[14] While learning can come from making mistakes and failing, too much of such negative "learning" destroys the pleasure in playing and may ultimately end the game. The most cited reason that players offer for cheating in games is *getting stuck* and being unable to progress any further. That failure happens because either the player or the game does not measure up in some way relative to the other.

Although researchers have begun to investigate the differences between play styles and the interests of men and women (and boys and girls), there is little information concerning the actual skill levels of different players across different types of games. It would probably even be difficult to determine what skills to measure and how to measure them—either in a game, over time, across game playing, or by any other yardstick. Even without such information, however, we can guess that player skill varies enormously, and the challenges that various games offer also differ, along with design competencies. And even among the best players, gameplay difficulties can occur, such as when a highly skilled 2D platform gamer moves to 3D FPS games for the first time. Different screen-reading tactics, methods for controlling the interface, and recognition of iconic elements all come together to create an experience that can be exciting and fresh, but also confusing and potentially discouraging.

Those situations occur with great frequency, especially as we move away from considering the abilities of the hard-core or power gamers to the more casual (and much larger) game-playing audience. Individual players run up against roadblocks to their game playing in many instances, including but not limited to:

- a puzzle they cannot solve
- an enemy who cannot be beaten
- a level with no obvious end point
- an unclear objective
- bugs that inhibit certain actions

Virtually every player I have talked with will use some form of help or cheat to get unstuck in the above situations, whether they define it as cheating or not. Such actions are perfectly rational, as without the help, it is unlikely that gameplay can even continue—the game is put aside in frustration and anger. Yet even as players know that they are trying to salvage some fun out of the game and have no intentions of further cheating, they still often try to justify their actions. For example, Mona explains that

> If I'm stuck on a level and just cannot figure out what to do next, I'll look at the walkthrough for just that part, but not for the whole game. In that way, I can get on with the game, but I haven't spoiled all of it.

Likewise, another player argues that guides:

> help me get through certain points where I just need to get to the next point and I'm not *seeing* what I need to see. It's probably 'cause I haven't had enough sleep and I've been overeating in front of the TV for the last

few days, but it's a, uh, that's what I use them for, more than anything else. And before I buy a guide I'll call my brother-in-law, Ray, and say "Ray! You've played this game, haven't you? What do I do? Here?" (Harmony, twenty-eight)

Even if players do not see these activities as cheating, they still justify the actions as legitimate in some way:

If I am stuck I will use walkthroughs. I also employ friends' help. I don't consider that cheating because you can justify it in odd ways. That is, using a walkthrough can be like a character's gut reaction. (George, nineteen)

I only use the help as a last resort. In the past when I didn't, I would not finish games when I got frustrated. (Ely, thirty)

Why would players try to legitimize an activity they don't see as cheating? In part, perhaps because cheating has a negative connotation to it and players are aware of such meanings. Many players have also stressed the importance of playing and winning a game "on one's own," and therefore, without outside help. The pleasure of a game often comes from achievements, and as players relate, when achievements come from consulting a guide or using a code—rather than the players' own ingenuity, creativity, or skill—the pleasure is hollow.

Such explanations can also tie back to gaming capital. Although guides and magazines can give players essential knowledge, and thus capital, overreliance (or perhaps any reliance, depending on the player) comes at a cost: admitting to an initial lack of gaming capital, at least in that particular situation.

While gaming capital has evolved, it has done so in interesting ways. Although industries have arisen to help players increase their enjoyment of gameplay, there is a striking contradiction at work. Players are not supposed to need help. If a person claims a certain amount of gaming capital, that capital bespeaks a certain level of expertise, which the player should possess. And so, the use of enhancement devices becomes furtive, in order to save face. Gamers in the know are not supposed to need such things—yet they do. So they may talk of only using them "when stuck" or "when a game is already beaten." Of course, not all players see gaming capital as limiting their options, but the coolness and "elite gamer" attitude fostered by such industries can work against as well as for their efforts.

These justifications, for whatever reasons, suggest that when players cheat to get unstuck, they are performing an *instrumental* action relative to gameplay. Codes, walkthroughs and hints are tools that players employ to restart a game that they cannot play—either because their skill level does not equal the games' imagined audience or because of faulty game design. It is not about extending or enhancing the game but about reentering it. Here, cheats are the "key" that allows players back into the game world and gives back the opportunity to re-create lost pleasure.

Finally, it should be noted that players themselves see these cheats for getting unstuck as "a last resort" and something that does have the ability to diminish their enjoyment. That could be due to either the concern that the use of outside information may destroy the pleasure of the epiphany or a fear of others' discovery of a player's lack of gaming capital. Yet players are willing to sacrifice some pleasure or admit to a lack of gaming skill if it means they can continue to play the game.

For the pleasure of the experience: it's fun to play god

I have cheated on certain occasions in some off-line shooter-type games, simply to make the game more enjoyable and long lasting (so I didn't have to start over again and again. (Drew, twenty-seven)

Sometimes it's good, at the end of a long, frustrating day, to put on the god cheat in *Quake III* and just mow opponents down left and right . . . . It can be very cathartic for me. (Mona)

Although less frequently mentioned, many other players also report cheating for the pleasures it can bring. For the most part, this group referred specifically to playing either single-player games this way, or in situations with friends where cheating was openly acknowledged and condoned by the group. Cheating for pleasure in multiplayer games is discussed in the last section of this part of the chapter, as there appear to be different reasons for that sort of cheating.

Here, contrary to the player using a cheat to get back into the game, a cheat is used to bring even more pleasure to an already-pleasurable experience. The player may have already completed and beaten the game once, or is curious about secrets or alternative options within the game. In such situations, the paratext surrounding games comes into play—players have read or heard about secrets within games, including things like side quests for powerful weapons, or ways to get the Golden Chocobo in *Final Fantasy IX* or the bicycle in *Crazy Taxi*. The information might have come from friends, Internet sites, or a strategy guide. Whatever the case, players are often invested in getting a complete gameplay experience, and so for many of them, that includes doing everything possible in a game.

In such situations, players may or may not see such activities as cheating. For those who do, they are careful to stress that they only do such things after they have beaten the game once already. Tom (twenty-one), for example, explains that

the help that I use is usually unlimited weapons; no damage; sniper-fire for all guns. I cheat so I can go back and have fun [but] . . . only when I have already beaten the game and started over with codes.

Relatedly, some players don't explicitly mention pleasure or fun as a reason to cheat but instead talk about wanting to "obtain everything," "uncover secrets," or "explore the game freely and more easily," or doing it "for the novelty." Here, enjoyment is tied to completion or a deeper knowledge of a particular game. Gamers are aware of all the extras now built into games, and are intent on experiencing as much of that content as they can. In that regard, the paratextual industry has succeeded in creating high expectations for game players about what *should* be part of regular gameplay and "how much" content they should be getting.

Cheating, in this instance, is not the instrumental action that it is when a player is stuck—it's more ludic in form. Cheats here are a playful expression for the player, intent on staying within a certain frame of mind, whether or not that action actually constitutes cheating or not. For those who do consider it cheating, it seems that certain instrumental obligations must be met first—such as finishing the game once or justifying the purchase through reference to spending a lot of money. At that point, the player can turn to (or see as justified) such actions. For those who don't consider it cheating, it is pure pleasure.

Time compression: hitting fast-forward

As Julian Kücklich explains, some cheats allow players to speed up the narrative of games and thus involve a "condensation of space."[15] Such cheats can take different forms, depending on the type of game being played— adventure gamers may consult a walkthrough to learn how to solve a puzzle more quickly, while FPS gamers might obtain a code to give them unlimited ammo and therefore clear levels at a faster rate. Importantly, though, the player is moving through the game at a presumably higher speed than they would "on their own."

Kücklich doesn't explore specific reasons for players choosing (or not choosing) such cheats, and although conceptually they may go together fairly well (the walkthrough hint and the unlimited ammo code), often players do see distinctions between them. As mentioned before, players tend to draw lines based on how "conceptually close" the cheat is to the game. For some players, walkthrough hints are OK, but codes are too similar to altering the structure of the game itself. Although both might achieve a similar end (that is, fast-forward), they do remain distinct for some players.

And yet, different players do employ such cheats. Players specifically mentioned using codes or walkthroughs to "get through a game as quickly as possible" to achieve some sort of completion. If a game had a particularly involved story, the story was frequently cited as a catalyst for the action:

> I could have figured it out, but I was in a hurry to get to the end. I wanted to see what was going on, what was coming next. (Harmony)

> I am more interested in the advancement of the game's story than the value I place on the game's ability to challenge me. (Steve, twenty-one)

Players can become involved in a particular story line, and want to see the conclusion without investing the required time to accomplish all the game-given tasks. And as many RPGs can require fifty-plus hours to complete, it's really no surprise that some players would want to arrive at the ending without spending the equivalent of more than an entire week of paid work to get there.

Such practices by game players do speak to the desire of some players for still-engrossing but less-lengthy games. Codes and hints can be fruitfully employed by the savvy gamer to tailor the gaming experience to their own time frame, but other players (or potential players) may be put off by the required time investments and not even attempt such games.

In counterpoint to wanting to witness story resolution, other players simply felt the need for closure with the game and wanted to hurry to the end point.

> Just to get a game over with. (Kris, twenty-four)

> When I give up on the game, so I don't want to invest the time to finish it, but I still want to see how it ends. I paid for it. I might as well see the ending. (Tim, thirty-two)

Here, the instrumental use of cheats returns, as they help players achieve a goal that is not entirely in line with the developers' original intent. The story isn't mentioned as a driving force for finishing the game, leaving us to speculate that players may also desire a certain amount of closure for its own sake—either being able to say that one has finished a game or the self-knowledge of completion. Some players also suggest that more interesting parts may be coming, and they wish to get past the "crap" and hopefully find more engrossing subject matter.

The instrumental nature of the cheat is in evidence, as it allows the gamer to move on to different games or activities that offer more promise of pleasure. In the case of those wishing to complete a story, the cheat may also allow pleasure in the knowledge of the story ending, if not in the actual gameplay.

Being an ass: multiplayer cheating

Finally, there's the person most of us think about when we envision the cheater. Playing against others, either online or in person, the cheater is the player who everyone else loves to hate.

> Sometimes I just feel like being a jerk online and will use cheat programs online. (Tim)

> I think I cheated (multiplayer) because I was an ass, and/or I wanted revenge against another player. (Victor, twenty-one)

> I have *definitely* cheated in games. I cheated in *Diablo II* online and I had to agree not to cheat before I started playing . . . . I like to have any possible advantage when playing a game online against people who do not necessarily want to play fair with me. (Pete)

Multiplayer cheaters were the definite minority of the players I interviewed. Players offered multiple reasons for such behavior, and most acknowledged that it was wrong or at least illegal to cheat in those ways. Several players admitted to doing such things as using aimbots and hacking the game code for the fun of causing distress and anger in other players. Others pointed to an already cheat-filled situation, and claimed that their own cheating was only to level the playing field. And one player mentioned his prowess in gaming, declaring that superior players had earned the right to cheat. By contrast, he felt that those without elite gaming skills were the ones not deserving of the greater abilities to be gained by cheating.

That last informant was illustrative of the "game the system" type of cheater who others have written about.[16] They tend to see themselves as elite gamers who have already surpassed the normal challenges offered by a game and so turn to gaming the game itself for exploits. In keeping with that approach, it would make sense for such players to express disdain for lesser-skilled players who attempt the same hacks. As Derek (twenty-one) explains,

> If a person knows how to play the videogame, if they've proven time and time again that there aren't many games that can keep them like, you know, that they can't beat, then I have no problem with cheating. It's the people who don't know videogames and then they decide they want to cheat so they can run off and play people who are way bigger than them and kill them. 'Cause that's just not, I don't know, I mean [if] you don't have any actual ability within the game, you shouldn't in a way be privy to that knowledge of how to soup your guy up.

Yet in addition to the act of earning the right to cheat, players such as Derek and others also engage in the activity as a way to cause trouble or disturb other players. Cheating in order to "be a jerk" or "an ass" focuses on the reactions of other players, and may not necessarily be tied to actual self-advancement in the game. While players may be breaking or bending rules to do so, they aren't necessarily better off at the end of the session. Such types of behavior tend to be categorized as what Chek Yang Foo and others have termed "grief play."[17]

Much like hackers, such cheaters are using the logics of code to demonstrate superiority over certain other players. For some this may be less directly confrontational, such as achieving great wealth by the careful deception of others (as a scam on Eve Online reveals), or it may be through actively defeating others in gameplay, by illegally (or unethically) acquired skills or items.[18]

I'll explore this concept and important exceptions to it in the next chapter. Yet it is fairly safe to say that the vast majority of game players consider the cheater as beyond the bounds of fair play—and often the cheaters acknowledge this themselves. Mostly, however, where the line between the full-on cheater ends and other activities begin to appear is a blurred one, which most players dynamically negotiate.

Conclusions

This chapter has investigated how players define and enact game-playing practices that could fall into the category of cheating. All players define cheating in a game as an activity that confers unfair advantage to the player. Yet that's where the consensus begins to break down. In their operational definitions, players identified different items and activities as cheating or not. From the purist to the purely social, cheating ranged from anything outside "one's own thoughts" in a single-player game to activities that had to make other players worse off. What can such a range of definitions tell us?

First, it reminds us of the diversity of play styles and practices that players bring to their games. Although it can be tempting to think only of the *Counter-Strike* hacker or the gold-buying player subscribed to an MMO, cheating, as defined by players themselves, can encompass a wide variety of actions. Second, that diversity points out the different ways that players make distinctions. For some players, the game world is defined quite narrowly—it is the game's code itself and the player—and all else is conceptualized as ideally out-of-bounds. That player wants to experience the game on its own terms, believing the game world to be cohesive enough to provide all the clues and skill builders necessary to complete it. Of course many games (or players) fall short of that expectation, at least occasionally. But that is how the purist approaches the game and sets about playing.

Next is the player who defines the game situation more broadly: the game world admits the game as well as help from other people, walkthroughs, and guides. Here, the line becomes the code of the game itself; altering it is the boundary line that players do not wish to cross—or at least during the first pass on a game. The physical code is the limit, yet the player allows other items and help into the game world.

Finally, there's the social player who only sees unfair advantage as something that can be expressed with other players present. Items and activities that are freely available to all are by definition not cheats; only secret activities used to best or gain advantage over others can "count." The game world in this instance must contain other players in order for cheating to potentially exist. And it must result in gain for the player.

If that's the range of how players define cheating, how do their actions measure up? It would be easy to argue that player definitions are based on ideal situations and their actions reflect actual playing difficulties, but while this is true to some extent, that explanation misses some key elements of cheating behaviors.

As mentioned, getting stuck is a major reason for cheating, and while making better games might diminish that problem, it will never be eliminated. Players have widely different skill levels as well as patience thresholds for different games, on different days, in different situations. Game developers will always be limited by deadlines and budgets to finish products, perhaps before they are all truly "done." There will always be times when players get stuck, or do not have ninety-plus hours to spend finding every secret item and location in a game. Likewise, even a twenty-hour game may be too long for some players, who would prefer to spend ten hours playing, see the ending, feel a sense of completion, and move on to another game. For all such reasons, people will cheat or use items others consider cheating.

Yet beyond instrumental reasons to cheat, there are purely ludic ones as well. Being playful—running around with ninety-nine lives or a bobble head—can be immensely satisfying for its own sake. It may have nothing to do with advancing the game or gaining skill. The player is gaining more enjoyment from the game, in a variety of ways.

The instrumental and the ludic, moreover, come together in social spaces, when the cheater enters the game. To be about more than grief play—which implies a solely ludic approach—the cheater incorporates instrumentality into his activities. The cheater gains the advantage and has fun in doing so. The enjoyment might differ from the form described above, as it often comes at the expense of other players (to be an ass), yet it is still about pleasure in the game.

To conclude, what does such knowledge tell us? Paratextual industries have created products and practices that play a contested role in players' experiences. They may contribute to the acquisition of gaming capital, but for some players signal its lack. Players carefully negotiate the use of such items in their gameplay, and there is a diversity of approaches in that use. Players are active and thoughtful, accepting and resisting various forms of guidance, help and cheats. Their activity indicates the complexity of the gameplay experience, which this chapter has only begun to explore. That investigation continues in the next chapter, which examines the cheater in greater depth. It asks who such players are, and how the cheater performs a critical role in the world of multiplayer games.

Notes

1 Or a computer, a keyboard, and a mouse.

2 See Gareth Schott and Kristy Horell, "Girl Gamers and Their Relationship with the Gaming Culture," *Convergence* 6, no. 4 (2000): 36–53; Pam Royse, Joon Lee, Undrahbuyan Baasanjav, Mark Hopson, and Mia Consalvo, "Women Gamers: Technologies of the Gendered Self," in *New Media & Society* (forthcoming); T. L. Taylor, "Multiple Pleasures: Women and Online Gaming," *Convergence* 9, no. 1 (2003): 21–46.

3 Hector Postigo, "Of Mods and Modders: Chasing down the Value of Fan-Based Video Game Modifications," in *Digital Games Industries*, ed. Jason Rutter (Manchester: Manchester University Press, forthcoming); Talmadge Wright, Eric Boria, and Paul Breidenbach, "Creative Player Actions in FPS Online Video Games," *Game Studies* (2002), <http://www.gamestudies.org/0202/wright/>.

4 T. L. Taylor and Mikael Jakobsson, "The Sopranos Meet *EverQuest*: Socialization in Massively Multiuser Games," in *Command Lines*, ed. Sandra Braman and Thomas Malaby (forthcoming).

5 Lawrence Lessig, *Code: And Other Laws of Cyberspace* (New York: Basic Books, 1999), 60.

6 "Do You Use Cheat Codes or Not?" *Electronic Gaming Monthly* message boards, 2002, <http://boards.gamers.com/messages/message_view-topic.asp?name=egm&id=zrcdr>.

7 Johan Huizinga, *Homo Ludens: A Study of the Play Element in Culture* (Boston: Beacon Press, 1950); Espen Aarseth, *Cybertext: Perspectives on Ergodic Literature* (Baltimore, MD: Johns Hopkins University Press, 1997). Elsewhere I critique the magic circle, as it suggests boundaries for gameplay that seem unrealistic in the contemporary world of games, where guides, fan fiction, and codes found in magazines (among other things) can appear and mediate gameplay at times apart from the actual playing of games. Yet the concept can still be helpful, I believe, in asserting that there is a boundary for games, which I believe are the rules of the game itself. Thus, the circle defines a conceptual rather than a spatial limit to games.

8 Huizinga, *Homo Ludens*, 8.

9 Aarseth, *Cybertext*, 124.

10 Aarseth, *Cybertext*, 91.

11 Oftentimes, even the guides themselves advise players to use them sparingly, in order to not spoil the excitement of figuring things out on their own. One of the guides to *Myst* at GameFAQs.com admonishes players to try and play through the game without consulting the more detailed walkthrough, unless the player is absolutely stuck. Additionally, the commercial strategy guide for the Nintendo game *Legend of Zelda: Majora's Mask* actually seals the information about the final battle and end of the game in a separate envelope at the back of the guide.

12 J. Barton Bowyer, *Cheating: Deception in War and Magic, Games and Sports, Sex and Religion, Business and Con Games, Politics and Espionage, Art and Science* (New York: St. Martin's Press, 1982), 300–301.

13 Mike Laidlaw, "Cracking Pandora's Box," The Adrenaline Vault, <http://www.avault.com/articles/getarticle.asp?name=pandbox>.

14 Success is obviously a loaded term here, and could include grief players who measure success through the levels of discomfort they cause in others players as well as more traditional players who try to follow the game's various success markers.

15 Julian Kücklich, "Other Playings: Cheating in Computer Games" (paper presented at the Other Players conference, IT-University of Copenhagen, December 2004), 4.

16 Chek Yang Foo, "Redefining Grief Play" (paper presented at the Other Players conference, IT-University of Copenhagen, December 2004); Chek Yang Foo and Elina M. I. Koivisto, "Grief Play Motivations" (paper presented at the Other Players conference, IT-University of Copenhagen, December 2004).

17 Foo, "Redefining Grief Play"; Foo and Koivisto, "Grief Play Motivations."

18 Nightfreeze, "The Great Scam," <http://static.circa1984.com/the-bigscam.html> (accessed March 1, 2005).

References

Aarseth, Espen. *Cybertext: Perspectives on ergodic literature*. Baltimore, MD: Johns Hopkins University Press, 1997.

Bowyer, J. Barton. *Cheating: Deception in war and magic, games and sports, sex and religion, business and con games, politics & espionage, art & science*. New York: St. Martin's Press, 1982.

Foo, Chek Yang. "Redefining grief play." Paper presented at the Other Players conference, IT–University of Copenhagen, December 2004.

Foo, Chek Yang, and Elina M. I. Koivisto. "Grief play motivations." Paper presented at the Other Players conference, IT–University of Copenhagen, December 2004.

Huizinga, Johan. *Homo ludens: A study of the play element in culture*. Boston: Beacon Press, 1950.

Kücklich, Julian. "Other playings: Cheating in computer games." Paper presented at the Other Players conference, IT–University of Copenhagen, December 2004.

Laidlaw, Mike. "Cracking Pandora's box." The Adrenaline Vault. <http://www.avault.com/articles/getarticle.asp?name=pandbox>.

Lessig, Lawrence. *Code: And other laws of cyberspace.* New York: Basic Books, 1999.

Nightfreeze. "The great scam." <http://static.circa1984.com/the-bigscam.html> (accessed March 1, 2005).

Postigo, Hector. "Of mods and modders: Chasing down the value of fan-based video game modifications." In *Digital games industries*, ed. Jason Rutter. Manchester: Manchester University Press, Forthcoming.

Royse, Pam, Joon Lee, Undrahbuyan Baasanjav, Mark Hopson, and Mia Consalvo. "Women gamers: Technologies of the gendered self." In *New Media & Society*. Forthcoming.

Schott, Gareth, and Kristy Horell. "Girl gamers and their relationship with the gaming culture." *Convergence* 6, no. 4 (2000): 36–53.

Taylor, T. L. "Multiple pleasures: Women and online gaming." *Convergence* 9, no. 1 (2003): 21–46.

Taylor, T. L., and Mikael Jakobsson. "The Sopranos meet *EverQuest*: Socialization in massively multiuser games." In *Command Lines*, ed. Sandra Braman and Thomas Malaby. Forthcoming.

Wright, Talmadge, Eric Boria, and Paul Breidenbach. "Creative player actions in FPS online video games." *Game Studies* (2002). <http://www.gamestudies.org/0202/wright/>.

84

GIRL GAMERS AND THEIR RELATIONSHIP WITH THE GAMING CULTURE

Gareth R. Schott and Kirsty R. Horrell

Source: *Convergence*, 6(4), December 2000, 36–53.

Abstract

This paper describes an investigation conducted into the current accessibility and allure of gaming platforms for females. In order to investigate one of the most developed areas of new media, a traditional feminist approach of explaining factors that exclude females from new media technologies was avoided in favour of a focus upon the experiences and attitudes of females who already view themselves as 'gamers'. Synonymous with 'grrl gamer' and 'game girlz' this paper uses the term 'girl gamer' to describe females who possess an aptitude for the games that currently define the contours of the gaming culture. In-depth interviews and ethnographic game-play observations conducted with a small sample revealed that 'girl gamers' possess an alternative playing orientation, style of play, the importance of cultural competency in game preference, as well as knowledge on the ways gaming is embedded in household dynamics.

Introduction

At present, computer games represent one of the most developed of the new media technologies. Over the last 30 years interactive multimedia has expanded from network-based games to stand-alone games, and moved from a position of controlled presence in arcades to potentially unlimited access in homes everywhere. The origins of the 'explosion of screen-based entertainment'[1] can be traced back over three decades to when *Pong* (Atari) (electronic ping-pong) became one of the first computer games to be made commercially available for domestic use. By the end of the 1970s popular arcade games like *Space Invaders* (Atari) and *Pac-Man* (Atari) were available on the Atari, the first widely popular home game console.[2]

By retailing at a fraction of the price of multimedia computers, the game consoles available today (*Dreamcast, Nintendo 64*, and *Playstation*) serve to make computer gaming more accessible. It is now common for a successful console game to have sales of well over a million units,[3] often surpassing 'chart-topping music CD's'[4] and competing directly with the financial returns of the cinema.[5] Indeed, the industry as a whole is currently worth more than ten billion dollars and growing.[6]

Technology = masculine

At the heart of academic understanding of computer games and games consoles is the widely held conviction that technology embodies a culture which is expressive of masculinity.[7] Male designers who have developed games' have traditionally preserved male dominance within the gaming industry based on their own tastes and cultural assumptions'.[8] Computer games such as 'sport simulations', 'beat 'em ups', 'shoot 'em ups' and 'adventure games' that incorporate fantasy and human violence[9] are said to maintain gender differences in play[10] and affect the degree of female participation in computer play.[11]

In the early 1990s Eugene Provenzo's content analysis of games available on the Nintendo platform revealed that games contained a small number of female characters in mostly submissive and marginal roles. For Provenzo, stereotyped portrayals of gender embody the culture in which games exist as well as reveal its prevailing attitude towards women.[12] Indeed, examples of sexism and misogyny are easily found within the annals of computer games. An extreme case is *Custer's Revenge* (Atari VCS), an infamous early eighties game which allowed players to have sex with an Indian squaw tethered to a pole[13] or in less liberal terms 'had nothing less than rape as its goal'.[14]

Today, the number of female characters contained within games has increased and with it their function has altered from 'window dressing' to active figures and principle characters. Characters such as Lara Croft (*Tomb Raider*, Eidos), Tina (*Dead or Alive*, SCEE), and Xiaoyu (*Tekken 3*, Namco) now represent powerful action figures that feature in popular games. Although gender representation has altered during the last decade, game developers openly state that their rationale for the inclusion of female characters is based upon the premise that they appeal more to the average boy gamer than an equivalent male character. As Herz concludes, 'when it comes to video games, teenage boys are the ones with the positive female role models'.[15] A game such as *Tomb Raider* may have sold over 16 million games, but the majority of its players remain male.[16]

The androgynous game

Although numerous sources confirm that gaming is a heavily male-oriented culture, it is not an exclusively male pastime. The saturation of gaming culture now means that an estimated 30 per cent to 50 per cent of families in the USA 'own or rent game systems and buy or rent games'.[17] Coupled with this is an estimation that 14 per cent to 25 per cent of the total gaming market can be attributed directly to females who game.[18] Despite the lack of equity between male and females within the gaming culture, games such as *Pac-Man* (Atari), *Tetris* (NES), *Baku Baku* (Sega), *Myst* (Cyan), *Riven* (Cyan), *Sonic the Hedgehog* (Sega) and *Abe's Odyssey* (GT Interactive)[19] are noted for their cross-gendered appeal. Furthermore, game-play has recently extended beyond traditional game narratives to include games that involve rapping (*PaRappa the Rapper*, SCEE), dancing (*Spice World*, SCEE; *Beatmania*, Konami) and composing music (*Fluid*, Sony; *Music*, Codemaster). Despite facing stiff opposition from gaming purists who have labelled such developments as 'games which are not games' and a 'passing fad',[20] they represent attempts to open-up and extend the gaming market.

There is also evidence to suggest that within the disproportionate number of females who game, there are girl gamers who pursue their interest in an active fashion. For example, a *Games White Paper* published by the Computer Entertainments Software Association (CESA) in Japan, reported that females recently made up one-fifth of the attendance at the Tokyo Game Show.[21] Furthermore, there now exist female-owned game companies (eg Her Interactive, Girl Games, Girltech & Purple Moon), female game designers (eg Trina Roberts; Lorne Lanning), female-oriented web sites (eg Just4girls, Q.Girlz) and organisations of girl gamers (eg DieValkarie, Clan PMS, Game Grrls, Quake Grrls) which together serve to represent, support and encourage 'girl gamers'.

Towards a study of girl gamers

Gill and Grint state that there is no longer a need to justify whether 'relations between gender and technology deserve attention; that argument has already been won'.[22] However, there remains a need to examine the issues raised by different technologies. The present study recognises the exigence for counterbalancing the non-participation of females in computer technologies with accounts of the factors that cause and maintain girl gamers' interest in a male dominated culture.[23] As Orr Vered notes it 'It's time for a different type of analysis to be brought to bear on the question of gender and computer game play'.[24] By examining females who already possess an aptitude for computer gaming our aim was to address the different ways in which females are positioned in relation to gendered technologies. Amongst theorists who discuss gender-technology a need is identified for understanding the motivation of females who currently engage with the gaming culture 'without transforming the direction of technological development'.[25] In this way, the link between masculinity and technology is retained and understood in the context of girl gamers who negotiate the male encoded culture of gaming. Thus, the present study sought to approach the entangled relationship between gender and technology by conducting an exploratory study of the meanings that female games console users attribute to computer gaming.

Methods – target sample

Green, Reid and Bigum have argued that research concerned with computer games is essentially examining children's culture.[26] While we accept the existence of a gaming culture, we questioned whether computer gaming is correctly defined as children's culture, given the number of games which now carry an '18 certificate'.[27] With this in mind, the present study aimed to examine both children and adult girl gamers. The authors were particularly interested to discover whether adult females gamed at all, or whether it is primarily the province of younger children.

The sample for the study was achieved by distributing an open letter within a large health organisation that employs a diverse workforce. The letter outlined the research and requested members of the workforce to nominate themselves or other females (daughter, granddaughter etc) who might be interested in participating in the study. The sampling method can broadly be described as a 'snowball technique', as first contacts either directly entered the study or led researchers to other respondents. This strategy functioned as an effective platform for locating girl gamers from both age ranges. Nominated individuals were then approached and screened for the study. Although data was collected on all responses to the open letter, this paper describes the data generated from females selected for in-depth study. The group comprised of both children (mean age = 7.9) and adults (mean age = 29.3), with the adult occupations ranging between full-time mothers, clerical officers and managerial positions.

The significance of the setting and methodology for the study

Given the focus on adult as well as children gamers, the present study was conducted on weekends and week-day evenings in the context of girl gamers' homes. The aim was to address gaming as a free-time leisure activity. Therefore it was necessary to distinguish gaming from school or work related computer use. Furthermore, research has already suggested that female identity as gamers is contextually-restricted, in that gaming in male dominated environments 'is not socially rewarding for females'[28] and therefore generally avoided. Instead, research has shown that females possess a tendency to play computer games at home over and above other contexts.[29] For these reasons and others (outlined below) arrangements were made for the second author of this paper to visit respondents in their home at a time when they would conceivably play computer games.

Beyond the physical space in which the games are played it was also recognised that game play takes its players to tombs (*Tomb Raider*, EIDOS), factories (*Abe's Odyssey*, GT Interactive), castles (*Spyro the Dragon*, SCEE), islands (*Crash Bandicoot*, SCEE) and different planets (*Riven*, Cyan). In order to provide a comprehensive account of the experiences of girl gamers it was considered necessary to account for both these locations within the methodology employed to collect data. To achieve this, interviews constituted the primary source throughout each session. However, this was combined with an observation of females' game-play within the context of a 'gaming interview'.[30]

Given the moral and social concerns that perennially surround the use of computer games[31] an attempt was made to avoid inviting socially desirable or adult responses during the interview. To achieve this interviews were couched as discussions with a fellow girl gamer, interested in exploring the experiences of other girl gamers. In the tradition of ethnographic research, the interviews were closer in character to conversations. Yet, as Hammersley and Atkinson state 'they are never simply conversations' as an agenda was maintained and control was retained over the proceedings.[32] In line with this thinking, the concept of a 'gaming interview' was also devised to facilitate a more 'play like' atmosphere and generate questions about female playing experiences as they occurred. Once the interviewer had established a rapport with the girl gamers, a request was made to either view or participate in any of the games specified during discussion. The interviewer also brought her own games to the interview in order to share gaming preferences with the participants and facilitate the commencement of the 'gaming interview' scenario.

Unlike arcade games where gamers play(ed)/paid for time, home games consoles have changed the continuous and short-term nature of game play, thus, permitting interpersonal communication during the course of play. Although this depends on the nature of the game being played, junctures within play generally enable communication and tactical discussion between players. The problems that require solving within adventure games often transcend the physical dexterity required by the joystick controller. Decisions concerning direction, orientation, utilisation of discovered objects are often more pressing and benefit from the input of others. From a methodological perspective, this allowed interviews with girl gamers to continue whilst games were in play. In addition to this, the gaming interview provided direct access to the girl gamers' playing style and habits, generated new questions and permitted the girl gamer to express their views on gaming whilst engaging directly with the technology. The benefits of initiating interactivity within play were thus twofold. Firstly, it allowed the researchers to emphasise their approval of gaming, which secondly, facilitated the interaction between the girl gamers and the female researcher.

Findings and discussion: practicalities of playing

The first section of the interviews sought to discover how girl gamers gain access to gaming, that is, whether girl gamers own or merely have access to a console. With girl gamers only representing a comparatively small proportion of the gaming market, it was important for us to explore whether girl gamers are unaccounted for or unrepresented in game content, primarily because their access to the gaming culture is achieved through secondary access to consoles owned by others.

On the whole, respondents owned the games consoles on which they played. Exceptions were generally found amongst older adult respondents with families, one of whom used her sons' games console. In such cases, access to gaming was initially spurred and then maintained by male interests and playing habits. Likewise, the type of games played under these situations was also invariably determined by the preferences of the console owner. Although part of the rationale for inclusion in the interviews was the degree to which females described their interest in gaming as more than a passing trend, those who experienced secondary access to game consoles revealed little desire for ownership or strict control of their playing experiences.

In contrast, child participants and adult participants in their early twenties owned their own consoles. However, similar to the position of those who have secondary access to consoles, it was found that ownership did not always secure or determine girl gamers' relationship with their console. The following extract typifies the obstacles that girl gamers face in their access to their game consoles. In this extract, one of the girl gamers revealed that she faced stiff competition from her father for access to her own console:

Child Gamer: *. . . my father's on it usually . . . I hardly get to play because my father's on it all the time. At about half past eight . . . my father starts playing on it, and about ten o'clock he's still playing on it and I've got to go to bed.*

Interviewer: *Do you ask him to let you play?*

Child Gamer: *Yes . . . but he gets on different levels and he gets onto them for me as well, he saves them onto my memory card.*

Interviewer: *So does your dad think you are playing the games together?*

Child Gamer: *Yes.*

This situation was based upon a common perception, evident in all the discussions, that males are 'the experts' when it comes to knowing what is required and how it is achieved. In all cases males constituted a vital frame-of-reference for girl gamers' gaming practices.[33] In doing so, male gamers represented players that they looked up to yet did not aspire to emulate, a finding that may be explained by girl gamers' playing style (discussed below) as well as the distance maintained between males as experts and girl gamers as novices. As the previous extract showed, male access to girl gamers' consoles was often presented or explained as support or collaborative play, when in fact what was described entailed little explanation, guidance or communication from male counterparts. Another example highlights this:

Interviewer: *When you play together on a game, who holds the joypad?*

Child Gamer: *We both do, but my [male] cousin does mainly . . . when it is a new bit that we haven't done.*

Interviewer: *Why don't you get to play on the new bits?*

Child Gamer: *Well he is better than me, he's been on different levels and things, he has got further than anyone else on it.*

212

Interviewer: *So when do you get to hold the controls?*
Child Gamer: *Mostly . . . You know when there's a bit which you can't do, and you do it loads of times. You know what you have to do, It's just you can't do it.*
Interviewer: *So does he tell you what you need to do? Or what's going on?*
Child Gamer: *No, not really, I just try to copy what he does. I usually get killed so he gets to go back on it.*

By adopting the position of 'watcher'[34] girl gamers appear to reinforce the positive association between masculinity and technology, which in turn elicits a sense of female inferiority in relation to gaming competence. Indeed, the act of 'stepping aside' to give others access to one's consoles was further confirmed and illustrated as a gender issue by a mother who is only permitted to play on her sons' console in their absence. In this instance, the sons do not have to compete for playing time with their mother in the same way that girls appear to with their fathers, brothers or cousins. Overall, the discussion with girl gamers did not present the home as a gaming context that possesses an operational philosophy of equal access and opportunity. Instead, gaming rights appeared to be embedded in existing social dynamics and gender hierarchies, a conclusion that was supported further by findings that relate to the way gaming becomes an issue within household politics.

Playing preferences

From the range and variety of games available to players, girl gamers were extremely consistent in their selection of a small number of games noted for their cross-gendered appeal. Girl gamers showed a preference for 'role play games' (RPG's) in which players adopt the role of protagonist in a quest. More specifically, girl gamers selected RPG's that contain an animal or creature (*Spyro the Dragon*, SCEE; *Crash Bandicoot*, SCEE) as its principle character, rather than a highly gendered male or female character. All the games identified were 'androgynous games'[35] and hence mainstream best-sellers, which meant that they were also available to the girl gamers who do not purchase their own games. However, it should be noted that those who have secondary access to games consoles played 'androgynous games' to the exclusion of a large range of other more traditional games.

Even though RPG's commonly possess some overarching purpose that justify their activities, the goals embodied within the narrative of the game did not correspond with girl gamers' reasons for playing. Instead, discussions with respondents were focused around the freedom that RPG's gave to exploration of its virtual environment for the accumulation of symbols that possess general life enhancing qualities. All girl gamers professed a liking for non-purposeful exploration, and stated that they generally avoided playing in a competitive fashion (against the game or other players). Furthermore, high-risk competitiveness (situations which carried the risk of losing a playing life or termination of the game) were perceived as requiring high levels of manual dexterity and commitment and deemed less enjoyable. Thus, girl gamers revealed a distinctive style of play that incorporated a high degree of open interpretation of game-objectives.

Other sources have previously revealed a female preference for games that are rich in character description and well-developed stories. Although the present study confirmed this finding these factors described the context of girl gamers' play rather than their motivation or playing style. Little intent to compete against the game or complete all of its constituent elements was demonstrated by girl gamers who were able to sustain their interest in a game by playing solely on demo disk versions. Available as promotional material, demo disks only contain a small percentage of a game to secure consumer interest:

[In the context of a discussion of their favourite games.]

Child Gamer: [Shouts] *Spyro . . . but we're are having a different Spyro now.*
Adult Gamer: [in response] *Yes we are having a new Spyro now.*
Interviewer: [directed at Child Gamer] *Oh are you?*
Child Gamer: *Yeah, with all the levels on it.*
Adult Gamer: *We've been playing it on the demo disk we got from a magazine.*
Interviewer: *So you've only just started playing Spyro then?*
Adult Gamer: *No, we've played it for ages, we . . .*
Child Gamer: [interrupting] *because there's new places*
Adult Gamer: *No it doesn't go as many places that one . . . . It's enough for us, with some games, to play the demo disk because we aren't that interested in finishing everything, we just like to run around and pick things up.*

Likewise, in other discussions with girl gamers, the titles of favourite games given to the interviewer were sometimes only possessed on demo disk and not the full software-package. In this way, appreciation of the story-line was non-linear. The study therefore revealed a discrepancy between the narrative text as a motivating force which attracts and maintains girl gamers' play and the narrative text as a motivator which determines progress towards game completion.

In the context of the information gathered on girl gamers' software preferences, girl gamers were also very forthcoming about the types of games that they disliked. As one participant declared:

Adult Gamer: *I also like the silly little ones like the Tetris thing, I like them, but I don't like the big involved games . . . I don't like them.*
Interviewer: *What do you mean by involved?*
Adult Gamer: *The involved games, the strategy games, I like a game when you just run around and pick stuff up.*

Respondents also indicated that they believed gaming was strongly biased in favour of males. In explanation of this supposition, it was argued that:

214

Adult Gamer: *They are very boyish in the fact that they tend to be football games or rugby games, and even the driving games tend to be rally racing type stuff, they are quite aggressive aren't they?*

Interviewer: *Yes, perhaps they are.*

Adult Gamer: *I mean I like Spyro . . . he's a very gentle little dragon.*

It was commonly stated that more boys play because so many of the games are in fact 'blokey games, y'know things like shoot 'em ups'. Referring to the disproportionate amount of games that are released with only male gamers in mind, girl gamers highlighted the lack of real choice available to them:

Child Gamer: *There are like more boy games coming out for the Playstation, I get Crash Bandicoots because they are my favourite games and because there's not much girl games out like. The only girl game I've actually got is the 'Spice Girls'* [reference to Spice World the dancing game].

Interviewer: *Would you like to see more games which have more for you as a girl?*

Child Gamer: *Yes, I think there should be more girl games coming out because there is a lot of boy games and they like, . . . you don't understand them because they are like for boys. Like there's football games and everything.*

Interviewer: *But I see you have football posters on your wall, why don't you play football games?*

Child Gamer: *I don't like the football games that are out, because it's hard to play because you've got to . . . try and get it off another player, and if you don't really know what the rules are . . . it's hard.*

This girl gamer not only recognised that gaming culture has direct links to existing male culture, but also there are ways in which such games presuppose a certain level of cultural competence. This and other similar comments were notable for the way computer games are not perceived as neutral artefacts by girl gamers, but an embodiment of the knowledge and practices of a male culture.[36] Thus, with reference to the range of games played by females, girl gamers revealed that their experiences outside the context of gaming did not in any way facilitate their ability to 'learn how to learn'.[37]

Stereotyped images in games

Questions relating to the *Tomb Raider* series were used to address girl gamers' attitudes and opinions towards the highly gendered images within games. Although one of the most successful and popular games of the 1990s, *Tomb Raider* is a good example of a game that appears to offer more for males than females. Indeed, the game's protagonist, Lara Croft, was featured in *The Face* magazine as one of the most popular twentieth century icons. Conforming to stereotypical perceptions of female beauty,[38] its popularity with males is not only documented by the selling power of the product, but also exemplified by *Playboy's* attempt to feature the human Lara Croft representative in their magazine.[39]

None of the respondents named the multi-million selling *Tomb Raider* as a game they favoured, although all had experience of playing it. However, it was not necessarily the case that the explanation for girl gamers' dislike of the game was purely an issue of gender stereotyping. Interestingly, girl gamers' negative responses were also linked to their playing preferences and approach to gaming. Many of the girl gamers revealed that their dislike for *Tomb Raider* was based on what they felt to be the inadequacy of the controls:

Child Gamer: *She's ok,* [Lara Croft] *but it's hard to move her . . . when I played it I couldn't work out how to do things like jump. She just flattens herself on these thorns, and if I got her over the first ones, there's another lot of thorns and I couldn't get her over them.*

Although essentially exploratory in nature, the virtual environment of the tomb was perceived by most as too claustrophobic and requiring a high level of joypad manipulation for effective navigation. Girl gamers also identified that they did not appreciate the intense nature of the problem solving tasks required to proceed in the game.

Inevitably the exaggerated physique of Lara Croft also figured in girl gamers' explanations for their dislike of the game:

Adult Gamer: *Her boobs are too big, huhuhuhu well the Lucozade advert, I don't think anyone looks at the Lucozade, well the men don't, but I mean it is pathetic really, I mean I have played the games . . . but her as an individual is a bit over the top.*
Interviewer: *What do you mean by pathetic?*
Adult Gamer: *Well it's like, Lara Croft is like curvy and everything, whereas the blokes that she's shooting are straight figures . . . they're all ugly. Anyway, I prefer the games where you don't have to just keep shooting.*

One of the most notable aspects in this extract is the way that the respondent seeks to balance the *Tomb Raider* games by including highly gendered male characters. Parallel to the phenomenon of Lara Croft, Poole has noted that Bandai, the company behind Duke Nukem the 'testosterone-dripping digital hero', are claiming that their protagonist receives a great deal of female interest.[40] In this instance, the attraction of *Duke Nukem* (3D Realms) is located within the large spin-off industry generated by the game, including cards, posters and action figurines. Unlike male interest in Lara Croft, female interest in Duke Nukem does not appear to include the software in which he appears.

It is also important to point out that the unpopularity of Lara Croft as a protagonist, within our sample, did not rule out female characterisation as something that girl gamers would like to see in place in games. Interestingly, one member of the child sample revealed that she was in the process of designing her own game, using the co-star of *Crash Bandicoot* (SCEE), Coco Bandicoot as her heroine. Currently, Coco is not an interactive character, but one that appears in the animated clips between levels. She declared that:

Child Gamer: *I'm trying to design a game, but I haven't finished it yet.*

Interviewer: *Can you tell me about what you've done so far?*

Child Gamer: *I've started to draw the characters . . . because everybody knows about Crash Bandicoot, so I've started to make a game with Coco Bandicoot. I've drawn the characters, I've either got one or two, I've got them in my file over there.*

Interviewer: *Can I have a look?* [finds a blue file and pulls out a folded piece of paper with pencil illustrations on it]

Child Gamer: *That man is called Neo Cortex, and he's starred in Crash Bandicoot one, two and three, and Wooky Witch is our new character we've tried to design.*

Interviewer: *Tell me about Wookey Witch.*

Child Gamer: *Well she's, when Coco Bandicoot's gonna try and get past her, she's gonna like either have a magic cloak or something and you've got to try and steal it off her, and she fires her magic lightening bolts at you.*

Interviewer: *What made you want to have new characters then?*

Child Gamer: *They're always men, the baddies and goodies and I like Coco but you can't be her.*

This particular girl gamer sought to extend the boundaries of interactive play to include character preference. This simple alteration would permit males and females to retain the game-play of the Crash Bandicoot games, but with the option of Coco as a principle character. Likewise, younger girl gamers also identified that they would still play the now unfashionable dancing game *Spice World* (SCEE) which features the 'Spice Girls', if it could be altered to include current pop sensation 'Steps' or other neutral characters. Thus, in these instances it appears that the key to increasing the longevity of some games would be to offer players greater flexibility in terms of characterisation rather than alter the nature of the game-play. This type of player choice is only currently available in arcade length games such as beat 'em ups. Thus, given this finding it would be interesting to pursue the impact of character choice upon girl gamers' playing behaviours.

Communication with others

The present study was also interested in exploring how girl gamers fit into the existing channels of communication within the gaming culture, in addition to what extent they had set up their own networks of communication with other girl gamers. In response to an enquiry regarding the type of actions participants take when they experience difficulty within a game, girl gamer's responses varied. Nevertheless, the interdependence that traditionally occurs between gamers and the support mechanisms of gaming culture (the web, magazines and official solution guides) were not evident in girl gamers' responses. Instead girl gamers highlighted individual persistence, male intervention, resetting the level, restarting the game and game termination as responses to obstacles. Common within all these responses was a lack of concern with the numerous problem strategies available to gamers:

Interviewer: *Do you use the cheats that you can get in gaming magazines?*
Adult Gamer: *I don't no, I'm not that involved. I'll play the games, but I'm not involved like [Boyfriend] is. He'll just play and play it until he finishes it, whereas it doesn't bother me if I finish it or not.*
Interviewer: *When you get stuck and you can't go any further, what do you do?*
Child Gamer: *You just keep working at it.*
Interviewer: *What if that doesn't work, do you use cheats?*
Child Gamer: *No, I guess I ask someone else, like my Dad, he can sometimes help me.*

The last extract appears to confirm Favro's suggestion that gaming unproblem-atically promotes communication and social interaction.[41] However, girl gamers provided examples of the way male status as 'expert' led to bias in game-related interaction. Although girl gamers revealed that they receive games or gaming magazines from males, many also provided instances of receiving either restricted software (see 'playing preferences') or incomplete knowledge:

Child Gamer: *I've got one magazine but some of the pages that I needed had been ripped out.*
Interviewer: *That's a bit mean.*
Child Gamer: *He reckons it was his baby brother who done it, but I don't know who done it, but I think he done it because it's that particular spot.*
Interviewer: *Why doesn't he want you to get there?*
Child Gamer: *He doesn't want me to be as good as him.*

This extract exemplified the pseudo-communication found between girl gamers and male counterparts, as well as actions that subvert female progress and main-tain male status as the 'expert'.

In contrast to early research that took the arcade as its focus,[42] game consoles have brought research into the home. Yet, irrespective of their domestication, game consoles continue to occupy a position in the public domain through game retailers. Attention was also given to the nature of girls' gaming activities, in particular alternative locations for their gaming. When asked whether they try out new games on playing-posts in shops, none of the respondents reported that they did. The responses indicated that shops, like arcades, are a male preserve. This attitude is perhaps best summarised by one of the young gamers, who stated that she sometimes watched boys play new games in shops, but has never had the courage to participate in that particular setting. Adult gamers, however, revealed that gaming occasionally occurs in the company of friends. However, it was commonly stated that they rarely instigate social gaming, neither do they actively participate when it does occur. Again, the processes of play[43] were revealed as affecting female playing practices with male involvement typically leading either to the exclusion of girl gamers, or girl gamers to exclude themselves.

Gaming and household politics

Adult participants revealed that the amount of time males devote to playing games constitutes a source of contention within the home. In relation to other everyday activities for girl gamers the older respondents spoke of how their time was divided between several other activities, including domestic labour. With particular reference to domestic chores, girl gamers stated that even though they enjoy gaming they are unable to attribute as much importance to it as males do.

Interviewer: *So how often do you play now?*

Adult Gamer: *Not as much because there's always something else to do . . . in the house you'll always find housework. And I think that's the other thing, the time commitment really. I mean it's important for my husband to know how Spyro works but it's more important for me to have the dinner cooked! I mean I want to be able to do it, but* [shrugs shoulder].

A number of examples were provided of the perceived imbalance between male and female gaming habits in relation to domestic chores. In such cases, male gaming habits appeared to be the cause of friction between partners:

Adult Gamer: *Sometimes things have got to be done. No one ever cleans this place, me included, but it'll be me that ends up doing it, because* [partner] *be like 'just let me finish this'.*

Likewise:

Adult Gamer: *Well* [partner] *didn't come to bed 'til about three o'clock last night, because he was, a friend has lent us a game at the moment, Soviet Strike and he has to finish it, he had to work this out so he didn't come to bed 'till about three o'clock.*

Interviewer: *How did that make you feel?*
Adult Gamer: *That was alright, I'd rather he did it in his time, it's when it gets in the way of other things that it bothers me.*
Interviewer: *Such as?*
Adult Gamer: *Like when we are all waiting for him so we can go out, or when there's things that need to be done around the place. You know its not life or death.*

For adult gamers it would seem that male gaming habits compete with other activities while girl gamers' gaming is often consigned to second place following housework. Therefore, for adult gamers it appeared that gaming slots into the existing nexus of domestic power. If this finding is taken in conjunction with Sefton-Green's[44] contention that today, a necessary condition of adulthood is the regressive ability to play, the fact that females appear to experience several barriers that serve to limit or deny their opportunities for play warrants a more focused investigation.

Conclusions

To make broad generalisations from a small exploratory study would seem imprudent, as it may produce an overly restrictive image of the girl gamer. Yet, it is possible to state that the girl gamers investigated in this study did not fit the profile of the masculinised heavy gamer.[45] Instead it has been possible to identify gaming characteristics that appear specific to girl gamers but also extend the profile of gamers. Thus, in the face of a priori criteria for identifying gamers, the findings of this study not only contradicted the traditional stereotype of the gamer, but have also initiated an alternative profile of the gamer that may situate further research into the girl gaming phenomenon. Understanding of girl gamers would therefore benefit from a wider and larger scale survey of the experiences of the average girl gamer within the UK. In particular this study has also revealed that adult gamers are an interesting phenomenon that would benefit from further study, specifically focused upon gaming within the family setting and the domestication of technology.

In answer to the question, 'Who are girl gamers?' this study firstly identified girl gamers as a group that are drawn from a broad age range. This was a group that enjoyed gaming as a secondary activity, in the sense that their absolute playing time was constrained by several self-imposed sanctions. Despite the wider availability of gaming consoles, the restrictions placed upon playing time were caused by interactions between several factors. Factors included the presence and dominance of male gamers, the salience of contrasting female/familial social roles and the self-efficacy levels of girl gamers in relation to their playing style and gaming preferences. The gaming interview was vital in revealing how girl gamers possess not only distinct playing tastes, with reference to the type of games they play, but also the style which they adopted in-play that is connected to their playing objectives.

Specifically, girl gamers identified a preference for third-person role-play games that contain animal/creature based characters rather than highly gendered human figures. In addition to these factors, games also needed to allow girl gamers the freedom to explore the virtual setting of the game. This was supported by the finding that girl gamers rejected games such as sports games and violent, combat focused games that are not open to creative interpretation. Girl gamers also revealed their awareness of the sexism in games and claimed to desire a more balanced portrayal of males and females in games, as well as greater flexibility in character choice. Thus, in gendering the technology, this study revealed that girl gamers require a specific combination of characterisation and game-play.

With reference to girl gamers' experiences of gaming culture the study produced some interesting findings. Although gender difference in time commitment has consistently been reported, with boys playing more than girls,[46] this study has identified possible explanations for such differences in the frequency of playing. Girl gamers believe that they experience gaming culture as secondary gamers, as owning a console does not guarantee them playing rights, neither does it allow them to excuse themselves from housework, as it does for males. Girl gamers do not extend their playing habits to engage in game play outside the home; neither did they show any evidence of participating in the wider gaming culture. No evidence was found for an alternative culture or female gaming networks. Instead, progression in play largely relied on their interdependence upon dominant male gamers, which in all cases constituted a primary frame-of-reference for their gaming activities. Irrespective of the active role assumed by some high profile girl gamers, it is possible to conclude from this data that girl gamers overwhelmingly negotiate their play through, and in relation to, a social space encoded as male. Thus, as long as the public face of gaming continues to be male dominated, girl gamers will continue to be perceived as residing on the margins of gaming culture.

Notes

1 J. Sanger, J. Wilson, B. Davies and R. Whittaker, *Young Children, Videos and Computer Games: Issues for teachers and parents* (London: Falmer Press, 1997), p. 6.

2 M. Kinder, *Playing with Power: In movies television and video games* (London: University of California Press, 1993).

3 'Interactive Entertainment Software: Rapidly maturing market', *Screen Digest*, June (1997), pp. 129–36.

4 J. Watts and F. Islam, 'Playstation 2 Arrives to Tease the Emotions', *The Guardian*, 14 September 1999, p. 23.

5 S. Poole, *Trigger Happy: The inner life of videogames* (London: Fourth Estate, 2000).

6 J. Cassell, and H. Jenkins, 'Chess for Girls?: Feminism and computer games', in *From Barbie to Mortal Kombat: Gender and computer games*, eds. J. Cassell, and H. Jenkins (Cambridge, MA: MIT press, 1998).

7 R. Gill and K. Grint, *The Gender-Technology Relation*, (London: Taylor & Francis, 1995). J. Wajcman, *Feminism Confronts Technology*, (Cambridge: Polity Press, 1991). P. Glissov, G. Siann and A. Durndell, 'Chips With Everything: Personal attributes of heavy computer users', *Educational Studies*, 20, no. 3 (1994), pp. 367–377.

8   J. Cassell and H. Jenkins, p. 25. L. Haddon, 'Electronic and Computer Games: The history of an interactive medium', *Screen: Technological relation*, 29, no. 2 (1988), pp. 52–73.

9   M. Griffiths, 'Computer Game Playing in Early Adolescence', *Youth & Society,* 29, no. 2 (1997) pp. 223–236. J. B. Funk, G. Flores, D. D. Buchman and J. N. Germann, 'Rating Electronic Games: Violence is in the eye of the beholder', *Youth & Society*, 30, no. 3 (1999) pp. 283–312.

10 K. Orr Vered, 'Blue Group Boys Play Incredible Machine, Girls Play Hopscotch: Social Discourse and Gendered Play at the Computer', in *Digital Diversions: Youth Culture in the Age of Multimedia*, ed. J. Sefton-Green (London: UCL Press, 1998).

11 T. W. Malone, 'Toward a Theory of Intrinsically Motivating Instruction', *Cognitive Science*, 5 (1981) pp. 333–370. P. M. Greenfield, 'Video Games as Cultural Artefacts', *Journal of Applied Developmental Psychology*, 15 (1994) pp. 3–12.

12 E. Provenzo, *Video Kids: Making sense of Nintendo* (London: Harvard University Press, 1991).

13 *Edge*, 'Parental Advisory Explicit Content', UK Edition, Future Publishing, June (1999), pp. 68–77.

14 L. Haddon, p. 62.

15 J. C. Herz, *Joystick Nation: How video games gobbled our money, won our hearts, and rewired our minds* (London: Abacus, 1997) p. 177.

16 J. Cassell and H. Jenkins.

17 Ibid. p. 14.

18 Ibid.

19 P. Wilson and K. Stuart, 'Essential Playtest: Abe's Exodus', *Essential Playstation*, 10 (1998) pp. 72–75.

20 *Essential Playstation*, 'Games Which Are Not Games', 10 (1998) pp. 36–40.

21 S. Poole.

22 R. Gill and K. Grint, 'The Gender-Technology Relation: Contemporary Theory and Research', in *The Gender-Technology Relation*, eds. R. Gill and K. Grint, (London: Taylor & Francis, 1995), p. 2.

23 S. McNamee, 'Youth Gender and Video Games: Power and control in the home', in *Cool Places: Geographies of youth culture*, eds. G. Valentine and T. Skelton (London: Routledge, 1997).

24 K. Orr Vered.

25 J. Wajcman, p. 25.

26 B. Green, J-A. Ried and C. Bigum, 'Teaching the Nintendo Generation', in *Wired Up: The electronic media*, ed. S. Howard (London: UCL Press, 1998).

27 Edge (June, 1999).

28 M. Griffiths, p. 235.

29 Durndell, P. Glissov and G. Siann, 'Gender and Computing: Persisting differences', *Educational Research*, 37, no. 3, (1995), pp. 219–227. J. Giacquinta, J. Bauer and J. Levin, *Beyond Technology's Promise: An examination of children's educational computing at home* (Cambridge: Cambridge University Press, 1993). K. Gilliland, 'Curriculum Development for Gender Equity in Computer Education', in *Technology in Today's Schools*, ed. C. Wagner (Association for Supervision of Curriculum Development, 1990). K. Inkpen, M. Klawe, J. Lawry, K. Sedighian, S. Leroux and D. Hsu, 'We Have Never-Forgetful Flowers in Our Garden: Girls responses to electronic games', *Journal of Computing in Childhood Education* 5, no. 2, (1994), pp. 383–403. L. Haddon, 'Explaining ICT Consumption: The case of the home computer', in *Consuming Technologies: Media and information in domestic space*, eds. R. Silverstone and E. Hirsch (London: Routledge, 1992).

30 C. M. Begly, 'Triangulation of Communication Skills in Qualitative Research Instruments', *Journal of Advanced Nursing*, 24 (1996), pp. 688–693. M. Hammersly and P. Atkinson, *Ethnography: Principles and practice* (London: Routledge, 1997).

31 M. Griffiths, 'Video Games and Aggression', *The Psychologist*, 10, no 9 (1997), pp. 397–399. H. Jenkins, 'Prof. Jenkins Goes to Washington', (circulated e-mail: "Henry Jenkins" henri3@mit.edul999). P. Keegan, 'US Marines Train to Kill Using this Game. So what does it teach the other 20 million or so people who play it?' *The Guardian: G2*, 1 July 1999, pp. 1–3. J. Sefton-Green (ed.) *Digital Diversions: Youth culture in the age of multimedia* (London: UCL Press, 1998).

32 M. Hammersley and P. Atkinson, p. 152.

33 H. W. Marsh and J. W. Parker, 'Determinants of Self Concept: Is it better to be a relatively large fish in a small pond even if you don't learn to swim as well?', *Journal of Personality and Social Psychology*, 47 (1984), pp. 213–231.

34 M. L. Benston, 'Women's Voices/Men's Voices: Technology as language' in *Technology & Women's Voices: Keeping in touch*, ed. C. Kramarae (London: Routledge Kegan Paul, 1988).

35 J. Cassell and H. Jenkins.

36 J. Wajcman.

37 K. Orr Vered.

38 J. Cassell and H. Jenkins.

39 V. Dodd, 'Lara Croft Saved from Playboy', *The Guardian*, 15 July 1999, p. 6.

40 S. Poole.

41 P. J. Favro, 'Games for Co-operation and Growth – An alternative for designers', *Softside*, 6 (1982), pp. 18–21.

42 L. Haddon.

43 K. Orr Vered.

44 J. Sefton–Green.

45 P. Glissov, G. Siann and A. Durndell. K. Roe, and D. Muijs, 'Children and Computer Games: A profile of a heavy user', *European Journal of Communication* 13, no. 3 (1990), pp. 181–200.

46 M. Griffiths, 'Amusement Machine Playing in Childhood and Adolescence: Comparative analysis of video games and fruit machines', *Journal of Adolescence*, 14 (1991), pp. 53–73.

85

INTRODUCTION (EXCERPT) TO
VIDEO GAMES AROUND THE
WORLD

Mark J. P. Wolf

Source: Mark J. P. Wolf (ed.), *Video Games around the World* (excerpt) (Cambridge, MA: The MIT Press, 2015), pp. 1–12.

With the enormous growth of the World Wide Web in the last two decades, the rise of mobile platforms and casual games, and an increasing number of game creation programs, the entrance requirements to the global video game industry are lower than ever. Small video game companies are appearing all around the world, each hoping for a hit that will bring it international attention and fame, both of which can spread much faster due to the Internet. With this rise in game production, many more countries have their own video game industries and their own national histories of video games, many of which are only now beginning to be recorded. And yet, thanks to foreign imports and indigenous productions, many national video game histories are already decades old even though the majority of them are not widely known beyond their own borders.

Video game histories typically follow the highlights, innovations, and advances made in the field, and naturally this can only be done using the resources available to researchers. In the United States, the first researchers were journalists or hobbyists looking back on the medium as it grew, such as the multipart "Electronic Games: Space-Age Leisure Activity" by Jerry and Eric Eimbinder, which first appeared in the October 1980 issue of *Popular Electronics*, and books such as George Sullivan's *Screen Play: The Story of Video Games* (1983) or Scott Cohen's *Zap!: The Rise and Fall of Atari* (1984). Interest in video game history picked up during the 1990s and saw the publication of David Sheff's *Game Over: How Nintendo Zapped an American Industry, Captured Your Dollars, and Enslaved Your Children* (1993) and Leonard Herman's *Phoenix: The Fall and Rise of Videogames* (1994). Soon after came Steve Kent's *The First Quarter: A 25-Year History of Video Games* (2000), later renamed *The Ultimate History of Video Games: A History from Pong to Pokemon—The Story Behind the Craze That Touched Our Lives and Changed the World* (2001). As nostalgia grew for video games, mass-market books with color photography appeared, such as Rusel DeMaria and Johnny L. Wilson's *High Score! The Illustrated History of Electronic*

Games (2003) and Van Burnham's *Supercade: A Visual History of the Videogame Age, 1971–1984* (2003). In the decade following that, many more books on video game history appeared, including two of my own, *The Video Game Explosion: A History from PONG to PlayStation and Beyond* (2007) and *Before the Crash: Early Video Game History* (2012). Other books have discussed the spread of video games, such as *Gaming Globally: Production, Play, and Place* (2013), edited by Nina B. Huntemann and Ben Aslinger, and an email discussion list, Local Game Histories [LOCALGAMEHIST], has been started by Melanie Swalwell and Jaroslav Svelch as a resource for the global community of game historians.

Most video game history books, however, are produced largely for a North American audience who remembers the games and so the books are thus compiled from the resources available in North America. After the rise of Nintendo following the North American Video Game Industry Crash of 1983, some Japanese history would be included and perhaps some information on Europe. But even in the pre-crash era, video game production and play was occurring around the world as foreign imports and home computers quickly spread. Research in computer science was already underway in multiple countries, with discoveries and developments occurring simultaneously and independently. Games, both amateur and professional, were made and circulated. Hobbyist groups, demoscenes, and communities of enthusiasts formed as early as the late 1970s, and written works including newsletters, magazines, journal articles, reviews, and books appeared, but they typically did not travel beyond their nation's borders. Even into the 1980s and 1990s, national histories of video games would remain largely unknown outside their countries of origin due to language differences and cultural divisions. This continued until the 2000s, when international conferences on video games began to bring together researchers from different countries. The chapters of *Video Games Around the World* attempt to describe the events of various national histories to an English-speaking audience, and many were compiled from primary research when no secondary sources were available. Some of these national histories appear here for the first time in the English language, and some for the first time in any language.

Readers will note that the chapters here vary greatly in terms of length, scope, style, and focus. Although all contributors were given a list of criteria to follow (namely, the history of video games in the country or region, the reception of foreign imports, domestic video game production and exports, indigenous video game culture and how it was influenced by national history, video game company profiles, video game content description, the role of academic video game studies, and the future of video games in the country or region), it was not always possible to cover all these areas. Video game production varies greatly from one country to the next, and where there is less production there is usually even less scholarship on games. While here in the United States one might take for granted that events will be thoroughly documented and that those documents will be safely filed away in an archive, where they will be preserved and made accessible to researchers, this is not the case in many parts of the world (and sometimes not in the United States either, for that matter). Those areas suffering from poverty, political instability, and minimal infrastructure naturally have other priorities, and some cultures do not place the same value on documentation and preservation, or they lack the necessary resources or inclination to do so.

When compiling this collection, there were two approaches that could be taken; I could try to include as much of the world as possible, even though this meant that chapters would vary considerably, or I could include only those chapters written by established academics with all the necessary resources available to write a complete history even if it reduced the global nature of the book's coverage that I originally intended. I have gone with the first option; however, the book described in the second option is still present here, and those who would prefer it can simply set aside those chapters that do not meet their needs. And even the longest chapters here can only touch upon all the various aspects of a national history of video games and suggest an outline of their contours.

As an editor, I have also chosen to allow a variety of voices throughout the book rather than try to homogenize them all into a single style, in order to preserve some of the cultural differences that one inevitably encounters in a project of this scope. Most of the contributors are also natives of the countries they are writing about, so in addition to researching video game history, they have lived through it, experiencing it firsthand, with a deep understanding of the culture in question as well as the prevailing zeitgeist. As noted in the "Contributors" section, many of them are also game designers and founders of game companies, giving them a firsthand perspective on the industries they discuss. Each country or region's unique situations and circumstances affected how their national video game histories developed and the shape that video gaming took; for example, the long history of computer science in the United Kingdom and Scandinavia, the prevalence of mobile games in Africa, Mexico and New Zealand's many arcade games, Brazil's large number of master's and doctoral theses, the Dutch industry's large percentage of serious games, the demoscenes of Eastern Europe, the PC Bangs of South Korea, the warnets of Indonesia, and so forth.

One may also note differences in terminology, which I have, for the most part, included here. For instance, although "video games" is arguably the most common term used to refer to the medium (at least according to Internet search engine results), other terms, such as "computer games" or "digital games" are also used and suggest a different context in which games arose. While people in the United States typically first encountered video games in the arcade or on a home console connected to a television set, leading to the common use of "video" games, in other parts of the world, particularly those where television did not have as strong a presence or had yet to even make any inroads at all, video games were more associated with home computers or even mobile devices, leading to the use of other terminology to describe them, such as "computer games," "digital games," or "electronic games." I have thus decided not to standardize some of the terminology throughout this book, to allow this cultural variation to manifest itself. As the difference in terminology demonstrates, the level and usage of technology and other resources differs greatly from one place to another, and it is to these that we next turn.

Laying the groundwork: infrastructures necessary for video game industries

A video game industry, even video games themselves, need infrastructure to support them. In the case of video games, we can identify three levels of infrastructure, each built upon the ones below it, which are necessary for a national industry to take root.

At the first level, there are basic needs such as access to electrical power, verbal and visual literacy, and lifestyles that include leisure time for gameplay. Electrical power, needed for the operation of video games, whatever kind they might be, may be distributed by power lines from a central production facility, in the form of batteries, or supplied by solar cells. The first of these three requires a certain level of industrialization, which in turn requires a certain amount of capital and the commercial and governmental means to control and regulate it, while the last two are less centralized but still require an industry to produce them or, at the very least, to import them. In any case, there is an ongoing energy expense for the user beyond the cost of the game and the platform it runs on, and a reliance on a technology that may be considered a luxury. And even electricity is a luxury that many do not have; as recently as 2013, around 1.3 billion people were still without access to it.[1]

Video game play also often requires verbal and visual literacy and some experience with media conventions. Not only do video games have text (at least in manuals and on menu screens, if not embedded within the games themselves), their visuals are often complex and fast-moving and depend on visual conventions borrowed from other media, such as conservation of screen direction and off-screen sound from cinema and television, word balloons from comics (for example, in many Nintendo games), and spatial constructions seen and navigated from a first-person perspective. While most cultures that have video games have already experienced film and television, these media still form the basis for an intuitive understanding of how video games work, and those cultures lacking such experiences are less likely to adopt video games as readily.

Finally, leisure time available for gameplay is necessary for video games, especially those requiring dozens of hours for their completion. Even casual games collectively can take up hours of one's time, hours which may not be available in agrarian cultures or cultures in which the work needed for subsistence takes up much of the day, or among the poor whose long hours in farm fields or factory sweatshops leave little time for relaxation. As mentioned above, there is also the cost of the systems and games themselves, which requires at least a small portion of disposable income. Thus, a certain level of economic development is also at the base of the first level of infrastructure.[2]

Once the first level of infrastructure is satisfied, the next level includes a certain amount of technology, technological know-how, and access to a system of game distribution and marketing. The first of these involves screen technology such as a television set or computer monitor, which the user must own before buying the console or computer system that will be attached to it; or, in the case of arcade games, there must be arcades or other places where the machines can be exhibited and available to the public. In many countries, home computer games are more prevalent than console-based games because of the relatively high cost of consoles (which are more limited in their capabilities) compared to home computers (which are usually cheaper and more multifunctional). Another technology is a system of telephony, either in the form of landlines or mobile phone towers and networks, which are needed for online games and mobile games. These often require Internet service providers (ISPs) as well. And the presence of the Internet does not guarantee the reliability and bandwidth needed to play online games, the requirements of which are a moving target as games continue to evolve.

Naturally, a certain degree of technical knowledge and expertise is necessary for the installation, use, and maintenance of these technologies, which together amount to a technology sector in a country's economy, and this, in turn, requires some degree of training for employees and users alike. Telephony and the Internet almost always involve connections to the rest of the world's communications systems, with all their conventions and protocols, and for many countries this will also include involvement with foreign communications companies.

A system of game distribution and marketing that is accessible to consumers is also necessary for video game culture to emerge. While today the Internet provides a forum for discussions about video games and a venue for their marketing and distribution, in earlier times this was accomplished by events at arcades, home computer clubs, magazines, bulletin board systems (BBSs), advertisements in hobby shops, and gatherings at conventions, demoscenes, warnets, PC Bangs, and so on. In the late 1970s and 1980s, home computer culture made it possible for users to create their own games and trade them, and the rising interest in computer games encouraged the importation of games and console systems, often by companies in related industries. As Melanie Swalwell writes in her chapter about New Zealand, "For some of the companies involved in the manufacture and sale of console (and arcade games), video games were just one of the various electronics design and manufacturing enterprises in which they were involved. Fountain was a well-known electronics company, producing record players, stereo systems, clock radios, and even microwave ovens. David Reid was the name of an electronics store. As far as arcade machines went, Rait made audio amplifiers, whilst Kitronix's products included heat sinks, guitar amplifiers, and printed circuit boards." On the other hand, some companies importing games had little or nothing to do with electronics; as Humberto Cervera and Jacinto Quesnel tell us in their chapter on Mexico, it was a meat-packing company that held the rights to import the Atari VCS 2600 into Mexico.

Once a country has attained the infrastructure of the first two levels just described, a third level of infrastructure becomes possible, which allows for the development of an indigenous game design and production industry. This level includes game designers, developers, programmers, and other professional staff, corporate structures to stabilize and maintain an industry, the necessary investment capital, and a large enough user base to make larger-scale productions financially feasible. Schools and training programs have aided the development of a skilled work force, and since the appearance of the World Wide Web, digital technologies such as game engines and game creation software, as well as the ability to collaborate interactively over long distances, has made it easier for independent producers to work anywhere in the world.

Even when all these things are present, however, the success of the industry will still depend on the successes of individual companies, and those successes will depend on the creation of video games that consumers want to play if profits are to be made (and they are made not only through game sales, but through membership subscriptions, sales of in-game merchandise, licensing, and advertising). Nothing can guarantee a game's popularity, as history has shown; the balance between conventions and innovations, and familiarity and novelty, along with the right kind of content, is difficult enough for anyone to achieve. The actual creation and marketing of games, as well as their content, is determined by a variety of factors, including the tensions present within the video game industry.

Tensions in national video game industries

Much of video game history (and for that matter, history in general) depicts enduring struggles between opposing forces over time, as well as the effects that produce and are produced by these tensions. The following sections look at some of the tensions present in national video game histories, which vary in importance from one country to the next. Although each of them is described in terms of one thing versus another, they should each be considered as more than just a simple binary opposition; each is a spectrum of possible positions, many of which will be found coexisting alongside each other. As can be seen in the chapters in this book, these forces largely determine the shape of an industry and the games it produces.

Indigenous production versus foreign imports

Every country that has video games has experienced the domination of foreign imports. For all countries except the United States, where they originated, video games arrived as an element of a foreign culture and one that threatened to displace local culture, or at the very least, would need to be assimilated. As Wesley Kirinya writes in his chapter on Africa, "Some of the games that used to exist in the traditional cultures, for example, Mancala and Bao, also faded away as they would be seen as 'backward' by the urban 'elite.'" In places like Africa, which had already experienced colonization by foreign powers, video games could be seen as yet another form of foreign cultural influence. Even in the United States, ever since Nintendo eclipsed Atari following the crash of 1983, foreign home game systems have been dominant, beginning with the importation of the Nintendo Entertainment System (NES) in 1985. Even as of late 2014, only one of the three top-tier video game systems (the Nintendo Wii U, PlayStation 4, and Microsoft Xbox One) is made by an American company. While the crash may have given foreign industries a respite, allowing them to pull ahead, other venues since then such as online gaming and mobile gaming have also reset the stage and given smaller companies the means to reach large international audiences.

Thus, the tension between foreign imports and indigenous production can be found in every country that has video games, and how this tension is managed varies greatly from one to the next. In almost all cases, the entry of foreign imports preceded indigenous video game production, establishing conventions and audience expectations that shaped the country's domestic video game industry and its output. The situation is similar to that faced by the film and television industries of many countries during the twentieth century; the importation of Hollywood cinema and American television programming was cheaper and easier than producing film and television programs domestically, and domestic projects rarely had budgets that could compete with Hollywood. The result was that national cinemas were displaced by Hollywood product to such an extent that governments intervened with quotas (as in postwar Britain), laws keeping foreign income within the country, or laws limiting foreign imports (such as Italy's Andreotti Law), as well as coproductions that were international in scope and were designed for a pan-European audience instead of merely a national one. Similar solutions can be found in national video game industries and are described in the chapters here.

At the same time, however, the distinction between foreign and domestic companies and games is an increasingly problematic one, since both console-producing companies (such as Nintendo and Sony) and major game-producing companies (such as Electronic Arts, Rockstar Games, and Ubisoft) have branches in multiple countries and continents. Each of these branches employs a local labor force, and, as a result, their products may even reflect the national cultural context. Furthermore, branches of foreign companies are often closely linked to local companies.

Just as programmers left Atari and began other companies such as Activision and Imagic, foreign branches of companies can seed national industries by hiring and training local designers who then leave to start their own companies. For example, as Dominic Arsenault and Louis-Martin Guay relate in their chapter on Canada, employees of the Canadian branch of Electronic Arts, known as EA Canada, left to start several of their own third-party studios, greatly enlarging the Canadian video game industry. As we see in Peichi Chung's chapter on Singapore, some governments even encourage foreign studios to enter their countries with the expectation that they will train local talent who will then start their own local companies. However, the opposite can also occur, since successful local companies are sometimes bought by foreign companies—for example, the Australian studios Beam, BlueTongue Entertainment, and Ratbag Studios, which were purchased by Info-grames, THQ, and Midway Games, respectively (see Thomas H. Apperley and Daniel Golding's chapter on Australia). And once the parent companies decide to cut back, some of these national branches are closed, sending professionals back into the job market again.

Sometimes foreign companies outside the video game industry can also play an important role, as in the case of the Timex Corporation in Portugal, which assembled its home computers in the country (see Nelson Zagalo's chapter), or the meat-packing company mentioned above that brought the Atari 2600 into Mexico. Imports don't always make it into countries either; as Melanie Swalwell tells us in her chapter on New Zealand, "Global distribution anomalies appear to explain the fact that some widely available consoles, such as the Colecovision, Intellivison, and the Vectrex, did not make it to New Zealand." Finally, foreign imports and indigenous production can be combined in such a way as to threaten both industries in the form of pirated versions of games.

Legitimate industry versus piracy

The degree to which piracy is present in a country depends on the efforts made to control it, governmental attitudes regarding patents, copyrights (and their infringements), profit margins, supply and demand, and even cultural attitudes toward copying and ownership. While many countries face software piracy due to the ease of reproducing digital media such as CD-ROMs, DVDs, and other optical discs, some countries also have pirated consoles in their black marketplace as well.

Piracy generally occurs due to the desire for lower-priced merchandise, especially when the population in question already is subject to low wages and economic hardship. Lower-priced pirated merchandise makes it harder for legitimate industry to compete and thus drives away legitimate outlets and companies even as it spreads video game culture among those who would not have been able to afford it otherwise. Pirated goods hurt foreign imports as well and often appear just as fast as the new games do. Consumers, however, can sometimes consider piracy a subversive activity; as Anthony Y. H. Fung and Sara Xueting Liao write in their chapter on China, "While the disregard for copyright is, in general, seen as the piracy of intellectual property, consumers in China (as they argue), see it as resistance against the dominance of the concept of copyright and patents. Local businesses also conceive of it as a counterforce against the giant multinational companies." Governments, then, may use piracy as a way of controlling foreign imports and influence, deliberately limiting them by making it difficult for profits to leave a country. As Humberto Cervera and Jacinto Quesnel explain in their chapter on Mexico, piracy can lead to brand loyalty that continues into legitimate industry when consumers are later able to afford legitimate products.

Piracy can also help determine the relative balance between the various sectors of the video game industry. For example, online games that require monthly subscriptions and access to a company's servers are less vulnerable to the loss of profits than standalone games that can be copied and sold; thus, in areas with high rates of piracy, companies may find online games more profitable. While statistics do not appear to exist regarding the number of programmers and other technical personnel who get their start in pirated games and later use their experience to make the transition into the legitimate industry, piracy can provide training for local workers who want to get into the video game industry and may make it easier for legitimate companies to find skilled employees. The competition between legitimate and illegitimate producers also mirrors, to some extent, another tension in the industry between mainstream and independent (or "indie") productions.

Mainstream industry versus independent productions

In the early days of video game production, games were typically created entirely by single individuals, opening production to anyone who was interested, and hobbyists could even begin to form their own companies (for example, in the Czech Republic, as Patrik Vacek tells us in his chapter). As games grew more sophisticated and elaborate, with more complicated hardware, they required larger design teams and game budgets, making it more difficult to enter the industry. By the late 1980s, only larger, mainstream companies were able to program games for state-of-the-art systems. By the end of the 1990s, triple-A game budgets were in the millions of dollars, and by the early twenty-first century, games such as *Grand Theft Auto 4* (2008), *Red Dead Redemption* (2010), and *Star Wars: The Old Republic* (2011) had budgets of USD $100 million or more. Few companies can compete at this level, and even games that are expected to do well due to their ties to existing franchises can eventually fail, such as the MMORPG *Star Wars Galaxies* (2003–2011), which began well but alienated players when changes were made.

Thus, different levels of games and game budgets exist. Since the 2000s and the rise of casual games and mobile gaming, an increasing number of game development tools and software have made it possible for small companies to develop games, and with the World Wide Web, distribution can be done digitally and reach a global audience. In some countries, government subsidies are available to aid the local industry, as Thomas H. Apperley and Daniel Golding describe in their chapter on Australia, and in others, government policies, programs, and support encourage the local industry growth of small-to-medium-sized companies, as Peichi Chung tells us in her chapter on Singapore. Government involvement can also lead to game censorship laws or to self-regulating organizations supported by the mainstream industry (such as the Entertainment Software Ratings Board [ERSB] in North America and Pan European Game Information [PEGI] system in Europe), or governments may even ignore games and see them as harmless (as in parts of Africa). Such attitudes and initiatives, begun by the mainstream industry, are usually applied to independent productions as well.

While games are usually seen as entertainment by consumers, the recognition of video games' artistic potential can also aid indie productions that are more experimental in nature, calling attention to new directions and possibilities for games. Museum exhibitions also help to highlight innovative games and game technologies, some of which may have commercial potential, and game journalism and academic scholarship can also promote such games. Like the film industry, successful innovations that begin in independent or experimental productions often make their way into mainstream productions, and successful indie companies occasionally grow to join the mainstream as well, blurring the divide between mainstream and indie productions. But gauging the marketplace and attempting to appeal to consumers is no longer something limited to national scope. Especially in smaller countries with limited markets, consideration of the global marketplace has become increasingly important.

National marketplace versus global marketplace

As mentioned earlier, foreign imports often set the tone, conventions, and audience expectations for video games within a national marketplace. Already-established hardware platforms and game engines may place limits or restrictions on game production, marketing, and distribution, and existing game genres may determine how games are perceived and experienced by an audience. Local game development companies are often enlisted to assist with the creation of games for multinational companies and foreign franchises, which have the global marketplace in mind. National audiences, especially in smaller countries, may not be large enough to recoup the cost of more expensive games, leading companies to reduce game content that is considered too nationalistic and thus not as exportable (as discussed in Songsri Soranastaporn's chapter on Thailand).

A wholly national aesthetic, then, may become harder to develop, since games with more nationalistic details may not sell as well on the international market, and the more expensive game development is, the more likely the international market will need to be targeted to return a profit. Like cinema, national languages sometimes give way to more internationally used languages such as English, so as to broaden the potential audience of a game. But whereas a two-hour film can be easily dubbed or subtitled with another language, games requiring dozens of hours of gameplay, with many contingent situations, may have more content to be translated, raising the cost. One of the most extreme examples of this is *Star Wars: The Old Republic* (2011), which reportedly contains more than two hundred thousand lines of recorded dialogue.[3] And yet there are still many games that are strongly rooted in their respective cultures, such as *Adventures of Nyangi* (2007), *Quraish* (2007), *Capoeira Legends* (2009), *The Spirit of Khon* (2010), and many other games mentioned in the chapters of this book.

Yet while corporations are concerned with selling games as broadly as possible in the global marketplace so as to maximize profits, gamers who are interested in something different may wish to explore games that are rich in localized content, and some games have managed to frame their unique cultural qualities in ways that distinguish them from their competitors, increasing their sales. With international distribution made easier by the Internet, more such opportunities become available as time goes on. Games that rely mainly on graphics as opposed to text, and those that have more recognizable game mechanics, may appeal and be playable regardless of culture and language barriers; and games that find success in their national marketplace may be able to reinvest profits in English-language (or other-language) versions for the global marketplace. Better still, games can be designed from the start to have multiple languages built in to them and their marketing. For example, Afkar Media has an English-language Web page promoting its game *Quraish*, which involves Islamic history (see http://www.quraishgame.com/qe_index.htm), and the game itself features interfaces in both Arabic and English. Even in the area of censorship, which differs from one region to the next, games can be designed with multiple systems in mind. In their chapter on Australia, Thomas H. Apperley and Daniel Golding describe how *Fallout 3* (2008) was altered globally due to requirements for Australian classification. In some cases, governments actively support games that promote national culture, for example, the Indonesian MMORPG *Nusantara Online* (2009). As Inaya Rakhmani and Hikmat Darmawan write in their chapter on Indonesia, "*Nusantara Online* was developed based on sociological, archeological, and historical theories that speak of Indonesia's cultural roots. The characters, social system, architecture, and even the virtual map are consistent with Indonesian cultural history in combination with mythological characters, legends, and folklore." Video games can also be coordinated with other media, and the relationship between them constitutes the last of the tensions to be explored in this section.

Video games versus other media

In the United States, video games became a venue for the adaptation of properties from other media as early as the late 1970s and early 1980s—for example, the Atari 2600 cartridges *Superman* (1979), *Raiders of the Lost Ark* (1982), *E.T.: The Extraterrestrial* (1982), *M*A*S*H* (1983), and *Krull* (1983). Today, video games are another venue for vast, transmedial franchises with works appearing in film, video, books, comics, games, websites, computer software, and other media. Video games have also become a medium of origin for transmedial franchises as well, as so many successful games have demonstrated. Thus, in industrial terms, video games are more often coordinated with other media, rather than simply competing with them, but culturally, video games have displaced other media and cultural activities taking users' time and attention away from them. As a result, tensions can exist between video games and other media, with one media industry driving another or providing content for it as video game industries integrate themselves into the broader media industry landscape.

Since a complete description of video games' place within broader media contexts requires detailed and in-depth discussion of the histories of all the other media in a given national context, this tension can only be touched on within a single chapter. Even so, many of the chapters here show how video games are related to home computer industries, which arose around the same time; film and television industries, from which ratings systems were adapted; and other industries that provided models of regulation and corporate structures for video game companies, addressing some of the same problems such as piracy, censorship, and lack of funding. As with the other tensions discussed, the universal situations faced in every country reveal the forces shaping video game industries, while the specificities of each national context reveal the variety of ways such forces can balance against each other.

A global portrait

In the global portrait of the video game industry collectively provided by the chapters of this volume, many overarching trends and connections are present but implied, due to the volume's division by country or region. For example, the availability of off-the-shelf hardware and software tools for game design coupled with the growing market for mobile games and the Internet as a form of distribution and delivery have reduced the overhead necessary for starting a game design company, so much so that they are now possible even in economically depressed parts of the world. Ideas are finding their way into the global marketplace much faster (and spreading their influence faster), while increasing collaboration and border-crossing erodes the traditional boundaries of national industries. Mobile games and MMORPGs can quickly propagate far beyond their national origins and are designed with the global market in mind. Hits such as *Angry Birds* (2009) from Finland and *Pou* (2013) from Lebanon demonstrate that top-selling games can come from companies in smaller national industries. Unlike the older model of an initial national release followed by later releases on other continents, simultaneous worldwide releases offer the lure of greater profits obtained in a shorter amount of time; increasingly, multinational corporations are up to the task. As of this writing, in March 2014, the most recent global blockbuster was *Grand Theft Auto V* (released worldwide on September 17, 2013) by Rockstar Games, a multinational video game developer and publisher with offices in the United States, England, Canada, Scotland, and Japan (and a former studio in Austria). With a reported development and marketing budget of USD $266 million,[4] *GTA5* made $800 million in its first day of sales and reached $1 billion after three days, making it the fastest-selling entertainment product in history.[5] Only with the anticipation of a global audience—and the means for simultaneous worldwide release—are such successes possible.

Collaborations, company ownership, branch office locations, and franchised intellectual property (IP) are crossing national boundaries more than ever before. For example, The LEGO Group, a Danish company, hired Traveller's Tales, a British company, which is now a subsidiary of the US Company Warner Bros. Interactive Entertainment (itself owned by conglomerate Time Warner Inc.), to produce LEGO-themed video games, and to do so, Traveller's Tales outsourced some of the work to the Argentine company Three Melons. The games were then programmed for systems from the U.S. and Japan.[6] Thus, the companies influencing the final form of the LEGO games are located in at least five countries on four continents. This is not unusual; according to a 2008 *Game Developer*

Research survey, 86% of game studios used outsourcing for some aspect of game development.[7] So just as many national video game histories are finally being written, the growing shift toward transnational game development is eroding and reconfiguring the very concept of a national industry. What is more, such transnational exchanges also enrich the cultures they impact while at the same time establishing video game conventions on a global scale. The balance between the differentiation needed for novelty versus the homogenization that allows familiarity is something that needs to be examined on a global scale, as games are outpacing the academic study of them. Thus, beyond merely offering a look at neglected areas of video game history, it is hoped that *Video Games Around the World* can provide a foundation for such comparative study, which has only barely begun. Along with the appearance of more national histories, this appears to be the direction that video game history is heading.

Notes

1 According to *World Energy Outlook 2013*, available at http://www.worldenergyoutlook. org/resources/energydevelopment/ (accessed March 12, 2014), and http://www.iea.org/ topics/energypoverty/ (accessed March 12, 2014). Sources vary slightly; for example, the World Bank, quoted in The Washington Post, gave 1.2 billion as the figure (see http://www. washingtonpost.com/blogs/wonkblog/wp/2013/05/29/heres-why-1-2-billion-people-still-dont-have-access-to-electricity/ (accessed March 12, 2014)).

2 For statistics on leisure time around the world, see http://www.oecd.org/berlin/42675407.pdf, http://www.nationmaster.com/graph/lif_lei_lei_tim_lei_tim_acr_act_oth_lei_act-leisure-time-across-activities-other, and http://www1.vwa.unisg.ch/RePEc/usg/dp2008/DP-14-En. pdf.

3 Apparently, the game currently holds the world's record for the "Largest Entertainment Voice Over Project Ever"; see http://en.wikipedia.org/wiki/Star_Wars:_The_Old_Republic.

4 According to Kirsten Acuna, "'Grand Theft Auto V' Cost More To Make Than Nearly Every Hollywood Blockbuster Ever Made", *Business Insider*, September 9, 2013, available at http://www.businessinsider.com/gta-vcost-more-than-nearly-every-holly-wood-blockbuster-2013-9 (accessed February 24, 2014).

5 See Dave Thier, "'GTA 5' Sells $800 Million In One Day", *Forbes*, September 18, 2013, available at http://www.forbes.com/sites/davidthier/2013/09/18/gta-5-sells-800-million-in-one-day/ (accessed February 24, 2014); Andrew Goldfarb, "GTA 5 Sales Hit $1 Billion in Three Days", *IGN*, September 20, 2013, available at http://www.ign. com/articles/2013/09/20/gta-5-sales-hit-1-billion-in-three-days (accessed February 24, 2014); and Caroline Westbrook, "Grand Theft Auto 5: Game smashes records to become 'fastest selling entertainment product ever' after passing $1bn mark", *Metro News*, September 21, 2013, available at http://metro.co.uk/2013/09/21/grandtheft-auto-5-becomes-fastest-selling-entertainment-product-ever-after-passing-1bn-mark-4061933/ (accessed February 24, 2014).

6 In particular, LEGO video games were made for Nintendo systems (Game Boy Advance, Game Boy Color, GameCube, Nintendo 64, Nintendo DS, Nintendo 3DS, Wii, and Wii U), PlayStation systems (1, 2, 3, 4, PSP, and Vita), Microsoft systems (Xbox, Xbox 360, and Xbox One), and the Windows and OS X operating systems.

7 See "Survey: Outsourcing in Game Industry Still on Increase" by the staff of *Game Developer Research*, April 2, 2009, available at http://www.gamasutra.com/php-bin/ news_index.php?story=23008 (accessed February 24, 2014).

86

BALANCING THE TENSIONS BETWEEN RATIONALIZATION AND CREATIVITY IN THE VIDEO GAMES INDUSTRY

F. Ted Tschang

Source: *Organization Science: Innovation at and across Multiple Levels of Analysis*: 18(6), November–December 2007, 989–1005.

Abstract

This paper investigates the forces that influence creativity in the video games industry. We adopt a qualitative approach to guide the development of grounded theory across multiple levels of analysis, including the industry (consisting of multiple actors), organizational, and individual creator levels. Our study shows that business and production interests currently drive the rationalization of video game production. There is a maturing trend, with product designs becoming well established as genres, and consumers and publishers desiring incrementally innovative games. This leads publishers to focus on acquiring intellectual property, and publishers and studios alike to make incrementally innovative sequels. The increasing complexity of products leads to further rationalization in their development. However, the need to satisfy consumers' continually evolving tastes and game developers' inclinations to be creative also creates tensions with these rational forces. Different actors balance these tensions differently. Studios may seek to balance these by shifting between more and less innovative products, by creating original intellectual property to increase their bargaining power with publishers, and by iterating and repositioning products during development to adapt them to the market. Publishers may enhance their portfolio by hiring highly creative designers into their stable. New products are created through combinative creativity, that is, the recombination of existing ideas from different sources into new products. The connection of combinative mechanisms with the balancing behavior at the firm level provides a means for understanding the evolution of innovative products and, therefore, industries.

1. Introduction

As industries evolve, product innovation usually gives way to efficiency considerations and process innovation (Utterback 1994). Abernathy and Utterback (1978) suggest that the rate of product innovation is highest in the emergent, or fluid, phase of an industry. That phase is usually associated with many entrants and design variations. Eventually, the market locks into a specific, dominant design that is based on certain firms' superior technology, productivity, fit with the market, and capabilities (Anderson and Tushman 1990, Henderson and Clark 1990, Klepper and Simons 2000). This cycle occurs because technological discontinuities offer better substitutes for the older dominant technology: Periods of dominant designs are followed by product variation, which are followed by new dominant designs (Anderson and Tushman 1990). It is yet to be determined whether this traditional model of industry evolution occurs over a broad spectrum of industries, especially those that are purportedly oriented around the need for their outputs—and therefore their employees—to be creative, i.e., the creative industries.

Creative industries have been defined to include a broad range of sectors such as film, video games, advertising, publishing, software, and computer services (Department for Culture, Media and Sport [DCMS] 1998). In this paper, we confine our definition of creative industries to the cultural industries (e.g., films) as well as entertainment sectors such as video games. One unique feature of creative industries is their use of intermediaries, who act not only as judges of talent and capability (i.e., gatekeepers), but also as financiers and distributors (Caves 2000). Creative industries are defined as much by the creative acts of specific individuals as they are by project teams or firms (Caves 2000, DCMS 1998).

Although they are characterized by the continual development and renewal of intellectual property (IP), firms within creative industries also tend to mature over time. Just as in manufacturing industries, product decisions in these firms tend to become more market driven as the firms mature. This is true, for instance, in the prevailing high-budget but conservative views of the major Hollywood film studios (Epstein 2005). The film industry's maturation was accompanied by certain film genres becoming design standards, with films within those genres accounting for most of the industry's revenue (De Vany 2004, Epstein 2005). Creative products such as films and video games are increasingly complex and costly to develop, which in turn leads to a rationalization of the production or product development process. *Rationalization* is defined in this paper as the predominant focus on business interests or productivity-oriented production processes, usually at the expense of creativity. In creative industries, rationalization or the pursuit of rational interests can constrain creative practices such as impromptu acts or serendipitous discoveries.[1] An example is the adoption of processes such as detailed scene-by-scene scripts that improve the efficiency of film production, but that could curtail creative on-the-spot ideas during production.

Economic forces such as vertical integration and the consolidation of the industry into a few large generalist firms can reduce innovation in the creative sectors (Mezias and Mezias 2000). Furthermore, entertainment products and services such as films are notorious for having (1) a hits-oriented nature (i.e., a small subset of products responsible for generating the larger proportion of the total revenue); (2) a short product life cycle in the marketplace (Epstein 2005, Hirsch 2000, Robins 1993); and (3) difficulties in predicting product acceptance (De Vany 2004). All these factors tend to reinforce the conservative nature of new product decisions, fostering incremental innovations (where *incremental innovations* typically involve minor changes to the products' components).

Nevertheless, as Lampel et al. (2000, p. 266) note, "Competition in cultural industries is driven by a search for novelty. However, while consumers expect novelty in their cultural goods, they also want novelty to be accessible and familiar." Large firms arise with industry maturity, but specialist firms arise with resource partitioning; this last development, in turn, stimulates innovation in film genres or classes (Mezias and Mezias 2000). Tensions arise, such as the tensions between profit maximization and creative forces (Glynn 2000), and those between individuals and broader systems (such as institutions) when the individuals assert themselves during the creative value-creation process (Eisenmann and Bower 2000, Lampel et al. 2000, Starkey et al. 2000). In other words, the maturation and evolution of creative industries tend to be driven by a broader, ongoing tension between forces for creativity and those for rational (e.g., business) interests. In part because of this tension, particular creative industries may not settle down to a dominant design and the subsequent long phase of incremental innovation, as occurs with traditional manufacturing industries.

Our objective in this paper is to explore how these opposing forces play out at various levels as a particular creative industry evolves (as seen through the perspective of selected individuals and firms), and what the implications are for our understanding of how dominant designs occur. Specifically, we use qualitative data collected over a three-year period to study how the tensions between creativity and rational interests are *balanced* (i.e., resolved) within the video games industry.[2] Our paper is organized as follows: Section 2 discusses our research focus and methodology. Section 3 describes the evolution of the industry and how industry actors have provided a rationalizing influence on creativity. Section 4 illustrates how industry actors balance their needs for creativity with the more rational needs of production and commercial interests. Section 5 provides a synthesis of the balancing efforts of the game development studios, and discusses how the findings relate to the literature. Finally, §6 presents conclusions with implications for the industry and for future research.

2. Research focus and methodology

2.1. Research focus

Our research focus is the U.S. video games industry (hereafter, the games industry). Video games are sophisticated products that combine advanced software technology with content and interactive qualities. The games industry is growing and is increasingly respected; it reached $7.3 billion in gross revenue in the United States in 2004, not far behind the U.S. film industry's gross box office receipts of $9.53 billion that same year.

The games industry is similar to other creative industries in a number of ways. For instance, games require their workers (known as "developers") to perform significant amounts of creative thinking, and games need to satisfy consumers' evolving expectations. However, game development differs from the development process of other creative industries in that it needs computer programming, design, project management, and substantial amounts of testing (Bethke 2003). In addition, the design process tends to be ongoing during development, with the design affecting other components such as the programming code (or "code") as the development proceeds (Tschang 2005). Game development is complex, and games need rational structuring, i.e., to be developed systemically to improve productivity and to ensure the certainty of the games' development. This suggests a similar process to the rationalization of commercial software development (Paulk 1995, Chrissis et al. 2003). This combination of rational and creative aspects can cause tensions in game development similar to those seen in other creative industries.

As with other creative industries, the games industry has three main actors: independent studios, publishers, and consumers. The studios do the creative work: They design and develop the games. Publishers serve as gatekeepers and provide almost everything else, including financing and distribution. Publishers also supplement the independent studios with resources for testing and for developing components like the art, or develop products themselves in their own development studios. Consumers directly and indirectly influence the games' development when they communicate their needs and abilities to studios and publishers. As we show in §3, the interactions among these three actors strongly influence innovation within the industry.

Given our interest in how creative industries evolve, it would be useful to understand how we measure creative output, or innovation, in game designs. Game designs "determine what choices the player will be able to make in the game-world and what ramifications those choices will have on the rest of the game" (Rouse 2001, p. xviii). Although there are several ways to measure individual creative output (see, for example, Sternberg 1998), it would be more appropriate for us to adopt measures specific to the games industry. One such measure involves specifying whether a particular game is an innovation within or between genres, or whether it is a new genre. A particular genre (or definitive type of game) can be uniquely defined by a combination of components. Usually, these are the form of *gameplay* (definable as "the formalized interaction that occurs when players follow the rules of a game and experience its system through play" [Salen and Zimmerman 2003, p. 303]); the particular visual style (such as a three-dimensional [3D] perspective); and sometimes the genre-specific story or background, such as the fantasy setting and heroic quest that is common to role-playing games. The game's design generally encapsulates all these aspects (with gameplay following from the game's design), and thereby forms the heart of a game's distinctiveness. On the one hand, a *new genre* can be defined as a radical innovation (Henderson and Clark 1990). On the other hand, games that extend a genre while imitating established forms of gameplay, visual styles, story, and means of integrating these components (e.g., how the storyline fits the game) can be considered as incremental innovations of an existing genre. Some observers are concerned that the industry is largely creating games with increasingly detailed content that promotes cinematic quality and *immersiveness* (defined as the quality of being in a realistic virtual environment), rather than new forms of gameplay (Dobson 2006).

2.2. Methodology and approach

To study the issues of interest within the games industry as thoroughly as possible, we used qualitative data collection, analysis, and reasoning methods as developed in the literature (Glaser and Strauss 1967, Lincoln and Guba 1985, Miles and Huberman 1994, Yin 1994). In particular, we adopted Lincoln and Guba's (1985) process involving (1) purposive sampling, (2) the inductive analysis of the data, (3) the development of grounded theory, and (4) the projection of next steps.

In our first stage, we sought emergent research themes from our initial interviews with a range of senior managers and experienced individuals within the industry.[3] We conducted interviews in March 2003 with 19 interviewees drawn from 17 firms. Each person interviewed was a lead designer or studio head (and almost all of the latter were involved in game design as well). About half of these interviewees were considered to be at the top of their profession, and most of the rest had been involved in key roles in well-known studios or on well-known games. Each interview lasted between one and two hours. As advocated in the literature (e.g., Eisenhardt 1989), we used semistructured, open-ended interviews, designed to allow phenomena to emerge rather than to seek only confirmation of prior views. We also attended trade and game development conferences, including the Electronic Entertainment Expo (E3) in 2002, and the Game Developer's Conference (GDC) in 2003 and 2004.

Our objective at this stage was to understand how creativity was practiced in the industry, what creative practices and processes looked like, and what factors influenced these creative practices. We partly redirected our focus as themes emerged during the interviews. Several characteristics of creative practices were revealed during this first stage of the research. One was the observation that creative individuals, including designers, work in groups on projects, and within larger social and industrial contexts that influence or constrain their creativity. An example of this was the observation by three interviewees of the tensions between their creative natures and the more conservative nature of publishers. These interviews, as well as secondary information that we later collected on the industry, suggested a trend toward incremental innovations, i.e., increasingly immersive games, games of the same genres, sequels, and games with similar gameplay.

We also collected secondary information, such as project *postmortems* and articles from the industry's main trade publication—*Game Developer*. Postmortems are reports written after project completion that detail the lessons learned, specifically identifying the helpful or damaging factors that influenced each project's development. Factors ranged from production-related issues such as scheduling to product development issues such as design and technology, and to external relationships such as those between the studios and publishers and between the studios and consumers. Of our set of 76 postmortems, 40 were of sequels to existing games or of games based on licenses. We defined games made with licensed IP or sequels as our cutoff for determining whether a particular title was *incrementally innovative*. Incrementally innovative games essentially extend a genre and do not involve significant changes in gameplay. Following Miles and Huberman (1994), we analyzed the postmortems using established protocols for coding and classifying their content. These were initially used to seek phenomena, but later also served to validate issues emerging from the fieldwork, such as the association between incremental innovations and products whose development was focused on meeting consumers' expectations.

In the next stage, to better understand how creativity occurs and could be constrained, we designed a follow- on cycle of purposive sampling to clarify how individual designers work in project settings. We used an ethnographic approach to systematically examine the design and product development process across time, across designers and teams, and across projects. Our ethnographic studies were of the four studios (each labeled with a fictional name).[4] One studio (IGF-Winner) was started by an individual during our research period. The second studio, Strategy Games, specialized in city-building games and was formed with 12 developers (later rising to 20). The third was a well-known studio: RPG Games, with 25 developers. The fourth studio, Action Games, had 20 developers, and made console action games. We made multiple visits to each of the four studios, conducting site visits in March, June, and July 2003; March 2004; and February 2005. We spaced our visits to each studio to try to capture as much of the product cycle as possible, as well as the creative and development-related phenomena occurring over that cycle; we succeeded in capturing an entire product cycle across all studio visits. As part of the ethnography, we sat in during 45 formal and informal team meetings, and conducted formal interviews at these studios with most of their personnel in residence, covering, in all, 41 developers. Finally, we informally interviewed more than 50 other developers and publishers' employees at game developers conferences (GDCs) and elsewhere.

We repeatedly visited studio sites, focusing on understanding the roles of designers as well as other emerging themes. We observed two related ways by which studios balance the different tensions between creativity and rationality: (1) by design considerations and iterations that designers created during a project; and (2) by how studios chose their next products to address problems and issues encountered with previous products, particularly innovative ones. We also recorded other observations, such as the fact that developers were generally avid game players, who tested games by thinking consciously as users throughout the development process. In later analysis, we examined the postmortem data to validate our observations on the tensions that were occurring in the industry and the ways in which these were being resolved by studios' balancing and adaptive mechanisms.

3. Rationalization in the games industry

We now describe the maturing of the games industry in terms of the actors' behaviors and the production processes.

3.1. The evolution of the games industry

It has been said that "if the 1970s were characterized by innovation and the 80s were about expansion, the 90s were a time of maturation" (DeMaria and Wilson 2002, p. 243). Several of the major genres were established by the early 1990s. These major genres included the first adventure games, which were based on versions programmed in 1972, the first-person shooter, popularized by *Wolfenstein 3D* in 1992 and *Doom* in 1993; the first role-playing game, popularized by *Akabeleth* in 1980, itself the forerunner to the *Ultima* series; and various simulation and strategy subgenres, including the first flight simulation game in 1979 and the first city-builder game in 1989. However, even in the 1990s, innovation continued within genres, and a few new genres were added: the real-time strategy genre (*Dune II* in 1992); the music genre (*Parappa the Rapper* in 1996); the massively multiplayer online role-playing game (MMORPG) genre (*Ultima Online* in 1997); and the virtual-life genre (*The Sims* in 2000). The studio head of Strategy Games noted that innovation did occur between genres in the 1990s, but that many games tended to be very focused within established boundaries.

Table 1 shows the recent trends with the 20 top-selling computer games from 2000 to 2004. A remarkable trend is that of first-person shooter games, which are some of the most immersive, visceral, and controversial games available (Kushner 2003). The number of such games steadily increased from one title in 2000 to seven in 2004. Table 1 also shows how other genres or categories have peaked or declined. Data on the different genres of computer games ranked by the proportion of purchases reveal that, in 2004, strategy games were most popular (26.9%), with family and children's (20.3%), first-person shooters (16.3%), role-playing (10%), adventure (5.9%), sports (5.4%), and action (3.9%) genres constituting the remainder (Entertainment Software Association 2005). In contrast, by far the most-played console game categories were action (30.1%) and sports (17.8%), followed by first-person shooters (9.6%), children and family entertainment (9.5%), racing (9.4%), role-playing (9.4%), and fighting (5.4%). While this data reflects the preferences of the total market for each genre, Table 1 reflects specific hit games and their genres, which are of equal if not greater interest for this study.

243

Table 1 Counts of top 20 computer games classified by genre/subgenre, 2000–2004

Genre or subgenre	2000	2001	2002	2003	2004
First-person shooter	1	1	2	4	**7**
Role-playing games	1	2	2	2	**3**
Real-time strategy	4	4	1	**5**	2
Action	1	1	1	0	0
Virtual life	2	4	**6**	5	4
Business strategy	3	3	2	3	3
Action-adventure	0	1	**2**	0	0
Flight simulation	0	0	0	1	1
Sports simulation	0	2	**4**	0	0
Other simulation (e.g., city building)	**4**	2	0	0	0
Other (education, casino, trivia)	**4**	0	0	0	0

Source: Author's summaries based on NPD Funworld data cited by the Entertainment Software Association, which are available on request.

Note: Unique peak numbers are in bold.

New genres tend to be created and old ones survive by an evolutionary process (Tschang and Szczypula 2006), in part because game developers themselves are serious consumers. For example, MMORPGs had roots in multiuser dungeons (MUDs), which in turn had roots in text-based adventure games. MMORPGS also had roots in early online games and role-playing games (DeMaria and Wilson 2002). Similarly, by increasing their immersiveness via 3D technology, other genres or subgenres such as real-time strategy and role-playing games have extended their life spans.

3.2. Industry actors and their interactions

One early designer who had eventually left the industry noted,

> 1986 is when the diversity of the games industry peaked and then slowly started narrowing, then in 1990, the narrowing process accelerated and all through the late 80s and early 90s, I was ranting at the industry saying "That we've got to broaden, not narrow," . . . by about 1993, 1 realized that I had lost.

Starting in the 1990s and going into the 2000s, several factors dictated a more professional and corporate image of games: Large publishers emerged, IP became increasingly important, and project and team sizes increased. The rise in incremental innovations can be traced to how the objectives of different actors shifted over time, and how these actors interacted with one another to seek certainty by developing within well-understood genres.

3.2.1. Publishers

Our analysis suggests that two issues characterize publishers: their focus on IP and their tendency to control the development process. As one studio head noted,

> . . . the publishers are reading one another's hype and telling you that gamers (i.e., consumers) don't want X, Y, and Z. That's what interests me about creativity . . . how it's completely dominated by people who are not creative. It's completely dominated by the business people.

Publishers themselves do not see it that differently:

> Like other entertainment companies, our business is based on the creation, acquisition, exploitation, and protection of intellectual property . . . in the form of software code, patented technology, and . . . "content." (Electronic Arts (EA) 2005)

Increasing project cost has driven publishers to bank on combining established gameplay with interesting IP that are potentially interesting to consumers. One well- known designer and studio head, who once worked for a major publisher, observed that the games industry is

> becoming a service industry like Hollywood. I think it's pretty sad . . . it seems that right now the thinking is that the only guaranteed hits are the games based on hit films. When they write a $30 million marketing budget or whatever, why take a risk on anything else.

Publishers generally consider *content* IP (used interchangeably with IP hereafter) to be the most valuable part of a game (Roch 2004). Content IP includes the art, story, and game world, where the *game world* is defined as the game's setting, including the background, history, and types of objects within it. The game world distinguishes each game's fictional world and environment from all other games'. While this IP had traditionally been developed by the games industry itself, the links between games and other industries, especially the film industry, have increased. In fact, of the top 25 console games in 2002, only two used original IP that the video game studios themselves developed (meaning that they were not based on licenses from movies or were not sequels to prior games).

Publishers are also interested in IP because mass- market tastes are often defined in many media around how IP is acquired. EA explicitly states that its goal "is to develop titles which appeal to the mass markets" (EA 2005, p. 21). Three of our postmortems note that publishers strongly encourage studios to make their games more user friendly. This also relates to the nature of the industry, which focuses on hits. As EA notes, "our business is driven by hit titles" (EA 2005, p. 21). EA's most successful games are its franchises. These are highly incrementally innovative in nature and occur largely within the established genres. For instance, EA owned 9 of the 10 top sports game titles in 2005 (McDonald 2005). EA itself recognizes that it is primarily not in the business of innovating: "We have developed, and it is our objective to continue to develop, many of our hit titles to become franchise titles that can be regularly iterated" (EA 2005, p. 22).

There has also been a tendency for publishers to create internal studios so that they can exercise more control over resource allocation and the game development process, such as the exercise of quality control and scheduling (Roch 2004). In 2003, the top 20 publishers sourced only about 45% of their released titles from independent studios (Donovan 2004). Publishers have built internal studios primarily through acquisitions (Rogers 2004). However, some observers suggested that in the well-known case of EA's acquisition of Westwood Studios, EA might have acquired the studio more for the sake of acquiring the studio's IP than for the studio's capability. Westwood's talent and capability were eventually absorbed into EA's Los Angeles office, which itself was eventually heavily scaled back. Other publishers, too, have behaved very assertively—if not rapaciously— in pursuing studio acquisitions and IP (Pham 2002). One interviewee noted that although EA had given him a blank slate several years ago and had subsequently approved his fairly innovative game, EA likely would not have funded his game today, given its desire to achieve higher sales for each game. Despite this focus on IP, sales of film-based game titles at EA have suffered recently, in part because rushing the games out to coincide with a film's release date or emphasizing the designs less than the content IP can eventually hurt these games' chances of success (McDonald 2005).

3.2.2. Early designers and the rise of the studio

Most early video games, and even some in the late 1980s, were developed by one, or at most two, developers (as seen in profiles by DeMaria and Wilson 2002). According to the head of Strategy Games, there was more experimentation during this early period, possibly because games could be designed and developed by a single individual in a matter of months. This, in turn, involved a lower cost of failure and allowed considerable risk taking.

Over time, however, project- and team-based studios emerged. These studios typically maintain a core full-time workforce of talented employees in preparation for new projects (Bethke 2003). In many project teams, the designer was and still is the center of the development effort (e.g., Warren Spector who designed *Deus Ex* at Ion Storm-Austin). Nevertheless, it was largely recognized by our interviewees that, in current teams, the designer is not necessarily the key actor in completing the game, and that a team's efforts are also critical for a game's development. It was also noted by one interviewee that because not all studios have a star designer, they will often seek to maximize team input to compensate for the missing creative functions of such a designer.

Most new genres tend to arise from forms of gameplay invented by individual designers (see DeMaria and Wilson 2002). Traditionally, an individual's creativity is seen in how lead designers came up with the core concept that underlies an entire game and its detailed game design. The creative vision of the initial designer or design team would also shape on a daily basis how other developers implemented the game.

Our interviews with lead designers revealed that they create new game concepts by using their diverse backgrounds, imagination, inspirations, and insights. New genres require even greater degrees of variance in thinking styles, and the designers tend to be exposed to domains significantly different from games. For instance, in conceptualizing the game *Parappa the Rapper*—the definitive game for the music games genre—the rap musician Masaya Matsuura "had the inspiration to play a TV (video) game as if it were a musical instrument" (Baba and Tschang 2001, p. 501).[5] *PC Gamer*, one of the leading consumer game review magazines, went so far as to dub some of these designers Game Gods—those with the capabilities to make innovative games.

Publishers heavily influence the type of game the studio makes. The publishers' greatest influence may be at the conceptualization or preconceptualization stage, when the publisher decides on the genre it wants, in effect subjugating the initial creative process to a rational decision. The head of the independent studio RPG Games notes how studios decide on new game ideas:

> Sometimes it's design driven . . . like, "Oh, I have an idea for a game." Sometimes it's market driven, as in, "Well we really should be doing a first-person shooter." Sometimes it's publisher driven. Publishers come to you and say, "We have a game we want done."

In many cases, studios will take at least part of the lead from publishers. The head of Strategy Games noted that, in 2005, his firm sought to scour the archives of IP from older media (e.g., films) for franchises on which they could hinge their games. However, he also noted,

> I also think there's a lot more room for originality and creativity. Some of the most interesting things in the world are not the things that 5 million people like. They are the things that 200,000 people like. There's still plenty of room to do that and make money on the PC, but the problem is that the publishing model has gotten where the publishers can't make money unless things are really huge, and they put a lot of money into it.

The publishers' advantage in resources has given them a position of strength in negotiations with studios, with the publishers usually retaining the rights to the IP pertaining to the characters and game world, and studios owning only the programming code. As explained by the head of Action Games, publishers usually fund the game's development, and therefore seek most of the royalties, with the studios only starting to see royalties if the game becomes a *hit* (which we define as a game that sells at least one million units). Unfortunately for the studios, few games become hits.

A studio head, one who had previously worked for publishers, observed that the publisher's conservative nature may stem from the fact that many publishing heads themselves know very little about games or game development. Some publishers came from outside the games industry and were funded by other sectors or private financiers. In fact, tensions occurred even in the early days of the industry. For instance, one of Atari's early CEOs came from outside the industry, and had a low regard for developers, seeking to ensure that they got as little recognition or reward as possible (DeMaria and Wilson 2002, pp. 40–41).

Finally, it has also been noted that retailers can influence studios and publishers. As explained by a studio head, retailers of games tend to have limited shelf space, which means they can carry only the more popular titles, further constraining the potential for developing creative games.

3.2.3. Consumers

Consumers also strongly influence the publishing and development decisions in the games industry. Although the typical game consumer used to be a male under 30 years of age (most often between 13 and 19), games are increasingly being played by other age groups and by females. The typical consumer tends to buy games within genres rather than games combining different genres. The consumer's taste for familiarity as well as desire for novelty also contributes to the tension in game design. As the postmortem of the *Age of Empires II* game notes, "The game business is brutal to those who fail to move forward with the times, but it's also equally brutal to those who experiment too much and stray from the expectations of the players" (Pritchard 2000, p. 53).

Our analysis revealed that consumers directly engage with the studios and rationalize game development in two ways. First, consumers offer feedback to the developers on their experience interacting with the game. For instance, design meetings often involve developers' ongoing iterative fine tuning of the overall game's design (as seen at Strategy Games), as well as the refining of the level designs[6] (as seen at Action Games), to improve their playability. As a result, hit games (e.g., Blizzard's *Warcraft* series and Valve's *Half-Life*) were not necessarily the most innovative, but were certainly the most well tuned. Of the 17 postmortems that explicitly indicated concern with how consumers or fans would perceive the game or gameplay, 11 were classified as incrementally innovative games, i.e., as sequels or based on IP licenses. For instance, a sequel called *Unreal Tournament*, according to its postmortem, relied strongly on "direct communication with the gaming community . . . . Nearly every employee . . . frequented message boards dedicated to the subject" (Reinhart 2000, p. 52).

The second way in which consumers engage with studios is by becoming developers themselves. As we found in our interviews, many studios ensure that their developers are also serious players of games, because that helps in the game development and tuning process. At Irrational Games, "In all our interviews (of potential employees), one of our most pressing questions to ourselves was 'Does this person get games?'" (Chey 1998, p. 54).

Designers' roots have changed over time, especially as the designer's role has become more niche oriented. Many well-established lead designers entered the industry as programmers. Partly because of this programming side and the smaller scale of projects, these earlier designers were able to independently conceive of, prototype, and implement innovative gameplay. However, more-recent designers have come straight from university and made their way into teams through general or nontechnical paths, usually beginning as testing personnel and then moving up to become level designers. The combination of specialized level-design positions with the availability of level-design tools has made the design process more general and more accessible. This, in turn, has allowed more game players who do not have formal programming training to become designers after receiving on-the-job training.

3.3. Rationalization of the game development process

The need to manage the increasing size and complexity of games and their development has resulted in a search for process improvements, not necessarily driven by concerns such as cost minimization, which are traditionally seen in other industries. The complexity of games can be measured in various ways, including (1) the scale of the effort and resources engaged (cited by interviewees), (2) the number of lines of code (cited by postmortems), and (3) the richness of game content, such as the complexity of individual graphic objects and environments. The latter is largely driven by the availability of ever more powerful computing and game console platforms (Gallagher and Park 2002, Schilling 2003). Since the early 1990s, advances in 3D technology have led to increasingly immersive games. Team sizes have also increased with project complexity. A sample of 48 firms from our postmortem data (from 1998 to 2002) show the average team size to be 20 developers; today, larger studios—such as those within EA—report 100 or more developers on a single team. This trend is partly due to the increasingly detailed content of the games, which has necessitated increases in the numbers of artists and animators within each team, as well as the increasing need to localize content to multiple countries and their languages.

As a consequence of these influences, game development is becoming more rational and process driven. There is a preoccupation with production-related issues (e.g., the tight schedules), product development–related issues (e.g., the need to concurrently develop different components), and organizational issues (e.g., communication problems within the team) (Tschang 2005). In fact, the three studios in our ethnography started out with no full-time producer for their first projects, but eventually hired producers to handle scheduling and resource management issues. Development costs also increase with scale, and various industry accounts indicate that costs have gone from a few hundred thousand dollars per game about 10 years ago, to several million dollars or more for a high-quality game today.

Furthermore, increasing project and team sizes has led to the emergence of hierarchies (i.e., lead members who coordinate the work of the personnel in each particular area, e.g., art or design) and the partitioning of work within project teams. Even in fairly innovative games such as the RPG game *Deus Ex*, structure is important: "There can only be one boss for a project, there can only be one boss for each department, and department heads have to answer to the person heading up the project" (Spector 2000, p. 57).

A lead designer of various U.S. and UK studios noted that this specialization or division of labor has reduced the individual's creative scope:

In the past, the core game may have been developed by two or three people. You now may have ten people in the team but seven of them are cut off from the process, because they are specialized. But you still have the same three (core design) people . . . I am sure everyone in the team will still be able to contribute ideas. It is just that the amount they contribute will become smaller and smaller because there are so many more ideas coming in . . . . It just may limit the amount of creative input individuals in the team have (although) they can focus more on their specialized area.

At an extreme, as pointed out by three interviewees, a significant number of developers in some projects are not even informed on a regular basis as to the designs' evolution. However, a trade-off may exist because encouraging creativity not only empowers team members to contribute innovations and details by fully using their talents, but also helps to motivate them. (At least 10 postmortems indicated that a project heavily relied on and encouraged team members' creative inputs.)

Another trend is the changing nature of the designer's role. Many lead designers act less as visionaries or conceptual idea generators and more as coordinators and negotiators with the team on a more rationally defined design, e.g., one that is designed to a publisher's requirement or someone else's vision. This suggests a rationalization of the designer's role, and a potential reduction in the opportunities to come up with significantly creative ideas.

Yet another trend is the increasing reliance on development practices that improve project performance. An examination of the postmortem data suggests the use of two development practices to mitigate the uncertainty or reduce the effort of making creative products. The first is the use of prototyping by studios to ensure that the basic concept's gameplay is workable, and to create demonstrations to gain publisher funding. The lack of prototyping can also cause problems when unproven concepts fail, or when they need substantial tuning, as indicated in the postmortem on *Thief: The Dark Project* (Leonard 1999). The second is the use of software tools to help automate the process of developing code and content. This includes the use of software such as editors and scripting tools to help create level or scenario designs, and animation packages such as *Maya*, which also improve artists' and animators' productivity. However, Crawford (2003) points out that this could be focusing designers on further exploiting (e.g., being more productive with) designs rather than exploring (i.e., being more experimental with) designs.

In summary, it is evident that a rationalization has occurred—within markets (with the changing of preferences) and in the development process. Figure 1 summarizes the several ways in which these rationalizing influences affect product creativity, both in terms of how they are demanded and how they are produced. (The direction of influence is shown with either a positive or negative sign.) This rationalization was a significant cause of the large number of incrementally innovative games being released by the games industry. We estimated from publicly available data sources that of the top 20 publishers' game titles in 2002, the percentage of new releases based on licensed IP was about 36%, the percentage based on sequels to past video games was about 56% (both of which can be used as rough measures of incremental work), and the percentage of new releases based on original IP was only about 25%. (These add up to more than 100% because some titles were dual categorized.)

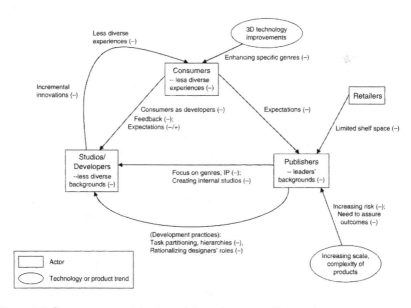

Figure 1 Influences on creativity that reinforce incremental innovation

Most of the relationships shown in Figure 1 are negative as far as their impact on the creativity of products. In §4 we will illustrate how studios and publishers also seek creativity to generate products that are more than incrementally innovative, in the hope of creating greater revenue, fame, and, therefore, self-determination.

4. Industry- and firm-level mechanisms to foster creativity

While simultaneously adjusting to rationalizing influences (i.e., production issues like efficiency, as well as business interests), the games industry has had to ensure that at least some creativity is preserved. This involves innovating, mostly incrementally, but occasionally radically (i.e., with new genres). Successful new games are not simply replicas of established games, but must contain something new to satisfy consumers' need for novelty without departing so much from the valued parts of the genre or original game (as in the case of sequels). For instance, in *Command and Conquer: Tiberian Sun*, the major issue was "[how] to maintain the feel of the original. When making a sequel, the question that always has to be answered first is, how far do you stray from the original game to make it compelling, yet still familiar?" (Stojsavljevic 2000, p. 47). We will next explore industry mechanisms and the behaviors of different actors that help foster creativity as the games industry matures.

4.1. Industry-level competitions

At the industry level, game competitions such as the Independent Games Festival (IGF), held every year at the GDC, provide publicity for innovative developers who do not have a publisher's support. The IGF provides a forum for showing independent work, in much the same way that the Sundance Film Festival provides a forum for independent movies. Its goal is to highlight and reward the bright ideas and innovative concepts that may not be commercially saleable yet, but that could become hits. Unfortunately, the IGF has only partly achieved its goals: Independent games are usually not polished enough to succeed as a commercially saleable product, or might not have a team strong enough to convince a publisher of the game's prospects. Our interviews at the IGF highlighted the difficulty that even IGF winners face in securing support and gaining business success. For instance, over the course of three years we repeatedly interviewed an independent game designer whose Web-based game won the best overall and best design awards at a recent IGF. Shortly after he won the competition, he sought to scale up his work by forming a company, IGF-Winner; he had hired 16 employees by mid-2005. However, as of our last interview, most of the projects that IGF-Winner had obtained were publisher dictated. None of the ideas generated by IGF-Winner, with the exception of the founder's award-winning game, had been accepted by publishers. Another IGF finalist noted that it was not easy to get Web-based game distributors such as Popcap—let alone the publishers—to list his independently developed games.

4.2. Publishers' attempts at balancing creativity

Although many mainstream publishers largely seek incremental innovations, some also engage in a portfolio diversification strategy by hiring innovative independent studios for specific projects, or by hiring genre creators or other highly creative designers and preserving the intellectual space for them to create new products. There are few proven creative geniuses husbanded in this manner by publishers. The small group includes Will Wright and Peter Molyneux at EA, Shigeru Miyamoto at Nintendo, and Masaya Matsuura at Sony Computer Entertainment. EA essentially allowed Wright free rein to create new concepts after EA acquired Maxis, the studio that he had co-led (Keighley 1998). However, one reason for this was that Wright already had a successful track record and considerable name recognition.

Increasingly, even reputable designers working within publishers' internal studios have to sell their ideas to project team members. One well-known designer at a publisher's studio noted that it was necessary for him to obtain buy-in on his innovative ideas from a wider cast of people, including the people who approve the projects, as well as his own team members, to move forward with his ideas.

4.3. Studios' attempts at balancing creativity: product strategy over time

For the most part, independent studios drive creativity and innovation within the games industry. Spin-offs from existing studios usually occur when employees leave to pursue fresh game design ideas, or to gain independence from existing employers. In some cases, they attempt to be innovative immediately with their first products. Often however they work on established and incrementally innovative IP from publishers.

Our analysis of published postmortems and ethnographic data on our three studios—Strategy Games, RPG Games, and Action Games—offers insights into how studios attempt to foster creativity within the constraints imposed by the rational influences of publishers and consumers. Table 2 presents the sequence of products and accompanying events at these three studios. As the studios move from one product to the next, they shift from innovative to less innovative games, or vice versa. In particular, Strategy Games and RPG Games backtracked with regard to innovation during subsequent game development; this backtracking was prompted by considerations such as the businesses' survival and the need to appeal to publishers' interests.

After Strategy Games' innovative first game came out in 2005, the studio found that some consumers of previous city-building games were confounded when their new game added a second layer or model—a society simulation—to the traditional city-building experience. As a result of that experience, Strategy Games' second product adapted only the city-building mechanics of its first product to a publisher's IP. The studio head further articulated what the studio had learned from that experience:

Table 2 Evolution of studios in the ethnography and sequence of products developed

	Action games	RPG games	Strategy games
Origins of the firm	Started out as a spin-off of a publisher's internal development studio (by former employees). Leveraged its programming (technology) competency.	Started out as a spin-off from another studio. Leveraged its experience in making RPG games as well as in content IP creation (e.g., good stories etc.).	Started out as a spin-off of a publisher's internal development studio. Leveraged its experience in making city-building games.
First product	Worked on third-party IP (incremental innovation); directly negotiated with comic book IP owner, then with publisher.	Sequel to a well-known game (incremental innovation) widely regarded for its gameplay; based on individual's vision.	Worked on own IP with combinative (gameplay, 3D) innovation that saw limited success; secured final funding from venture capitalist; based on individual's vision.
Second product	Worked directly for publisher sequel (project not completed).	Own IP (with combinative gameplay innovation) that became a success; individual and small group inspired.	Change (less innovation) Working on sequel to publisher IP using same game *engine* (defined as the core code); only reusing a subset of the first title's gameplay (i.e., the city-building aspects).
Third product	Worked on game with comic IP that publisher had rights to (incremental innovation).	Own IP (combinative innovation) (project not completed).	
Fourth product(s)	Change (more "content IP creation") Working on own IP; attempting to develop own IP and to market it to publishers, based on team member's proposal.	Change (less innovation) Worked on sequel to second product (incremental innovation that was partly self-distributed). Also worked on two sequels to publisher IP (incremental innovations).	

Source: Author's interviews and ethnographic cases.

Note: Combinative innovation refers to innovation that is more than incremental by combining features of two or more genres together to significantly change the gameplay or manner of interactivity.

> The first thing is that I think a franchise name is much more important than people may want to admit . . . . It's already a big risk to strike out to make a new franchise. You're taking on a whole big challenge when you do that—a big challenge with publishers, a challenge with retailers.

He further reflected that "if I had to start over again, I might go to a publisher and say, 'Hey, you guys have that *Spell Force* game. We want to do a sequel to that [by adapting Strategy Games' game design].'"

RPG Games had a different experience. After developing two successful products (one of which was an innovation), it had to weather difficulties with false starts and one incomplete product, and sought to sustain itself with two incremental sequels based on publishers' requests. By their own admission, the sequel to their second game was also incrementally innovative, but helped them to reap more of the returns from the original IP that they had developed earlier. Interestingly, all three sequels that they worked on won accolades and awards even though they involved only incremental innovations: They enhanced gameplay as well as introduced compelling characters and stories that were similar to previously successful characters and stories from the original titles on which they were based.

Action Games began with a strong, albeit incrementally innovative, first product. However, the issue became not too much innovation, but rather too much publisher control over the IP. Despite its technical competence, Action Games had to cede a fair degree of control of its second and third products to publishers. One publisher wanted to dictate the game's design, and the other was concerned with onscreen representation of the IP. An additional issue was the studio's low visibility in the market because the publishers took most of the credit. For their fourth product, Action Games sought to develop their own unique content and to continue to build on their own programming code, which the studio head and employees believed might help achieve more bargaining power with publishers.

The issue of publisher control raises another extreme situation—where completed work is lost when contracts are cancelled. Two studios that we interviewed suffered when their publishers decided not to continue with the studios' nearly completed projects. As a result, all of the game design, code, and content was abandoned and largely not reused.

To circumvent these fates, other studios have tried to leverage IP in different ways. For example, a studio could attempt to become a publisher itself. This was the path successfully followed by Blizzard, which became part of Vivendi Universal's holdings. Two other studios in our interview sample tried a different strategy. Both focused on concept and pure IP creation for other interested parties, including film studios. This moved them upstream in the IP-value chain, making their strategies similar to those of the film industry.

Innovation requires studio lead designers to combine features from different games or genres, or to use other means to develop innovative gameplay. This is especially true of innovations that are more than incremental in nature. Innovations at Strategy Games and RPG Games were initially conceptualized by their respective studio heads. The innovative city-building game at Strategy Games combined two levels of simulation—a society simulation as well as a city-building simulation—in effect revamping the city-building genre. Similarly, the head of RPG Games noted, "We'll always bring to the table a big tool set with these RPG elements. However we take it to the first-person shooter genre so you can play with a different experience." In another combinative situation, concept brainstorming sessions at Action Games were observed to involve designers creating lists of features that would define their game.

The making of innovations or attempts to secure better terms may require that studios explore alternative funding and distribution paths to conventional publishers. With its first game, Strategy Games attempted to work with a venture capitalist-investor that wanted to enter the industry. However, Strategy Games eventually had to rely on an established publisher as well, because the venture capitalist lacked experience and capability in marketing and distributing games. RPG Games adopted a different strategy to bypass publishers by partly selling the sequel to its second product directly to consumers via the Internet.

4.4. Balancing at the project level by tuning designs and repositioning products

Even as studios attempt to foster or introduce innovation in their products, they have to be mindful that the games they develop suit their consumers' and publishers' needs. One way of balancing to help ensure a design's success is for teams to evolve games through the project development cycle by iteratively tuning and testing them. Such iterative tuning and testing for optimal play experience ensures wider acceptance of the eventual product by consumers (Tschang 2005). In almost all the design meetings we attended at Action Games and Strategy Games, developers considered game features and details in view of consumers' expectations, and sought to fine-tune gameplay to meet perceived needs. In part, this was due to the intricacy of the games and the uncertainty of consumers' responses to design changes. Even in the somewhat incrementally innovative game *Rise of Nations*, which was a next-generation real-time strategy game, "we didn't know which [ideas] would work" (Train and Reynolds 2003, p. 36). Many teams use prototyping to help understand consumers' reactions to their games. Sometimes teams change designs because the initial designs do not work well, or because the designers want to make improvements. As a result of this uncertainty, some studios even adopt the alternative design philosophy of designing on the fly or as the game's development proceeds, as opposed to developing the full design upfront. There are also cases of major redesigns late in the product cycle: Despite having a nearly completed first version, the incrementally innovative *Half-Life* underwent a major overhaul at a late stage, which helped make it a great success (Birdwell 1999).

A second way of balancing at the project level is to reposition games and their designs expressly for (rational) marketplace concerns. As development proceeds, studios may make changes to the packaging (e.g., title and selling points) of the game, or to the design and content of the game, so as to satisfy potential publishers. In some cases, game developers need to reposition an innovative concept or game in development to find either an initial or a new publisher; in other cases, developers need to satisfy an existing publisher. For instance, the Strategy Games studio head and lead designers considered repositioning their innovative city-building game halfway through the development cycle to fit with new publishers and their market interests. The repositioning alternatives they considered ranged from changing the game's name to considering a different game with the same game engine, gameplay, and visual perspective. The latter would have entailed a completely different background and context—and, therefore, new art work, sound, and detailed designs. Ultimately, these developers stayed with the initial game and content. At least four postmortems also note the need to match ideas to publishers' expectations: The postmortem for *No One Lives Forever*, for example, states "the project mutated constantly in order to please prospective [publishers'] producers and marketing departments" (Hubbard 2007).

5. Discussion: the studio's balancing act

Our discussion of industry data and events traced how the games industry has matured, and how interactions among different industry actors and increasing rationalization within the industry have resulted in games that are increasingly incrementally innovative over time. Firms—particularly independent studios—have struggled to satisfy consumers' simultaneous but conflicting urges for novelty and familiarity, while conforming to the publishers' and market's rationalizing influence.

5.1. Balancing at the firm and project levels

In general, studios perform a balancing act by shifting from innovative to less innovative products or vice versa. Sometimes, as with RPG Games, they go back and forth. Studios seek to innovate because they might want to test the innovativeness of a design, or to make a name for themselves beyond simply contracting work from a publisher. They innovate by developing their own original content, forms of gameplay, or both. Figure 2 represents this balancing behavior with a model of studios' decisions on product innovations. At the beginning of the design process, a studio chooses an initial level of innovation in gameplay terms. The decisions that follow, however, depend on whether the product becomes a hit.

A combination of these two factors—the extent of product innovation and the extent of success—yields three major types of product strategies, each with at least two states and two substrategies. In the first strategy of developing new genres, a hit might lead to an incrementally innovative sequel (e.g., *The Sims* was followed by many expansion packs, as well as by *The Sims* 2). However, if

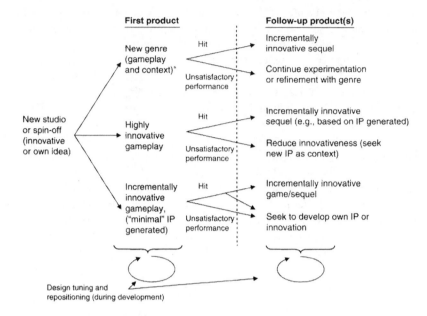

Figure 2 Balancing product innovations within game development studios

* Based on interview data.

the product is not a hit, the designer may continue to work on and refine the emerging genre. In the second strategy, success also dictates making similar but incrementally innovative sequels, especially if valuable content IP has been generated by the initial success (e.g., RPG Games' second product). If the game is not a hit, part of the innovative gameplay and code might be salvaged and reused with new content (usually consisting of well-known IP) in successive products (e.g., Strategy Games' second product). Depending on consumers' feedback, this might also involve simplifying gameplay. In other words, the studio tends to backtrack innovatively by retreating to a less risky application of its innovation. The third strategy involves starting out with incrementally innovative products. If these are hits, or at least provide contract work that can sustain the studio, the studio may take the option to continue to develop and introduce incrementally innovative products. A studio adopting such a strategy might also be sustaining itself until it can be in a position to innovate more substantially later (e.g., RPG Games' fourth products). If the incremental innovation strategy does not work, for instance, because it allows the publisher to dictate terms, a studio might try to innovate by creating more of its own IP and/or design innovations. In this way, the studio may gain more favorable bargaining terms with publishers, among other things (e.g., Action Games' fourth product). In summary, forces tend to push studios into performing balancing acts on innovation, regardless of their starting state of innovation.

258

Balancing can occur not only between projects, but also within a particular project as studios try to manage uncertainty and adapt their products to the marketplace. Figure 2 shows the two mechanisms discussed earlier by which studios adapt designs to suit the marketplace: tuning and repositioning of innovations. Both tuning and repositioning can also be done for incrementally, as well as radically, innovative games. Both can also involve minor or major redesign.

5.2. Understanding the phenomena

Our findings can be interpreted through various perspectives in the literature. The influence of rational forces on incremental innovation can be seen through the lens of institutional *isomorphism*, or the institutional forces that constrain organizations to resemble one another. Our findings on firms' balancing behavior adds to our understanding of how creative-rational tensions are resolved in creative industries, and our illustration of studios' product strategies and adaptive behaviors sheds light on the combinative nature of creativity in the industry.

Our study shows that rationalization in the games industry might involve studios and publishers making increasingly similar products, often with similar processes. An explanation for this organizational similarity may involve more than market mechanisms, and, in fact, our study may support an isomorphic explanation.[7] The desire of large publishers such as EA to influence independent studios with their processes and technologies is not unlike the coercive form of isomorphism, that is, the "formal and informal pressures exerted on organizations by other organizations upon which they are dependent" (DiMaggio and Powell 1983, p. 150). Cultural industry studies on nonprofit professional theatres (Voss et al. 2000) and Hollywood's film studios (Epstein 2005, Mezias and Mezias 2000) have also shown that the tensions between artistic and financial agendas are often resolved by the domination of one particular force—the pursuit of financial security and stability. As Epstein (2005, p. 107) notes of Hollywood's major studios, "The main task of today's studio is to collect fees for the use of the intellectual properties they control. . . . It is now essentially a service organization, a dream clearinghouse rather than a dream factory." In like fashion, game development studios have also paid overwhelming attention to their external constituents—publishers and consumers.

The notion of *mimetic isomorphism*, i.e., isomorphism due to uncertainty in the environment, also helps to explain the imitative behavior of the studios. The concept of ambiguity in goals and means (March and Olsen 1976) provides a rationale for this notion: "When goals are ambiguous . . . organizations may model themselves on other organizations." In this way, "uncertainty is also a powerful force encouraging imitation" (DiMaggio and Powell 1983, p. 151). The unpredictability of consumers' reception to new game designs (especially those that enable new forms of gameplay), and increasing product complexity, create significant uncertainty. The tendency of independent studios to imitate or learn from one another partly results from their need to manage the risks of this uncertainty.

The production of well-understood products that have immediate market interest is a related means of countering this problem. Furthermore, as outputs become similar—e.g., with the increasing dominance of immersive 3D games—the use of common scripting, graphics, and other software tools are becoming de facto parts of the process. This in turn is leading different firms to undertake similar tasks and routines as another way to combat uncertainty. Some idea of the importance placed on mutual learning can be seen by the popularity of the postmortems in *Game Developer* magazine as well as by the numerous conference sessions at the GDC that detail the lessons learned by studios on their projects.

Finally, the trend towards professionalization in the industry means that a normative form of isomorphism might be at work. At least some of the rationalization in the game development process appears to be similar in spirit to the rationalization trend in the computer software industry, which is now strongly influenced by the software engineering discipline (as developed by authors such as Chrissis et al. 2003 and Paulk 1995).

In summary, institutional characteristics can influence isomorphic behavior, which includes phenomena that occur at multiple levels, involves a variety of actors, and is caused by rational influences operating over long periods of time.

In seeking to move beyond the influence of rationalization and its effect on incremental innovation, studios also try to strike a balance between creativity and rationality. The issue of balancing creative with rational interests is analogous to the general organizational tension identified between explorative and exploitative processes (March 1991). Learning or technological change involves adaptation and a "delicate trade-off between exploration and exploitation," where exploitation involves the refinement and extension of existing competencies (March 1991, p. 85). Furthermore, this adaptive feature of organizations involves a tendency "to substitute exploitation of known alternatives for the exploration of unknown ones, to increase the reliability of performance" (March 1991, p. 85), presumably as a means of addressing the ambiguity that organizations face (March and Olsen 1976). Although this is largely described for the organizational level (March 1991), our study also illustrates such tensions occurring at multiple levels and across a variety of actors.

The issue of creative-rational tensions and the need to balance them has also been encountered in studies of other creative industries. As Lampel et al. (2000) note, novelty and familiarity are necessary ingredients for developing creative products, yet they create a tension because firms and other actors seeking to achieve both. For example, creative-rational tension occurs between commercial motivations and artistic license (Glynn 2000, Voss et al. 2000). A similar tension occurs between two types of authenticity: individual creative expression, and *manufactured authenticity*, defined as the rational attempt to craft an artist's persona to attract the attention of customers, critics, and others (Jones et al. 2005). Similarly, a game's design requires balancing the more rational interests of the market (e.g., tuning games to make them playable or usable by consumers) with the interests of developers in making a creative product. Publishers, too, have

260

diversified their portfolios by contracting with external studios to make products that are more creative.

These tensions can be resolved in other ways. Resolutions are sometimes achieved by emphasizing either a dominant deliberate or emergent strategy. In the case of emergent strategies, "authenticity evolves and changes over time, requiring the feedback of and interaction among interdependent participants" (Jones et al. 2005, p. 897). Similarly, the adaptive behavior of game development studios, which involves creating and backing away from innovations, has an emergent quality. Other studies have also noted that such tensions are usually resolved by a balance or negotiation between the artists or creators and other stakeholders, as in the case of professional orchestra musicians confronting the rational business interests of the institution's management (Glynn 2000).

At the industry level, the balance between these conflicting interests may involve the creation of new firms, as shown with Mezias and Mezias's (2000) examination of the emergence of specialized film studios. This was also the case for the game development studios in our study, where the spin-off process allowed them to begin pursuing a more innovative path.

Creativity is a central instrument for individuals and firms to achieve greater returns through exploration, and more generally, in their search for balance in their efforts at innovation. Creativity underlies development of the next dominant designs, linking innovative behavior in the form of an organizational model of search and adaptation to the evolution and possible emergence of such designs. From our data, a potentially important creative mechanism for innovating or even adapting products is combining features from past games, a mechanism that we term *combinative creativity*, resulting in combinative innovations. The concept can be used at multiple levels. The idea of combinative capabilities was put forward by Kogut and Zander (1992, p. 392), who follow Schumpeter in thinking of innovations as "new combinations of existing knowledge and incremental learning." When operationalized, the term *combinative* may refer to the combination of ideas from one domain or industry with another through the sheer creativity of individuals and teams. This is not uncommon among leading product design companies (Hargadon 2003). At the cognitive level, combinative creativity is related to constructivism, a philosophy of learning based on the premise that our understanding and representation of the world reflects our experiences. In games, constructivism involves cross-fertilizing ideas from previous games and other media, including books and films (Tschang and Sczcypula 2006). We have further shown in this paper that these innovations can also arise from splicing gameplay and features from other games or genres to create a fusion product that may not closely resemble the gameplay of the constituent genres.

In the games industry, combinative creativity can lead to the refinement of genres' new dominant designs (i.e., genres) or products that in their culmination of features become the defining representatives of such genres. We have provided a basis for explaining how combinative creativity can enable a sequence of incremental innovations that may evolve into new genres or games that are definitive examples of new genres. An example of this is the *Grand Theft Auto* series, which evolved from a driving game with a *top-down view* (i.e., where the game is viewed from above, as in a map) to a 3D driving game (which gives a first-person view) that was lauded as a breakthrough product for its highly immersive nature and emergent gameplay (i.e., for the flexibility of play that it allowed users).[8] Combinative creativity may be a fundamental mechanism to be considered in terms of how technological trajectories and dominant designs occur. In fact, combinative creativity may weaken the influence of dominant designs because it can facilitate fusion products that are in-between dominant designs, as with RPG Games' second product. It may even extend the life of a dominant design, as seen in the extension of the RTS genre's popularity through the use of 3D technology. These insights might provide a basis for formulating an alternative means to conventional models (such as the product innovation-to-process innovation model [Utterback 1994]) for understanding how industries evolve. The manner in which combinative mechanisms shape industry evolution could be further researched. The combinative creative mechanism is analogous to the recombinative form of evolutionary change based on genetic cross-over mechanisms as seen in complex adaptive systems (CAS) modeling approaches (Axelrod and Cohen 1999, p. 23). CAS approaches could thus be suitable for further investigating how the adaptive and creative behaviors of firms are related to the evolution of designs and dominant designs.

To make sense of the relationships between the different actors and forces in the games industry, it can also be useful to investigate the commonalities within the class of structuration models. In particular, the use of technology could be institutionalized in an organization's practices, thereby limiting the potential creativity of users (Orlikowski 1992). The situation we observed in the games industry can be viewed as structuration occurring at multiple levels: An aversion to innovation may emerge as a norm when consumers and publishers become familiar with certain genres, and when studios become familiar with the production of those genres. However, as our study points out, this is balanced by the inherent desire of individuals to be creative, and the need to meet consumers' demands for some level of innovation.[9]

6. Conclusions

Our objective in this paper was to explore how different forces interact at various levels as a creative industry evolves, and to study how the tension between creativity and rational influences is resolved. As the games industry has evolved, certain unique games have defined new genres, that is, dominant designs. Interactions among the industry actors—publishers, studios, and consumers—have reinforced a trend toward incremental innovations based on these genres. Recent criticisms of the lack of innovation in the industry suggest a growing awareness of this problem (Dobson 2006, Roch 2004). Tensions are created with this rationalization because consumers also expect innovative aspects in new games. The need for increasingly immersive games with detailed content will make it harder for studios to excel in all dimensions, i.e., to create innovative and enjoyable gameplay that responds to consumers who seek immersive experiences. A key challenge in the industry is the management of these tensions. Different actors accomplish this with a variety of balancing behaviors. Creative individuals are responsible for bringing about radical innovation, which results in new game genres. Recognizing this, some publishers seek more innovation by altering their portfolio to include successfully creative designers. Independent studios and their designers also balance creative and commercial interests by adapting their behavior with regard to product strategy (e.g., making their next products either more or less innovative, or shifting their focus to include creating their own IP), and by tuning and repositioning designs during projects.

In light of the uncertainty in this industry, strategies for initial success might be risky, especially for inexperienced teams. It may help firms to recognize that the process may involve balancing innovations and combinative creativity. To survive over the longer run, firms may need to be aware of the potential for innovation balancing strategies to help products evolve and succeed. These strategies also provide learning opportunities, e.g., how various kinds of combinative innovations can influence success. The "AAA" (i.e., highest production value and cost) titles such as *Grand Theft Auto 3* and *Sims 2*, both of which are sequels to innovative games, are examples of how the twin objectives of innovative gameplay and costly immersive qualities can be managed within successful product evolution strategies that may not have been dictated beforehand.

The risk-averse nature of many publishers also makes it difficult for designers to convincingly demonstrate new and innovative gameplay. The question is, at the industry level, can ladders containing progressive amounts of resources be made available to support a sequence of products, including their sequels, to improve new forms of gameplay, thereby attracting consumers? Firms may need to explore newer market niches where highly refined content is less important than providing innovative gameplay or unusual experiences.

Studios also need to manage a variety of other factors including internal resources, externally available resources (which are mostly controlled by publishers), and other objectives such as the perceived need to produce immersive polished games. One issue for further study would be whether other models exist that can effectively build internal capability that could be connected to external resources while minimizing risks. Another potential area of research involves whether the building of particular capabilities and resources helps differentiate studios from one another, and whether the mix of these capabilities and resources constrains or helps studios as they develop and evolve a sequence of products.

Finally, we might ask whether current institutions and incentives are optimal for promoting innovation, or whether new institutions or intermediaries with different incentives and different risk-mitigating behaviors are needed, e.g., publishers that act more like venture capitalists, or better online distributional models that fund and create game industry versions of the long-tail business models currently seen in some film- and Internet- content industries (Anderson 2006).

Acknowledgments

The author thanks the special issue's co-editor, Professor Susan Taylor, and two reviewers for their invaluable comments and guidance; Arun Kumaraswamy for his support and suggestions on various drafts; and Amritha Mani for her research assistance. The author also thanks participants in seminars at the Ministry of Economy, Trade and Industry's Research Institute of Economy, Trade and Industry (Japan), Yuan-Ze University (Taiwan), and the Institute for Infocomm Research (Singapore), where parts of this study were presented. The author acknowledges the financial support of the Wharton- Singapore Management University (SMU) Research Center.

Notes

1 We use the term *creativity* as a general term referring to both the output (with unique and interesting qualities) and the activity (i.e., creative thinking) that generates the output. Also, we consider creative output and thinking to be the same as innovative output and thinking.

2 Technically, the term *video games* refers to console games, i.e., games played on consoles such as Sony's Playstation, Nintendo's GameBoy, or Microsoft's Xbox. In this paper, however, we use video games (or games) to refer to both console games and to so-called computer games (i.e., those played on personal computers).

3 All interviews were conducted in confidentiality, and the names of interviewees are withheld by mutual agreement. Most of our interviewees were developers of computer games, although several interviewees (and one studio on which an ethnographic study was developed) made console games.

4 The four firms—Action Games, RPG [role-playing games] Games, Strategy Games, and IGF-Winner—were given fictional names that reflected their primary characteristic (e.g., the typical genre of game that they made). All other studios in the paper are referred to by their actual names.

5 Likewise, Will Wright's first big success—*Sim City*—was a city-building simulator/ strategy game known for its sandbox kind of open-ended, goalless type of play. He was inspired as he toyed around with a scenario editor for another game, and discovered that he had more fun building things onscreen than tearing them down; he then combined this with models from Jay Forrester's studies on system dynamics (Rouse 2001). Similarly, *The Sims* was created by Wright after he spent two years researching books from architecture and other fields; he first attempted to make an architectural simulation, but this became more fun to play with as a virtual doll house. Another example is that of Chris Crawford, who has labored for more than 20 years to build his interactive storytelling technology. An early prototype appeared as *Siboot*—a game partly stemming from his ongoing research at Atari into components of interactive storytelling, but that was actually stimulated in a flash of insight by a tragic event—the agonizing death of a pet.

6 *Level design* is the practice of plotting paths through or creating scenarios for segments of the game that the consumer must traverse in the course of playing.

7 Over the course of our interviews, studio heads hardly ever discussed the conditions of competition or notions of competitiveness. Nevertheless, there is some element

of competition in the market. Thus, alternative views to isomorphism might involve rational or market mechanisms (see DiMaggio and Powell 1983 for a discussion). Bounded rationality forms of decision making may also factor in the industry (March and Olsen 1976, Simon 1979). For instance, publisher behavior that categorizes games and seeks new titles according to their genre could be a form of heuristic-based behavior. However, given the evidence we have presented, it is unlikely that these are the main reasons for the similarity seen across organizations. The industry's behavior toward innovations is more likely to be a complex combination of rational and isomorphic factors.

8 Other examples come from the games that have become definitive representatives of new genres. When traced, these games appear to have their lineage in predecessors that contained significant elements of their gameplay, but which did not capture the genre in as definitive a way as these games. Examples of this include the definitive first-person shooter *Wolfenstein 3D* and real-time strategy game *Dune II*. Writers feel that the first instance of specific real-time strategy gameplay (i.e., containing "harvest [resources], build [buildings], conquer [opponents]" actions, all performed in real time) appearing was in the console title *Herzog Zwei*. This predated the 1992 *Dune II* by three years. However, elements of real-time strategy appeared even further back in other games, such as *The Ancient Art of War* in 1984. Whether and to what extent these games influenced the designers of *Dune II* is an open question, but *Dune II*'s designers did play many of these earlier games.

9 Other related approaches that may be structurally appropriate for mapping onto the models in this paper include frameworks that permit the incorporation of multiple frames or perspectives (e.g., Orlikowski and Gash 1994) and multiple levels of analysis in a structuration model (DeSanctis and Poole 1994).

References

Abernathy, W. J., J. M. Utterback. 1978. Patterns of innovation in industry. *Tech. Rev.* **80**(7) 40–47.

Anderson, C. 2006. *The Long Tail: Why the Future of Business Is Selling Less of More.* Hyperion, New York.

Anderson, P. C., M. L. Tushman. 1990. Technological discontinuities and dominant designs: A cyclical model of technological change. *Admin. Sci. Quart.* **35**(4) 604–633.

Axelrod, R. M., M. D. Cohen. 1999. *Harnessing Complexity: Organizational Implications of a Scientific Frontier.* Free Press, New York.

Baba, Y, F. T. Tschang. 2001. Product development in Japanese TV game software: The case of an innovative game. *Internet. J. Innovation Management* **5**(4) 487–515.

Bethke, E. 2003. *Game Development and Production.* Wordware Publishing, Plano, TX.

Birdwell, K. 1999. The cabal: Valve's design process for creating half-life, http://www.gamasutra.com/features/19991210/birdwell_01.htm.

Caves, R. E. 2000. *Creative Industries: Contracts Between Art and Commerce.* Harvard University Press, Cambridge, MA.

Chey, J. 1998. Irrational Games' *System Shock 2. Game Developer* **6**(11) 52–59.

Chrissis, M. B., M. Konrad, S. Shrum. 2003. *CMMI: Guidelines for Process Integration and Product Improvement.* Addison-Wesley, New York.

De Vany, A. 2004. *Hollywood Economics: How Extreme Uncertainty Shapes the Film Industry.* Routledge (Contemporary Political Economy), Oxford, UK.

DeMaria, R., J. L. Wilson. 2002. *High Score! The Illustrated History of Electronic Games.* McGraw Hill, Osborne, Berkeley, CA.

Department for Culture, Media and Sport (DCMS). 1998. *Creative Industries Mapping Document 1998.* Department for Culture, Media and Sport, London, UK.

DeSanctis, G., M. S. Poole. 1994. Capturing the complexity in advanced technology use: Adaptive structuration theory. *Organ. Sci.* **5**(2) 123–147.

Crawford, C. 2003. *Chris Crawford on Game Design.* New Riders Games, Berkeley, CA.

DiMaggio, P. J., W. W. Powell. 1983. The iron cage revisited: Institutional isomorphism and collective rationality in organizational fields. *Amen Social. Rev.* **48**(2) 147–160.

Dobson, J. 2006. Indie developers on how to fix the game biz. Industry News, Gamasutra. http://www.gamasutra.com/php- bin/news_index.php?story=10643.

Donovan, T. 2004. Top 20 publishers in games. *Game Developer* **11**(9) 10–18.

Eisenhardt, K. M. 1989. Building theories from case study research. *Acad. Management Rev.* **14**(4) 488–511.

Eisenmann, T. R., J. L. Bower. 2000. The entrepreneurial M-form: Strategic integration in global media firms. *Organ. Sci.* **11**(3) 348–355.

Electronic Arts (EA). 2005. *10-K Filing.* Securities and Exchange Commission, Washington, D.C. (June 7, 2005).

Entertainment Software Association. 2005. Essential facts about the computer and video game industry. Entertainment Software Association, Washington, D.C.

Epstein, E. J. 2005. *The Big Picture: The New Logic of Money and Power in Hollywood.* Random House, New York.

Gallagher, S., S. H. Park. 2002. Innovation and competition in standard-based industries: A historical analysis of the U.S. home video game market. *IEEE Trans. Engrg. Management* **49**(1) 67–81.

Glaser, B., A. Strauss. 1967. *The Discovery of Grounded Theory: Strategies of Qualitative Research.* Wiedenfeld and Nicholson, London, UK.

Glynn, M. A. 2000. When cymbals become symbols: Conflict over organizational identity within a symphony orchestra. *Organ. Sci.* **11**(3) 285–298.

Hargadon, A. 2003. *How Breakthroughs Happen: The Surprising Truth About How Companies Innovate.* Harvard Business School Press, Cambridge, MA.

Henderson, R. M., K. B. Clark. 1990. Architectural innovation: The reconfiguration of existing product technologies and the failure of established firms. *Admin. Sci. Quart.* **35**(1) 9–30.

Hirsch, P. M. 2000. Cultural industries revisited. *Organ. Sci.* **11**(3) 356–361.

Hubbard, C. 2007. Postmortem: Monolith's *No One Lives Forever.* http://www.gamasutra. com/features/20010608/hubbard_01.htm.

Jones, C. J., N. Anand, J. L. Alvarez. 2005. Manufactured authenticity and creative voice in cultural industries. *J. Management Stud.* **42**(5) 893–899.

Keighley, G. 1998. Simply divine: The story of Maxis software. *Game Spot,* http://www. gamespot.com/features/maxis/.

Klepper, S., K. L. Simons. 2000. Dominance by birthright: Entry of prior radio producers and competitive ramifications in the U.S. television receiver industry. *Strategic Management J.* **21**(10–11) 997–1016.

Kogut, B., U. Zander. 1992. Knowledge of the firm, combinative capabilities, and the replication of technology. *Organ. Sci.* **3**(3) 383–397.

Kushner, D. 2003. *Masters of Doom: How Two Guys Created an Empire and Transformed Pop Culture.* Random House, New York.

Lampel, J., T. Lant, J. Shamsie. 2000. Balancing act: Learning from organizing practices in cultural industries. *Organ. Sci.* **11**(3) 263–269.

Leonard, T. 1999. Looking glass's *Thief*. The dark project. *Game Developer* **6**(7) 50–58.

Lincoln, Y. S., E. G. Guba. 1985. *Naturalistic Inquiry*. Sage Publications, New York.

March, J. G. 1991. Exploration and exploitation in organizational learning. *Organ. Sci.* **2**(1) 71–87.

March, J. G., J. P. Olsen. *1976. Ambiguity and Choice in Organizations*. Universitetsforlaget, Bergen, Norway.

McDonald, D. 2005. Hollywood to EA: Bring it on. *Wired Magazine* (August).

Mezias, J., S. Mezias. 2000. Resource partitioning and the founding of specialist firms: The American feature film industry, 1912–1929. *Organ. Sci.* **11** 306–322.

Miles, M. B., A. M. Huberman. 1994. *Qualitative Data Analysis*. Sage, Thousand Oaks, CA.

Orlikowski, W. J. 1992. The duality of technology: Rethinking the concept of technology in organizations. *Organ. Sci.* **3**(3) 398–427.

Orlikowski, W. J., D. C. Gash. 1994. Technological frames: Making sense of information technology in organizations. *ACM Trans. Inform. Systems* **12**(2) 174–207.

Paulk, M. C. 1995. *The Capability Maturity Model: Guidelines for Improving the Software Process*. Addison-Wesley, Reading, MA.

Pham, A. 2002. Consolidation seen among game firms. *Los Angeles Times* (Oct. 7).

Pritchard, M. 2000. Ensemble Studios' Age of Empires II: The Age of Kings. *Game Developer* **7**(1) 52–58.

Reinhart, B. 2000. Epic Games' Unreal Tournament. *Game Developer* **7**(5) 46–58.

Robins, J. A. 1993. Organization as strategy: Restructuring production in the film industry. *Strategic Management J.* **14** 103–118.

Roch, S. 2004. The new studio model. Gamasutra. http://www.gamasutra.com/features 20041029/roch_01.shtml.

Rogers, D. L. 2004. The end game: How top developers sold their studios, Part 1. http://www.gamasutra.com.

Rouse, R. 2001. *Game Design: Theory and Practice*, 2nd ed. Word-ware Publishing, Plano, TX.

Salen, K., E. Zimmerman. 2003. *Rules of Play: Game Design Fundamentals*. MIT Press, Cambridge, MA.

Schilling, M. A. 2003. Technological leapfrogging: Lessons from the U.S. video game console industry. *Calif Management Rev.* **4**(3) 6–32.

Simon, H. A. 1979. Rational decision making in business organizations. *Amer. Econom. Rev.* **69**(4) 493–513.

Spector, W. 2000. Ion Storm's Deus Ex. *Game Developer* **7**(11) 50–58.

Starkey, K., C. Bamatt, S. Tempest. 2000. Beyond networks and hierarchies: Latent organizations in the U.K. television industry. *Organ. Sci.* **11**(3) 299–305.

Sternberg, R. J., ed. 1998. *Handbook of Creativity*. Cambridge University Press, Cambridge, UK.

Stojsavljevic, R. 2000. Westwood Studios' Command & Conquer: Tiberian Sun. *Game Developer* **7**(2) 46–54.

Train, T., B. Reynolds. 2003. Big Huge Games' Rise of Nations. *Game Developer* **10**(7) 36–41.

Tschang, F. T. 2005. Videogames as interactive experiential products and their manner of development. *Internet. J. Innovative Management* **9**(1) 103–131.

Tschang, F. T., J. Szczypula. 2006. Idea creation, constructivism, and evolution as primary characteristics in the video game artifact design process. *European Management J.* **24**(4) 270–287.

Utterback, J. M. 1994. *Mastering the Dynamics of Innovation*. Harvard Business School Press, Cambridge, MA.

Voss, G. B., D. M. Cable, Z. G. Voss. 2000. Linking organizational values to relationships with external constituents: A study of nonprofit professional theatres. *Organ. Sci.* **11**(3) 330–347.

Yin, R. K. 1994. *Case Study Research: Design and Methods*, 2nd ed. Sage Publications, Thousand Oaks, CA.

87

CONVERGENCE AND GLOBALIZATION IN THE JAPANESE VIDEOGAME INDUSTRY

Mia Consalvo

Source: *Cinema Journal*, 48(3), Spring 2009, 135–141.

For contemporary media scholars, convergence means more than technologies or content coming together in one box.[1] It instead alludes to the convergence of content across media platforms, and the joining together of media producers and consumers in the production and negotiation of that content—through user-generated content, greater feedback mechanisms for consumers, or fan-driven media campaigns. Yet apart from a sidebar mentioning the importance that both Western and Japanese fans have played in the global popularity of Japanese anime, most examples that Henry Jenkins cites in *Convergence Culture*, and the majority of work done by other media scholars, focuses on Western media products and companies.[2]

This essay addresses that omission and advocates further investigation regarding the Japanese game industry by studying three companies successful in developing and publishing games, along with a range of other activities. Those companies are Bandai Namco, Square Enix, and Konami. I chose these three for several reasons. First, all released annual reports for 2007, which formed the starting point of analysis. Second, the companies have had long histories and have all weathered multiple console releases, as well as evolving cultural, technological, social, and political developments. None of the three are principally console manufacturers, like Sony and Nintendo. Those companies would make comparisons more difficult, as hardware and software production are different undertakings. And finally, I chose companies that acted as both developers and publishers and who had diversified holdings. Not *all* Japanese videogame companies are this diverse in their ownership and business strategies; it is exactly their diversity that makes these three companies particularly interesting and important.[3]

This essay investigates how these companies are negotiating the "convergence culture" that Jenkins writes about. Next, it examines how they are responding to a problem unique to Japan—the graying of the nation. Lastly, it questions how globalization plays a role in Japanese game business strategies.

First, however, let me give a brief description of each company. The oldest is Bandai Namco. Bandai began in the 1950s producing various toys, mostly metallic cars. It created the Sailor Moon and Power Rangers brands, released Tamagotchi in 1996, and in 2005 acquired Namco.[4] Namco started out producing mechanical rocking horses, later acquiring the Japanese division of Atari and entering the coinoperated game market. In 1980 Namco released the global blockbuster *Pac-Man*, and in 1993 the company merged with Aladdin's Castle Inc., to become the world's largest arcade company.[5] Bandai Namco now comprises business units that include game development, arcades, toys and toy-related products, spa facilities, tourist hotels, online services, anime production, and restaurants.

Konami incorporated in 1973, when it began to manufacture amusement machines.[6] It created the hit arcade game *Frogger* in 1981, and has since produced some of the best-known games in game history, including the *Castlevania* (1986–2008), *Contra* (1987–2007), *Silent Hill* (1999–2008), and *Metal Gear* (1987–2008) series, along with *Dance Dance Revolution* (1998) and the soccer series *Winning Eleven* (1995–2008). Currently, Konami has three business segments. Its Digital Entertainment segment comprises home videogame software, card games, and amusement arcade machines. The Health and Fitness segment operates sports clubs and develops health-related products and services. Lastly, the Gaming and System segment develops, manufactures, and supplies gaming machines and casino management systems.

The final company, Square Enix, is the product of another merger, in 2003, of two Japanese developer/publisher stalwarts best known for their *Final Fantasy* (1987–2008) and *Dragon Quest* (1986–2008) series. Enix was founded in 1975, while Square began operations in 1986. Square Enix continues to release games in the *Final Fantasy* and *Dragon Quest* series, along with developing games for emerging markets in China and Korea. In 2005, Square Enix acquired Taito Corporation, which started operating in 1953 as a manufacturer of small vending machines. Taito went on to expand its arcade business, developing the global hit *Space Invaders* in 1978. Square Enix segments its business into numerous areas, including offline games, online games, mobile phone content, publications, and amusements.

Convergence culture meets Japan's media mix

Jenkins writes how content moves across platforms, as well as how media consumers interact with content, identifying sites of negotiation where convergence occurs.[7] One site transforms media franchises from a central text with derivative works related to it to, instead, places where "each media manifestation makes a distinct but interrelated contribution to the unfolding of a narrative universe."[8] If thought about as a continuum, universes range from encapsulating a strong "center-periphery" model to systems that are much less centralized.

The "center-periphery" model was first widely exploited in the West with the success of George Lucas's *Star Wars* series in the 1970s and 1980s. Although most often credited with creating a market for media-related consumables and collectibles, *Star Wars* also helped establish the idea of a media universe, creating opportunities for further consumption, but also for providing new pieces of the *Star Wars* story (as well as adaptations) through novels, comics, and videogames. During that time, most of what was released was created by professional storytellers (or designers) rather than by fans of the series, a situation that would change quickly.[9]

Western media corporations have mostly continued to follow a "center-periphery" paradigm, claiming a particular canon for some universe, either through films *(Star Wars)*, books (Tolkien and Middle Earth), or a television series *(Star Trek)*. In contrast, the background that companies such as Bandai Namco and Konami have in toys and amusements sets up a different form of engagement with the world of cross-media and cross-product promotion; unlike in the American model, here central characters or a theme or world are created, then gradually filled in by various media products, none of which may take center stage.[10] Bandai's Gundam character line, for example, began in 1979 as part of an anime series, followed by a toy series in 1980, a series of movies starting the next year, and continuing with new toy lines, anime (TV) productions, films, and videogames. Importantly, these are all key components of the Gundam universe, with no one piece being the center. Such assemblages constitute what Ito terms a "media mix" which includes games "as one component of a broader media ecology that includes anime, manga, trading card games, toys, and character merchandise."[11]

Bandai Namco stresses such linkages, calling them synergies, which "integrate character merchandising with technical development capabilities and a location network."[12] That synergy includes the networked arcade game *Mobile Suit Gundam,: Senjo-no-Kizuna* (2007)—which sixteen people can play concurrently—and the 2006 construction of the theme park "Namco Wonder Park Hero's Base." In similar ways, Square Enix draws from elements of its business to expand the *Final Fantasy* universe, which has never featured a core text or storyline, but instead creates features and elements that make each iteration of *Final Fantasy* feel familiar (including the appearance of specific animal races such as the chicken-like chocobos, a character named Cid, crystals, and a common currency). Currently Square Enix takes the *Final Fantasy* universe and uses films to tell some stories ("Advent Children"), games to tell more (including games such as *Crisis Core* [2007], which steps outside the numbered franchise and tells a story of a character from *Final Fantasy* VII [1997]), and other products or services to keep the universe expanding. Other elements include the MMOG, *Final Fantasy* XI (2002), mobile phone games such as *Dirge of Cerberus: Lost Episode* (2006), collectibles, music CDs, and mp3's from the games.

The graying of Japan

Top sellers in places like the United States and Europe draw from developers and publishers spread around the globe. One European Top 20 list, for example, includes games from Nintendo, Konami, Activision, EA, Ubisoft, and Sega.[13]

In contrast, Japan remains insular in its appetite for game titles. Charts listing the top one hundred games sold in Japan in 2005 show the first non-Japanese game listed being the #70 title *Ratchet & Clank 4* produced by Insomniac Games in California. In 2007, the first non-Japanese entry was Rockstar Games' *Grand Theft Auto: San Andreas* at #35, selling slightly more than 400,000 copies. To compare, the top seller in 2007 was *Wii Sports* (Nintendo), which sold almost two million units, and #2 was Monster *Hunter Freedom 2* (Capcom) for the PSP with almost 1.5 million units, suggesting that Western games have a rough time gaining entry or popularity in the Japanese market.[14] Because of those historical tendencies, Japanese game companies have found a ready market at home, with little fear of outside competition.

However, even if game and related product sales in Japan are favorable (as they have been for Konami), and even if Japanese game companies have had a near monopoly on game sales in Japan itself, convergence and a turn to global audiences are becoming necessities not options. Much has been made of the declining birth rate in Japan—the "graying of Japan"—with two annual reports specifically concerned with the aging of the Japanese market as a "risk factor." In this context, the possibilities of convergence help to shore up a games market that has started to contract due to the shifting demographics of Japanese society. This challenge in part drives the creation of game-related products such as Square's 2001 film *Final Fantasy: The Spirits Within* (Hironobu Sakaguchi and Motonori Kakakibara), to spur potential interest beyond the traditional core of young boys and men. A converged media culture has added more revenue flows, as Japanese game companies have placed greater emphasis on going global with their media mix—something that they have been doing for years with varied degrees of success—as another key way of managing the declining local market.

Going global with a converged culture

The media mix or convergence culture which Japanese companies have been developing has of necessity made its way to Western markets, often beginning through unofficial channels. Jenkins explains that "western youth is asserting its identity through its consumption of Japanese anime and manga [. . .] A new pop cosmopolitanism is being promoted by corporate interests both in Asia and in the West."[15] Scholars have begun to map this trend, pointing to how anime fans see the material as more complex and thought-provoking than most Western media, as well as how "all things Japan" come to be seen as "cool" in the West.[16] That trend has historical roots which span at least 150 years, with similar fads or interest in "all things Japanese" influencing the Impressionists in Europe, and other intellectuals and middle class citizens as time passed, as Susan Napier has noted.[17] Games (and their related products) appear to be another piece of that Japanese cultural "cool," on which the media industry capitalizes.

Steady calls for globalization of a media mix in annual corporate reports may seem puzzling, since games from Japan have been an integral part of the history of the game industry since Nintendo revitalized the US market in the mid-1980s.[18] From that time, Japanese game developers, publishers, and console manufacturers have gone from dominating output to, at minimum, assuming a central role in the industry's continuing development. Yet financial documents reveal another view of Japanese companies. While Bandai Namco, Square Enix, and Konami all have global operations, percentages of income and sales gained from abroad are rather meager. Across the three, the Japanese market accounts for three-quarters or more of sales and revenue. The remaining income is gathered from North America, Europe, and Asia. ("Asia" here refers to a select few countries—China, Hong Kong, Taiwan, and Korea—and is a minor player.) It is easy to see why Japanese companies are so nervous about their shrinking domestic market: it represents the vast majority of their sales. Consequently, Japanese companies are desperately seeking to diversify, and do so in ways that go beyond a few internationally known blockbuster titles or series. Even if revenues are comparatively small, the global operations of Japanese game companies have been key to the development of the industry generally, as Japanese games and firms have contributed much in the way of cultural (if not economic) influence on the global games industry.

Yet now, those companies desire to broaden their markets, expand operations, or more carefully develop opportunities for international sales. Konami talks of "bolstering overseas business development," while Bandai Namco states that one of their "key business strategies . . . is strengthening overseas businesses."[19] Square Enix reports that overseas sales from games such as *Kingdom Hearts II* (2005) and *Final Fantasy XII* (2006) "contributed substantially to earnings and profits."[20] Bandai Namco also realized gains from abroad, which "supported domestic operations," which had seen a decline in sales and profits in the past year.[21] In the 1980s and 1990s Japanese companies produced a disproportionate share of software and hardware sold globally, meaning that even poorly localized games could sell well. Early game fans derided the translation and localization efforts of those games, which often featured badly broken English. Yet the development of a more competitive global market with more companies and genres of games that might be regionally appropriate has changed the parameters for competition. Japanese companies must now be more diligent in how they pursue overseas markets, carefully developing or adapting selected media products that (re)deploy successful product universes.

Thus Konami will have employees in North America, Europe, and Asia "create, produce and offer products and services targeting local markets . . . [and] each local operating base will [also] build a system that will enable the global rollout of certain products and services."[22] Echoing interests in convergence, Konami sees opportunities both for global successes like *Metal Gear*, as well as the creation of content tied to particular regions and interests, that is, not simply Japanese content repackaged for sale elsewhere.

Bandai Namco is moving their strategy beyond localization of Japanese products and the development of overseas content: "Instead of development that is based on the framework of 'products for Japan' and 'products for overseas' we

273

will emphasize cooperation between Japan and overseas bases and implement worldwide development from the planning stage."[23] What this might mean is the development of content that in its raw form might draw from common themes, characters, or universes, but is then localized or "culturalized" to respond best to the interests of a variety of markets. Perhaps this indicates the formation of another layer or level to convergence. In addition to a fictional media universe drawing from a theme or character to create a diversity of content across multiple media platforms, convergence might entail that process working across regions and markets as well, carefully adapted not only for a technical platform, but for particular communities or nation states. Convergence just gained another order of complexity.

Conclusions

This essay has applied the concept of convergence to a slice of the Japanese game industry, to see how they are adapting to new demands. Japanese companies like Bandai Namco or Konami have a broadly diversified set of business segments, managing businesses that would seem to have nothing to do with games or even amusements. Yet at the same time, they have certain segments, such as toys and arcades, which help them create greater synergies or convergences across media forms as well as fictional universes. Japanese game companies operate primarily in domestic markets, where they dominate, and are now trying to diversify their revenue streams through more skilful use of their media mixes, and through the (re)capture of global markets, which have become much more demanding in terms of quality of content and familiarity of products. It can be done. Many Western individuals claim to love anime for its complex themes and lack of simplistic endings, suggesting that there is still interest in Japanese products abroad, in games, in anime, and in many other related artifacts. Yet how wide that market may be is an open question. Japanese game companies will need to consider such questions and challenges as they move forward with plans for greater expansion. They have moved beyond the creation of basic product lines to more sophisticated and inter-related products, as well as from the export of crudely localized products to more carefully "culturalized" ones. They are also questioning whether one-way exports are the answer, or if simply setting up offices abroad and having them make "local" games and artifacts is the right approach. For now, they continue to struggle with the logics of convergence, in a constantly changing global media universe.

Notes

1 Henry Jenkins, *Convergence Culture: Where Old and New Media Collide* (New York: New York University Press, 2006); Henry Jenkins, "The Cultural Logic of Media Convergence," *International Journal of Cultural Studies* 7, no. 1 (2004): 33–43.
2 Jenkins, *Convergence Culture*, 156–161.
3 Other contenders considered, and to be expanded on in a future edition of this paper, include Capcom, Sega, Koei, and Atlus.

4 For more on the history of these companies, see Bandai's official history at http://www. bandai.co.jp/e/corporate/history.html and a Wikipedia entry profiling the company at http://en.wikipedia.org/wiki/Bandai (accessed October10, 2008).

5 Information taken from http://en.wikipedia.org/wiki/Namco (accessed October 10, 2008).

6 Konami Corporation, *Annual Report 2007*. Tokyo, Japan.

7 Jenkins, "The Cultural Logic."

8 Jenkins, "The Cultural Logic," 40.

9 More recent franchises such as the Harry Potter books have entered a playing field where readers-turned-fans have also become active producers in the Potterverse. The fan site HarryPotterfanfiction.com, for example, boasts over 50,000 stories and podcasts created by fans, and receives over 40 million hits per month.

10 Perhaps the best-known example would be Sanrio's Hello Kitty, which started life in 1974 simply as a brand, with content waiting to flesh out the form.

11 Mizuko Ito, "The Gender Dynamics of the Japanese Media Mix." Paper presented at the Girls and Games Workshop, UCLA, 2006.

12 Bandai Namco Games, *Annual Report 2007*. Tokyo, Japan.

13 "Top 20 Publishers 2007*," Game Developer* (2008). Available online at http://www. gamedevresearch.com/top-20-publishers-2007.htm (accessed October 10, 2008).

14 *Wii Sports* may be an unfair comparison, as it came free with the Wii console; thus I have included the #2 ranked game as a better comparison. "2005 Top 100 Best selling Japanese console games," *The Magic Box* (2006), available online at http://www. the-magicbox.com/Chart-BestSell2005.shtml; Daemon Hatfield, "The Japan 100, 2007 Edition," IGNi2008), available at http://ps3.ign.com/articles/845/845026pl.html (accessed October 10, 2008).

15 Jenkins, "The Cultural Logic," 41.

16 Susan Napier, From Impressionism to Anime: Japan as Fantasy and Fan Cult in the Mind of the West (New York: Paigrave, 2007).

17 Napier, *From Impressionism to Anime*. See also Mia Consalvo, "Visiting the Floating World: Tracing a Cultural History of Games Through Japan and America." Paper presented at the *Digital Games Research Association Conference*, Tokyo, Japan, September 2007.

18 Mia Consalvo, "Console Video Games and Global Corporations: Creating a Hybrid Culture," *New Media & Society 8*, no. 1 (2007); David Sheff, *Game Oven How Nintendo Conquered the World* (New York: Vintage, 1994).

19 Konami, 15; Bandai Namco, 9.

20 Square Enix Company Limited, *Annual Report 2007*. Tokyo, Japan.

21 Bandai Namco, 9.

22 Konami, 16.

23 Bandai Namco, 14.

88

VIDEOLOGY

Video-games as postmodern sites/sights of ideological reproduction

Simon Gottschalk

Source: *Symbolic Interaction*, 18(1), Spring 1995, 1–18.

Abstract

As new technologies, video-games are becoming increasingly popular among today's pre-teens and teenagers. Relying on systematic observation of videogames found in public arcades, participation in them, and engagement with the relevant literature, I explore eight central assumptions of "videology": the ideology which organizes these games. While suggesting that these assumptions articulate and exaggerate problematic ideological themes, I also explore the relationship between videology and a postmodern culture or moment.

Introduction

It has now become a cliche to assert that both our private and public environments are becoming increasingly computerized, robotized, and otherwise invaded by a multitude of new technological devices such as television sets, Virtual Reality, computers, VCRs, work-out machines, invisible cameras, video-games, and so forth. Although these devices are appreciably different from each other, they share with many others the characteristics of having emerged relatively recently, of constituting an "electronic environment" (Ellis 1983; see also Ross 1991; Anderson 1990; Diani 1992; Chen 1987), of being based on a logic of simulation, and of being associated by many theorists with the shift from a modern to a postmodern society, culture, and consciousness. Of course, the postmodern shift is predicated on much more than a simple association with these new technologies, but such a shift is importantly informed by their presence and multiplication.

For example, in his analysis of the works of Lyotard, Foucault, Derrida, and Baudrillard, Poster (1990) discusses the still elusive transformations engendered at the cognitive and macrosocial levels by the introduction of television, computers, and other new technologies constituting the "mode of information." Focusing on TV, the FAX machine, and the computer, psychologist Gergen (1991) suggests that these "technologies of social saturation" "populate the self," encouraging "multiphrenia" and other little understood experiences. While Agger (1992) and Denzin (1992) discuss the transformative influence of television on sociological theoretical concerns, Clough (1992) problematizes the relationship between sociological modes of representation and existing modes of mass communication, and Pfohl's (1992) self-reflective postmodern ethnography simulates the impact of the televisual logic on his experiences of self, epistemology, and politics.

Meanwhile, various scholars not necessarily associated with postmodern perspectives are also reflecting about the puzzling sociological effects of television in particular. Postman (1985) suggests that this device might very well precipitate important transformations in our cognitive functioning and in the possibilities for and engagement with serious political discourse. Mitroff and Bennis (1989) suggest that television might collapse our conceptions of reality and obliterate our capabilities to engage with it, and Meyrowitz (1985) suggests that our "sense of place" is constantly disoriented by the televisual blurring of once-clear social boundaries and categories (see also Ross 1991; Silverstone 1989; Gottschalk 1993).

Investigating the growth of more advanced technologies such as Virtual Reality, journalist Rheingold (1991, p. 17) posits the emergence of a "reality-industrial complex" whose dimensions, structure, resources, and possibilities we are barely beginning to imagine. In a recent article, Chayko (1993) also suggests that the increasing presence of Virtual Reality requires symbolic interaction theorists to reevaluate existing definitions of "the real" (see also Heim 1993). It is also fairly obvious that, beyond their most visible effects and uses, many of these new technologies will interact with older ones, merge with newer ones, and continue to transform our macro and micro-social environments in unfathomable and—some say—hallucinatory ways.

In sum, empirical and theoretical explorations of the effects of many new simulational technologies reveal that they have profoundly changed our global and social landscapes as well as the cognitive, emotional, and behavioral codes with which we engage them. The rapid rise and dissemination of postmodern theory must at least to some degree also be understood as a consequence of—and response to—the changes unleashed by this electronic revolution.

Video-games

Suddenly a new medium—and a new market opportunity—has opened up in the place where Hollywood, Silicon Valley and the information highway intersect. Games are part of a rapidly growing world of interactive amusements so new that nobody knows what to call them
—Dickerson and Jackson (1993, p. 68)

As the offspring of the coupling between a television screen and a computer, videogames constitute new simulation technologies which are enormously popular among male teenagers and which constitute a large and lucrative industry. According to Provenzo (1991, p. 8) the total 1990 sale for the Nintendo corporation amounted to $3.4 billion, and total sales for the entire video-game industry for that same year were $4 billion, encouraging the rapid emergence of new companies. In February 1989, 16 of the 20 top selling toys in the country were video-games or video-game related, 12% of all American homes owned Nintendo systems, and during the 1987, 1988, and 1989 Christmas seasons, Nintendo was the single best-selling toy, commanding 23% of the total $11.4 billion spent on toys in 1989 (Provenzo 1991, pp. 12–13). Kinder (1991, p. 88) reports:

> In the United States alone, consumers spend more on video-games— about $9 billion a year, including some $8 billion for coin-op and $1 billion for home games—than on any other form of entertainment, including movies and records. One game alone, Atari's awesome Asteroids earned about as much just in its best year ($700–$800 million) than the biggest money-making film of all time, *Gone with the Wind,* has made in four decades of screenings.

As Provenzo's study (1991, p. ix) also reveals:

> There are currently 19 million Nintendo game playing machines in the United States. The overwhelming majority of these game machines are owned by children. In addition to the games, there are Nintendo television programs, Nintendo books and magazines, Nintendo movies and video tapes, Nintendo lunch boxes, even Nintendo cereal, as well as social codes and traditions based on the Nintendo games and their characters.

And a recent *Time* magazine article (Dickerson and Jackson 1993, p. 68) also declares that the video-game industry has become "a global moneymaking machine that is gobbling up some of the most creative talents in Hollywood . . . . Globally, game revenues exceed $10 billion each year, and the worldwide sale of a single hit can top $500 million."

In this article, I explore "videology": the system of interrelated ideological assumptions which organizes video-games. Although we might minimize the importance of toys and games as indicators of anything sociologically or culturally significant, it might be useful to recognize that beyond their immediate pleasurable manipulation, toys are also cultural objects, socializing agents, carriers of the dominant ideology, "instruments of a larger, political, and cultural hegemony." (Provenzo 1991, p. 115) As Barthes (1957, pp. 63–64) suggests in *Mythologies:*

> Contemporary toys essentially represent an adult microcosm . . . [they] *always signify something,* and this something always carries social

inscriptions; it is constituted by myths or technologies of modern adult life: the army, the radio, the postal service, the medical institution, school, air travel, transportation, science. *Literally* representing the universe of adult functions, toys inevitably prepare the child to accept them all, constituting in him [sic], before he can even think, the alibi of a nature which has always created soldiers, postal workers, and vespas (translation mine).

Similarly, in his research on video-games and the world of play and games in general, Toles suggests that such a domain of activities "allows for a subtle expression of the ways of perceiving consensual reality held by a culture. Games serve as extensions of social man [sic], giving new meanings to social structures which have become so familiar that their meaning is forgotten or obscured as we conduct the routine activities of everyday life" (cited in Provenzo, 1991 p. 72).

Video pleasures

There has been a considerable amount of research carried out by psychologists exploring various aspects of video-game playing. These include: the motivations behind their uses, their presumed addictive qualities, the cognitive strategies involved in the games, the pleasures they provide, and other various effects (Turkle 1984; Malone 1981; Greenfield 1984; Dominick 1984; Anderson and Ford 1986; Loftus and Loftus 1983; Morlock 1985; Graybill et al. 1985). Among sociologists, researchers have investigated the relation between the use of video-games and gender (Kaplan 1983; Kiesler 1983), personality and other demographic variables (McClure and Mears 1984), patterns of consumption (Panelas 1983), relationship with deviant behavior, sociability and academic performance (Ellis 1983), and family dynamics (Mitchell 1985).

Whereas many psychologists explain the essential pleasures of video-games by using Skinnerian, Freudian, Kleinian, and cognitive models, Fiske (1989, pp. 77–93) adds that playing video-games also produces important *semiotic* pleasures. By allowing players to metaphorically transfer the power of control and meanings from machines, and the sphere of work, society, school, and parents to the self, videogames create a series of interesting inversions from normal everyday life. For example, by comparison to the player's location in the machine-dominated sphere of labor, the player does not work *with* the machine but *against* it. In contrast to the factory, improved speed and skill on the part of the player does not bring higher profits to the owner/ producer but to the player him/herself who saves money by extending play-time. Additionally, skilful video-game playing demands an "excess of concentration" which results in:

a release, a "loss of self," of the socially constructed subject and its social relations . . . . "Losing oneself" (in a text or a game) is for Barthes the ultimate "eroticism of the text," which is experienced at the moment when culture collapses into nature or when the ideological subject reverts to the body . . . . The physical intensity with which the games are played produces moments of *jouissance* that are moments of evasion of ideological control (Fiske 1989, p. 93).

Although video-games are not the only games which allow such pleasurable loss- of-self experiences, their requiring energetic intervention in and control of a dynamic and colorful TV-like screen seems to constitute important and unique features of these games. Taken together, the player's necessary identification with electronic icons through their activation in spectacular, fast-moving, and action-packed decors, the high-tech visual, aural, and—sometimes kinetic—stimuli of video-games, and the instantaneous translation of digital impulses into televised events produce a total and high-tech "visceral" (Stallabrass 1993) environment. Such features might be especially attractive to young people who can now actively participate in electronic spectacles, control them, and master them, rather than passively watch them.

Another significant aspect of video-games that differentiates them from other games is that their ending is known in advance. The very essence of the games can be summarized as the prolongation of the player's already doomed electronic survival. Upon inserting a coin in the slot, the player knows that the machine will always win. Whether a player can make the game last 20 seconds or 20 minutes, s/he will always run out of time, "fuel," planes, tanks, ammunition, "energy," protective shields, or "lives." Yet, although the machine always wins, the essence of "video pleasure" consists in outsmarting it, if only for a while, and in extending the game to long sessions so that a single coin gives as much pleasure/time as possible. Fiske (1989, p. 93) thus calls video arcades "the semiotic brothels of the machine age" and suggests that, although "the video arcade and the machines in it are bearers of the dominant ideology," they also allow space for a loss of self and resistance where the player becomes, temporarily, an empowered author. For Fiske, these "moments of evasion" from the dominant ideology are central dimensions of video pleasures.

Whereas Fiske emphasized the empowering pleasure of resistance derived through skilful video-playing, I want to concentrate here on "videology"—the system of interrelated assumptions that video-games articulate. Following Provenzo's (1991, p. 32) contention that video-games are "symbolic systems" which select cultural ideas for amplification and others for reduction, I situate these acts of resistance within this broader symbolic system and propose that it articulates problematic assumptions which frame and inform the pleasures perhaps too readily celebrated by Fiske.

Context and texts

The observations I report were gathered in the video arcades located in most of the major casinos/hotels which crowd the Las Vegas "Strip." Besides and beyond the ubiquitous walls of slot machines, Las Vegas casinos/hotels are also central tourist sites complete with concert halls, mini-zoos, movie theaters, shops, rides, art galleries, and video arcades. Being prohibited from gambling by Nevada laws, children and teenagers visiting the casinos often congregate in the video arcades where they also participate in the casino/hotel economy by playing video-games. Not surprisingly, these arcades are usually located in the areas of the casino most removed from the central gambling areas: close to the exits or to the various shopping sections, and sometimes on different floors. Interestingly, the very location of these video arcades in expensive casinos/ hotels may very well indicate that the fears of antisocial behavior parents and politicians once associated with video arcades (Fiske 1989; Ellis 1983) may have been significantly reduced.[1]

Because video arcades are public areas accessible for observation and participation, I chose to limit my investigation to video-games which are located in those sites. Accordingly, I do not include in this analysis video-games which can be played on TV consoles at home. As such, the extent to which the eight videological assumptions I explore here also organize home video-games should constitute the object of future research. By comparison to the private space of home where one can play video-games on TV or computer consoles which might be located in a wide variety of settings, arcades are highly structured spaces. They construct meanings which coincide with those articulated by the games and, as Stallabrass remarks (1993, p. 93), "form a digital phantasmagoria, far more menacing and effective than the piped music and the plastic trim of the shopping-mall."

Upon entering the video arcade, one is immediately assaulted by an overpowering cacophony emanating from the different consoles. The sounds of repetitive electronic notes merge with that of male martial voices ordering guns to shoot, with the sound of flying bullets, exploding bombs, crashing planes, revving engines, screeching tires, vicious kicks, and the moans, groans, and screams of electronic victims. These sounds of speed and violence hailing male teenagers as subjects of videology are reinforced by a continuous bombardment of colorful signals, pictures, and numbers urgently flashing from the screens. Human presence is not required in the video arcade for this ambience to exist. When unused, neither are the consoles of video-games silent nor are their screens idle. Instead, they are locked in computer programs which project repetitive sequences of sounds and colorful moving graphics. These depict the object of the various "missions," the main characters involved in them, situations the player is likely to encounter, instructions on how to operate the electronic gadgetry, the names of the champions of these games, and so forth. It seems that whether a player decides to operate them or not is relatively unimportant. The consoles are always "alive;" they "communicate;" they challenge and generate excitement without the need of human interference. In such a situation, players become temporary insertions in a continuous electronic text. This is the first message of video-games, which is conveyed simply by the context of their location in arcades and their very design.

Videological assumptions

My observations of and engagement with a wide variety of these games lead me to suggest that they are organized by eight interrelated assumptions which constitute what I call "videology." When analyzed in and outside of the arcade context, I find that videology both: (1) amplifies several cultural orientations which have much currency in everyday life, and (2) expresses important themes which several theorists associate with an emerging postmodern culture and consciousness.

First assumption: it's a violent world after all

The central organizing assumption of videology is unarguably that of violence. Although the humans, machines, robots, animals, and mutants that video-games simulate are technically capable of a wide range of activities, videology translates these objects into violent, dangerous, and destructive ones. The game titles written in attractive colorful letters on the sides, fronts, and hoods of the video-games consoles are quite explicit about this obsessive theme permeating the electronic playground: *Car Riot, Street Fighters, Crime Fighters, Guerilla Attack, Contra, Elevator Action, Cyberpolice, Battle of the Solar System, Air Battle, Beast Buster, Captain Commando, Archrivals, Shootout, Wrestlefest, U.N. Squadron, Final Fight, Crime City, Buster Brothers, Operation Wolf, Terminator, Thunderblade, Rampage, Danger Zone, Pit Fighter, Total Carnage, Mortal Kombat, Final Blow, Wrestle War, Mechanized Attack, Punch Out, Road Blasters, Lethal Enforcers, Desert Assault, Air Inferno, Shark Battle, Vendetta, Desert Commander, Fire Line, Lethal Weapon,* and even—in the age of anorexia and the fitness craze—*Food Fights.*

Of course, not all video-games contain violent themes, but in an overwhelming majority of them, violence is the basic assumption, the given. The only relevant question posed by videology is not whether a particular situation calls for negotiation or violence but how efficiently can violence be administered. By rewarding violence with more points, credits, and play-time, videology also sends clear messages as to what "pays" and "works" in the games and, perhaps, also "out there."

By selecting the theme of violence as central both *within* and *across* the games, by associating it with a broad range of objects, situations, and types of encounter, videology amplifies the cultural importance of violence and positions it as the axial and organizing rule of its logic. In videology, violence is not one among the many behaviors humans, animals, or machines sometimes participate in. It is the most typical behavior we can expect from these various entities constituting our (real or fantasized) environment.

The videological construction of machines, animals, and humans into dangerous entities is also replicated in the simulation of temporal decors. Thus, whether simulating the past (Wild West, medieval times), the present (Third-World jungles, inner cities), or the future (alien planets, postnuclear urban landscapes), videological texts also indicate that, no matter what particular point in time and space one "enters," it is inevitably a violent one. Past, present, and future are thus invariably simulated as an electronic slaughterhouse and a "paranoiac environment" (Skirrow 1986, p. 130; Provenzo 1991).[2]

Second assumption: the other is violent

Videology essentially organizes the majority of the games around the predetermined confrontation between a single entity (machine, human, mutant, animal) and a multitude of "others" (machines, humans, mutants, animals). When video-games simulate texts of battling humans, the "hero" (the one the player identifies with through activation) is overwhelmingly young, white, muscular, and male. The others-as-enemies are overwhelmingly male, often browner or yellower than the hero, are sometimes assigned foreign-sounding names, and, when they speak, do so in heavily accented English or in altogether unrecognizable languages. This is an ironic aspect of videology, considering that many of these games are manufactured in Japan and Taiwan.

That many of these confrontations are simulated in decors reminiscent of Third World jungles or "inner" cities is also indicative of underlying cultural and political messages of videology children learn while blasting as many "others" as possible with patriotic zeal. Thus, whereas in many games, the enemies/others are depicted as "natives" or "terrorists" battling in Third World jungles, the Persian Gulf, or airports, in others, they are hostile chiefs of state and their malevolent cronies implicated in hostage-taking or drug-smuggling activities. In still others, they are represented as delinquent youth terrorizing inner city neighborhoods, banks, homes, and (usually young white) female residents. Both the "Third World" jungle and the inner city are thus simulated as dangerous breeding grounds for criminals and as free-fire zones where excessive violence is always already the only logical strategy. Not surprisingly then, while the player's (hero's) own "lives" are valuable, limited in number, and monitored by flashing warning signals, the "others'" lives seem unimportant and expendable, as swarms of them electronically hurl themselves at the hero's bullets, bombs, kicks, and missiles, and vanish off the screen as soon as they have been killed (see Stallabrass 1993).

Third assumption: violent individualism

A related aspect of this videological paranoid violence concerns its individualistic nature. Even though many games are designed to enable two individuals to play side by side (Smith 1983), most players prefer to play alone against/with the machine. This preference makes sense considering that the scenarios of these games are most frequently organized around a single entity launched against hordes of others. Thus, although the design of many video-games allows two people to play side by side, they most often can only play one at a time rather than as a team. Even when two people do play simultaneously, the rapid circulation of entities on the screen and the very construction of the scenario reduce all choices of strategy to that of *chacun pour soi* (each person for him/herself). Thus, among the 40 top-selling violent games reported by Player's Poll, "virtually all are based on the rule of an autonomous individual acting on his or her own" (Provenzo 1991, p. 127). The imposition of this theme of the young white male hero who single-handedly defeats countless others articulates and extremizes deep-seated ideological myths of individualistic and violent conquest. The electronic hero whom the player activates and identifies with neither cooperates nor negotiates nor organizes with others. He maims, bombs, kills en masse, and dies alone.

Fourth assumption: helpless in videoland: the place of women in video-games

My observations confirm that women are underrepresented in video arcades (Fiske 1989; Provenzo 1991; Kiesler 1983) and that videology constructs them as highly stereotyped subjects. Simulated most often as a young, white, oversexed, and defenseless victim, she is rarely depicted as an active agent participating in whatever mission the game involves. Provenzo's (1991, pp. 108–109) research reveals that of the 47 top-selling games covered, "a total of 115 males and 9 females were identified. Male versus female figures predominated by a ratio of nearly 13 to 1 . . . approximately 30% of the games contained scenarios in which women were kidnapped or had to be rescued as a part of the game." As Skirrow (1986, p. 129) remarks, "women are not there as rewards, they are the landscape, the scene in which the performance takes place."

For example, at the beginning of one game, a bruised young white woman is depicted with a torn shirt, looking terrorized. She implores the player for help in eliminating her assailants and then disappears from the screen, never to be seen again, as the object of the game really consists of destroying the "others" rather than in rescuing her. In still another game, upon its conclusion, a holographic depiction of a scantily dressed and attractive young white woman appears on the screen. Lying on her side, she talks directly to the player and seductively asks him to insert more coins and play another round. The act of additional p(l)aying is thus interpreted as a move that will bring both her and the p(l)ayer conspirational pleasure—a situation not unlike other transactions organized around the expending of cash in exchange for the promise of pleasure uttered by a suggestive female voice. Fiske's idea of videogames arcades as "semiotic brothels" (1989, p. 93) may be more than just a metaphor clarifying the nature of "video pleasures."

The meanings this videological under/misrepresentation conveys to the primarily male players are not hard to fathom: Women are objects of temptation and violent rescue/appropriation but are usually excluded from active participation in the meaningful aspects of the electronic world. Women are simulated as characters who are "acted upon rather than as initiators of action" (Provenzo 1991, p. 100). Depicting women as invariably in need of being rescued through violent male intervention, videology reinforces and exaggerates gender stereotypes for young male and female players. This ideological bias partly explains the overwhelming

284

male presence and female absence in video arcades. Kiesler (1983) also makes the interesting observation that when female teenagers do visit video arcades, their behaviors there mimic those of the women of videology. They rarely play and most often act as an audience witnessing male prowess. As Turkle (1984) and others also explain, given that video-games represent a first important entry point of the child into the computer world, women might be disadvantaged in this area as their participation in video-games is importantly limited through their sexist simulation in videology.

Fifth assumption: violent no to drugs

Another interesting assumption of videology concerns the juxtaposition of drugs and violence. Besides explicitly embedding drugs within invariably violent contexts, videology goes one step further. As suggested earlier, when unused, arcade video screens are not idle but project sequences of images and sounds. In many cases, unused video screens display as part of this sequence an image of the seal of the F.B.I., with a caption underneath stating, "Winners don't use drugs."[3] In one game, this slogan is uttered by the hero of the game as he looks at the potential player with authority and determination.

This juxtaposition of images/texts which contain an official condemnation of drugs embedded within an implied celebration of excessive violence endorses additional important ideological messages. More specifically, it communicates that excessive violence is acceptable when it is unleashed on the "drug problem." As prologues to commando-like missions where patriotic Marines bomb and kill "Third World" natives in decors simulating Central American jungles, messages such as these might significantly contribute to socializing young players into accepting as *normal* similar scenarios when they appear "for real" on television screens or on the front page of daily newspapers.

This same logic often applies in games where the player activates/identifies with a (usually) white policeman risking his electronic life in a drug-bust mission carried out in decors reminiscent of those depicted on *America's Most Wanted, Cops, F.B.I.,* and similar TV "infotaining" programs glorifying the everyday professional practices of the official agents of social control. Symbols of the political, military, and legal institution thus preside over, encourage, and reward the efficient and systematic elimination of those who are involved in the drug trade, and of those who evidently couldn't "just say no."

Sixth assumption: from screen to shiny screen: videology and intertextuality

Video-games often simulate characters or texts which were/are/will be simulated on other media screens, especially television and cinema. From the Mario Brothers to RoboCop, Hulk Hogan, Star Wars, Tron, the Teen-Age Mutant Ninja Turtles, Airwolf, Batman, Indiana Jones, Bart Simpson, the Terminator, and so forth, videology icons often refer to characters whom players recognize from previous encounters on the multiple screens of the mediascape. Indeed, it is often difficult to establish whether a particular media icon traces its electronic roots back to the screen of television, cinema, or video-games. While Stallabrass (1993, p. 85) remarks that the "mutual dependence" between video-games and cinema is increasing, journalists Dickerson and Jackson (1993, p. 72) report that "at Sony Interactive, every movie script that Columbia buys is screened by the video-game department for its game potential . . . . In some cases the movie script is actually changed to add what Sony's creative team calls IPMS—interactions per minute— to make for a better game . . . . In some cases, extra footage is shot on location to provide additional material for the games."

The global range of these icons' circulation and claims to authenticity are further enhanced through their reproduction on everyday objects such as lunch boxes, cereal boxes, pens, children's shoes, notebooks, postcards, bumper stickers, posters, ties, socks, baseball caps, T-shirts, and so forth. Video-games thus represent a growing sub-program of a much broader and "ever-expanding entertainment supersystem" based on "transmedia intertextuality." (Kinder 1991, p. 1) According to her:

> In order to be a supersystem, the network must cut across several modes of image production; must appeal to diverse generations, classes, and ethnic subcultures, who in turn are targeted with diverse strategies; must foster "collectability" through a proliferation of related products; and must undergo a sudden increase in commodification, the success of which reflexively becomes a "media event" that dramatically accelerates the growth curve of the system's commercial success (pp. 122–123).

Individuals consuming these everyday objects branded with a reproduction of these icons in some sense also proclaim their position as subjects/spectators of the "entertainment supersystem" or, to quote Guy Debord (1983), of the "society of the spectacle" whose boundaries are rapidly reaching global dimensions and where "staying tuned is the chief political act" (Poster 1990, p. 136).

But besides simulating the prominent icons of the entertainment supersystem, video-games also simulate texts which refer to real mass-mediated events such as the Gulf War, the invasion of Panama, World War II, the Vietnam conflict, and so forth. With its ability to simulate texts/icons which belong to radically different spheres (Bart Simpson or/and General Noriega), videology may thus contribute to and accelerate the collapse of the boundaries between fantasy and reality, a collapse introduced long ago by television logic. Like television, videology flattens the difference between mass-mediated serious events and cartoonish fantasies by reproducing both on its colorful screens, and subjecting both to its (il)logic. It is only a while before Bart Simpson goes to Vietnam or before Batman captures General Noriega on the screens of video-games.[4]

Seventh assumption: hyper-s(t)imulation

The videological simulation of excess allowing the "loss of self" mentioned above by Fiske (1989, p. 93) deserves further attention. As Skirrow (1986, p. 121) remarks, video-games "attempt some kind of totalising experience which demands our undivided attention, temporarily eclipsing all other worlds." Turkle (1984, p. 82) suggests that "for many people, what is being pursued in the video-game is not just a score but an altered state." Her respondents indeed describe the effects of the games with a Zen-inspired vocabulary, explaining that such games allow for intensely pleasurable "centered" feelings and sharply aware mental states.

In video-games, then, the pleasure of the loss of self takes a particularly interesting form which resonates with various depictions of postmodern culture as one of electronic simulation and excess.[5] By comparison to many other loss-of-self practices involving meditation, visualization, and concentration in sites where sensorial stimulation has been minimized as much as possible, losing oneself in video-games requires first immersion in, and then mastery over, the vertigo of electronic excess. By "plugging" into the game, the player finds him/herself inserted in an orgy of hyperstimulation consisting of attacking others, flying bullets, flashing signals, noise, speed, movement, and megalomaniac destructiveness available at one's fingertips or in one's fist clenched around the joystick. That teenagers and younger children achieve this pleasurable loss-of-self experience through the strategic administration of excessive violence in the midst of electronic chaos will be discussed further below.

Eighth assumption: modern pleasure for rules and postmodern rules for pleasure

Videology articulates an additional type of pleasure overlooked by Fiske, a pleasure which might become increasingly important in the midst of a social world constantly and rapidly transformed beyond recognizable logic. As Skirrow suggests:

> Part of any account of the popularity of video-games must be the fact that the games represent very powerfully the breakdown of boundaries characteristic of postmodern culture: boundaries between fantasy and science, between high-tech and primitivism, and between play and real life . . . . As the explosion in information and technology in the last few years has made the possibility of division seem infinite, the difficulties incomprehensible, and solutions remote, the popular imagination appears to have taken flight either into a world like those presented by the pop videos where signs not anchored to anything seem to suggest and encompass everything or into model environments like those of video-games where systems still have their own limited and understandable—though strange—internal coherence (1991, pp. 118–122).

Accordingly, although video-games texts produce an excess of visual and aural stimuli rapidly circulating on the screen, videology also offers the promise of reliable rules. To some degree, the videological message embedded in the games postulates that beyond and beneath this chaos of electronic excess, there exists an organized set of rules, a decipherable computer "order" where pleasure, control, and survival are possible once one has accepted its (il)logic and successfully cracked its code. For Greenfield, "part of the excitement of the games surely must lie in this process of transforming randomness into order through induction" (1984, p. 112). For Turkle:

> Unlike the real world, the game universe always conforms to rules. There is violence, murder, and theft, but the rules for what can happen and how to handle it are precise . . . . Their constraints are those imposed by rule systems, not by physical reality or moral considerations (1984, p. 79).

In sum, if anybody with a quarter to spend can play *at* video-games, video *pleasure* requires the player's total immersion in the electronic text, trust in the existence of a code imposed by invisible experts, and the self-affirming and empowering experience of its incremental mastery. Predicated on the ability to rapidly discriminate between circulating signs (some hostile, some neutral, and some friendly), and to appropriately respond to them, such a pleasurable mastery involves a skillful and rapid navigation in a chaotic electronic text, a navigation propelled by strategic violent moves administered digitally.

In videology then, the modern pleasure of discovering the rules of a seemingly random electronic text is implicated in the postmodern rules for experiencing electronic pleasure. In other words, in order to experience a pleasurable loss of self in the midst of electronic excess, one must first immerse oneself in the "logic" of videology and accept its rules so as to decipher them. If those rules appear "illogical" when compared to those organizing everyday life and the physical world (Turkle 1984, p. 79), they also replicate the (il)logic of other media texts where anything is indeed (graphically) possible.

Conclusions: video-games as postmodern sites/sights of ideological reproduction

Whereas Fiske suggested that video-games represent sites or practices of resistance against the dominant ideology—moments of evasion from its grip— I have focused here on the assumptions of videology, the broader context within which this resistance is situated. As I have shown, the pleasure of video-game, this loss of self *cum* control players seek to attain, is framed and predicated by eight interrelated assumptions. When examined outside of their electronic context and translated into everyday language, such assumptions can be seen as intensifying problematic ideological orientations. These hail and re-inscribe the young male p(l)ayers as subjects of a decidedly violent, paranoid, individualist, racist, sexist, militarized, and oversaturated electronic New World Order whose trigger-happy patriotic young white male agents brutally enforce a "zero-tolerance" policy toward drug-smugglers and a great variety of others, while keeping women "in their place." In contrast to Fiske's celebration of the pleasurable resistance video-games allow, I emphasize here that such resistance and pleasure rest on the tacit acceptance and reproduction of these assumptions.

The first videological assumption which organizes the vast majority of the games posits that excessive violence characterizes time, space, and human and nonhuman entities. It is the given, the foundation of video-games texts. The second and corollary assumption implies that whatever is not-self (the polymorphous "other") is most probably hostile, dangerous, and involved in unacceptable activities. Since these others' presence and circulation signify one's electronic "death" and the end of video pleasure, their brutal elimination is the quintessential means *and* ends of a majority of video-games. The third assumption premises that people essentially administer and experience violence individualistically in a world where the only person one can truly count on is oneself. The fourth assumption implies that, while women are always white, young, and attractive, they are essentially passive decorations flaunting their bodies, victims whose sole raison d'etre is to be rescued/appropriated by male characters/players. In videology, this task is most often accomplished through a spectacular and violent confrontation with the "other." Through the juxtaposition of quasi-official symbols simultaneously expressing the political/legal/military institutions' condemnation of drugs and their celebration of violence, the fifth assumption of videology communicates that the institutions so symbolized approve the use of excessive violence when its aim is the elimination of illegal drugs and of those "others" engaged in their traffic. The sixth assumption of videology confirms its insertion in a wider entertainment supersystem: the global mediascape whose icons are reified, kept "alive," and authenticated through their constant circulation as electronic signals on media screen and as everyday material objects consumed by citizens/spectators. The seventh assumption communicates and exaggerates the reality of electronic excess, an excess which simultaneously contains risks and tensions on one hand, and opportunities for pleasurable loss-of-self through mastery on the other. The eighth assumption affirms the existence of reliable, decipherable, and systematic rules, a purely objective computer "order" which promises control and survival in the midst of electronic excess, an order with "little moral complexity or ambiguity" (Stallabrass 1993, p. 90), unencumbered by the "limitations of physical laws, compassion, negotiation, or due process."

The last three assumptions (one's insertion in an entertainment/spectacle supersystem, the normality of electronic hyper-s(t)imulation, and the increasing organization of everyday life by a computer [il]logic) articulate and amplify important social and social psychological characteristics which authors such as Baudrillard (1983, 1970); Pfohl (1992, 1990); Kroker and Cook (1990); Kroker, Kroker, and Cook (1986); Gergen (1991); Anderson (1990); Gottschalk (1994, 1993) and others have associated with an emerging postmodern consciousness and moment.

While these three interrelated postmodern assumptions/characteristics constitute novel parameters complicating an assessment of the impact of video-games on players,[6] they also indicate that such effects cannot be understood in isolation from the broader social and electronic context of which they are part. Thus, for example, if engagement with violent texts/games does sometimes generate therapeutic and cathartic outcomes, the nature and dynamics of such outcomes might be significantly transformed by: (1) the unique technological properties of video-games and the kind of participation they require, and (2) the positioning of violence as the axial principle rather than as the exceptional and cathartic crisis point, but also by (3) *the interpenetration* of these games within a broader mediascape where the boundaries between "the real" and the spectacle are themselves becoming increasingly blurred.

What happens when the "real" world provides a diminishing contrast with the world of play and when both increasingly seem to become a series of interrelated electronic spectacles, remains an open question that requires further research. For example, many journalists have commented that televised military operations in the Gulf war looked like scenes on a video-game screen. In situations where the real looks like its simulated version and where the simulation approaches the real to the point of *virtual* reality, one's perceptions of the real, of one's actions and of their effects on others, might become substantially altered.[7]

As s(t)imulating machines, video-games enable active participation, encourage the mastery of various skills, and translate those into spectacular and instantaneous screened events. They obviously produce intense pleasure and allow for momentary and imaginary empowering experiences. As socializing agents, they might offer more pleasure than television-watching and might thus displace it as a site/practice of ideological communication. It is unfortunate but hardly surprising that the obvious talent necessary for the writing of such sophisticated video-games programs is channeled into the invention of ever more convincing aural and visual experiences of violence, faster and more precise responses to digital impulses, and other technical priorities. Presently, the channeling of such talent into the simulation of texts which could communicate a radically different worldview and encourage equalitarian, cooperative, and conciliatory skills remains outside of (v)ideology.

Acknowledgments

The author wishes to thank Dmitri Shalin, Andrea Fontana, and David Dickens for their comments and suggestions on earlier versions of this article. Thanks also to an enthusiastic and anonymous reviewer.

Notes

1 On the other hand, casinos/hotels are constantly monitored by a network of omnipresent but concealed cameras which—as one casino worker told me—can observe absolutely everything and everyone within the casino boundaries. The casino and its attached tourist areas are also constantly patrolled by a multitude of armed and unarmed security

personnel in both uniform and plain clothes, talking/listening to their walkie-talkies—to invisible others. The adult fantasyland many associate with Las Vegas casinos is also a high-security zone, a buzzing Panopticon where multiple and mobile hidden electronic/human eyes are constantly watching the human traffic.

2 See, for example, Burgin (1990) for an exploration of the paranoid dimension of post-modern culture.

3 This videological assumption might be limited to video-games found in video arcades.

4 The most revolting expression of this mixing of genres appeared in the form of a vide-ogame produced by a German underground network of video-games programmers. Simulating the decor of a concentration camp, the object of the game was to dispose of inmates in the most efficient way. The German government banned the game upon learning about it.

5 See, for example, Baudrillard (1990, 1983, 1970); Chen (1987); Kroker, Kroker, and Cook (1990); Kroker and Cook (1986).

6 This assessment becomes especially problematic when considering that video-games are constantly improving in their sophistication and enable a growing range of experiences. New hybrid machines combining virtual reality and video-games are already being mar-keted by SEGA and other corporations.

7 The puzzling nature of the Gulf War for many Western citizens/spectators might be a consequence of this accelerating electronic spectacularization of warfare (see Baudrillard 1992; Stallabrass 1993).

References

Agger, Ben. 1992. *Cultural Studies as Critical Theory.* London: Falmer Press.

Anderson, Craig A., and Catherine M. Ford. 1986. "Affect of the Game Player: Short-Term Effects of Highly and Mildly Aggressive Video-games." *Personality and Social Psychology Bulletin* 12(4): 390–402.

Anderson, Walter Pruit. 1990. *Reality Isn't What It Used to Be.* San Francisco: Harper & Row.

Barthes, Roland. 1957. *Mythologies.* Paris: Editions du Seuil.

Baudrillard, Jean. 1970. *La Societe de Consommation: Ses Mythes, Ses Structures* (Consumption Society: Its Myths and Structures). Paris: Gallimard.

Baudrillard, Jean. 1983. "The Ecstasy of Communication." Pp. 111–159 in *The AntiAesthetic: Essays on Postmodern Culture,* edited by Hal Foster. Port-Townsend, WA: Bay Press.

Baudrillard, Jean. 1990. *Fatal Strategies.* New York: Semiotext(e).

Baudrillard, Jean. 1992. *La Guerre du Golfe N'Aura Pas Lieu* (The Gulf War will not Take Place). Paris: Galilee.

Burgin, Victor. 1990. "Paranoiac Space." *New Formation* 12: 61–75.

Chayko, Mary. 1993. "What is Real in the Age of Virtual Reality? 'Reframing' Frame Analysis for a Technological World." *Symbolic Interaction* 16(2): 171–181.

Chen, Kuan-Hsing. 1987. "The Masses and the Media: Baudrillard's Implosive Postmodernism." *Theory, Culture & Society* 4: 71–88.

Clough, Patricia T. 1992. *The End(s) of Ethnography.* Newbury Park, CA: Sage.

Debord, Guy. 1983. *The Society of the Spectacle.* Detroit: Black & Red.

Denzin, Norman K. 1992. *Symbolic Interactionism and Cultural Studies: The Politics of Interpretation.* Cambridge, MA: Blackwell.

Diani, Marco (ed.). 1992. *The Immaterial Society: Design, Culture, and Technology in the Postmodern World.* Englewood Cliffs, NJ: Prentice Hall.

Dickerson, John F., and David S. Jackson. 1993. "The Amazing Video-game Boom." *Time* (September 27): 67–72.

Dominick, J.R. 1984. "Videogames, Television Violence, and Aggression in Teenagers." *Journal of Communication* 34:136–147.

Ellis, Desmond. 1984. "Video Arcades, Youth, and Trouble." *Youth and Society* 16(1): 47–65.

Ellis, Godfrey J. 1983. "Youth in the Electronic Environment: An Introduction." *Youth and Society* 15(1): 3–12.

Fiske, John. 1989. *Reading the Popular.* Boston: Unwin Hyman.

Geist, Christopher D., and Jack Nachbar (eds.). 1983. *The Popular Culture Reader.* 3rd edition. Bowling Green, OH: Bowling Green University Popular Press.

Gergen Kenneth. 1991. *The Saturated Self.* New York: Basic Books.

Gottschalk, Simon. 1993. "Uncomfortably Numb: Countercultural Impulses in the Postmodern Era." *Symbolic Interaction* 16(4): 351–378.

Gottschalk, Simon. 1994. "Currents in the Field, Ethnographic Derives, and Popular Voices: A Postmodern Imagination." Paper presented at the 1994 Stone Symposium, Urbana, Illinois.

Graybill, Daniel, Janis R. Kirsch, and Edward E. Esselman. 1985. "Effects of Playing Violent versus Nonviolent Video Games on the Aggressive Ideation of Aggressive and Nonaggressive Children." *Child Study Journal* 15(3): 199–205.

Greenfield, Patricia Marks. 1984. *Mind and Media: The Effects of Television, Video Games, and Computers.* Cambridge: Harvard University Press.

Heim, Michael. 1993. *The Metaphysics of Virtual Reality.* New York: Oxford University Press.

Kaplan, S.J. 1983. "The Image of Amusement Arcades and Differences in Male and Female Video Game Playing." *Journal of Popular Culture* 16: 93–98.

Kiesler, S., L. Sproull, and J.S. Eccles. 1983. "Second-Class Citizens." *Psychology Today* 17(3): 41–48.

Kinder, Marsha. 1991. *Playing with Power: From Muppet Babies to Teenage Mutant Ninja Turtles.* Berkeley: University of California Press.

Kroker, Arthur, and David Cook. 1986. *The Postmodern Scene.* New York: St. Martin.

Kroker, Arthur, Marilouise Kroker, and David Cook. 1990. "Panic USA: Hypermodernism as America' Postmodernism." *Social Problems* 37(4): 443–459.

Loftus, Geoffrey R., and Elizabeth F. Loftus. 1983. *Mind at Play: The Psychology of Video Games.* New York: Basic Books.

Malone, Thomas W. 1981. "What Makes Computer Games Fun?" *BYTE* (December): 258–277.

McCabe, Colin (ed.). 1986. *High Theory/Low Culture: Analyzing the Popular.* New York: St. Martin.

McClure, R.F., and F.G. Mears. 1984. "Video Game Players: Personality Characteristics and Demographic Variables." *Psychological Reports* 55: 271–276.

Meyrowitz, Joshua. 1985. *No Sense of Place.* New York: Oxford University Press.

Mitchell, Edna. 1985. "The Dynamics of Family Interaction around Home Video Games." *Marriage and Family Review* 8:121–135.

Mitroff, Ian, and Warren Bennis. 1989. *The Unreality Industry.* New York: Birch Lane.

Morlock, Henry, Todd Yanto, and Karen Nigolean. 1985. "Motivation of Video Game Players." *Psychological Reports* 57: 247–250.

Panelas, Tom. 1983. "Adolescents and Video Games: Consumption of Leisure and the Social Construction of the Peer Group." *Youth and Society* 15(1): 51–65.

Pfohl, Stephen. 1990. "Welcome to the Parasite Cafe: Postmodernity as a Social Problem." *Social Problems* 37(4): 421–422.

Pfohl, Stephen. 1992. *Death at the Parasite Cafe: Social Science (fictions) and the Postmodern.* New York: St. Martin's Press.

Poster, Mark. 1990. *The Mode of Information.* Chicago: University of Chicago Press.

Postman, Neil. 1985. *Amusing Ourselves to Death.* New York: Viking.

Provenzo, Eugene F. 1991. *Video Kids.* Cambridge, MA: Harvard University Press.

Rheingold, Howard. 1991. *Virtual Reality.* New York: Simon and Schuster.

Ross, Andrew. 1991. *Strange Weather: Culture, Science and Technology in the Age of Limits.* London: Verso.

Silverstone, Roger. 1989. "Let Us Then Return to the Murmuring of Everyday Practices: A Note on Michel de Certeau, Television and Everyday Life." *Theory, Culture & Society* 6: 77–94.

Skirrow, Gillian. 1986. "Hellvision: An Analysis of Video Games." Pp. 115–142 in *High theory/Low Culture: Analyzing Popular Television and Film,* edited by Colin McCabe. New York: St. Martin's Press.

Smith, R Sue. 1983. "Coin Detected in Pocket: Videogames as Icons." Pp. 145–156 in *The Popular Culture Reader,* 3rd edition, edited by Christopher D. Geist and Jack Nachbar. Bowling Green, OH: Bowling Green University Popular Press.

Stallabrass, Julian. 1993. "Just Gaming: Allegory and Economy in Computer Games." *New Left Review* (March/April): 83–106.

Turkle, Sherry. 1984. *The Second Self: Computers and the Human Spirit.* New York: Simon and Schuster.

89

TOO MANY COOKS

Media convergence and self-defeating adaptations

Trevor Elkington

Source: Bernard Perron and Mark J. P. Wolf (eds), *The Video Game Theory Reader 2* (New York, NY: Routledge, 2008), pp. 213–235.

Within the general trend of media convergence, the relationship between the film, television, and video game industries present a particularly interesting love–hate dynamic. On the one hand, visual and interactive media show increasing aesthetic and procedural similarities. Video games have generally become more narrative-based and increasingly draw upon film-like special effects and celebrity-power to stand out in the marketplace. Likewise, the technologies used for computer-generated imagery (CGI) in film are more and more often the same technologies used to develop video games, to the point that artists and technicians are able to move between the two industries with increasing fluidity. This process of convergence is expedited by the rapid expansion of the video game market and the horizontal integration of the media industry. The parent companies that own film and television studios are also increasingly invested in video game development, making synergistic collaborations between film, television, and video game developers commonplace. Major film releases like *Spiderman 3* (Sam Raimi, 2007) and the *The Lord of the Rings* films (Peter Jackson, 2001, 2002, 2003) are accompanied by video game adaptations, classic films like *The Godfather* (Francis Ford Coppola, 1972) and *Scarface* (Brian De Palma, 1983) are licensed for interactive media, and more video games are adapted to film, such as *Doom* (Andrzej Bartkowiak, 2005) or the *Tomb Raider* films (Simon West, 2001; Jan de Bont, 2003). And yet, licensed adaptations are commonly dismissed by critics and players as nothing more than cynical attempts to cash in on hype. Films based on video games usually do not fare well among critics and audiences, though they are capable of performing well at the box-office. Likewise, video games based on films receive a generally hostile reception from game reviewers and players. Rather than successfully drawing on the synergistic advantages of cross-media development and promotion, licensed film-to-game adaptations in particular must overcome a long history of critical and commercial failure.

But are licensed adaptations, when viewed as products in themselves and not as part of a larger media trend, qualitatively any worse or better than their competitors? Does the perception that licensed adaptations are inferior in quality bear up to analysis? And if so, then why is this the case? In order to answer these questions, it is useful to narrow the scope of inquiry. The challenges faced by video games adapted from film and television licenses can be seen as a problem of integrating often incompatible industry processes and potentially resistant social orders. That is, the consistent critical panning of licensed games can be framed as the result of incompatible production practices between film studios and game studios, as well as the resistance of critics and fans with incompatible expectations drawn from the original medium. The process of making a good film is not the same process as making a good game, and the elements that make a film good may not translate well into game form. Consider, for example, the mixed reception of films that attempt some level of interactivity such as *Clue* (Jonathan Lynn, 1985), in which audiences could choose from one of three endings and which was largely received as a vaguely interesting publicity stunt. Likewise, various attempts to use home video technology for interactive movies, where the home viewer is offered decision points throughout the film, have never developed into more than a minor niche market of video sales. In light of these tensions, it is useful to think in terms of what film scholar Mette Hjort, under a different context, has referred to as self-defeating productions.[1] In discussing the process by which many films are co-developed across national lines, Hjort advances the idea that film co-productions, in her case among Nordic nations, are potentially self-defeating if they fail to account for the split interests of their audiences. Serving two or more sets of audiences risks antagonizing the divisions within those audiences by serving too many masters and none well. The concept of self-defeating productions can be usefully broadened to apply to cross-media adaptations as well, in which products created to appeal to more than one audience of consumers can conceivably fail to appeal to any by including multiple elements that please one audience and actively antagonize another, such that no audience is wholly satisfied. Video games based on film and television licenses must attempt to appease two audiences: fans of the original license, who expect a certain adherence to its details, and fans of video games, who expect adherence to common notions of gameplay. Reconciling these expectations presents a fine line bordered on one side by numerous possible mistakes and on the other by a long history of previous failures.

Critical reception of licensed games: the numbers

But how pronounced is the problem, really? Licensed games with narrative components continue to appear on the market at a rapid rate, which would seem to suggest that success of some form can be found here. If these games are so unpopular, why would companies continue to make them? Would not sales reflect the problem, and thus discourage this kind of development? After all, game publishers are in the business to realize a profit. Clearly, successes do occur, and sales charts are filled with games based on the most recent blockbuster film titles. However, sales of this type are difficult to separate from the general level of marketing saturation associated with most leading film licenses. Licensed video games often benefit from the "opening weekend" strategy that has been at play in the film industry over the last decade and more: film studios, particularly in the case of blockbuster action titles of the type licensed games are commonly based on, look to recoup their investment in the initial days of the films' international opening, as a way of counteracting any potentially negative word of mouth.[2] As part of this media barrage, games based on movies can accomplish something similar, debuting with strong sales well before the critical reviews reach consensus and word of mouth spreads. As such, commercial success would seem at least initially to be a poor measure of game quality for anybody other than the game publishers that benefit from those sales, for whom financial success will always necessarily be the bottom line.

Where the problem of evaluating the "quality" of a game becomes most clearly identifiable is in the reception among critics and game-playing audiences. Compiling a broad sample of product reviews provides a useful index of how critical audiences, and potential consumers, are reacting to a particular game or a particular genre. Warner Brothers Interactive Entertainment took this logic to its extreme when it announced in May, 2004, that in order to discourage game developers and publishers from damaging their intellectual property by developing poor quality games, it would begin using a fluctuating royalty rate for game publishers based on critical response, drawing from results in sites like GameRankings (www.gamerankings.com) and Metacritic (www.metacritic. com). The policy, devised by the division's chief Jason Hall as an attempt to hold publishers responsible for producing inferior products, was wildly unpopular among game developers and game critics, who argued that game quality did not have a direct correlation to game sales, with many high-rated games selling poorly and many low-rated games selling well, and more tellingly, that game reviews are far from objective.[3] Attempting to pin an objective royalty scheme to a subjective index presented game developers with a seemingly impossible situation. Games that reviewed well but sold poorly would not have significant revenue to draw royalties from, and games that sold well but ranked poorly would be punished by the policy. So why use critical response as an index of industry status at all? While game reviews are subjective, and any one review is a poor indicator of the game's reception by other reviewers or its potential sales, game reviews do offer a sense of the *perceived* quality of particular games and a specific genre. As consumers themselves, video game reviewers provide some insight into consumer reception that reaches beyond sales figures. More importantly, despite developer assertion that quality and sales are not necessarily related, a recent study found that there is in fact a direct relationship between reviews and sales, with highly-rated games selling up to five times better than titles with lower-scoring reviews.[4] Developers, publishers, and licensors should be paying attention to review scores, as they seem to suggest how a game will perform in the marketplace, individual exceptions aside.[5] Moreover, the problem that Hall attempts to address, poorly-developed games damaging healthy intellectual property, is not simply a matter of video game developers and publishers exploiting trusting film studios by foisting inferior products onto unenlightened audiences. Rather, the problem is systematic, a flaw engrained within the current methods by which licensed games are developed, and game reviewers and audiences are keenly suspicious of the role film studios play in this process, as will be discussed below.

In this light, analyzing the review statistics compiled on Metacritic proves a useful case in point. The site collects reviews from stable game sites and compiles the results into aggregate statistics based on a 100-point scale, with separate rankings for critic reviews[6] and fan reviews, resulting in a meta-review that gives a broad sense of what people are saying about a particular game. Of the thousands of games reviewed on the site, hundreds are developed directly from a film or television license, whether as part of a major release like the video game adaptation of *Spider-Man 3* (Treyarch, 2007) or a retroactive attempt to market an older license, such as the quickly forgotten adaptation of *Miami Vice* (Atomic Planet Entertainment, 2004). At the time of writing, reviews for over 1500 games developed for the Sony PlayStation 2 (PS2) between 2000 and 2007 are aggregated on the site.[7] Review data was collected initially on September 10, 2005, and again on October 10, 2007. Average scores for PS2 games are relatively stable across time, dropping slightly from 69.1 in 2005 to 67.9 in 2007. These scores put the average game review within the "Mixed or Average Reviews" category for the Metacritic site.

However, the aggregate review numbers for video games paint a very different picture. In September, 2005, there were 1099 PS2 games listed on the site; of that number, 106 were directly based on a film or television license, a ratio of roughly 10:1. Of the licensed games, the average aggregate score was 61 out of 100, a full eight points below the average, though still within the "Mixed to Average Reviews" category. However, these numbers do not immediately reveal that nearly one quarter of the games reviewed, 22 out of 106, fell on or below 49, in the "Generally Unfavorable Reviews" category. By October, 2007, the picture is notably different. In the intervening two years, an additional 448 games were aggregated, resulting in an overall average of 67.9. Of those additional games, 109 were based on film and television licenses. For all scores in the database, the ratio of all games to film and television adaptations drops to roughly 7:1; more significantly, the ratio of all games to adaptations released between September 2005 and October 2007 drops to nearly 4.5:1. Most tellingly, the average aggregate score of film and television license-based games developed between September, 2005 and October, 2007, fell to 56.9.[8] Three conclusions become clear. One, that film and television adaptations consistently score lower than the average across the reviews aggregated by Metacritic. Two, film and television adaptations are occupying a larger portion of games released in a given year. Three, and most importantly, these games are receiving lower and lower scores over time. Put succinctly, video game developers and publishers are releasing more film and television adaptations at a faster rate, as a larger percentage of their release schedules, and these games are less and less popular with critics. It begs the question: Why? Are the commercial incentives simply too great? As noted above, critical reception and sales numbers show direct correlation. Are publishers simply willing to ignore critical response and keep delivering the same unpopular product in the hopes of finding a statistically exceptional hit with consumers? Or is the baseline of sales for lukewarm titles still enough to make them profitable? The evidence would seem to suggest both rationales as distinct possibilities.

Self-defeating adaptations

So why do film and television adaptations fare so poorly with critics? Two possibilities seem likely: either the games are truly worse than other games on average, or critics just do not like adaptations, whatever their individual merits. Setting aside the second possibility for the moment, the possibility remains that film and television adaptations are simply not as good as non-adaptations, that there is something intrinsic in the adaptation process that results in an inferior game. Perhaps the difference between the media is too vast; the parameters of video games are too vastly different from film to make for good adaptations. And yet, both critical and financial successes do occur. So what's the secret? Or rather, what's the problem?

In an interview for the video game industry site Gamasutra, Rodney Greenblat, the artist who helped shape the groundbreaking *PaRappa the Rapper* rhythm game for the Sony PlayStation (NaNaOn-Sha, 1997), discussed the franchise's development across media. The game's success in Japan spawned an animated children's show, but for Greenblat, the results were messy. Conflicts over design and copyright among different branches of the franchise owner, Sony, led to continuity errors, narrative inconsistencies, and a sacrifice of the original game's vision. As Greenblat notes:

> Sony Creative owned the copyright, and Sony Computer had ownership of just the game . . . they didn't care, because it was raking in all this money for Sony even if it was just two different divisions . . . but when the animation people came in, and then Fuji TV . . . it just got [to be] this whole mess. Just too many people.[9]

When the series appeared on Japanese television, it became clear that significant differences between the game audience, comprised largely of adolescents and above, and the animated series, which was targeted at children, made it difficult to realize any cross-media synergy. Fans of the game were not interested in a children's television show, and fans of the series found it difficult to master a game designed for adolescent developmental skills. This internal conflict of franchise management resulted in a self-defeating project. The term underscores the idea that media convergence, despite its apparent ability to smooth over differences in media, actually creates an *increased* awareness among audiences of the particularities of form and content across media, and consequently requires developers to be more aware of the limitations of each medium and more responsive to the vicissitudes of various audience demographics. Media convergence is not an industry curative that makes production conditions easier; if anything, it increases the level of complexity. Thus the term "selfdefeating" suggests projects in which the different goals of the various license-sharers stand in direct conflict, even contradiction, to each other, so that not only do they sacrifice consistency and continuity, they effectively achieve negative synergy, as each product antagonizes the contrasting audience.

So how do adaptations commonly defeat themselves? It is useful to look at the critical reception of four film-to-game adaptations from the height of the previous console generation: *Van Helsing* (Saffire, 2004), *Enter the Matrix* (Shiny Entertainment, 2004), *The Lord of the Rings: The Third Age* (Electronic Arts, 2004), and *The Chronicles of Riddick: Escape from Butcher Bay* (Starbreeze, 2004).[10] By analyzing specific critical response to these games, certain common faults and uncommon strengths in design as well as central challenges facing the current models for adapting films to video games begin to coalesce. The relative success and failure of individual cases suggests three things: one, games have arrived as a culturally and aesthetically competitive narrative space to film and television as opposed to a simple licensed ancillary; two, that players reject video games that rely heavily upon cinematic conventions; and three, that what video game consumers seek from adaptations is not a simple, interactive rehearsal of film events but in fact further expansion of a narrative world via an engaged relationship with an interactive medium. Failure to accommodate these factors results in a poorly-rated game.

The most common form of film-to-game adaptation is the direct adaptation, in which a video game closely, even slavishly, follows the film narrative by directly turning film events into interactive experiences. While certain exceptions do occur, they are generally the most criticized games on the market, seen as cynical attempts to exploit the hype of a particular film release. Saffire's *Van Helsing* adaptation exemplifies common weaknesses of the genre. *Van Helsing* receives a 63 on Metacritic, based on 32 professional reviews. Comments about the game ranged from lukewarm to savage, with one reviewer concluding, "*Van Helsing* is a shining example of what's wrong with games based on movies."[11] So what went wrong? Critics point to shallow, unchallenging gameplay, mediocre graphics, and a narrative based directly on film events, eliminating any element of suspense. More importantly, critics point to the limited options offered players as they are shuttled along a linear level design in order to work through events mandated by the film; any notion of emergent or creative gameplay is limited by the strictly linear narrative, thus stripping the title of a crucial interactive element. And finally, critics point to perhaps the most common complaint about film-to-game adaptations: an overreliance upon cut-scenes. This design weakness means that players are not rewarded by events within the interactive game space, but in fact play up to a certain point, at which the game engine takes over and delivers a canned cinematic. Not only does the design choice rupture the flow of interactive space, it also undoes the basic idea of games, which is that they are subject to player control.[12] It is a flaw seen repeatedly in the games discussed below.

A second type of film/game convergence can be found in what Henry Jenkins has called "transmedia storytelling," in which each media product contributes to an overall narrative world, suggesting that single storylines are less important than the unfolding of an entire narrative world. The most notable example of this genre is the various products associated with *The Matrix* films (Andy and Larry Wachowski, 1999, 2003, 2003), where the various short films, games, books, and other products supplement and expand the world established by the films. Interestingly, critical and commercial reception of *The Matrix Reloaded* and *The Matrix Revolutions* was notably more negative than for the original film. Despite earning collectively over $800 million at the box-office, revenue fell markedly from the second to the third film, and both films saw significant drop in revenue after the opening week, suggesting a word of mouth effect that cooled interest from the first film. Critical reception of the films focused on the tangled narrative, apparent plot holes, undeveloped tangents, and shallow characters. Roger Ebert tempers his admiration for *Revolutions* by noting "the awkward fact that I don't much give a damn what happens to any of the characters" before concluding with a significant wink that "finally I measure my concern for [Neo] not in affection but more like the score in a video game."[13] Likewise, the video game component *Enter the Matrix* received a lukewarm 65 across 34 reviews, and Jeff Gerstmann writes in his GameSpot review that "the game serves as little more than an advertisement for the film—it doesn't have a story that stands on its own, and the gameplay doesn't really offer anything that we haven't seen in better games."[14] Similar to Joe Dodson's review of *Van Helsing*, Gerstmann notes the game's tendency to sacrifice gameplay for special effects and cut-scenes, emphasizing the significant error of taking interactivity out of the hands of the player at key moments. In other words, the reviewers of the game *and* film argue that in trying to be more like each other, the texts manage to sacrifice the strength of their own medium without realizing the strengths of the other, thus leading to a self-defeating project achieving negative synergy.

A more positive example of transmedia storytelling can be found in Electronic Arts's *The Lord of the Rings: The Third Age*. While the initial games from *The Lord of the Rings* project are typical interactive walkthroughs of the film events, EA's *The Third Age* attempts something near transmedia storytelling by allowing players to direct original characters pursuing their own adventures in the larger world of Middle-earth. Characters at times intersect with film events, providing the larger picture of what happened before, elsewhere, or after the heroes of the movies pursue their quest. Reactions to the game were generally favorable, and the title received 75 across 38 reviews. Criticism, when offered, focuses specifically on the common flaw of mirroring narrative and cinematic convention over interactivity. In her review for GameSpot, Bethany Massimilla notes the game's tendency to communicate narrative exposition through cut-scenes in which Gandalf reveals information about characters and events, rather than through characters interacting with each other or the game world. She argues that "you are explicitly told what has happened and what will happen instead of actually seeing it happen, and it serves to somewhat distance the player from the whole experience."[15] However, in general, this critic concludes that game play compensates for the weakness and offers a compelling experience, and more importantly, fans of the books and films will enjoy the chance to explore Middle-earth and interact with the major characters while augmenting the clear narrative lines set by Tolkien. Where *The Third Age* fails is in its attempts to be more like a film; where it succeeds is where it plays upon the strengths of the game medium and offers players the chance to fully explore a larger fictional world.

Escape from Butcher Bay offers a third category of film/game convergence, drawing upon the Chronicles of Riddick world initially launched by the sleeper success *Pitch Black* (David Twohy, 2000) and its sequel, *The Chronicles of Riddick* (David Twohy, 2004), but pursuing a separate narrative not directly reliant upon film events. The game receives an aggregate score of 89 across 84 reviews, placing it high among games reviewed for the Xbox console. GameSpot reviewer Greg Kasavin notes:

> *The Chronicles of Riddick: Escape From Butcher Bay* is one of those exceedingly rare types of games that delivers exceptionally high quality through and through and single-handedly ups the ante for all similar games. The fact that it also happens to be based on a movie franchise— something that's usually a bad sign for a game—makes it all the more incredible.[16]

Escape from Butcher Bay is often framed as that rarest of products, the critically successful film-to-game adaptation. Players guide Riddick as he escapes from the maximum-security prison Butcher Bay, a necessary offstage event that takes place prior to the events in the films. The obvious advantage for developers here is that, beyond general faithfulness to the film world and the facts established by the films, they are not hemmed in by the film narrative. They can more easily avoid the temptation to make the game like a film, as in this case, there are no specific film events that need to be related within the game narrative and there are no film sequences to be directly adapted as cut-scenes or gameplay elements. Instead, players shift from the film's third-person perspective to an interactive first-person perspective in order to further explore an appealing fictional world without being hampered by the specific constraints of the film or by the film medium. Unlike other transmedia storytelling, in which games like *Enter the Matrix* and *The Third Age* contribute one piece that directly relies upon the contents of the films, *Escape from Butcher Bay* takes one relatively minor detail and expands it into its own narrative territory without being too reliant on the films it licenses.

So what does this review of reviews tell us? To return to the example provided by Rodney Greenblat, it becomes clear that media convergence does not play out on a level field. Far from it. Film and television license-owners have to date largely dictated the course of game development, treating video games more or less like traditional ancillaries. Most of the qualitative problems arise from treating video game development as an afterthought, leaving developers hard-pressed to devise ways to work around the film schedule and agenda. The most common strategy, the direct adaptation, is also demonstrated to be the least popular among game players, resulting in a self-defeating project in which the film and game do not achieve synergy beyond name recognition and initial hype. Those games that do break out of this basic mold, like *Escape from Butcher Bay*, not only receive critical praise, but seem better positioned to reap comparable financial reward. Indeed, as Henry Jenkins argues in *Convergence Culture: Where Old and New Media Collide*,[17] story worlds are increasingly more important than individual stories, as consumers become fans of fictional characters and settings and look to the individual texts, be they films, video games, or novels, to offer further details and stories within those worlds. Creating a game that is a straightforward rehashing of the film or television product offers nothing new to the consumer in terms of new ideas or details, instead trading on an oversimplified appeal to interactivity in place of novelty. This rings particularly true for licenses within already popular narrative settings like Tolkien's Middle-earth, the Wachowski Brothers' Matrix universe, or J. K. Rowling's Harry Potter world. Part of the appeal to film studios and video game publishers for adapting works within these settings is that they come with established fanbases pre-disposed to buying additional products that further develop these worlds. However, as suggested by critical response, many of these video games in fact serve to further alienate that fanbase. Given the reception of games like *Escape from Butcher Bay*, it is clear that adaptations can succeed critically as well as financially. So why do so many of these games go wrong? As the reviews above suggest, some of this is directly due to the design of the games themselves, potentially hampered by their over-reliance upon the original intellectual property and upon the aesthetics of film and television in the first place. However, there is more than an aesthetic problem at stake here.

It is possible that in fact there is nothing qualitatively wrong with film and television adaptations, and that this is simply a case in which video game reviewers are negatively prejudiced against adaptations from the outset. As the reviews above suggest, many critics work from the assumption that adapted video games will be of inferior quality unless proven otherwise, and note with pleasure when a game overcomes that expectation or knowingly report when it does not. Perhaps the problem lies less with the games than with the critics. Maybe a game based on a film or television license simply cannot get a fair assessment. There are many possible reasons why reviewers might be ill-disposed toward adaptations. The legacy of poorly reviewed adaptations alone suggests that further adaptations will simply go on to fit the established mold. Likewise, Eric Peterson, a game developer who has specialized in adaptations such as *Flushed Away* (Monkey Bar Games, 2006), points out that most video game adaptations are based on children's film and television and are targeted toward that audience, which immediately affects their reception among adult reviewers:

> Reviewers frequently don't give kids games a fair shake—some don't even bother to review them, either because they aren't "cool," or don't appeal to their demographic. When these games are reviewed, they are often compared to games for older audiences, and which have longer development cycles.[18]

It is not surprising that a game like *Flushed Away*, with its appeal to juvenile humor, would not resonate with an adult reviewer. Indeed, the same study that found a correlation between high reviews and high sales also found that mature-rated titles have the highest average Metacritic scores and the highest average gross sales. This may be a reflection of the age and interests of the average game player skewing toward the ESRB M-for-mature rating. A broader consumer base, paired with a quality game, should result in higher sales. Reviewers, as average game players, may not understand adapted games targeted at children and thus review them negatively, while the kinds of games that reviewers do favor, mature-rated games, fare best commercially. Children's games fare poorly among critics already; with many adaptations falling into that genre because of their licensed material, it is predictable that their average review scores would also average below the norm. Nevertheless, games based on children's licenses such as *Happy Feet* (Midway Games, 2007), while receiving a 49 or "Generally Unfavorable Reviews" score on Metacritic for its PS2 version, have performed very well in the marketplace. The game shipped 1.8 million copies by January, 2007 (Seff, 2007).[19] So while mature-rated games rate high and sell well, other games that do not rate high nevertheless can offer financial incentives, which is a clear motivator for why they continue to be released despite general panning among reviewers.

Interestingly, despite noting that children's games rate poorly among reviewers, Peterson goes a long way to offering additional reasons why adapted games generally receive poor ratings and are expected to be of poor quality by reviewers. As he states the case, adapted games like *Flushed Away* are expected to be "just another movie-based game with shallow gameplay that was rushed out the door" (Peterson). But as Peterson admits, these types of games, whether for children or otherwise, usually have shorter development cycles, meaning that less time is available to develop innovative game design and polish the overall quality of the game. For better or worse, most adapted games *are* rushed out the door, with most being pushed to ship simultaneously with the release date for the film. But even games that are not rushing to ship for a box-office date, games like *Miami Vice* where the original intellectual property is already in the marketplace, are still reviewed poorly. In an example similar to Rodney Greenblat's experience on *PaRappa*, Peterson discusses his experience developing *Dinotopia: The Sunstone Odyssey* (Monkey Bar Games, 2003). Early in the development cycle, the licensors decided that the game should reflect coming narrative changes planned for the series. When these changes proved to be unpopular among series fans, they held the game accountable. "Dinotopia fans were outraged because they thought that we, as developers, had decided to change the world they loved" (Peterson). Moreover, because licensors were co-developing unreleased content with the game developers, it meant a high level of involvement from multiple parties during the game development cycle, with changes to the series directly impacting the design of the game. "We were like taffy, being pulled between licensor, sub-licensor, and publisher, all of whom wanted something different. We still got the game done, but at a heavy price. Everyone felt like they were forced to make a game they didn't believe in" (Peterson). The resulting game scored poorly in reviews, receiving a 50 on Metacritic. Development experiences like Greenblat's and Peterson's go a long way to suggesting why many game adaptations are of such poor quality. Game developers, often working under shortened production schedules, are put in the middle of conflicting interests from licensors, publishers, and other parties such as celebrities connected with the game. Whereas constant change is often the rule in film development, the impact of last minutes changes and ongoing design fluctuation is far more detrimental to game development, where design, art, and programming efforts often take months or years of work to produce results. The problem, in a nutshell, is that game development cannot respond well to competing interests and the design fluctuation it brings. In trying to serve so many masters, from the licensors on one end to the fans on the other, the potential result is a self-defeating product, a game that pleases nobody, be they licensor, publisher, developer, fan of the property, or fan of games. In order to understand the problem better, it is useful to turn to a developer that has a history of getting it right, the studio behind *The Chronicles of Riddick: Escape from Butcher Bay*.

Too many cooks working too fast

Johan Kristiansson, CEO of Starbreeze Studios, the developer behind *Escape from Butcher Bay*, offers valuable insight into the licensed-game production cycle. He identifies two specific issues that compromise the quality of games based on film and television licenses: one, conflicts of development time and schedule, and two, conflicts within the design approval process.[20] The average Hollywood film takes roughly twelve to eighteen months to move from pre-production to completed postproduction, depending upon a myriad of complex factors including the completeness of the script when green-lighted, necessary revisions, production factors like set-building and special effects engineering, and post-production elements such as digital effects and post-processing. The average AAA-title game, a nomenclature reserved for industry-leading titles from major publishers intended for the broadest audience usually across multiple platforms, averages 24 months or more to move from the design stage to a release-ready gold disc. Immediately, one can see the direct conflict in schedules. More often than not, a game developer would need at least a six month lead in order to deliver a game ready to be released simultaneously with a film. But if the project has not yet been greenlighted, there is no license or approved concept to work with. This leaves most game developers with two options: remain faithful to the film production schedule and shorten their own development cycle, or ship a game potentially months after the marketing campaign for the film is over. Generally, developers choose to capitalize upon film marketing by maintaining the film's release schedule, and attempt to make up the difference in a variety of ways, by either hiring more employees, working extra hours, underdeveloping parts of the game, or adapting their design. The last two factors, in particular, can result in inferior game quality: art assets seem incomplete, music is of poor quality, game play is simplified, and narrative content closely mirrors that found in the film. However, depending upon the status of the script, securing a license for a greenlighted project is no guarantee that the film concept is firmly in place. Film studios routinely revise scripts, sometimes to a significant degree, right up to and through the production phase. Unfortunately, game development is much less flexible in its design phase, as it can take weeks of multiple employees' efforts to institute features mandated by the film design. An off-the-cuff decision by the filmmakers can potentially run into weeks of wasted effort for game developers. Change, however, is inevitable, and if the film changes, then the game must change accordingly or run the risk of design discontinuity and potential self-defeating status.

Kristiansson provides an example in the development of *Escape from Butcher Bay*. Starbreeze Studios secured the license to make games based on *The Chronicles of Riddick* universe before the sequel script was complete; not having seen the script for the film, the team based its game pitch on what it knew of the Riddick character from the original film, *Pitch Black*. Faced with a 20-month development schedule, unusually long for a film because of its abundance of special effects and CGI sequences, the team debated setting its game as a sequel or a prequel to the films; given that the film script was still undergoing development, they ultimately opted to avoid direct conflict by developing a prequel to film events, leaving them a greater degree of design freedom. However, conflicts were not completely eliminated. For example, game designers created a backstory that explains Riddick's ability to see in the dark that did not correspond to the explanation ultimately reflected in the script. The game developers were fortunately able to change their design accordingly (Kristiansson), but the potential for significant problems increases the further along in the development process conflicts take place. The more developed a game is, the greater is the impact that design changes can have.

The second issue that Kristiansson directly identifies as problematic for developing games based on films is the increased complexity of the approval process. Unlike a traditional game or film, in which approval generally follows a hierarchy limited to and within the production company and the publisher/studio, licensed games, in this case film-based or otherwise, must gain approval from parties outside the direct line of game development. In the case of a game based on a film or television license, the approval process usually has three major steps: studio/publisher, license holder/film production team, and talent, usually the film's director, major stars, and similar parties. In addition to the usual game development approval steps that entail several levels of designers and executives within the studio and the publisher, a licensed game design must clear two additional hurdles: the license holder and film production team, and the talent, usually the film's director, major stars, and similar parties. In the case of *Escape from Butcher Bay*, the approval process outside the studio included the publisher, Vivendi Universal Games, and the film production team as managed through Vivendi Universal Films. Vin Diesel was also entitled to his own approval; fortunately in this case, Diesel has a welldocumented interest in games, so much so that he created his own company, Tigon Studios, to oversee his involvement in this and future game projects. Each step in the approval process includes the possibility of suggested changes, which, as already stressed, presents a time-sensitive set of variables in game development.

The approval process is particularly thorny when dealing with independently-owned corporations sharing aspects of an IP license, as in the case of *Escape from Butcher Bay*, for which Starbreeze Studios contracted with Vivendi Universal to produce a game. Multimedia entertainment corporations with divisions devoted to the various aspects of contemporary entertainment would seem to have a clear advantage. Sony, as one example, has divisions devoted entirely to film, television, music, and games, and as such, would seem ideally positioned to streamline the design and approval process. However, even here, the possibility of conflicting creative visions is clear, as Greenblat found during the development of the *PaRappa* television series, where competing divisions within the same company behaved in ways similar to a licensors pulling the development in different directions.

Process-based conflicts like those described by Kristiansson do not entirely account for games like *Miami Vice, American Chopper* (Activision Value, 2004), or *The Great Escape* (SCi Entertainment Group, Pivotal Games, 2003). While all three are based on successful and potentially valuable film and television licenses, they are not entirely subject to the same production or marketing pressures as the usual film-to-game adaptation. *Miami Vice* was published years after the television show ended, presumably leaving the development team free to dictate its own schedule with ample time for developing a polished game, and yet the game received an abysmal 27 rating on Metacritic. *American Chopper*, based on a successful series already well established on television by the time the game was in development, likewise presents a different scenario from adapting a summer blockbuster. The cost of producing a reality-television series is substantially less than that of producing, for example, the *Van Helsing* film, and as such, the possibility that the greater financial stakes involved in filmmaking necessarily

306

dictated design process does not necessarily apply to the *American Chopper* television license. One could imagine that the game developers would be on a more level playing field with their television counterparts, consequently able to negotiate a favorable design and schedule. And yet, the game received a 47 rating on Metacritic. Likewise, *The Great Escape*, based on a film classic with an established following, is nevertheless an older license that has long since recouped its investment through theatrical release, video sales, and other licenses. In theory, it would present a prime opportunity to invest the time and care necessary to develop a high-quality game capable of reviving the license's appeal. The game received a 57 on Metacritic.[21] Individually, these games have their specific flaws; collectively, they suggest that the game industry is still seen by the larger entertainment industry as a place to realize easy money by developing quick products that attempt to exploit license appeal without providing game quality.

The challenges discussed above are largely procedural issues, but the one element they all have in common is essentially a social factor: the current "illegitimate" status of the game industry. Despite healthy profits, explosive growth, and significant future market potential, many people still envision the typical game player as an antisocial seventeen-year old sitting on the living room sofa. This perception of diminished social significance pervades the entertainment industry. In her address at the 2005 Game Developers Conference, game development guru Kathy Schoback outlined predicted cost of AAA-title development for next-generation consoles, anticipating that costs could go above $20million, mandating a break-even sales number of roughly one million copies. Despite the social and economic significance reflected in these kinds of numbers, as Schoback quipped, "we're still not as cool as Hollywood."[22] Likewise, in his opening "state of the industry" address at E3 Expo 2005, Douglas Lowenstein, at the time President of the Entertainment Software Association (ESA), made a point of dispelling the urban myth that the game industry is larger than the film industry, noting "it never has been true . . . . In truth, the worldwide film industry stands at about $45 billion and the worldwide video game industry checks in at around $28 billion."[23] In the same address, Lowenstein outlines six fundamental issues in establishing social legitimacy for the video game industry, or as he puts it, "what will it take for the game industry to be as big or bigger than the film industry at some point in the future?" Among these issues, Lowenstein identifies the need to expand the market base for games, and in general his agenda calls for increasing appeal to female and casual gamers through better and different game design, arguing that more variety in what is offered to game buyers will increase the variety of people who will buy games. But what remains significant about Lowenstein's remarks is the pointed assumption that games are currently seen as a less socially acceptable or legitimate form of entertainment media. As he states the case:

> Acceptance in the culture is the key to legitimacy. None of us were alive when film first came on the scene but historians will tell you it was not regarded with great and instant acclaim. Our industry is just thirty years old

and has produced more than its fair share of classics. No doubt, many more will come. But if we as an industry aspire to the same cultural and artistic credibility and stature achieved by other major forms of entertainment, our creative community and our publishers will have to eschew some of the historically easy and successful formulas for commercial success and draw consumers into some new kinds of interactive entertainment experiences that more often ennoble our industry.

Remarks like Schoback's and Lowenstein's reflect the position of the contemporary entertainment industry, that it often plays the little brother role to the larger film industry. While making such clear-cut distinctions between the two industries is problematic given the sizeable investment of companies like Sony, Vivendi Universal, etc. in both media, nevertheless, when it comes to licensed adaptations development, video games clearly take a backseat to film and television. It is standard procedure that a game studio developing a licensed franchise gives some level of creative approval to the licensor; paradoxically, the reverse is hardly ever true. Even Bungie, creators of the enormously successful *Halo* (2001, 2004, 2007) franchise and with all of Microsoft's business acumen behind it, eventually gave up creative control of the *Halo* film license to Universal and Fox, though reports assured that Microsoft executives and designers would be guaranteed "'extensive' consultation."[24] Eventually, the film was postponed due to conflicts within the project.

Developers like Kristiansson and Greenblat describe in clear terms the challenges presented to game development when their creative agenda is subject to the approval of a party whose agenda is set by film or television dynamics, completely different media with different production and audience demands. This is perhaps understandable, given the differences in potential revenue. But the situation does give rise to avoidable conflicts in creative agendas, conflicts that potentially result in self-defeating productions.

A suggested solution: centrally managed development

The failures of transmedia development, as best seen in the critical reception of video game adaptations of film and television licenses, have and will continue to call for central project management. Current industry practice resists this kind of central planning by allowing the initial or most costly Intellectual Property (IP) commodity to set the agenda for the rest of the associated products. The film or TV script is written, the production schedule is planned, and it is up to the other associated developers to find a way to work around or within that frame, regardless of how this might impact their usual development practices. However, to successfully develop a project across media, the various development parties would benefit from ground level coordination in order to create a fictional world in which there are equal opportunities for high quality products across media. If these projects are not centrally managed, they quickly degenerate into situations where what is good for the film or television series is not good for the game and vice versa, pitting the interests of each medium and each license-holder against the central concept of the intellectual property. Rodney Greenblat's experience with *PaRappa* provides further illustration of this point:

> When *PaRappa 2* came out, the animated series came out in Japan, and [there were] too many people involved for me . . . [The show's producers] decided that they wouldn't let anyone from the game team side work on the TV side, they didn't want to pull anyone from the game development for the TV show development. And then they wanted to slate the show for little kids, 5 year olds or something, mostly to sell toys.
>
> And I wasn't into that, because I was like "Everyone knew teenagers loved *PaRappa*, so let's do a teen show." But [Sony] wanted to sell toys, so [the show's producers] made a little kids version of *PaRappa*. (Hawkins)

Greenblat goes on to note how, because of the lack of central design and franchise management, the various parties quickly pursued design decisions that best fit their medium and market needs, regardless of how these development decisions fit into the larger franchise:

> I would get rushes for each episode and make corrections, and they wouldn't even do anything about it! Characters kept on changing and messing up . . . in the game PaRappa could drive a car so you figure he's 16 or 17, but in the show he's sitting in the third grade and his antics were based on what 8 or 9 year olds are doing? It just got all nutty . . . and then I think [all the various parties] all fell apart . . . [A]ll those companies just scattered and did their own things. (Hawkins)

The problems created by a lack of central project management are more than simple issues of continuity. When the various products within a franchise pursue different goals and, in this case, different market demographics, the result is a self-defeating project in which any original audience is actively alienated by the new products, while a new, cohesive audience is difficult to achieve, as the products no longer make sense with regard to each other. What appeals in the game is contradicted by the television show, and vice versa. Again, what is realized is the worst of both worlds with the advantages of neither; the sacrifice culminates in a loss of franchise synergy.

This kind of central project management calls for central roles for the design and production teams. One suggested solution is the New Studio Model offered in October of 2004 by Stuart Roch, a ten-year games industry veteran and producer of *Enter the Matrix*.[25] Roch's model revolves around a core team of developers that build the game technology, allowing the studio to bring in guest designers to lead the game design. The goal of his model is to allow IP originators from other media like film or print to direct games based upon their fictional universe and accentuate their narrative strengths without falling into the traps discussed previously in this essay. The New Studio Model also places the administrative hassles on the shoulders of the publishers and producers, who are best suited for these tasks, rather than the artists creating the game. It is perhaps no coincidence that Roch is an executive producer at Shiny Entertainment, the developers of *Enter the Matrix*, as this model would serve well for a Matrix-like project. However, this model is designed specifically as a solution for developing games. It does not entirely account for the demands of transmedia or multimedia development, in which multiple projects are developing simultaneously, potentially pulling the core creative talent in numerous directions. A more radical solution is required: a central design and production team that develops the core narrative world including game and film scripts, characters, art design, gameplay, and other elements in order to insure that each element logically fits into the larger whole without sacrificing one text's needs for the demands of another. The implementation of these designs can then be managed by the individual studios. Projects like *Enter the Matrix*, *The Lord of the Rings*, and *The Chronicles of Riddick* have already moved definitively in this direction. Likewise, game publishers and developers are becoming savvy to the advantages of co-developing original content with film and television partners from the earliest stages. Midway's *The Wheelman*[26] is a case in point. Intended as a new creative franchise for Vin Diesel and developed in tandem with his game development company Tigon Studios, the initial idea was conceived as a game and film project from the beginning. The game was developed first, with the film script then written based on the game design.[27] This allowed the game developers to work closely with Diesel and deliver a solid game that is still consistent with the film. The film then becomes an additional text within the fictional world initially introduced in the game.

The challenges to this model are in part financial and pragmatic. Who provides the capital and assumes the risk for a transmedia project of this nature? How are the profits shared? Who has final say over the inevitable conflicts? To date, these risks have largely been shouldered by the film studio, as the majority of licensed adaptations or transmedia projects are generated by film narratives. Moreover, most transmedia projects to date are based on pre-existing franchises in an attempt to minimize risk, the logic being that if an audience for this narrative world already exists, then sales for new commodities within that world are more likely than for original IP. Working from existing narrative worlds also allows film and game developers to capitalize upon works already created and essentially "market tested" by fans. Working from a pre-existing world reduces the time and money required to develop intellectual property, and appealing to an established fanbase likewise reduces the risk of developing original IP that consumers may ultimately find uninteresting or unconvincing. As such, it seems likely that licensed franchise development will continue hand-in-hand with media convergence for the foreseeable future.

The larger issue at hand is the necessity of changing the perception of the video game industry as a lower stakes, less legitimate offshoot of the entertainment industry in general. As Douglas Lowenstein summarizes the issue, "acceptance in the culture is the key to legitimacy." Acceptance of this kind largely comes with time, as successive generations embrace video games and developers emerge to address different market demands, expanding the video game market beyond its current demographics and encompassing older, gender-balanced, and ethnically diverse audiences. Moreover, the continuing success of the game industry will be in part its own solution to the problem of legitimacy. As the cost of developing video games increases at the same time that the video game buying market is expanding, studios will necessarily have larger financial stakes in codeveloping licensed franchises and will be better positioned to demand better terms for development, potentially leading to higher quality games.

The term "media convergence" carries with it the idea that all media are moving toward the same spot, a central ground in which texts begin to behave similarly, thus mandating a similar approach to developing a film, a game, or any other related product. However, not only are the narrative and design demands different between a successful game, a successful film, or any other medium, each medium likewise offers different strengths and weaknesses. Moreover, the successful management of a film, television series, or game presents its own practical production challenges. It requires different skills, resources, and schedules to develop different media commodities. Rather than thinking of film-to-game adaptations as a pale, interactive imitation of the original film, they should be conceived of as their own legitimate products requiring their own forms and deserving quality development. In order for the evolving practice of transmedia storytelling to result in works that will be well-accepted by consumers and reviewers alike, the production methods and social positioning have to evolve accordingly.[28]

Notes

1 Mette Hjort, "From Epiphanic Culture to Circulation: The Dynamics of Globalization in Nordic Cinema," in *Transnational Cinema in a Global North: Nordic Cinema in Transition* (Detroit, MI: Wayne State University Press, 2005), 191–218.

2 Brian Jay Epstein, *The Big Picture: The New Logic of Money and Power in Hollywood* (New York: Random House, 2005). The means by which Hollywood realizes a profit on films is far more complex than counting box-office profits, as Epstein convincingly demonstrates. Most Hollywood films are considered a success if they manage to break even on theatrical sales when counted against the cost of distribution and marketing. Instead, studios depend upon home video sales, global television rights, and ancillary sales, including game licenses, to push the title into a profit.

3 Rob Fahey, "Warner Bros. Plans Penalties for Poor Quality Licensed Titles" *GamesIndustry.biz* (26 May 2004). Available online at <http://www.gamesindustry.biz/content_page.php?section_name=pub&aid=352>.

4 Leigh Alexander, "M-Rated Games Sell Best," *Game Developer* (October 2007): 5.

5 However, a controversy within the video game industry erupted in late 2007 that suggests a more complex relationship between high-rated games and high game sales. On November 30, 2007, *Penny Arcade* (<http://www.penny-arcade.com>), an industry site that hosts a popular comic series, game reviews, and forums and organizes an increasingly important annual game industry conference (PAX), reported on the firing of

outspoken game reviewer Jeff Gerstmann from GameSpot, a leading game review site. Penny Arcade alleged that Gerstmann had been fired after his "savage flogging" of Eidos Interactive's title *Kane & Lynch* (Io Interactive, 2007) had led Eidos to pull "hundreds of thousands of dollars worth of future advertising from the site" and pressure GameSpot's parent company, CNET, to discipline Gerstmann ("The New Games Journalism" *Penny Arcade* (November 30, 2007). Available online at <http://www.penny-arcade.com/2007/11/30#1196409660>). Representatives from CNET, GameSpot's parent company, later denied that Gerstmann was fired for his review, asserting that "we do not terminate employees based on external pressure from advertisers"; however, they declined to comment on whether Eidos had attempted to apply any such pressure on GameSpot for the review (Kyle Orland, "GameSpot Denies Eidos Pressured Firing of Gerstmann" *Joystiq* (November 30, 2007), available online at <http://www.joystiq.com/2007/11/30/gamespot-denies-eidos-pressured-firing-of-gertsmann/>). The ensuing controversy, in which Gerstmann, Eidos, CNET, and various other interested parties weighed in with often conflicting accounts of what had happened, led to vigorous conversation on video game forums on the nature of corporate influence within the game review industry. While separating the business and content departments as a means to avoid these types of ethical conundrums is a standard practice in mainstream journalism, the possibility that video game publishers might essentially buy good reviews and punish bad reviews through the application of advertising funds called the validity of all video game reviews into question, at least in the eyes of some. It also further complicates the reliability of drawing conclusions based on game sales vs. game reviews, as video game publishers with the highest selling games also tend to have the most advertising funds, at least in theory suggesting that they can influence the rating of their video games and possibly further incite sales. It is a controversy particularly relevant to this essay, as Gerstmann's reviews on other video games are quoted as a means to demonstrate a larger argument. However, the lack of a clear conclusion as to why Gerstmann was fired from GameSpot and whether Eidos had any influence on the decision is itself indicative of the difficulty of ascertaining the relationship between reviews, advertising, and sales. It is an area of inquiry that clearly calls for more research; in the absence of that research, this essay must rely on the current state of thought on the issue.

6 Metacritic does not report aggregate scores for video games until at least four critic reviews have been collected.

7 The Sony PlayStation 2 was chosen as an analytical basis as it provides the largest pool of reviews to draw from and was the commercially dominant console platform during its technological generation. Review data was originally collected on September 10, 2005, and again on October 10, 2007. Games that did not yet meet the minimum four-review limit were not considered as part of the data collected for this analysis.

8 The average for all film and television adaptations between 2000 and 2007 fell to 59.

9 Matthew Hawkins, "Interview: Rodney Greenblat, Creator of Sony's Almost Mario," *Gamasutra.com* (July 5, 2005). Available online at <http://www.gamasutra.com/features/20050705/hawkins_01.shtml>; hereafter cited as Hawkins.

10 Due to *Escape from Butcher Bay*'s exclusive release on the Microsoft Xbox console, these scores are for versions on that console. The other three games discussed were also released as PS2 and PC versions. In 2007, a revised and expanded version was released for the Xbox 360 and PS3, titled *The Chronicles of Riddick: Assault on Dark Athena*. It is also worth noting that although two of the games discussed (*Van Helsing* and *Escape from Butcher's Bay*) are from the same publisher, Vivendi Universal, they are from different development studios and significantly different in design.

11 Joe Dodson, "Review: *Van Helsing*". Available online at <http://gr.bolt.com/games/ps2/action/van_helsing.htm> (accessed July 21, 2005).

12 It also conversely points to the unpopularity of interactive movies, rupturing as they do the receptive experience that underlies film viewing. However, the question of choice

and spectator activity in the experience of film perception is a broad field of research and is beyond the scope of this essay.

13 Roger Ebert, "Review: The Matrix Revolutions," *Chicago Sun-Times* (November 5, 2003). Available online at <http://rogerebert.suntimes.com/apps/pbcs.dll/article? AID=/20031105/REVIEWS/311050301/1023>.

14 Jeff Gerstmann, "Enter the Matrix Review" *GameSpot.com* (20 May 2003). Available online at <http://www.gamespot.com/ps2/action/enterthematrix/review.html>.

15 Bethany Massimilla, "The Lord of the Rings, The Third Age Review," *GameSpot.com* (November 4, 2004). Available online at <http://www.gamespot.com/ps2/rpg/tlotrthethirdage/review.html>.

16 Greg Kasavin. "The Chronicles of Riddick: Escape From Butcher Bay—Developer's Cut Review," *GameSpot.com* (December 10 2004). Available online at <http://www.gamespot.com/pc/action/chroniclesofriddick/review.html>.

17 Henry Jenkins, *Convergence Culture: Where Old and New Media Collide* (New York: New York UP, 2006), 20.

18 Eric Peterson, "A License to Review," *Game Developer* (October 2007): 64.

19 Ascertaining precise sales numbers for games can often be difficult, as publishers often report only the number of games shipped as a way to circumvent issues of game returns and the sale of used copies.

20 Johan Kristiansson, Private interview (August 10, 2005); hereafter cited as Kristiansson.

21 Scores for all three games are for PS2 console version.

22 Kathy Schoback, "The Economics of a Next-Gen Game," *Game Developers Conference 2005* (March 9, 2005).

23 Douglas Lowenstein, "E3Expo 2005 State of the Industry Address," E3Expo 2005 (May 18, 2005). Available online at <http://www.theesa.com/archives/2005/05/e3expo_2005_sta.php>. Making easy comparisons between the economic status of the video game vs. the film industry is difficult, as the significance depends entirely upon how one defines the scope of each industry and how wide one casts a net for figures. Lowenstein's numbers are based on software sales vs. box-office sales. As noted previously, the majority of contemporary Hollywood's revenue comes from home video sales, international television sales, and product licensing. Profit calculations based on these numbers would project Hollywood's annual revenue at a much higher number.

24 Wade Steel, "Halo Film Planned for 2007: Fox and Universal to bring Master Chief to the silver screen," *IGN.Com* (August 23, 2005). Available online at http://xbox360.ign.com/articles/644/644458p1.html.

25 Stuart Roch, "The New Studio Model," *Game Developer Magazine* (October 2004): 6.

26 At the time of writing, *The Wheelman* is scheduled for release in 2008. In the interest of full disclosure, it should be noted that the author of this essay is an employee of Midway Games at the time of writing, but works for a different development studio on a different IP.

27 Rebecca Murray, "*The Wheelman* to be Both a Video Game and Feature Film," *ABOUT. com* (February 28, 2006). Available online at <http://movies.about.com/od/dieselvin/a/wheelman022606.htm>.

28 This essay is a revised version of papers I delivered at the 2005 Future Play Conference and at the 2006 SCMS conference. The Future Play version is available as "How a Salad Bowl Can Improve Transmedia Storytelling: Integration and Convergence in Film and Game Development." Available online at <http://www.futureplay.org/docs/papers/2005/paper176_elkington.pdf>.

90

THE CENTRALITY OF PLAY

James Newman

Source: *Best Before: Videogames, Supersession and Obsolescence* (excerpt) (New York and London: Routledge, 2012), pp. 149–160.

Within academic game studies, it is well documented that digital games are essentially made through the act of play, and while terms like 'interactivity' are rejected by some (e.g. Aarseth 1997) as being ideologically charged, the fact remains that the performance of the player impacts greatly on the structure, form and aesthetic of the game (see Eskelinen 2001; Moulthrop 2004). Most obviously, many digital games make use of branching, non-linear structures or 'narrative trees' that are traversed by players making self-conscious choices (go left; enter the building; etc.). The course of the gameplay experience might be markedly different for players making different choices, with some sections either present or omitted and even wholly new narrative branches or ending states revealed. Moreover, game structure might be contingent on other performance factors. One branch might open up only if a sequence is completed in a particular manner (e.g. within a specific time limit, or having collected a specific number of items) or by demonstrating a particular prowess (e.g. having lost no 'lives').

More than this, videogame play actually describes a variety of related but significantly different practices and performances that are contingent on the differential motivations of players, as well as their skill. Play may be articulated in terms of the 'completion' of games in the fastest possible time, the acquisition of the highest score, or by tackling the challenges in a 'pacifist' mode, dispatching only those enemies that actually bar progress and cannot be avoided. Players may seek to use as few additional capabilities or weapons as possible or may be driven by a desire to acquire every last item of inventory available, even those that are tangential. Play may involve exploring as much or, indeed, as little of the gameworld as possible by engaging in 'complete' or 'low per cent' routes to completion. As such, while some players may never complete a game like *Super Mario Bros.*, others are able to finish the job in just five minutes. For example, see the recordings of superplay at *Speed Demos Archive*, with Andrew Gardikis's 4:59 run the latest to shave seconds off Scott Kessler's 5:11 performance, and one second off his own 5:00 run performed in 2007 (Gardikis 2010). Note also Gardikis's (2008) 19:40 100 per cent time for an all-stages run that does not utilise any of the warp zones.

Additionally, as I have discussed elsewhere (e.g. Newman 2008), the video recording and online sharing of gameplay has become a significant part of the culture of videogames, with players keen to demonstrate their knowledge of the game's potential and their mastery of the system (see also Lowood 2005, 2007 for more on the emergence of 'superplay' and the online collection at the *Speed Demos Archive* for resources). What is notable about these various playings is that they are often characterised by forms of customisation, personalisation and the self-conscious modification of technique and strategy. Players often explore and perform with their games to – and even beyond – destruction, with strategies and tactics exploiting not only the range of moves and capabilities outlined in instructional manuals but also a host of bugs, glitches and other inconsistencies in the operation of the game's code.

We need only look at fan sites such as ZeldaSpeedRuns.com for evidence of the ways in which the exploitation of glitches and bugs in the game have become written into the standard lexicon of gameplay (certain techniques are listed under the 'general knowledge' section, implying their widespread use, while others are coded as being available only to more sophisticated players or to facilitate specific types of play). For some players, even the limits of human ability are insufficient to explore games to their ultimate conclusion. Practices such as tool-assisted speedrunning (TAS) typically involve the use of emulation software and the ability to save the state of gameplay at any point (rather than using the game's own saving regime) so as to perform gameplay as a form of stopframe animation. Built up over many months, these TAS performances are often cast by their creators as artworks whose intention is to push at and beyond the boundaries of what is routinely achievable through play. In addition to the exploitation of the kinds of strategies we have seen deployed by other superplayers and speedrunners, TAS creators make extensive use of further glitches, bugs and other performance and code inconsistencies in games that either would require too great a degree of precision or whose execution is too variable to be used in standard play. *Super Mario Bros.*'s collision detections are a case in point, and recordings of TAS show seemingly impossible jumps through enemies that, in fact, utilise the vagaries of Mario's sprite detection routines and benefit from the ability to 'rewind' and re-record in the event of a failed manoeuvre.

Examples of this creative, exploratory play abound. The canonisation of 'Glitch Pokémon' through in-depth practices of writing, visual art and analytical textual production speak of fans' willingness to explore fully, process and assimilate their findings (see Rita Buuk n.d. and Mandy Nader 2004, while we have seen already the range of walkthroughs for games like *Goldeneye 007*, some of which document in meticulous detail the variety of ways missions can be failed. Discussions of 'cheating' in videogames (e.g. Consalvo 2007) reveal additional layers of complexity in relation to digital gameplay and further highlight the permeability of the game's rulesets and the willingness of players to deliberately play 'against the grain' to maximise their performative reward.

It follows that the ways in which games are played frequently diverge from the ways in which they were intended to be played by their developers and designers, with 'emergent' strategies yielding unanticipated, and impossible to anticipate, results. It will be clear that videogame play need only be obliquely concerned with the ostensible 'aim' of the game as documented in instructional manuals and frequently superimposes additional rulesets that are designed and regulated by communities of players. These might be comparatively straightforward (driving the 'wrong' way around a racing track attempting to avoid oncoming traffic for as long as possible; see Newman 2004 on *Gran Turismo and Ridge Racer*, for instance) or more obviously divergent (side-stepping large tracts of the game to access advanced weaponry before the logic of the narrative/ structure ordinarily allows, a subversive practice known as 'sequence breaking'; see Newman 2008).

In devising these new strategies and gameplay modes, players sometimes work alone, but very often operate within the context of a community of offline and online players sharing experiences and the results of their investigative playings. As such, gameplay is best understood as a practice that very often takes place within the context of, and is shaped and regulated by, a community of other players, whether this occurs through face-to-face collaborative play, talk and discussion or via the textual products of a fan-culture distribution network such as *GameFAQs* or *YouTube*. Specific tactics, techniques and strategies become available to players as they observe the performances and discussion of others, just as certain techniques are written into or out of the canonical lexicon of available gameplay strategies. Sites such as ZeldaSpeedRuns.com investigate and codify a range of techniques, including, for *OoT*, 'Power Crouch', 'Infinite Sword Glitch', 'Damage Buffering', 'Megajump and Hover Boost', and 'Megaflip', as well as the various 'Sequence Breaks' that allow the subversion of the game's narrative structure by avoiding areas or acquiring objects, techniques and capabilities out of their designated sequence. Conversely, players of first person shooters such as the *Halo, Call of Duty* and *Modern Warfare* series pour scorn on the use of grenade launchers whose accuracy and impact typically leaves them apparently unbalanced and appealing to putatively less skillful players. Their designation as 'noob tubes' reflects the shape of the weapons (typically grenade launchers or bazookas) and pejoratively constructs their use as suitable only for the new, unaccomplished and unskilled gamer (see, for instance, the discussion of 'noob tubes' at *Gamespot* UK (Essian 2011) and the Call of Duty Wiki's (n.d.) outline of the game's various weapons).

Most critically, the gameplay that results from these performances is often unpredictable, emergent and frequently travels in directions unintended and unanticipated even by the designers and developers of the gaming environments within which it is enacted. For these reasons, Sue Morris (2003) terms videogame play a 'co-creative' act in which notions of creator and user, developer and player are effectively blurred (this recalls Surman's 2010 discussion of the 'level creator' facility in *Sonic 2*). Not only do players operate on the system, rules and code to bring 'the game' to life (thereby engaging in play as a 'configurative' practice in Moulthrop's 2004 terms) but also players create their strategies and tactics for play with reference to the advice, guidance and norms of the communities of practice within which they operate. In some instances, this even appears to operate at the expense of the gameplay in its entirety.

Machinima, in which the interactive environments of games are used as the stage for the creation of decidedly non-interactive movies, is perhaps the most extreme and well-known example. Series such as Rooster Teeth's *Halo-based Red vs Blue* (see Delaney 2004) and Chris Brandt's (2005) virtuoso *Dance Voldo Dance* routine performed in *Soul Calibur* (see Newman 2008) move beyond the use of real-time game engines as pre-visualisation environments or prototyping tools and present critical spaces in which issues of masculinity and violence, for instance, are interrogated as well as operating as self-consciously reflective examinations of the modalities and conventions of game forms (see Wilonsky 2002; Marino 2004; Lowood 2005, 2007; Cannon 2007). Of course, the production of Machinima is by no means the only way in which gameplay mechanics are subverted and recast, and we might look to the appropriation of motion control systems such as the Wiimote, PlayStation Move and Kinect by experimental musicians and visual artists for further examples. Applications such as *OSCulator*, for instance, facilitate the use of Nintendo Wiimotes as well as accessories such as the WiiFit balance board and nunchuks to create motion-based interfaces for synthesiser plugins and digital audio workstations by converting game control signals to the protocols of audio control, namely OSC (Open Sound Control)/MIDI (Musical Instrument Digital Interface). Like Machinima, these uses do not mark the eradication of gameplay per se. *Prima facie, Red vs Blue's* removal of shooting from the First Person Shooter or *Dance Voldo Dance's* close choreography that eschews the brutality of combat in favour of erotic, balletic gyrations, might seem to have little to do with 'gameplay' if we define gameplay solely as the actions and performances that the game appears to have been designed to support. However, what these and countless other examples of the creative, investigative, transgressive performances of superplay demonstrate is the videogame's susceptibility not only to be played but to be played *with* (see Newman 2008).

In light of these observations and analyses, it is something of an understatement to suggest that play is important. Certainly, current strategies for game preservation recognise this, and both museum and software-based approaches orient themselves around making games available in playable forms. Whether concerned with the collection of the material objects of gaming or recreating games hardware and software systems through emulation, migration or virtualisation, it is self-evident that being able to play games is the key driver for these projects. And why should it not be? After even the brief discussion of the configurative, exploratory nature of play that we have seen above, with its unexpected, unanticipated contours and its use of emergent strategies and techniques, it is clear that games and 'play' go hand in hand. To paraphrase Kevin Kelly (2010), then, if we pose the question 'what do videogames want?', 'to be played', or at least, 'to be played with', must rank as one of the most convincing answers.

However, there are some important issues raised here. First, as we have seen, neither emulation nor museum strategies are able to unproblematically solve the issues of game preservation. Material objects deteriorate and inevitably disappear, while, as PVW and other projects have demonstrated, emulation presently offers 'acceptable' but significantly lacking recreations to play. Second, as contemporary game studies reminds us, play is more than a process of inputs and outputs into and from a system. It is a socially and culturally situated practice. Sensitivity to the ways games are actually used and what, as a result, are deemed to be the important qualities and characteristics of that game to its players who have learned to use it in specific ways and for specific purposes must then be a key aspect of any preservation activity. Noting these issues, Lowood poses some essential questions:

> There is a difference between preserving game technology and preserving game content, which includes gameplay. Is it necessary to play The Legend of Zelda on the original Nintendo Entertainment System, with the original Nintendo controller and a contemporary television set, in order to gain a historically valid experience of the game? The experience of viewing Birth of a Nation in a palatial theater with live music is different from viewing it on videotape, on our television, at home, and so is reading any rare book in a modern edition or format. Different, yes, but is that difference essential for scholarly research?
>
> *(Lowood 2004: 5)*

In fact, we can develop this point yet further. We might also ask whether attempting to play a game in the absence of the networks and sources of information that originally shaped and informed its playing is similarly problematic. It is certainly possible to argue that encountering a game in a gallery or archival context in the future is not only potentially jarring from a technological or historical perspective, but, in being stripped of the contextualising network of talk, discussion, demonstration and webs of investigation, the game is isolated as a comparatively free-floating text or exhibit rather than part of a suite of complex, interconnected social and cultural practices.

Dead pixels

Ultimately, the study of play reveals a variability, flexibility and malleability in the game that encourages us to view it not as a static object of preservation but as a set of resources to be engaged with and shaped through configurative, creative, exploratory practices. It is small wonder, then, that Guttenbrunner *et al.* (2010: 72) note that their ability to be played means that 'Digitally preserving interactive console video games is very different from digitally preserving static documents'.

318

As we have seen, neither museum- nor emulation-based approaches appear entirely satisfactory or viable as long-term solutions, by virtue either of the inherent shortcomings or the inconsistencies and differences in the experiences they deliver. Depending on our positions and allegiances, we might consider these shortcomings to be insurmountable problems that cast doubt on the efficacy of the entire project of game preservation or simply as a set of challenges that may be tackled through the deployment of increasingly sophisticated technological solutions. Certainly, Giordano's (see Sterling 2011) assessment strongly hints at the fundamental impossibility of game preservation, given the 'extreme fragmentation' we have noted and the intrinsic mutability and instability of games as forms that we see highlighted in examinations of games in and at play. Indeed, at this nascent stage in the development of game preservation strategy, reading discussions of the need to define 'good enough' preservation alongside judgements of what might constitute the 'acceptable' performance of an emulator in relation to its differential performance compared with original hardware and software might lead us to feel some sympathy for Giordano's position.

However, I wish to suggest that these issues only become problems because of the way we are presently approaching game preservation. The issues surrounding the long-term availability of original hardware and software systems or the variations in audiovisual representations and the interface mappings of particular emulators are problems only because the current objective of game preservation is to retain the playability of videogames in the future. If being able to play games in the future is the aim of game preservation, then the integrity of the experience offered to future players is, it goes without saying, of paramount importance. However, as we have seen, the attainment of this goal of duplicating the experiences of play through currently available means is, if not impossible, then demonstrably unattainable at present. This is not a problem, though, if we reconsider our objectives. Accordingly, I wish to suggest a somewhat radical and apparently counterintuitive alternative.

Let videogames die

By this, I mean to say that games as playable entities may have a limited lifespan and that the objective of game preservation need not be to artificially extend this in perpetuity, but rather, should be to document the period of the game's existence. This is not merely a pragmatic decision taken in the face of the difficulties encountered in deploying a museum or software approach, but rather, a considered position informed by a recognition of the importance of gameplay as a configurative act and as a socially and culturally situated practice. In short, play is not the outcome of game preservation but is its object. The capturing of games in and at play could and, I would contend, *should* be the core objective of game preservation. To be clear, this position is not opposed to emulation or the presentation of original hardware and software, and what is proposed here should not be read as a criticism of either of those approaches or projects. Nor does this position imply that emulation or playability have no place in the wider context of games preservation, interpretation and access. However, it does signal a shift in the focus of game preservation.

Of course, the proposal that game preservation broadens its attentions beyond the playable game is far from a revelation. As Vowell (2009: 12) notes,

> if we place too much emphasis on preserving only published games, we relegate much of the history behind games to the shadows. To challenge this over-emphasis on the game itself, we may consider whether a future historian can learn how a game was made by only playing it, or whether that historian could learn about the history of a development studio and the culture of the development team simply by playing their games.
>
> *(Vowell 2009: 12)*

Vowell goes on to produce a helpfully lengthy list of materials (and types of materials) that might accompany digital game objects and provide contextualisation for future scholars. Among these diverse materials, we find development documentation, budgetary information, PowerPoint pitches, press kits, demos and company newsletters. However, important though these materials are, their designation as context implies a continued centrality of the game as the unit of currency in game preservation. The position I am outlining here represents, in one sense, a reversal of this stance. The game, at least in its playable form, is 'dethroned', and ceases to be the object that is contextualised, interpreted and made sense of by these other materials which, in turn, potentially take on the role of archival documents of games and, most importantly, of gameplay. Among these 'other documents' I include video recordings of gameplay as well as the fan-produced walkthrough texts that we saw earlier in this book, as these represent some of the most comprehensive investigations of game structure, form and ludic opportunity that exist either within or outside game studies. It is worth pausing momentarily to consider the implications of this point. In order to document, record and capture gameplay, that most interactive, configurative and performative of practices, the most appropriate and effective tools reveal themselves to be decidedly non-interactive: static, plain text documents and linear video recordings. In relation to video, we might take a middle ground, as proposed by Guttenbrunner *et al.* (2010: 87), who recognise the benefits of video capture particularly in relation to the absence or failings of other contemporaneous strategies:

> The video approach was ruled out in this case study as it lacked interactivity, even though it scored highest in almost all other aspects. In cases where a suitable emulation alternative is not available (e.g., Sony PlayStation 2, Atari Jaguar) it can be the best option until an interactive alternative does become available. It can also be a complementary strategy to emulation for quick access or to verify

future emulators' visual and audible compliance. Video recordings of users playing the game can serve as an additional reference for the way games were played with special controllers and even in what context they were played.

(Guttenbrunner et al. *2010: 87)*

McDonough and Olendorf's (2011) assessment of the importance of interactivity as well as the dynamic and mutable nature of game structure and resources leads them to a similar conclusion:

> Preserving this dynamic component of games and virtual worlds has meant that a purely documentary approach to preservation through the use of screen shots, video capture of game play, textual walk through of game play, etc., was not sufficient. Such documentation might provide a useful supplement to our preservation efforts in many cases, but perhaps the most significant property of virtual environments is their interactivity, and so our efforts have tried to preserve this as much as possible.
>
> *(McDonough and Olendorf 2011: 91)*

The assumption that an emulation alternative will inevitability be available is, as we have seen, open to question, given the current state of hobbyist development and its tendency to reproduce the patterns of popularity and market share. However, we might question yet further the desirability of a playable solution, even if one were feasible. In its discussion of *Second Life*, the PVW team notes that

> The value and meaning of a virtual world is primarily derived from the actions and interactions of its players. Imagine stepping into Second Life, which doesn't even have the benefit of plotlines or non-player characters (NPCs), years after the last user signed off. The world would be empty; interactivity limited to the virtual equivalent of archaeology: examining buildings and prims in an attempt to build a picture of how Second Life was lived.
>
> *(McDonough* et al. *2010: 29)*

Elsewhere in the report, the point is reiterated in relation to *Everquest*, drawing attention not only to the significance of materials external to 'the game' in contextualising gameplay but also to the possibility of their status as the only source of information and documentation of practices and events that are simply impossible to deduce from fresh playing:

> Installing Everquest in 2050 will not reveal much about the virtual world that emerged from the software, how it was built or used, even if future writers and historians have access to everything needed to run a fully functioning version of the game. Certainly, there are important reasons

321

for preserving this software, whether as artistic or cultural content, for technology studies, or for forms of scholarship that treat digital games and virtual worlds as authored texts or artistic objects. Still, we also need to think about virtual world history in terms of events and activities, much as an archivist or historian would in the real world, and attend more carefully to preservation of forms of documentation in digital form that are external to virtual worlds as software environments.

(McDonough et al. 2010: 49)

Clearly, both *Everquest* and *Second Life* are online role-playing games or software environments that apparently differ from the comparative containment of console and PC games like *Sonic the Hedgehog* or *Doom*, and we might be tempted to consider the issues they raise to be non-transferable. However, as we have seen, gameplay is invariably socially and culturally situated, informed and shaped by discussions, practices and cumulative knowledges that are at once integral to and external from the game. While the presentation of contextualising documentary materials may serve to alleviate some of these issues by breathing some air into the vacuum of the encounter, there can little assurance that the *Street Fighter IV* player in 2050 will benefit from the a priori knowledge that contemporary players potentially bring, whether this is gleaned through discussions with friends, read in strategy guides, shared via fansites or learned through head-to-head competitive play. Let us not forget also that much of what constitutes *Street Fighter IV* is revealed only through repeated, skilful and selfconsciously directed play. If we factor in multi-player gaming and the availability of online competitive play, *Street Fighter IV* soon might appear as barren and deserted a place as *Everquest* or *Second Life*'s environments.

Consider also that games such as the *Final Fantasy, Legend of Zelda* and even *Super Mario* series present not only expansive worlds but worlds whose contours are revealed only through extensive, iterative play. We might well ask at what point the playable should be made available in the first place. In common with many games, *Super Mario Galaxy*'s environments change throughout the game. The act of play is literally transformative, changing the landscape, opening up some options while closing down others that have been completed or negated. Gameplay leaves an identifiable and indelible trace on the world. Indeed, as we saw in the case of Capcom's *Resident Evil: The Mercenaries 3D*, this trace is permanent and cannot be erased. Of course, regardless of whether it becomes hardwired into the code of the game, the trace of gameplay is both a function of informed choices and contingent on gameplay performance, prowess, skill and perhaps even luck. One path opens up because a player decides to fork left rather than right, while another is revealed because, while it is not declared in the gameplay, a player completed within or outside an unstated target time.

That so much of what games have to offer is based on contingencies of play must surely lead us to question the primacy of playable games in the game preservation project and encourage us to consider the possibility of a need to a shift the balance from game preservation towards *gameplay* preservation. In contrast to the position outlined by McDonough and Olendorf (2011) and Guttenbrunner *et al.* (2010), I want to suggest that recognising play as a vital part of what is to be preserved, rather than the outcome of preservation, might lead us to a re-evaluation of the role of the documentary approach. While for many it exists as a valuable supplement to the business of game preservation, I wish to suggest that a documentary approach is well suited to respond to the diversity of play and the susceptibility of games to the configurative, transformative acts of play as well as underpinning any project based around the presentation of playability. The centrality of documentary materials, of non-interactive means of gaining access to, and ascertaining the meaning of, a media form that is defined by its interactivity marks an important if somewhat controversial shift of focus.

Videogames are disappearing

To reiterate, this stance is not one that denigrates the idea of playable games, but rather, it is one that questions the extant centrality of playability in game preservation strategy. The continued ability to play remains a valuable and potentially useful means of contextualising and interpreting videogames, in much the same way as handling a replica or original medieval broadsword might give a sense of combat through its heft or the aura of its authenticity. However, just as the sword itself reveals little of the detail of the lived experience of knightly life, neither can the isolated playable game communicate the lived experience of gameplay. Ultimately, a strategy based around the comprehensive documentation of play as it exists now, and in all its diversity, lessens the severity of some of the anomalies we noted in relation to emulated versions of games, as these no longer have to stand as perfect replicas of the originals or, worse still, as a simulacrum that masks the fact that no singular 'original' ever truly existed, due to variations in components such as sound and graphics cards, joypads, multibutton mice and audiovisual display technologies. Moreover, the desperation felt in relation to the business practices that use up, wear out and 'retire' games may abate somewhat if we are sufficiently confident to allow games to die in their playable state. The onus therefore shifts to documenting as thoroughly as possible the game while it exists. At the very least, we might argue that the creation of a documentary record of gameplay, audio and visual performance must be a *predicate* for an emulation- or software-based strategy. Without a reliable and trustworthy reference point for comparison, how might we be able to judge the accuracy or efficacy of future attempts to recreate or resurrect? Far from being ancillary materials that flesh out the story of a given game, platform or series, or that help to enrich our appreciation or ability to interpret, I would assert that, even if only in terms of their ability to present a referential baseline, gameplay videos, along with walkthrough texts and the other products of fan cultures, are the foundations upon which all preservation effort must be built. As such, the creation and preservation of these comprehensive documentary materials must be a priority.

It is important to remember at this point that game preservation is not simply a project concerned with resuscitating old games. Certainly, the lens of game preservation thus far has tended to focus on 1980s-era titles, and this is at least in part because of the putative threat of their material disappearance, as well as the focus of grass-roots videogame emulation projects on consoles and Coin-Ops from this period (which, as we have seen, is perhaps a function of the technical feasibility of such undertakings). However, a concerted focus on a documentary approach (even, for that matter, if it remains part of a 'contextualisation' or 'reference point' strategy that still retains playability as its long-term objective) reconfigures preservation as a present concern. If we take on board the inevitability of the disappearance of games, which for at least some titles appears unanimously agreed a practical certainty – and we need only look at the documented failings of attempts to preserve *Second Life* in McDonough et al. (2010; see also McDonough and Olendorf 2011) or the business practices of retirement, the subsequent removal of online access to games and the lack of formal support and backwards compatibility for a compelling case – we find that a potentially liberating position unfolds, which encourages a concern for the present and future rather than a wistful sense of a lost past.

But what of the games that have already been lost? Might we be suggesting a 'year zero' approach to preservation? While there is little that documentation can do to capture the stories of play and development that help to explain and make sense of *Jet Set Willy, Sonic the Hedgehog or Parachute*, these games do continue to exist in some form. That their emulated, re-released selves are not identical to their original releases might present problems where the recreation seeks to stand for the original, but by treating the 2012 emulation as a continuation of the original game rather than its substitute we find the contexts of contemporary play a rich and productive area to document. The cultures and practices of retro gaming, the creation and use of games under emulation are, in and of themselves, vital areas in need of recording and documentation. As such, oral histories, annotated and narrated gameplay videos and walkthroughs as extensive archival documents of gameplay can deal with *Jet Set Willy, Sonic, Parachute et al.*, as they are now – 'now they are old', as Marvin (1988) might have it. Where the IGDA Game Preservation SIG urges action 'before it's too late', we might shift slightly and recognise that at some point it inevitably will be too late – too late to play these games in their original state, at least.

As we noted at the very beginning of this book, videogames are disappearing, and while it is natural to lament their passing, it does not necessarily follow that the realisation of games' vulnerability to material and digital deterioration, obsolescence and supersession should cast the project of game preservation as one primarily concerned with halting or interrupting these processes. The idea that we might be able to arrest the business and discursive practices that sit at the very foundation of the videogames industry in its broadest sense, and which are, in part, responsible for the disappearance of games and the diminution of their longevity, is ambitious, to say the least. Similarly, the contingency of ongoing access to games on technologies, systems, networks, intellectual properties and rights management systems that are in the control of organisations in whose interest it is to protect their proprietary nature and exclusivity ensures that any attempt to preserve systems and games in playable form beyond their commercially supported lifetimes inevitably operates from a position of disadvantage. Moreover, we have seen that techniques to recreate the conditions of play using different hardware and emulation software, and which attempt to side-step some of the dependencies on proprietary and unsupported technologies and systems that are beyond the control of preservation practitioners, bring with them their own issues in terms of the authenticity of their representations and experiences, as well as requirements for their ongoing support and development.

Ultimately, what is at stake here is the purpose of game preservation as a project. As we have seen, current game preservation work is underpinned by the desire to maintain or recreate games in playable form, which, given the apparent indivisibility of 'game' and the configurative 'play' that enacts it, appears to be a wholly natural position to adopt. However, I want to suggest that the focus on preserving playability is not the logical outcome of recognition of the importance of play. Nor is it the best way to tackle the disappearance of games, which, far from being the problem to tackle, is best conceived as the context in which preservation takes place. Videogames are disappearing and they will continue to disappear, for all the technological and commercial reasons we have seen throughout this book. It might seem an odd, even perverse thing to suggest, but perhaps their disappearance is not a problem per se, or at least might not be the problem best addressed by game preservation. Perhaps recognising that it will not be possible to play today's games in the future is not an admission of failure but a firm foundation upon which to plan.

The decision to embrace the extinction of games in playable forms, and the shift away from conceiving of play as the outcome of preservation to a position that acknowledges play as an indivisible part of the object of preservation, are not merely born of pragmatic frustration with the apparent impossibility of the project or the (im)precision of current strategies to prolong playability. Rather, the decision to focus on the documentation of gameplay as experience and configurative practice, in concert with development documentation and original or emulated playability as part of the wider body of contextualising materials, is born precisely of the recognition that play is not merely important, but that it is too important not to preserve.

Videogames are disappearing and, by default, so too is gameplay. The urgent aim of game(play) preservation must surely be to record as much as we possibly can about games, and the way they are made, played and played with, while they are still with us.

325

References

Aarseth, E. (1997) *Cybertext: Perspectives on Ergodic Literature*, Baltimore, MD: Johns Hopkins University press.

Brandt, C. (2005) 'Dance, Voldo, Dance: A Machinima Music Video', Bain Street Productions <http://www.buinst.com/madness/voldo.html>

Buuk, R. (n.d.) 'A Day in the Life of MissingNo.', *Team Rocket's Rockin* <http://www. trsrockin.com/missing.html>

Call of Duty Wiki (n.d.) 'Grenade Launcher', <http://callofduty.wikia.com/wiki/Grenade_Launcher>

Cannon, R. (2007) 'Meltdown' in A. Clarke and G. Mitchell (eds) *Videogames and Art*, Bristol: Intellect Books, pp. 38–53.

Consalvo, M. (2007) *Cheating: Gaining Advantage in Videogames*, Cambridge, MA: MIT Press.

Delaney, K.J. (2004) 'When Art Imitates Videogames, You Have "Red vs. Blue": Mr. Burns Makes Little Movies Internet Fans Clamor for; Shades of Samuel Beckett', *Wall Street Journal*, 9 April.

Eskelinen, M. (2001) 'The Gaming Situation', *Game Studies* 1(1), <http://www. gamestudies.org/0101/eskelinen>

Essian (2011) 'Are Noob Tubes Ruining FPS Games?', *Gamespot UK*, 2 March <http:// uk.gamespot.com/forums/topic/27593794/are-noob-tunes-ruining-fps-games&msg-id=328458417>

Garkidis, A. (2008) 'Super Mario Bros. Speedrun (nowarps). Best time 0:19:40', (performed 12 March), *Speed Demos Archive* <http://speeddemosarchive.com/Mario1.html#nowarps>

——(2010) 'Super Mario Bros. Speedrun (normal). Best time 0:04:59', (performed 24 October) *Speed Demos Archive* <http://speeddemosarchive.com/Mario1.html#norm>

Guttenbrunner, M., Becker, C. and Rauber, A. (2010) 'Keeping the Game Alive: Evaluating Strategies for the Preservation of Console Video Games', *The International Journal of Digital Curation* 5(1).

Kelly, K. (2010) *What Technology Wants*, New York: VikingPenguin.

Lowood, H. (2004) 'Playing History with Games: Steps towards Historical Archives of Computer Gaming', *Annual Meeting of the American Institute for Conservation of Historic and Artistic Works (Electronic Media Group)*, Portland, OR, 14 June.

——(2005) 'Real-time performance: Machinima and games studies', *iDMAa Journal* 2(1), pp. 10–17.

——(2007) 'High-performance Play: The Making of Machinima', in A. Clarke and G. Mitchell (eds), *Videogames and Art*, Bristol: Intellect Books, pp. 59–79.

Marino, P. (2004) *3D Game-Based Filmmaking: The Art of Machinima*, Scottsdale, AZ: Paraglyph Press.

Marvin, C. (1988) *When Old Technologies Were New: Thinking about Electric Communication in the Late Nineteenth Century*, Oxford: Oxford University Press.

McDonough, J. and Olendorf, R. (2011) 'Saving Second Life: Issues in Archiving a Complex, Multi-User Virtual World', *The International Journal of Digital Curation* 6(2) <http://www.ijdc.net/index.php/ijdc/article/view/185/252>

McDonough, J., Olendorf, R., Kirschenbaum, M., Kraus, K., Reside, D., Donohue, R., Phelps, A., Egert, C., Lowood, H. and Rojo, S. (2010) *Preserving Virtual Worlds: Final Report*, available at the University of Illinois IDEALS Repository at <http://www.hdl. handle.net/2142/17097>

Morris, S. (2003) 'WADs, Bots and Mods: Multiplayer: FPS Games as Co-creative Media', in M. Copier and J. Raessens (eds) *Level Up: Digital Games Research Conference Proceedings*, University of Utrecht (CD-ROM).

Moulthrop, S. (2004) 'From Work to Play: Molecular Culture in the Time of Deadly Games', in N. Wardrip-Fruin and N. Harrigan (eds) *First Person: New Media as Story Performance, and Game*, Cambridge, MA: MIT Press, pp. 56–70.

Newman, J. (2004) *Videogames*, London: Routledge.

——(2008) *Playing with Videogames*, Abingdon: Routledge.

Nader, M. (2004) 'The Secret of MissingNo', *Team Rocket's Rockin* <http://www.trsrockin.com/missingno_fic.html>

Sterling, B. (2011) 'Dead Media Beat: Federico Giordano, "Almost the Same Game"', *Wired*, 21 April <http://www.wired.com/beyond_the_beyond/2011/04/dead-media-beat-federico-giordano-almost-the-same-game>

Surman, D. (2010) 'Everyday Hacks: Why Cheating Matters', in R. Catlow, Garret, M. and C. Morgana (eds) *Artists Re:Thinking Games*, Liverpool: Liverpool University Press, pp. 74–7.

Vowell, Z. (2009) 'What Constitutes History?' in H. Lowood (ed.) *Before It's Too Late: A Digital Game Preservation White Paper* <http://www.igda.org/wiki/images/8/83/IGDA_Game_Preservation_SIG–Before_It%27s_Too_Late–A_Digital_Game_Preservation_White_Paper.pdf>

Wilonsky, R. (2002) 'Joystick Cinema: It's Man vs. Machinima when Video Games Become, Ahem, Movies', *Screen Entertainment Weekly*, 14 August.

INDEX